Against the Cold War

Against the Cold War

*The History and Political Traditions
of Pro-Sovietism in the British Labour
Party 1945-89*

Darren G Lilleker

I.B. TAURIS

LONDON · NEW YORK

Published in 2004 by Tauris Academic Studies.
an imprint of I.B. Tauris & Co Ltd
6 Salem Road, London W2 4BU
175 Fifth Avenue, New York NY 10010
www..ibtauris.com

In the United States of America and in Canada distributed by
St Martins Press, 175 Fifth Avenue, New York NY 10010

International Library of Political Studies 1

ISBN 1 85043 471 9
EAN 978 1 85043 471 9

A full CIP record for this book is available from the British Library
A full CIP record for this book is available from the Library of Congress

Library of Congress catalog card: available
Printed and bound in Great Britain by MPG Books Ltd, Bodmin from
camera-ready copy edited and supplied by the author

Contents

ACKNOWLEDGEMENTS

This research would not have been possible without the scholarship offered to me by Barnsley College. I would like to acknowledge the debt of gratitude to the college and the staff on the BA Humanities degree course: David Bills, Sian Edwards, Robert Fletcher, David Kiernan, Tony Hooper, Martin McMahon, Michael McMahon, Graham Mustin and Paul Wild. All of whom were immensely supportive to me throughout my studies and during my time as a postgraduate and lecturer at the college. I would also so like to offer my thanks to Keith Brock of the International Unit.

I also owe a debt of gratitude to my supervisors, Julian Birch and Michael Kenny, for all their help and support throughout my research and writing. There are also many others within the department who were supportive during my time in the Department of Politics at the University of Sheffield, particularly Ian Bache, Stephen George, Steve Ludlam, Pat Seyd, Martin J Smith and Paul Whiteley. I would also like to thank the office staff; Sarah Cooke, Sue Kelk, Katie Middleton, Christine Whitaker and Rob Collins who are fantastic on a daily basis.

Within the field of Labour and Communist history I found a great deal of support and made many friends along the way, this made my research both enjoyable and rewarding. Ray Challinor and Archie Potts both gave vast amounts of advice and information over several telephone conversations, I thank them very much.

This study also benefited from the help and encouragement of many people beyond academia, not all of whom I can mention here. The archivists at the Museum of Labour History, the Modern Records Centre and King's College London were enormously helpful. Those who agreed to be interviewed were all thanked individually, however I would like to reiterate my heartfelt thanks as much of this work relies upon their accuracy of recollection and willing participation. Sadly since being interviewed Frank

Allaun, John Platts-Mills and Jan Zilliacus have passed away, I trust I serve their memories in telling one small part of their stories.

Finally, and on a personal note, I would like to thanks my colleagues within the Political Studies Association Postgraduate Network for their friendship and support, Ralph Negrine for giving me my first full-time post and to Simon Cross and James Stanyer for making me welcome at Leicester, my friends in Wakefield for keeping me grounded in the real world, to Sue Lindley at Bournemouth University and Chris Jeapes for their help with preparing the manuscript, and finally Teresa, to whom I owe the greatest debts of all.

This book is dedicated to the memories of Gladys Mabel Price, Arritza bin Rashid and Jack 'Stig' Webster, all of whom were influential figures in my life.

Darren G Lilleker, Poole, March 2004.

INTRODUCTION

Pro-Sovietism and the British Labour Party

The British Parliamentary Labour party (PLP) is traditionally described as a coalition of left-wing traditions and ideologies. Wright described this coalition as fragile because the leadership was often torn between the policy outcomes imposed by the realities of governance and those prescribed by ideology.[1] The debate between approaches frequently divided the party. The leadership adopted a largely pragmatic and consensual approach to government, while the left argued that ideology should guide the party. The intra-party debate thus centred upon what was possible; the leadership maintained the stance that radical socialist policies were untenable for Britain and unpopular with the electorate. The left, in contrast, argued that socialist principles alone should determine policy and that, if the leadership showed determination in the pursuit of socialist goals, the electorate would respond favourably.

Thorpe argued that similar divisions existed within the traditional constituency of the party, the working class.[2] Britain has traditionally lacked a revolutionary socialist tradition and, therefore, any socialist political grouping intent on securing electoral success has had to adopt a centre-left or social democratic position. The democratic socialist left largely rejected this as an illegitimate constraint; they were not about accepting the mood, they sought to steer the mood in a more socialist direction.

The internal divisions in the British Labour party are amplified by the fact that the party was founded upon an alliance of autonomous organisations. This factor led Shaw to conclude that Labour was "neither socialist nor... a party".[3] He described the party as a confederation of societies that had amalgamated only because they represented, to differing extents, working class interests. This has led political analysts to define Labour's ideology not as socialism but 'labourism'; a coalition of group interests some of which can be described as ideological but, in general, are nothing more than political objectives derived from the interests of a single class.[4] We can therefore view Labour party policy as having emerged out of a loose collection of ideological traditions, restricted by a traditional non-radical tendency within the electorate and the party's structure and also by the existence of a largely right-wing parliamentary opposition. From this analysis we can recognise that socialist achievements, such as the nationalisation programme and foundation of the Welfare state, could only have been achieved in a consensual political atmosphere.[5]

There is no easy way to characterise those parliamentarians who became known as the left-wing of the PLP. The left-wing traditions, which filtered into the ethos of the Labour party, included the influence of Marxism and Trotskyism, libertarianism, intellectual humanism, Christianity and internationalism. It would be misleading to discuss the existence of a left-wing ideology, or indeed one definite labourist ideology. Across the party there existed divisions over the objectives that should be pursued, which were often dependent upon the individual's socialist ideals. Furthermore, each of the ideological concepts held had blurred boundaries and lacked definite objectives relevant to everyday politicking. Thus the left of the Labour party can be defined as a loose collective united only around broad objectives, that lacked a definitive ideological core.[6]

Historically high politics within the party has been viewed as a battle between left and centre-right factions, for example the Bevinite-Bevanite divide within the 1945-50 government, or the Healey-Benn split of 1981. However, by no means were these factions organised or cohesive. In fact the ideological divisions within the party can be viewed as existing in minutiae within the left. The left-wing did have a broadly defined policy objective; to improve the conditions of the party's traditional constituency, the working class. The central tenets of the left-wing agenda were state ownership of the means of production and a non-aggressive foreign policy. The latter would determine what defence was necessary for Britain. However the proposed strategies for achieving this agenda differed vastly. There was no single philosophy that acted as a guide for left-wing activity and the broad objectives were not explicit and liable to flux. However, these two tenets were the broadly unifying ideological features of the left-wing agenda.

THE LEFT AND PRO-SOVIETISM

The attitude towards the Soviet Union was one issue that separated the left. Most Labour left-wingers were at best antipathetic to Soviet Communism. Despite this, opposition to the Cold War did emerge out of Bevanism; the left-wing philosophy that enjoyed support of the majority of the left. The Bevanite mission was to unravel Britain's international ties that opposed the implementation of a socialist domestic policy.[7] They particularly opposed Atlanticism; the support for the Anglo-American special relationship, and argued that Britain should establish a neutral Third Camp in alliance with socialist European powers. Trotskyists largely agreed with the Bevanite principles, but their arguments were linked intrinsically to a more revolutionary tradition.[8] While these traditions became shaped within a world polarised by the Cold War the majority of left-wingers retained a fundamentally anti-Soviet perspective.

However there were a minority who did argue that a link existed between the Soviet model and the global socialist movement. These individuals were representative of the pro-Soviet tradition of left-wing politics. They held a sympathetic view of the Soviet Union, argued that it represented the only practical model of socialism and developed a theory for explaining any inconsistencies between the Soviet model and the Marxist template by highlighting that the regime had been beset by aggression since inception. This allowed these figures to develop a rationale for supporting and protecting the Soviet model from ideological and military attack. Pro-Sovietism became an ideological guide for action, those who possessed this sympathetic view of the Soviet model actively pursued strategies of opposition to the Cold War anti-Soviet rationale and attempted to build political, cultural and economic links between British society and the Soviet people and government. These activities were driven by events in the sphere of international relations and, in particular, the emergence of two camps; one socialist, represented by the Communist bloc, the other capitalist and led by the United States of America.

This international ideological dichotomy had existed since October 1917, but was only ratified as a bipolar division in 1946 by the Truman Doctrine and Churchill's Fulton speech. This division led some left-wingers to feel forced into making a choice between western reformist socialism and Marxist-Leninist state socialism. While the former achieved hegemony, and the Labour leadership adopted a largely Atlanticist policy,[9] there were those who opposed the anti-Communist rationale as defined by the Truman Doctrine. These figures pursued an active role in opposing the cross-party consensual foreign and defence policy. They argued that Britain's post-war foreign policy was Churchillian in origin and should be re-oriented by a Labour government. These individuals were a minority who existed on the fringes of both Bevanism and Trotskyism and it remains difficult to categorise them within the traditional party political left-right spectrum.

THE COLD WAR NARRATIVE OF PRO-SOVIETISM

When we are introduced to the pro-Soviet figures it is usually in pejorative terms. These definitions ignore the nuances in their political thought and fail to attempt to explain their activities and arguments as a tradition within Labour's ethos. Histories of the party have largely, and perhaps rightly, defined them as a group with insignificant influence and so worthy of little academic attention. Those who have performed studies of the left-wing, or indeed left-wing thought, have offered them little more attention. In fact we find them lumped together and written off as anti-thetical to Labour's traditional ethos. Jenkins used the phrase "neo-Stalinist left",[10] a view supported in Foote's work on the party's political thought.[11] Morgan, a little more charitably, defined the same group as "the far left fringe"[12] but also employed the pejorative terms "fellow-travelling left-wingers",[13] "crypto-Communists"[14] and "left-wing gadflies."[15] Thus they were consigned to history as the "loony left"; an image promulgated by the right during the 1980s. This perception was largely supported by the party leadership. Hattersley described them as members of the "illegitimate left".[16] This, Hattersley explained, included Trotskyites, Maoists and Stalinists. He recalled that Neil Kinnock, as party leader, was:

> Determined to remove what he regarded as parasites, cuckooing in Labour's nest – as much because of the electoral damage that they did as because of his undoubted opposition to their philosophy.[17]

Evidence suggests that the majority of the Labour party leadership shared this view of the pro-Soviet left.

A powerful Cold War espionage narrative, which classifies all those who were sympathetic to the Soviet Union as spies and traitors, reinforces this negative historiography. It has been the raison d'être of many writers to expose those who they allege were agents working on behalf of the Soviet Union. Blake Baker, Brian Crozier, Chapman Pincher and Nigel West have all devoted a significant amount of their writing and research to exposing the network of Communist agents active in Britain. This narra-tive is symptomatic of the fear of insurgent Communism that existed in Western societies. This was emphasised following the defection of Oleg Gordievsky and his subsequent collaboration with, Cambridge Professor and intelligence expert, Christopher Andrew. Revelations that Labour mem-bers were deeply involved in pro-Soviet activity are also extensive in Gordievsky's autobiography and in the work of Chapman Pincher.[18] The watershed for such revelations emerged during the early 1980s and ce-mented the opinion that there was a profoundly dangerous aspect to the 'loony left' press caricature. These works epitomise the public expression of the opinion that the West was constantly under attack and that there were those within the British parliament who sympathised with, and in-deed worked on behalf of, that Communist enemy power.

By the very nature, working as an agent for a foreign, enemy power is a clandestine activity. Therefore, it is difficult to prove or disprove com-plicity. The writers who alleged that those MPs who expressed pro-Soviet sympathies were Soviet agents depend upon this lack of clarity and rely on the willingness of their audience to believe their exposés. It should be noted, however, that this is an aspect of the Cold War mindset. On both sides of the global divide the attitude was zero-sum. Expressing pro-Soviet sympathies was equated to being an agent. The full gamut of agents, from Alger Hiss who passed information on the development of nuclear weaponry to the Soviet Union, to Will Owen, MP for Morpeth 1955-70, proven to have taken money from the Czech StB for non-secret information, were all defined under the narrow definition of agent of the Soviet Union.

The majority of literature on the subject is shrouded in sensationalism and relies upon a degree of innuendo. The best example of this authorship is Chapman Pincher. Developing the narrative following the conviction of Will Owen, Pincher, through several works, increased the atmosphere of suspicion claiming that there were more powerful, still undisclosed, Soviet agents within the Labour hierarchy. This notion was reinforced by others including Blake Baker, Brian Crozier and to a lesser extent Nigel West.[19] Pincher, as a journalist, sensationalised the story, alluding to individuals' treachery. An example of this is that throughout his works on the Labour party he stated that his contacts in the intelligence agencies had told him in private that there was a spy active in the Callaghan Cabinet. He also described Tony Benn, albeit completely inaccurately, as pro-Soviet.[20] Nowhere does he link the two statements, however, a connection can be made, and the reader can make whatever conclusion suits.

AGENTS: A QUESTION OF PERSPECTIVES
The term agent needs some clarification. We need to understand what it meant exactly to be an agent of the Soviet Union, from the perspective of the KGB, and how an MP would be recruited. An important source of information is Oleg Gordievsky. As 'resident'[21] in Britain 1980-83 he was party to many of the activities of the KGB and was able to define the terms used, and the type of work engaged in, by those MPs who were classified within the broad definition of agent. Gordievsky placed these MPs into three categories. An agent of the Soviet Union was an individual who did a variety of "little jobs" or "ran errands" under the influence of their Russian contact.[22] An agent, specifically of the KGB, supplied information directly to a KGB officer as Gordievsky himself was. During the 1970s a new term was introduced, the 'confidential contact'. These were very similar to the first category of agent of the Soviet Union. To be classified as such the individual had to have supplied information and followed KGB instructions on a significant number of occasions. Control, however, was limited and the relationship was often open and friendly. This is in stark contrast to the relationships described by Pincher.

It is within the latter category that most of the individuals analysed in this study would fall. Gordievsky accepted that they were not spies, and that their usefulness was limited, but that they were viewed as KGB assets. This perception was held because they were sympathetic towards the objectives of the Soviet Union and, because of this, were prepared to divulge information that was unobtainable through official channels and would reiterate Soviet arguments as their own. Due to their position of influence, and prominence in the press, they were seen as important and KGB officers, Gordievsky recalled, were encouraged to recruit as many of this type of contact as possible.

Evidence from other active Soviet agents reinforces Gordievsky's claim that penetration of the Western political structures was prioritised. Peter Gutzeit, the New York KGB station chief, when rationalising the requirement for extra expenses to aid the election campaigns of sympathetic would-be Congressmen and Senators, argued that this was necessary to "create a group of our people in the legislative bodies, define their political positions, and insert them there to actively influence events."[23] This indicates that there was a strategy to install and then control a sub-group of politicians within the legislatures of non-Communist governments. The purpose for this is clear. Josef Frolik, Czech StB operative in London until 1970, argued that MPs enjoy day to day contact with the governing forces of a country and so were placed in an ideal position; not only could they leak information on policy, they could also argue a certain line.[24]

Parliamentary agents were, therefore, viewed as being of the highest importance. Sir Martin Furnival Jones, a former Director General of MI5, stated:

> of all their British targets, Members of Parliament were the most vulnerable... [Furthermore] if the Russian Intelligence Service can recruit a backbench MP and he climbs to a ministerial position, the spy is home and dry.[25]

Gordievsky used the case of Norwegian politician Arne Treholt to emphasise the potential importance of sympathetic MPs. Treholt rose to the equivalent of Under-secretary in the Norwegian Ministry for Defence, potentially he could have become Minister had his Soviet connections remained concealed.[26] Similarly, Gordievsky listed Michael Foot as a favourable target for cultivation during his early career.[27] Had Foot been recruited the KGB would have had a potential Prime Minister under their influence. Gordievsky claimed that by the time of his residency Foot was no longer approachable, but had run errands for his predecessors. However, no evidence exists to substantiate the allegation. Furthermore, this was strongly repudiated by Foot, forcing Gordievsky to retract his statement.

⚬ Josef Frolik, Czech StB agent, also claimed to have handled three Labour party MPs. In Frolik's account of his defection he does not name them, though this was due to contemporaneous court cases against them. The individuals were, however, identified by codenames as Lee, Gustav and another unnamed man caught in a homosexual trap. Each, Frolik claimed, were paid for their services. Lee, identified as Will Owen, was solely interested in financial reward. According to Frolik he demanded free holidays and money and in return passed information of the "highest importance."[28] This description of Owen seems somewhat dubious, Owen was not party to important information, and the fact that he was acquitted from a treason charge on the 9th May 1970 substantiates these doubts.

⚬ Gustav was identified as the late Barnet Stross; Labour MP Hanley 1945-50, Stoke on Trent 1950-66. Information supplied by Ann Swingler indicates that he did indeed have extensive contact with officials of the Czech Embassy and with the Czech government itself through his role as President of the 'Lidice Shall Live' campaign, organised by himself and fellow MP Stephen Swingler. Regardless of this, it is questionable whether Stross imparted information during his contact with the Czech officials, however the StB viewed Stross as a sympathetic contact within the British parliament. The third man was of the greatest significance. Not only was he paid, but was also blackmailed over his homosexuality and therefore had a dual motivation for working for the Czech Embassy. Pincher revealed that this was John Stonehouse who, throughout his career, appears to have been motivated by promise of financial gain. Frolik viewed all three as equally guilty and described them as "parliamentary freeloaders" and warned others "there are no such things as 'gifts', 'retainers'... [or] 'consultancies'... there are only bribes."[29]

⚬ A further MP to be named as a contact and agent was Ray Fletcher, MP for Ilkeston 1964-83. This allegation by Vasili Mitrokhin, who was accepted as being highly reliable, comes directly from the files of the KGB. The allegation is that Fletcher published a critique of defence spending on the behest of the KGB and enjoyed extensive contact with the Czech Embassy and thus, it is implied, the StB.[30] The latter Fletcher admitted, but claimed the contact to be innocent. His widow, in response to Mitrokhin's revelations, alleged that Fletcher was used as a conduit between MI6 and Czech dissidents.[31] This appears an equally feasible role for Fletcher. He does not appear to have held a pro-Soviet perspective and *£60 a Second on Defence*, the pamphlet alleged to offer a pro-Soviet analysis, argued from a similar position to Cook and Smith's *What Future in NATO?* and reiterated the arguments of many critiques of defence spending produced by the anti-Soviet left. However, his writing shows evidence of a wealth of research into Soviet defence capabilities. This would have been carried out using the Soviet Embassy in London as a resource and, it is likely that, Soviet statistics were reproduced verbatim. Therefore some could argue that he had reiterated Soviet propaganda.

There were obviously sections of the party whose ideas were, at times, better suited to membership of the CPGB. Similarly there was also a minority that appeared blind to the faults of the Soviet Union due to the claim to being 'actually existing socialism'. However, there is no evidence to suggest that the majoritarian desire of these individuals was to undermine or overthrow British democracy. The pro-Soviet strand desired radical changes, along socialist lines, that could lead to the creation of a more progressive society. The Soviet Union represented this ideal in part, but not in entirety. What was paramount to their perspective was the opinion that progress could not be made in an atmosphere of Cold War and thus the two sides had to be reconciled.

Those who held pro-Soviet perceptions were identified and their ideals exploited by KGB officials. Gordievsky stated that this was particularly the case with the pacifistic strand. He related the method used by his one time superior Gennady Titov for gaining control over Norwegian politician Arne Treholt. Treholt had a bright future, until discovery, and Titov recognised this and flattered the young Norwegian by overstating the importance of his stance for achieving peace.[32] One particular phrase Gordievsky recalled was Titov telling Treholt "[y]ou are preserving world peace and saving Europe from nuclear war."[33] Such encouragement could have had a significant effect on figures such as Konni Zilliacus or Frank Allaun, whose entire careers hinged upon fighting for peace. We can not say with any degree of certainty tactics like this were, or were not, used on British politicians. What is obvious is that the potential was present. Furthermore this was standard KGB procedure and it is doubtless that KGB agents at least attempted to tap into the pacifist strand using this methodology.

In some cases a sense of importance as a political actor could have been a deciding factor. An ambitious backbencher that believed that their talents were not recognised, a characteristic of many of the left-wing, may have sought rewards elsewhere. Active sympathisers were told that they were highly regarded in Moscow, given presents, holidays, and even medals for their service. If we consider William Wilson, a self-confessed confidential contact during the second Cold War, he found that the PLP failed to recognise the common sense in his case for the recognition of the GDR or for developing a strategy of co-existence with Communism. However, to the Soviet officials he was an influential politician who, at crucial junctures, reinforced the Soviet line. Equally Konni Zilliacus was allowed to interview Khrushchev for research purposes. The impression is given that, to the Soviet leadership, Zilliacus particularly was a man of some importance. This is supported by the fact that Stalin felt it necessary to denounce Zilliacus when he switched his support to Tito. While Zilliacus maintained an independent perspective, refusing to adopt a purely pro-Soviet stance, his background and experience meant that KGB agents would have sought to cultivate him as an agent, may have sought to influence him with propaganda and did claim control over him when he reiterated their arguments. However, the reality of the relationship was vastly different from the Soviet perspective of Wilson or Zilliacus. This narrative provides some clues to why many MPs were categorised as agents without them entering into activities that they believed benefited the Soviet cause. In the zero-sum perspective of world affairs these individuals could not be seen as non-aligned but were either for or against. This explains why Zilliacus was classed as an agent and contact,[34] and why he was condemned as a traitor and fascist spy for supporting Tito's Yugoslavia in opposition to Stalinism.

In stark contrast, Frolik in particular argued, that the desire for funds to supplement the arguably meagre wages of a backbencher led some MPs to become agents. These were seen as the most reliable by their handlers, as Frolik argued, "a friend can drop out of the business any day, a paid agent never, we ensured they received money from us and signed for it."[35] The payment and receipt were very important, as this written proof of funds changing hands could be used as a lever to ensure the MP's future co-operation. On other occasions it was the MP's sexual proclivities which made them susceptible to blackmail and so be led to act on behalf of the Soviet Union. An example of how the KGB worked is illustrated by the case of Sir Geoffrey Harrison, British Ambassador to Moscow during the late 1960s. Photographs were sent to him of a sexual encounter he had with a young woman employed as a maid in the British Embassy. The KGB claimed that she was an agent, and offered to overlook the incident should he do them certain favours. Harrison reported the situation to the Foreign Office and was duly transferred.[36] Pincher inferred that the majority of others who found themselves in similar situations did not report such incidences.

This may have been particularly the case with homosexuals. Due to the stigma and illegality attached to this sexual preference for a large part of this period it appears that it was easier for the KGB to extract aid from them. Mitrokhin stated that homosexual Labour MP Tom Driberg was recruited in this way.[37] Pincher argued that Driberg had a dual role working for the KGB and MI5, a situation Driberg exploited in order to be open about his sexuality without fear of arrest.[38] However, there were also ideo-

logical affinities between Driberg and Communism. This is evident in
Driberg's portrait of his friend and former lover Guy Burgess who, Driberg
argued, had attempted only to create a "better understanding between the
Soviet Union and the West."[39] This is an identical stance to that adopted by
many of the pro-Soviet left-winger's. Therefore, though Driberg is argued
to have exploited the interest in him, there may have been other, both
ideological and personal, motivating factors.

       Therefore there is some substance to the allegations brought against
pro-Soviet MPs. However there remains little evidence to suggest that any
Labour MP acted as a slavish agent of the Soviet Union. Where there is a
body of evidence, for example the cases of Driberg, Fletcher and Zilliacus,
there is often a more complex picture than that offered by the majority of
commentators. This study, therefore, removes the subject from the connotations associated with the Cold War narrative and offers alternative perspectives of pro-Soviet activities. However it remains important to exam-
ine the authenticity of many of the claims made against the pro-Soviet
MPs.

TOWARDS A REJECTION OF THE ZERO-SUM
PERSPECTIVE

       The whole question surrounding the activities of the pro-Soviet
MPs, despite the traditional analysis of pro-Sovietism, is by no means zero-
sum. The zero-sum, agent or enemy, perspective was the product of a climate that encouraged paranoiac anti-Communism, caused by the fear that
the Communist ideology could become popular and subvert western democracy. This attitude was mirrored in Communist nations by an institutional narrow-mindedness, a feature of the societal control and all-encom-
passing totalitarianism, and a culture of fear. Therefore it is useful to explore the evidence that exists to undermine key aspects of the traditional
Cold War narrative relating to pro-Soviet individuals in the West.

       Oleg Gordievsky, as acting head of the KGB station in London
1979-82, was fully aware that officials did exaggerate the contacts they 'controlled' and their usefulness to Moscow. This justified both the official's
existence, and the expenses they claimed.[40] The fact that officials would
and did exaggerate does mean that some of the information Gordievsky
and Mitrokhin provided could be questionable. Although he is aware what
contacts he himself had, Gordievsky could not be certain, for example,
when naming Ian Mikardo as an agent of the Soviet Union and Zilliacus as
an agent of the KGB, specifically how great the contact, or element of
control, was. There is evidence that many MPs would have contacted East-
ern-bloc Embassies on several occasions for demonstrable reasons. For
example, Ian Mikardo needed permits and information to support his plans

for trading with Eastern Europe. Konni Zilliacus, on the other hand, would have developed a rapport with Soviet Embassy officials when arranging fact-finding visits and contact with his friends in the Soviet Union. Gordievsky explained that safeguards did exist in the Soviet system, preventing over exaggeration. He argued that any one who believes in the innocence of socialist politicians should "not underestimate the ability of a Westerner to lie."[41]

Vladimir Shaposhnikov[42] highlighted a further problem when gauging the culpability of a politician accused of acting as an agent. Most MPs enjoy legitimate contacts with the Embassies of foreign countries. Depending on their political persuasion, but more importantly on their reason for visiting, they were assigned a point of contact with the Soviet Union. This Embassy official, usually a KGB agent, would become their liaison. The Soviet representative would attempt to strike up a rapport, provided that the MP appeared sympathetic. If this relationship developed, the Soviet representative would draw them into conversation on mutually interesting issues, particularly party policy and member's attitudes to such issues as nuclear defence. The MP may have seen these discussions as informal, unimportant and possibly furthering East-West friendship. Equally much of what was discussed would have already been public knowledge. However, if the Soviet representative won an argument, putting forward a perspective which the MP agreed with, and found this later used in a debate in the House, or in a publication, that Soviet official could legitimately claim the ability to influence an MP.

Norman Atkinson, MP for Tottenham, 1964-87, himself named by Oleg Gordievsky as "a frequent and friendly guest"[43] of the Soviet Embassy, reinforced this argument. Atkinson argued that those who put forward allegations against left-wingers were only attempting to "make themselves a shilling or two."[44] He proposed that, as Prime Minister, Edward Heath often visited foreign Embassies, then in a speech in the House of Commons directly referred to that visit and conversations held with Embassy officials. These often included Eastern European Embassies, particularly the Yugoslav, and Heath's statements were on some occasions supportive to that nation. As Atkinson pertinently asked, did this make Heath the agent of any particular Embassy?

Contacts between left-wing MPs and Soviet officials are also obscured by the perception of those officials who held, what Shaposhnikov referred to as, the mindset of *homo sovieticus*. To the Soviet official there was no such thing as an open, frank discussion. Soviet society was built upon secrecy and the fact that the agent's task was to prove their capability at recruiting Western politicians to the Soviet cause meant that any contact had to be logged and reported to the Centre. To a British politician parliamentary debates are not secret, in fact most would have already appeared in the press. To the Soviet official any contact was an opportunity to gain kudos with the Centre and, for someone in Shaposhnikov's position, a chance to rise in the hierarchy. Furthermore, KGB agents believed that the MP, being willing to talk, may be willing to enter into some other form of collusive activity.

The insignificance of the content of discussions is reinforced by the recollections of those who dealt with the Soviet Embassy. MPs had frank discussions and often heated debates. Sometimes the MP would even concede an argument to his Russian debating partner.[45] State secrets were never involved and it should be noted that most of what was discussed had been in the press for days.[46] However all unofficial contact was viewed as potentially collusive, and all information classified as important. However the level of contact and degree of openness could wane. Gordievsky claimed that Ian Mikardo was, "in the fifties and sixties... regarded as an agent, and a very good one. But then after Czechoslovakia he faded away."[47] He and Jo Richardson, the latter named by Crozier as a confidential contact of the Soviet Union, had extensive contact with Soviet officials.[48] The dossier on each must have been extensive though solely, in all likelihood, referring to the trading network they organised. It is definite that Mikardo would have been viewed as of extensive use, due to the number of British businesses he introduced to the Soviet Union. However, this does not necessarily make him an agent in the sense of acting traitorously, though he was arguably a willing volunteer of help. To him this was a reciprocal venture that benefited both economies, not one or the other side in the Cold War. Furthermore, his trading network was in operation until 1977, so presumably his use would not have been exhausted by 1968. However he may have been a little less willing to enter into frank discussions and more critical of Soviet policy.

It must be remembered that the Soviet officials may have encouraged frank discussions from their British contacts, but this was not a luxury Soviet officials could enjoy. All they could do was reiterate the policy line set by the Politburo. Often the Soviet official tried to make MPs believe that they could talk frankly and independently about Soviet policy, and indeed this may have been possible beyond the confines of the Embassies and the myriad forms of surveillance. However, this was largely a ploy to increase informal contact between the official and the MP.[49] The objective was to gain a group of influential individuals that would work on behalf of the Soviet Union. However the inconsistencies between the MPs behaviour and the Soviet perception of them are notable and too great to ignore. Therefore it appears doubtful that the spy network in parliament, implied by Pincher and Crozier, actually existed. If any co-operation occurred be-

tween pro-Soviet MPs and their Soviet points of contact it was likely to
have been a discussion, between seemingly like-minded left-wing politicians, debating points that they were integral to the world view they shared.
It should not be assumed that they were discussing how they could aid the
Soviet Union in the ideological struggle against the West.

REDEFINING THE ROLES OF THE PRO-SOVIET MPS

This study offers two alternative definitions of pro-Soviet activism;
the 'change agent' and the 'conduit of understanding'. These definitions
classify these figures as political actors with ideological motivations and
clear objectives. These terms need some clarification. It should not be assumed that acting as a change agent entailed changing society or government on behalf of the Soviet Union. The aim was to change the climate of
opinion. The anti-Communist Cold War perception was based upon the
belief that nothing good came from the Communist bloc, this was characterised in myriad Cold War movies with the rationale that 'the only good
Commie is a dead one'. As one veteran pro-Soviet activist argued; "I didn't
like that and wanted to change these ideas."[50] Changing the perception of
the Soviet Union could lead to changing the societal perception of the
British government and even changing the nature of that government,
however this was not a necessary contingent of their activity.

While avoiding the pejorative connotations associated with the term
agent, change agent is a useful descriptive tool in outlining the role of
those who promoted the policy of the Soviet Union. This was very much
an agency driven activity. Their role was to highlight the progressive nature
of the Soviet world view, the advanced nature of the socialist society and
the desire for rapprochement and understanding among the Soviet leadership and people. In advancing these claims these individuals attempted to
alter the anti-Communist rationale which dominated the Western perception of the Eastern bloc. In putting themselves forward as a conduit for
pro-Soviet ideas they acted as the agency through which these ideas could
be disseminated, gain a broader audience and alter public perception and
thus governmental policy. The ultimate aim was to end the Cold War and
establish peace and global security, this would increase national prosperity
for all nations following the end of the arms race and enable socialist ideas
to spread across Western society. The hopes were that with rapprochement
the Soviet Union would be able to discard the 'bunker' or 'fortress' mentality, repression would end and a reformed, more democratic form of socialism could emerge. Arguably those who acted as change agents were of
great importance to the Soviet Union, particularly if they were figures with
a degree of influence.[51] Within society those perceived as most influential
were University and College lecturers.[52] In political circles however, the

MP was the highest prize. This meant that the Soviet Union, through front organisations, propaganda campaigns and direct approach, actively pursued those with political influence attempting to convince the individual that the ideals of the Soviet Union and the individual were identical.

There were various methods by which the official perceptions of the Soviet Union could be altered. Early examples are the attempts to convince Western socialists of the benefits of certain aspects of Soviet society, the planned economy being one key issue promoted throughout the 1930s. Later examples would be the attempts to convince pacifists that there was a real desire for peace within the Soviet Union and equally that the foreign policy of the Soviet Union espoused ethics that were absent from the policies of Britain and the United States. These notions were emphasised by many of those who form the remit of this study. Arguably these figures were of significance to the Soviet Union in terms of gaining a foothold within the British socialist movement. Karl Radek emphasised their importance in 1934:

> Their actions are of enormous political significance, and not only as a symptom of the state of feeling among the intermediate strata in the capitalist countries… they are hindering world imperialism in its effort to engineer a new and supreme crime, namely, an attack upon the USSR.[53]

Acting as a conduit of understanding occurred simultaneously, but not universally alongside, acting as a change agent. This meant actively participating in developing an atmosphere of mutual understanding. While many MPs, of diverse political ideologies, attempted to work with their Soviet counterparts, developing a relationship based upon mutual understanding is significantly different. The West was arguably as enigmatic and incomprehensible to the Soviet Communist as Communism was to Western politicians. Therefore gaining a group of individuals who were willing to explain British politics, particularly the decision-making and policy formulation processes, was important to the Soviet Union: particularly when these individuals encouraged further contact between the Soviet representative and other Westerners. These people were particularly important as they acted as conduits of understanding between the conflicting ideological and political systems. Soviet leaders acknowledged that for them to comprehend British political culture and Britain's response to global events, a broader understanding of the British system was required. This meant gaining an in-depth knowledge of the policy formulation process, the constraints under which governments operated and the economic priorities of the capitalist system. To gain this knowledge meant encouraging those within government to explain why decisions had been taken, the underlying rationale for policy and what future policy determinants were likely to be. This information enabled Soviet leaders to understand Western policy and predict how NATO, and the individual member states, would respond to Soviet actions.

It is difficult to determine how far this aided the Soviet Union. Nor can we ascertain the quality of information that they received, though both Gordievsky, as receiver, and William Wilson, one MP who discussed politics with a KGB agent, provide an indication that the information was unimportant and readily available from newspapers. What is important is that individuals were prepared to share information with the Soviet Union regarding Western domestic politics. Clearly, to the Soviet official, if an MP was willing to discuss political events and future policies there was the potential that, had war broken out, they may have remained an important source of information within the British government.

Equally links forged between British businesses and the Soviet economy, which had an underlying political agenda, were useful in ensuring that an element of public opinion was steered away from the anti-Communist perspective. Soviet leaders assumed that a greater understanding of Soviet policy aims would lead to a reduction in the effect of Western anti-Soviet propaganda. Therefore the combination of trade links, cultural exchanges and open contact between representatives of East and West was encouraged to ensure that a more inclusive pro-Soviet movement was created. These links were all founded upon mutual understanding. While the effects of this remain largely unquantified it is significant, in terms of Radek's view of this activity, that influential individuals were prepared to encourage the establishment of these links. Based upon an evaluation of those who entered into these activities, and their self-defined rationales, this categorisation of them as change agents and conduits of understanding can be put forward as a firm basis on which to found an analysis of the actions of the pro-Soviet MPs. Equally, when characterising pro-Soviet activity in these terms, this analysis also provides an alternative analysis of the Soviet Union's objectives when courting the British left-wing sympathiser.

This study attempts to redress the pejorative connotations associated with pro-Sovietism by separating the activities from the Cold War zero-sum perspective. Implicitly this analysis rejects the description of these individuals as fellow travellers, however there is one useful aspect to this expression. That is the 'right to alight'.[54] The 'fellow traveller' metaphor argues that all socialists were travelling in the same car, and that the ultimate destination was the Soviet model. However all passengers had the right to alight at any point on the journey. When looking at those pro-Soviet individuals, usually earmarked as fellow travellers of the Communist party, it is clear that the right to alight was utilised frequently. This dispels the slippery slope theory that hypothesises that once an individual developed pro-Soviet sympathies, and acted against the Cold War rationale, then they would automatically drift into becoming a Soviet agent. The activities pursued by those studied here clearly show differing gradations of pro-Soviet activity and different categorisations of utility to the Soviet Union of these individuals. Understanding this is important to developing an explanation of the pro-Soviet political strand. These MPs did not constitute a coherent movement and did not follow one single form of political activity. Pro-Sovietism was based upon an assortment of ideals, not all of which were subscribed to by every individual who displayed pro-Soviet sentiments, and had multi-faceted activities associated with it. The level of support for, and contact with, the Soviet Union depended largely upon the individual. Similarly the perceived use to the Soviet Union of some pro-Soviet MPs was far greater than was the case with others. Therefore, the level of activity and utility can only truly be measured through a study of the individual's activities and their motivations for adopting a pro-Soviet perspective of global politics.

STRUCTURE OF THE STUDY

This work plots pro-Sovietism as a trend within the broad church nature of the Labour party's ideology. While concentrating specifically upon the period post-1945, the focus upon the Soviet Union as an alternative to Fabian gradualism and the opinion that the future of Western Europe, as a group of independent, non-fascist nations, may well depend upon the actions of the Soviet Union emerged. The fact that these ideas remained on the fringes of labourism is of some interest, particularly when we understand the hostility with which such ideas were greeted.

The high tide for pro-Sovietism being overtly represented in the British parliament was the period after 1947, leading to the Labour party dismissing the main protagonists. This led to a protracted period of entrenchment where pro-Soviet ideas filtered into debates surrounding nuclear weapons, the future political organisation of Western Europe and the nature of the world order in the latter half of the Twentieth Century. Pro-Soviet campaigns were led from within organisations the rationale of which was to link progressive ideas to Soviet international relations, the support for which led to deeper, more interdependent, pro-Soviet links to be established by British Labour MPs. The return to prominence of left-wing figures willing to publicly denounce the Anglo-American special relationship in favour of more amenable relations with the Soviet controlled bloc led the party to once again take strong action against the amorphous institution that was its left wing.

This study seeks to explain why a section of Labour's left wing was drawn towards adopting a pro-Soviet perspective. In identifying and exploring the common denominators of the arguments and beliefs of the key pro-Soviet individuals, we are able to explain the central elements within pro-Sovietism. This allows us to establish a framework of understanding of pro-Sovietism. This analysis avoids attaching normative values to pro-Soviet beliefs allowing us to comprehend pro-Soviet activities within their context. This leads to the issue of perceptions to be introduced. Those who adopted the pro-Soviet oppositional stance were frequently criticised as anti-democratic, traitorous or bordering on the insane. A similar critique was developed of the Atlanticist, pro-nuclear grouping by their pro-Soviet opponents. While the reality of life under Communism became clear with the collapse of the Soviet Union, this should not purely be seen as an opportunity to prove the critics of pro-Sovietism correct. The end of the Cold War also allows us to understand why these minority positions were adopted without being constrained by the Cold War's zero-sum perspective.

The key questions this study asks are how were these arguments developed, what underpinned them and how the Soviet Union was used as the focus for a significant part of this oppositional stance. Equally interesting, however, is what led social democratic politicians to use a regime, frequently regarded as despotic and corrupt, as the focus for their socialist belief. In the course of studying these individuals the nature of their activities will be explained and contextualised, showing how political actors promote causes and gain broader support for their ideals. Finally it will be asked what impact they actually had upon the Labour party, the Soviet Union and in relation to public opinion. This study will categorise these figures as change agents and conduits of understanding and assess the extent to which pro-Sovietism acted as guide on the activities they pursued in their quest to encourage a peaceful, socialist world order to evolve.

1
BUILDING A PRO-SOVIET FIFTH COLUMN:

The Soviet campaign for support during the Cold War

The Marxist-Leninist revolutionary socialist doctrine contained a clearly global objective. The revolution should not be limited within one nation, to paraphrase Marx and Engels "the proletarians... have a world to win".[1] Lenin believed the creation of the Soviet Communist State could act as the catalyst for a European socialist revolution. He tried to give this rhetoric a practical dimension by ordering the Red Army deep into Poland in an attempt to provide military aid to the Spartacist movement in Germany. While the Western allies defeated the Red Army, this action substantiated the fears of Western governments that Bolshevism was an ideology of world domination. The fear that 'the Russians are Coming'[2] remained a chief tool for gaining public support during the Cold War, and was the rationale behind the McCarthy-led hunt for communists within the United States legislature and upper echelon of US society. Similar 'witch-hunts' were carried out in other Western non-Communist nations.[3]

Lenin had predicted that inter-ideological war was inevitable and necessary. Capitalism and communism could not, and should not, co-exist.

> The free federation of nations is impossible without a more or less prolonged and stubborn struggle of the socialist republic against the backward [capitalist] states.[4]

The workers, Lenin prescribed, supported by the Soviet government and its forces abroad, should plan to overthrow capitalism.[5] "Either the Soviet government triumphs in every country in the world, or the most reactionary imperialism triumphs."[6] The method for achieving this 'Soviet triumph' was not through military force but covert activity. Propaganda would be used to exacerbate hostilities within and between nations "tak[ing] advantage of this hostility... to incite one against the other."[7] Within capitalist nations

A Communist must… resort to all sorts of schemes and stratagems, employ illegitimate methods, conceal the truth, in order to get into the trade unions, stay there, and conduct the revolutionary work within.[8]

Willi Munzenberg, Lenin's personal adviser and Soviet propagandist, developed this policy within Western states. He argued that the Communist state required, what one Sovietologist described as, "transmission belts"[9] to disseminate revolutionary ideas. These conduits would promote Soviet policy "when [the Soviet Union] are lacking the necessary strength."[10] Munzenberg brought the idea to life when he established the Communist Youth International. This was originally the Association of Social Youth Organisations, an organisation that united the youth organisations of the world under a socialist banner. Munzenberg set about converting it to Soviet control. Alongside his Finnish contemporary Otto Kuusinen he pioneered the creation of myriad organisations throughout those nations whose foreign policy was hostile to the Soviet Union. Munzenberg saw the membership disparagingly as a 'Club of Innocents', particularly those of the Friendship Societies.

The operational activities of Munzenberg and Kuusinen, and proof that Soviet spies were active within Britain and the United States, fuelled the fires of anti-Communism. A situation evolved where any contact with Communists, or particularly representatives of the Soviet sphere of influence, could lead to an individual facing accusations that they were in some form of collusion with agents of the Soviet Union. Therefore official contact was minimal, at the highest level only and any form of entryism was prevented. This underpinned the Labour Party policy of proscription. The recognition by the party that certain organisations were conduits of Soviet propaganda, and tools of Soviet foreign policy, increased the fear that Soviet subversion was indeed a threat to party cohesion, electability and, indeed, British democracy.

This was only one aspect of the campaign designed to keep the Communists out of politics. Western propaganda promoted the perception that the Soviet Union was economically and politically corrupt and therefore contact with the regime, and its supporters, was perceived as unhealthy. This uniformity of message led to a rebuttal being transmitted by the Soviet Union and pro-Soviet organisations. In turn organisations were established to counter Soviet propaganda and infiltration.[11] An article in RIA Novosti's Daily Review outlined the Soviet campaign and its effects.

A system was maintained that included an office of correspondents, the Novosti Press Agency [and] the Houses of Friendship. They functioned, turned out products, some delegations made visits. A paradox system emerged. Despite an extreme hatred of Communism, the image of the USSR was much better than that of today's Russia.[12]

The Cold War was therefore fought mainly through propaganda campaigns and covert operations.

This activity was a key aspect of both superpowers' prosecution of the Cold War and fear of enemy infiltration dominated international relations and domestic security. The Cold War became not a race for global military domination, though both sides did create monopsonic markets for their arms and established ideological hegemony over regional security, the frontline of the Cold War was ideological. As Yuri Andropov, fifth leader of the Soviet Union, stated in an address to the Central Committee of the Communist Party of the Soviet Union [CPSU] of 15th June 1983;

> A struggle is going on for the hearts and minds of billions of people in the world. The future of mankind depends, in no small measure, on the outcome of this ideological struggle.[13]

While this was the Soviet perception of the Cold War it was equally recognised in the West that public opinion needed to be convinced that anti-Communism was the correct course of action. Fears existed that, while the majority of Western opinion was indeed convinced by the Cold War rationale, there existed an influential clique of pro-Communists, either in the pay or under the influence of Soviet propagandists and agents, who were attempting to reverse this negative perception of the Soviet Union.

The tactic utilised by the Soviet Union was the launch of an appeal to sympathisers to alter the perception of Soviet Communism. Propaganda was designed to attract those who argued for the adoption of a 'true' socialist agenda. It promulgated the twin beliefs that the Soviet Union adhered to true socialism and that it represented the progressive option in a zero-sum global dichotomy. The methods by which these messages were disseminated differed and are analysed separately below, however the paramount aim was to attract a variety of different influential individuals into the pro-Soviet coterie. The more difficult step was to encourage those individuals to act on behalf of the Soviet Union.

PRESENTING THE ALTERNATIVE: THE SOVIET PROPAGANDA CAMPAIGN

Initial reports of the political and social situation in post-revolutionary Russia were largely unfavourable. The correspondence of Malcolm Muggeridge to The Manchester Guardian reinforced the opinion that Communism was a new form of oppressive barbarism. This was perpetuated by official reports. It was thus necessary for the Soviet Union to encourage Westerners to visit the Soviet Union and offer an alternative, favourable, account of the regime: one it was hoped they would reiterate.

The first visitors to the Communist State equally reflected the zero-sum nature of the global dichotomy. There were those, such as John Reed and George Bernard Shaw, who fell in love with the society and political system; others, like Muggeridge and Walter Citrine, recognised a savage, barbaric and oppressive aspect to Bolshevik rule. It was the latter that became the received analysis. Muggeridge sent reports of cannibalism, state violence, enforced hardship, purges and growing inequality. These reports were to define the accepted perception of life under Communist rule. Those who dismissed this reality were individuals who desired the reality to be different. This led them to be criticised for their blinkeredness, or for allegations to be perpetuated that they were being paid by the Soviet Union to refute these stories. From these polarised perspectives the propaganda war began in earnest.

Stalin, a far more pragmatic leader than Lenin, attempted to gain acceptance from the world. This initially involved attempts to show that his policy did not involve spreading the Bolshevik revolutionary doctrine, this was encapsulated in the theory of socialism in a single country. Alongside this was the campaign to show that Communism was an advanced method of government. The achievements of planning and state control were publicised, leading many to accept that the future lay more with the ideas of Communist society than those of the capitalist world. The Soviet Union became, to those who desired such an icon, a living embodiment of the socialist meta-narrative. This was advertised in diverse ways, each aiming to convince the non-Communist of the benefits of that society, that it was more advanced than capitalism and represented the future for mankind. The supporters and purveyors of this meta-narrative argued that the Soviet Union was the epitome of the modernist ideal, Communism had redesigned the relations between man and society and was in the process of reshaping the future of politics. The objective of this was to gain support among idealistic but influential writers throughout the non-Communist world. The aim of this programme was simple: gaining acceptance, ending containment and encouraging others to adopt the ideas of socialism.

It is useful to look at the methods by which the Soviet Union attempted to create converts. This was a three-fold approach. Soviet publications in the form of pamphlets, books and journal articles argued the benefits of Soviet society and the Communist system. These were circulated through pro-Soviet organisations within the non-Communist nations. Secondly, and more important in convincing a broader audience, was encouraging others to promote the Soviet argument. The intended process was; encouraging individuals to read and believe the propaganda, and then to visit the Soviet Union so the arguments of the propaganda could be reinforced. The final step was to encourage the individuals to reiterate these arguments as their own. Thus there are three aspects to the creation of the pro-Soviet meta-narrative discussed above: Soviet-produced propaganda, encouraging non-Communists to visit, then encouraging those people to write a favourable account of their visit. A further aspect to this process, detailed later, was not adopted by all those who held pro-Soviet sympathies and entailed entering into further activities in support of the aims of Soviet policy.

Propaganda is the first line of attack when attempting to reach, and influence, a mass audience. In times of warfare it has been the primary tool for gaining support from the people for a cause, and attempting to undermine that of the enemy. It was the latter that Soviet propaganda was aimed towards. The ideology was disseminated in the name of the 'people' of the world, as distinct from those in government. The Soviet propagandists attempted to plant a seed, or in many cases nurture an already existent sympathy. The aim being to encourage influenced individuals to work on their behalf. According to Marx this was the role of the Communist Party, who would act as the leader of the proletariat.[14] In Britain the Communist Party [CPGB] became politically discredited and was unable to act as an agent of influence within the British socialist movement. Therefore, though it could still do Moscow's work, other independent advocates were required to substantiate Soviet arguments.

Early examples of these would be Beatrice and Sidney Webb, George Bernard Shaw and Denis Nowell Pritt. Depending upon the degree of Moscow's influence over those who produced the arguments, we see these secondary propagandist arguments staying true to, or varying somewhat with, the Moscow line. Pritt was completely slavish to the Moscow line; the Webbs privately faltered; later cases such as Konni Zilliacus or Frank Allaun allowed themselves to be critical showing clear differences in the degree of influence played by the Soviet Union.

Qualter argued that the true reason for this propaganda campaign was much more than simply gaining pockets of sympathy across the globe. But that "in any given situation the reaction of those so influenced will be that desired by the propagandist."15 This means that those individuals who became influenced would, at crucial points, argue and act on behalf of the Soviet Union. This is the accusation made against many of the pro-Soviet members of the Labour Party. Attaining active support was the ultimate aim of the pro-Soviet propagandist, particularly when it was possible to influence those in, or with proximity to, political power. Public meetings on the advanced nature of Soviet society, usually substantiated by an eyewitness account did attract some support. Equally a mass readership for material like enabled propagandists to set the agenda in favour of Soviet objectives. However five hundred ordinary members of western society, the average enjoyed by societies like the Society for Cultural Relations with the Soviet Union [SCR] do not have the influence of one in government.

Lenin argued that there were two distinct methods for achieving this objective. Propaganda, the printed word, and agitation, the spoken word. Once in full power of what was to be the Soviet Union he created the Department of Agitation and Propaganda (Agitprop). Under the control of these departments fell the Soviet press, publishers, radio and later television. Thus, all media within the Soviet Union spoke with a single voice, that of the Politburo: essentially the leader. Through this unitarianist reportage the 'cult of personality' of Stalin was cultivated, fear was spread, and Russians and westerners alike could be drawn to believe the rhetoric. In 1929 this Department was divided. The Department of Agitation and Mass Campaigns was given the task of controlling information reaching the Soviet people, creating the cult of Stalin. The second department rendered from Agitprop was the Department of Culture and Propaganda, the work of which was aimed beyond Soviet borders. This division of labour lasted for five years; Agitprop was re-ratified in 1935. The aim of Agitprop was to mobilise and control the Russian people, while publications were aimed at the non-Communist world. Both aspects aimed at attaining slavish support for Stalinism and Soviet Communism. Internally this was a great success; externally it succeeded only among a minority with an existent ideological link to Marxist-Leninism. Agitprop established a network of publishers and writers who would reproduce the words of the Politburo as their own. British Communists such as Robin Page Arnot, Rajani Palme Dutt and Tom Wintringham produced many publications, from voluminous books to short easily readable pamphlets,[16] all argued the Soviet line. Alongside these were the Soviet Union's own publications of speeches and data, showing the success of Communism, and key theoretical works.

The chief exporter of this propaganda was the Novosti Publishing Agency, created in the early 1960s to counter the anti-Soviet propaganda that had become the chief produce of departments of Western security organisations.[17] The aim of Novosti was to centralise the production of Soviet propaganda. It ensured that every publication leaving the Soviet Union for the international audience was written with 'partiinost'; absolute loyalty to the party. It also sought, by this centralisation, to increase output, particularly to those audiences that the Soviet Union believed were most susceptible to their arguments. Novosti collected and disseminated data on the achievements of the Soviet Union and published myriad forms of literature to advertise and extol the cultural heritage of the Soviet Union to the foreign audience. As Hazan explained, the role of Novosti was to "sell the Soviet

Union to the world."[18] Alternatively, from the unique perspective of the Soviet Union, "spread the truth about the Soviet Union in all continents."[19] Novosti was, and to an extent remains, a highly organised propaganda machine though now it is a business providing travel brochures and Russian literature to the world market. Under the Soviet regime its staff consisted mainly of intelligence officers; for example Kim Philby worked for Novosti after his defection.

The largest audience for Novosti publications were the English speakers of Britain and North America, at whom was aimed, between 1960 and 1970, a total of 58.8 million magazines and newspapers. To concentrate on the statistics for Britain in 1970 alone 161 titles on culture and education were released and a total of 10.5 million individual copies sold. Western Europe was also heavily targeted, particularly the FDR [West Germany], France, Spain and Italy. Though publications to the latter two were decreasing by 1970, there was a sharp rise in publications released in Spanish after 1975. These were mainly historical works on the Communist's role in the Spanish Civil War, information hitherto banned by the Francoist regime. A few figures on publications exported to Europe show where the Soviet Union believed the most sympathy lay. In 1970 out of a total of 50,587 titles released by Novosti 21,406 were for the English market, 18,374 aimed at the FDR. This was the heritage of the Soviet Union's propaganda campaign aimed hitherto at these two nations. The Soviet propagandists had created an audience which, though an insignificant minority of the total population, was increasing steadily. Unfortunately what cannot be ascertained is what positions in society this minority held. We do see that many West Germans held prominent positions on front organisation's international committees.[20] This does indicate a degree of sympathy for the Soviet Union among an influential minority.

A similar targeting pattern is apparent in radio broadcasts, though in this case most broadcasting hours are aimed at the USA. Targeting was all important, the cost precluded saturation, therefore Agitprop had to aim its service at existing customers in the hope that these people would encourage others to join the audience. Pamphlets could be passed on to others, newspapers sold to work colleagues and so the message could be disseminated. This is the practice of any movement wishing to draw public attention to their cause. This, however, was essentially the work of an enemy power and anyone who entered into this type of activity was technically guilty of a treasonous act. However, prosecution was reserved only for those who passed secrets to the East, not for those who imported propaganda to the West.

The targeting process did not just aim at nations, but at individuals within a nation. Organisations held lists of the sympathetic, as many advertising companies hold the names of those who may potentially purchase their produce. Any individual who had subscribed to a newspaper or journal, sent off for a pamphlet, visited the Soviet Union, or more significantly became a member of a pro-Soviet organisation would be targeted with further material.[21] Agitprop, and its network, also targeted independent organisations. Propaganda attempted to link Soviet policy with the aims of non-aligned organisations. Equally pro-Soviet activists pursued entryism to gain influence over the policies of various organisations.

An example of which would be the way that the Campaign for Nuclear Disarmament [CND] was courted. Ostensibly a pacifist organisation which united many strands of thought, CND was infiltrated by Communists. By the 1980s members of the CPGB or the British Peace Association [BPA], British affiliate to the World Peace Council, filled many key organisational positions. For example Gary Lefley, BPA National Organiser became General Secretary of CND in 1981. He was joined on the National Executive by five others named as CPGB members: Philip Bolsover, Duncan Rees, Stanley Bonnett, Chris Horrie and John Cox. Though none of these were prominent British Communists, they had been slowly promoted within the pro-Soviet network until they could gain a degree of control over the policy of an influential movement with a mass membership. Bolsover was, during the 1970s, a Morning Star editorial writer; here he gained respect within the British Communist movement. His elevation was then to a place of greater influence. The role of these Communists was to transmit the message that the Soviet Union supported the anti-nuclear, pro-peace campaign to the membership of CND.[22] Stalin argued that war was inevitable between imperialist, and therefore capitalist, countries; thus, he argued, the peace movement should actively fight the governments of the capitalist nations.[23]

Using myriad publications the Soviet Union disseminated this message to the broader audience. In the July 1950 issue of the World Federation of Democratic Youth [WFDY] magazine the Soviet Union was proclaimed the bulwark for peace, despite the fact that it had just become a nuclear power and was arming the North Koreans against the United States. Speeches that reinforced this notion, and argued the justice of Soviet actions, were propagated by Soviet propaganda agencies. The front organisations disseminated a similar message to its membership. Thus the image of the Soviet Union as being a nation based upon a socialist ideology desirous of peaceful co-operation was disseminated among idealists and intellectuals alike, encouraging the creation of a pro-Soviet strand.

The initial propaganda of the Lenin regime was aimed at nurturing support and recognition from the world's governments. There was a degree of sympathy during the interventionism of the Allies during the civil war. Lenin sought to exploit this among those Union leaders who had threatened strike action and so ended the intervention policy. Initially representatives of the working class leaders were invited to Soviet Russia to view the new society. It received the mixed reviews characteristic of later visits to the Soviet Union. George Lansbury filled Albert Hall to speak of the virtues of the 'First Socialist Republic', overwhelmingly though Labour politicians and Union leaders condemned it, General Secretary of the TUC 1918-25 Walter Citrine was particularly critical. Following virtual failure with the working class leaders it was the intellectuals who were invited to visit and encouraged to dispel the rumours that the Bolsheviks were nothing more than anarchistic iconoclasts, hell bent on shaping the world in their image. This equally had varying degrees of success. Early publications had a very small audience, so the only tenable strategy was to induce others into publishing. All that was required was to get prominent individuals who commanded respect to visit the Soviet Union, praise it in the highest terms, and publish their work. George Bernard Shaw was one such selected and he in turn introduced the Webbs who produced the greatest eulogy possible.[24]

Shaw, the Webbs and many contemporary intellectuals and writers from the democratic west, found the invitation to visit, subsequent guided tour, and the honour of being able to produce an exclusive report on the phenomenon of the Twentieth Century, too great an opportunity to miss. They left for the Soviet Union with great alacrity, ignorant of what was being laid on for them. The Soviet Union that they saw was a pageant from the time they set foot on Russian soil. They were treated like demi-gods, given the party line and sent home with money, in the form of a publisher's advance. All that was required of them was the production of a favourable account. This was not unique to the 1930s, or to the writers and intellectuals, the invitation was to remain a powerful tool of Agitprop. It appears that many visited the Soviet Union wishing to find their ideal and therefore blinded themselves to the faults. A pertinent example, in relation to this study, would be the Webbs. However, there were many others who made the pilgrimage to the Socialist Mecca.[25]

Theodore Drieser, a lawyer who has suffered an expensive divorce, extolled the simplicity of divorce in the Soviet Union. Equally, Alexander Wicksteed, a campaigner for equality for women, lauded the fact that under Communism women had equal rights to work, and childcare provision was provided by the state to enable them to do so. The perceived achievements under Communism could be attributable to the conversion to pro-Sovietism of Renee Short, who held similar ideals to Wicksteed and combined them with her perception of Soviet society. Others did not go to the Soviet Union in search of an advanced society. They wished to return to basics and view politics and society developing from a tabula rasa. Indeed for the Fabians like Shaw and the Webbs it was an experiment, possibly one to which they believed they could provide stimulus. For others the Soviet

Union could provide a sense of atonement, they were hardened capitalists, fully imbibed with the fetish for commodities, in Soviet Russia they could view a new simpler world knowing that they would return to their comforts.[26] A process existed by which any guest could be convinced that the Soviet Union represented their personal ideal.

＊   From arrival in the Soviet Union, the 'guest' would be pumped with a stream of data showing Soviet successes. They were booked into suites in the Metropole Hotel and dined on the finest foods. This experience led Shaw to believe that there could not be a famine in the Soviet Union.[27] During their stay the guests underwent an endless tour of factories, collectives or whatever their particular interest may be. Renee Short described her tour of the schools of Leningrad,[28] Platts-Mills the justice system.[29] This would provide the ultimate proof that the successes were real and worthy of published praise. Furthermore, implicit to these tours was the implication that these achievements should be actively protected from a hostile world.

Intourist was created in 1929 to co-ordinate the visitors programme in line with party policy. If one particular achievement required advertisement, then Intourist would take the guests there. Initially this was handled through Soviet businesses which would appoint an interpreter, often a KGB official. Intourist was used to centralise the organisation, it would be told who was arriving and when, and so be able to plan a programme around the visitor well in advance. During the peak period of visits, the 1960s and 70s, a London based company Progressive Tours, virtually subsiduarised by the British-Soviet Friendship Society, became the main tour operator. This worked closely with British front organisations and the Soviet embassy, and according to certain sources made a very good profit from this venture. Worker's exchange trips became a particular tool for gaining support.[30] Once a trading partnership was established British workers were invited to visit their Eastern European counterpart. During these visits attempts were made to indoctrinate their visitors with Marxist-Leninist ideas, a campaign which can be attributed as contributing to the emergence of revolutionary ideas during the 1970s and 80s.[31] The tour guides, often young women, were also employed to steer their guests away from what they really wanted to see and to what the party wanted them to see. Pamphlets were also left in hotels; these reinforced Soviet propaganda and no exposure to non-partiinost material was allowed.

＊   There were those who came back after this experience unimpressed. Andre Gide, a French writer, disliked the fact that he was allowed privileges by the so-called ultra egalitarian society.[32] Others could not ignore the conflicting reports. They, like Stephen Spender British poet and playwright, could not compromise what they were shown with the conflicting reports of their respected contemporaries. This was particularly the case among 1930s

Communists who renounced the Soviet Union in 1939 because of the Nazi-Soviet Pact. Others failed to make this transition because they saw the Soviet Union as representing a higher ideal, whether it was socialism, simplicity, or an advanced society is particular to the individual.

The alternative perspective of life and politics within the Soviet Union, as portrayed by propaganda and reinforced during guided tours, was presented by organisations and respected individuals. This was to be continued by many of the Labour MPs who constitute this study. There were three key ways in which this meta-narrative of the Soviet Union was presented to the West. Firstly the presentation of a purely alternative perception, this combated the image of the Communist as evil and sub-human as depicted in Western propaganda. Secondly, and importantly, the Soviet Union was extolled as an 'actually existing' socialist society, the embodiment of an ideal. This encouraged others to support and protect the regime, many hoping for the long awaited thaw in the leadership style. Finally, the Soviet Union was presented as a proponent for peaceful coexistence, the alternative to the United States which was argued to be an imperialist power. Those who presented this alternative picture of the Soviet Union facilitated Communist entryism into groups such as CND and campaigned for acceptance of the World Peace Council as a credible organisation. The latter created a situation which meant that many of those who adopted an anti-Atlanticist, or what is often described as a 'progressive' stance on world affairs, but were not ostensibly sympathisers of the Soviet Union, were drawn naturally into the pro-Soviet orbit as the perception was popularised that only the Soviet Union supported progressive political movements.[33]

THE PROGRESSIVE ALLY: THE SOVIET FRONT ORGANISATION NETWORK

One of the central tenets of the Labour left-wing was, and remains, the promotion of social and political reform and the adoption of a liberal democratic framework across the world. This was promoted through extra-parliamentary organisations established to oppose regimes which operated through oppression, segregation and suppression of all, or sections of, the populace. While to many the Soviet Union epitomised the antithesis of these 'progressive' ideals a strategy existed to counter this perception. The Soviet Union actively supported many organised movements, regional, national and international, which opposed non-progressive regimes. Examples of those organisations which directly received Soviet support, in the form of money and arms, were the African National Congress [ANC], the Palestine Liberation Organisation [PLO] and the Provisional Irish Republican Army [IRA]. This process was aimed at drawing the members of supportive organisations, such as anti-Apartheid and the Troops Out Movement, to also support these causes' benefactor. These ideologically non-aligned organisations were often funded indirectly through Soviet controlled umbrella organisations such as the International Association of Democratic Lawyers [IADL]. This support led to the progressive ideals of the organisation and its membership being allied to Soviet foreign policy aims, thus encouraging supporters of the ideals to join the pro-Soviet coterie.

John Platts-Mills, President of the Haldane Society and Executive Member of the IADL, acted as the link between Cominform and myriad British organisations, organising funding for offices, providing secretaries and linking them to non-British organisations with a similar remit. He accepted that the Soviet link was real, arguing it to be necessary and unavoidable:

> America, and Britain, supported all these monstrous leaders and disgusting regimes, only the Soviet Union stood for freedom and democracy they supported justice and so helped one who fought these regimes.[34]

Platts-Mills rationalises this as part of a struggle of good versus evil, the Soviet Union representing the good, a perception he developed during the Spanish Civil War. He refused to see that the ulterior motive for the Soviet Union's support for these organisations was to encourage the members to act on the behalf of, not only the particular organisation but also, the Soviet Union.

These organisations, often referred to as front organisations independent of their proximity to Soviet policy aims and Soviet control, because their innocent façade was perceived as a front for their real function: supporting Soviet policy aims, recruited from a broad section of the left-wing. Communists, Labour Party members, non-aligned socialists, pacifists and humanists supported the ideals these organisations represented. The Soviet leadership's underlying hope was that this broad alliance would draw the majority of socialists and progressive individuals into adopting a pro-Soviet perspective. This could only be achieved by linking the aims of the organisation with those of the Soviet Union and by fostering a recognition that it was the Soviet Union alone whose policy was supportive of progressive movements across the globe. Thus there was an active policy within many organisations designed to encourage support for the Soviet Union as being the progressive bulwark as an alternative to the 'imperialist' United States.

This was perhaps the most effective way of creating a stratum of support. Whether they were single-issue societies; such as the League for Democracy in Greece, organisations working at the international level; the

World Peace Council for example, or friendship and cultural societies like the British-Soviet Friendship Society, they attracted a wider spectrum of membership than the Communist Parties. This was the purpose in the mind of the man who can be credited for developing this network, Willi Munzenberg. Munzenberg's 'Innocents', particularly within the Friendship Societies, had the appearance of independence, but the societies' leaders were tireless workers on behalf of the Soviet Union.

      In Britain one man stamped his mark on several such organisations, D N Pritt. It appears clear that he was an agent of the Soviet Union.[35] For his devotion to duty, Pritt was awarded both the Lenin Peace Prize and the Stalin Prize. Pritt's main task, it would seem, was initially the creation of support within British intellectualism. Later he was a pro-Soviet lawyer, Labour MP and independent pro-Soviet voice in parliament.[36] The first organisation he became involved with was the SCR. Though he does not appear on the list of founders, he was a prime mover in its establishment. At this time he was not well known and therefore his name did not carry much weight. However, those who were influenced sufficiently into forming the SCR were, or would become, extremely prominent. The list of founders read as a who's who of the pro-Soviet or fellow travelling intellectual movement, it included G D H Cole, G B Shaw, Beatrice Webb, Leonard and Virginia Woolf and J B S Haldane. There are also individuals like Bertrand Russell and H G Wells who criticised the regime, but still wished to retain a link with the Soviet Union or at least an interest in its progression. The founding members of such an organisation are unimportant. What is important is control. Pritt was the first President, no records exist of how he was elected, however his role was to ensure that the society would adhere to the Soviet policy line. This society was to be joined by the British-Soviet Friendship Society [BSFS], formed in 1927.

      Following the Second World War various friendly societies were created to promote friendship with the Warsaw Pact nations. All had a similar raison d'être, advancing the Soviet cause. The broader membership may not have been entirely aware of this. The SCR, for example, provided language classes, film shows, exchange visits for entertainment or education and travel arrangements. However, the main purpose was introduction. From the time an individual crossed the step of the SCR office, and showed an interest, that person was regarded as a potential sympathiser. This was the route taken by many students of Slavic languages, or exiled Russian refugees, who wished to retain a cultural link. Jane Rosen, currently the librarian for the SCR recalled that three MPs, Ian Mikardo, Sydney Silverman and Julius Silverman were frequent visitors; all three were, as children, Jewish refugees from Tsarist Russia. The SCR was particularly unobtrusive with regards to its control, this was what can be characterised as a 'first base' organisation. Individuals who progressed further into the network would become more interesting to the Soviet propaganda machine. However, in joining the SCR their names were entered onto the mailing list. They would then be sent offers to buy Soviet literature, or sent gratis copies, their response was measured and the contacts increased or decreased reciprocally. The Soviet Cultural Attaches, who monitored these societies, did not want to enlist these people as spies; all that was needed was a sympathetic ear. It would be ascertained later as to how far they would travel on the metaphorical Moscow-bound car.

Organisations such as the BSFS present the best example of a front organisation. While there are scant records of the inner workings of the national body, viewing the archived material of some of the regional branches it is possible to gain an insight into how the organisation operated. The raison d'être of the BSFS was to promote friendship and understanding between the peoples, but not the governments, of the two nations. They encouraged the twinning of towns, exchange visits and held meetings and seminars; all these aimed at educating people on politics and life in Soviet society. They approached art galleries to hold exhibitions, colleges to allow Russian visitors to give a presentation and encouraged the establishment of local East-West trading links. The best available example is the Birmingham Branch, whose minutes from 1975-90 present a picture of the activities of the society. These show there was a clear political agenda.

The organisation's meetings reiterated the message of the Soviet Union, particularly enforcing the image of the Soviet Union as being pro-peace and anti-nuclear. The secretaries frequently invited MPs to speak at these events, asking them to promote certain issues, particularly easing the way for expanding existent trade and it is notable who accepted and who declined. Philip Crees, Chair of the Birmingham branch, denies involvement in approaching MPs, but recalled it did occur and that he thought that the political side of the organisation was promoted too heavily. Crees campaigned for rapprochement but believed that it was achievable using cultural links alone. However, the organisations national apparatchiks, for much of the period Andrew Rothstein and Gordon Schaffer, ensured that promoting political connections remained high on the agenda.

Arguably this was due to these societies close ties to the Soviet Union. While members claim these societies were self-funding, evidence suggests that a degree of control was exercised from the Soviet Embassy and that the Centre encouraged political ties being forged. MPs were encouraged to join, one, Coventry MP 1964-83 William Wilson, being Chairman from 1977 to its demise. He recalled that when concerts were put on, the Soviet Ambassador would only attend if an MP were speaking.[37] This indicates that the Soviet Union saw the BSFS purely as a conduit for information and support and so enforced a certain type of activity upon its members. The faithful, who occupied the top posts, filtered these directives down to the membership at the branch level. Crees recalled that it was the secretary who dealt with "head office". This secretary was not named, and has since died but, was a Communist Party member and dealt with preparing articles for publication and organising events. The secretary was the mechanism by which the Centre maintained control over the branch. Crees appears a little naïve in not recognising the control exerted by the Soviet Union, but remained a semi-respectable figurehead of the branch, living on ideals that were largely false.

Following the Second World War altering the global perception of the Soviet Union became the goal for many such organisations. Linking the Soviet Union with the ideals of peace and democracy, in opposition to the recognised perception in the West, encouraged influential and idealistic individuals to lend their support. In this period the front organisations took on a new facet; from aiming to gain a mainly passive membership, they now needed an active pro-Soviet fifth column. Radek and Kuusinen's role for them came to life as the bulwark of Soviet agitation. The network expanded exponentially throughout the world, the centre of which was the World Peace Council [WPC].[38] This became a very powerful asset to the Soviet Union, gaining many unwitting agents to the cause, particularly through its subsidiary organisations. The raison d'être was defined in a 1949 Cominform directive

> Particular attention should be devoted to drawing into this move-ment trade unions, women's, youth, co-operative, sports, cultural, educational, religious and other organisations, and also scientists, writ-ers, journalists, cultural workers, parliamentary and other political and public leaders.[39]

This was the fulfilment of the ideals espoused by Lenin and put into practice by Munzenberg and Kuusinen, the desire to gain a mass movement just below the governmental level. All that had to be achieved was, as Munzenberg stated, "spread[ing] abroad the doctrine that Russia is prepared to sacrifice everything to keep the world at peace."[40]

It is doubtful that the mass movement, which the peace movement became, believed Soviet rhetoric. However the perception, which became popularised, was that the Soviet Union was at least more inclined towards peace and disarmament than the West, particularly the United States which was characterised as a capitalist imperial power. Many Labour MPs shared this view, however this was seldom the result of exposure to Soviet propa-ganda. Some who held an anti-Atlanticist world view found their ideas shared by Soviet propaganda, others viewed the propaganda as a cynical ploy and rejected these arguments.[41] The individuals who became attracted by the image of the Soviet Union as the force for 'peaceful co-existence' were those who held existent beliefs in the Soviet Union. These beliefs were gathered through their perceptions of the historical relations between East and West and their perceptions of the nature of Soviet socialism. Many of the ideals of the pro-peace movement became reinforced by Soviet propaganda, this led many organisations to be tainted by association because of the proximity of the arguments.

Using the WPC as an example it is possible to show how a front organisation was utilised to promote the idea of the Soviet Union as a bulwark of peace and ascertain what led individuals to join. The image of this organisation was one of non-alignment and impartiality. WPC activities aimed at promoting an end to the arms race and in particular ending nuclear escalation. This was of course completely in line with Soviet desires as they were well aware that they were losing the arms race.[42] The initiative emerged following the first World Congress of Defenders of Peace held simultaneously in Paris and Prague in April 1949. This attracted delegates from seventy-two countries. We know that at least two British MPs attended the Parisian conference: Konni Zilliacus and Ian Mikardo. Goodman argued that this was an attempt to unite the worldwide communist movement following a period when control had slipped away from Moscow and at a time when communication was hindered due to keen defences and inadequate finances.43 The WPC was established as the executive body of the Partisans for Peace Congress, which claimed to unite the anti-fascist and anti-imperialist movements across the globe. The invitation placed in World Government News, the journal of the US based World Government Movement, claimed modest objectives.

> to continue discussions with the World Government Movement in different countries, to seek for points of agreement and joint activity, and to encourage participation by both movements in their respective conferences and congresses.[44]

Frederic Joliot-Curie defined the organisation's role in explaining"[n]o one man, no one country by itself, but all united together can defend peace and prevent war."[45] This was to become the central tenet of the WPC.

Joliot-Curie, scientist and Nobel laureate was the first WPC President and the French representative; however, he was not a member of the French government. Equally the United States representative 1949-53 was Paul Robeson, a man banned from public speaking in his own country. This is mirrored by many of the representatives. What it became, therefore, was an organisation with an international membership of intellectuals and artisans, all putting forward a pro-Soviet argument for peace while having little real influence. Essentially it was an agent of influence as were its members. The WPC did have input at, perhaps, the highest level, though was still unable to change policy. It was recognised by the United Nations and was often consulted during the formulation of policies around relevant issues. Therefore, as an agent of influence, it had achieved its greatest aim. Nevertheless it found itself unable to change the dominant rationale.

Communists historically dominated the leadership of the WPC. The greatest example is that of Romesh Chandra, who became President in May 1977 following the death of Joliot-Curie. His path to the heights of pro-Sovietism was through the Communist Party of India. Indian Communists became the most fervent supporters of the Soviet Union during the fight against Britain for independence. Chandra ensured that all WPC propaganda had a pro-Soviet, anti-Western slant attached to it. The central tenet of all WPC propaganda was world peace: Chandra argued "[t]he Soviet Union's military policy fully corresponds to these goals. It is of a purely defensive character".[46] Equally representatives of Soviet controlled governments dominated it. Poland, the Soviet Union itself, Cuba, the German Democratic Republic, and other Warsaw Pact nations held exponentially more seats than their size or influence should have dictated. Latin American regimes also feature highly, but usually for limited periods, then an ex-president, recently ousted by a coup is found acting as the country's representative. Usually a US backed military leader, a factor that reinforced the anti-American rhetoric of WPC propaganda, had exacted the coup. Any circumstance that indicated that the United States was an aggressor suited the WPC perfectly. The WPC did take harsher lines than would be expected on Hungary and Czechoslovakia, as did semi-independent Communist states, such as Yugoslavia and Romania. This could indicate that the Soviet Union did not have total ideological control. However, this was not how the WPC was perceived in the west. William Whitelaw, in his role as British Home Secretary denied access to Chandra in 1980 on the grounds that he was "a senior official of an organisation which is a disguised instrument of Soviet foreign policy... his exclusion is conducive to the public good."[47]

The irony of the WPC is that its members ratified the 'rules and regulations' which stated members should promote eight set objectives. These included respect for the right of people to sovereignty and independence, respect for the territorial integrity of states and, non-interference in the internal affairs of other nations. These, together with the objectives concerning nuclear proliferation were broken continuously by the Soviet Union, and not only in Hungary, Czechoslovakia and Afghanistan. In every Warsaw Pact nation and within the Baltic States there were desires for independence from Soviet military rule. This must have been obvious to those who represented the GDR and Poland and for many native Russians, however, this organisation constantly promoted the Soviet Union as the conciliatory and progressive superpower, an argument that gained strength as it became widespread. MPs are recorded as members, and one, James Lamond, MP for Oldham 1970-92 defended his affiliation in Parliament. He recognised its pro-Soviet nature, but saw it as the only organisation which co-ordinated the peace movement on an international scale.[48] He was convinced that the pro-Soviet argument was correct, as were many others. Viewing the organisation impartially we can see the attraction it held for people of a certain mindset. Members met anywhere in the world, represented many societies and ethnic origins and the agenda was centred around establishing a peaceful, co-operative future. Colour, race, religion, gender or politics was irrelevant, what was importance was a desire to work towards world peace. This was the attraction of the organisation.

Control cannot be reasonably disputed, even though members such as James Lamond claim they were completely unaware of it. The list of Joliot-Curie Gold Medal for Peace winners read as a 'who's who' of the Communist leaders and supporters of the world. Fidel Castro of Cuba, Salvador Allende of Chile, Brezhnev himself and Yasser Arafat chairman of the Palestine Liberation Organisation [PLO], a regular receiver of Russian arms. This type of organisation attracted those who desired world peace. They were then drawn into believing that the Soviet Union was the only nation that stood for peace. The Soviet Union did desire peace, but on their terms, not those of the western leaders, thus they encouraged an army of supporters to argue this cause on their behalf. The objective was to encourage these supporters to use their positions of influence to change the governmental and public perception of Soviet policy aims.

The WPC also forged links with Soviet backed paramilitary and liberation movements, particularly the PLO, Provisional IRA and the ANC and encouraged leading members of these onto the Presidential Committee. This led supporters of these movements; pro-Palestinians, Irish Nationalists and Black Rights activists, into the pro-Soviet orbit. Subsidiary organisations, established independently, were supported by front organisations. The Anti-Apartheid movement in Britain was funded by the Haldane Society, which indicates they enjoyed the sponsorship of Moscow, as was any organisation that opposed British involvement with Northern Ireland.

John Platts-Mills, President of the Haldane Society, organised annual grants to be transferred from the Haldane Society's fund to more than twenty different organisations that opposed Anglo-American policy and supported various global liberation movements. The fund was entitled the "international liberation fund" established jointly by the IADL and the WPC, undoubtedly the money came from the Soviet Union. No accounts for the

Haldane Society are available, however Platts-Mills defended his role arguing that "someone had to support these causes, no so-called democratic government would".[49] Equally Libya, Cuba and Vietnam had their own friendship and support organisations which were backed by the Soviet Union. Possibly all but the top echelon of these organisations could have avoided being fully aware of the extent of Soviet support.

. When looking at those front organisations which survived beyond the Soviet Union it is telling that they were poorly funded in their latter years. In 1994 Paul Mercer[50] recorded them as being mainly run from one address; 27 Old Gloucester Street, London. This was a single office that controlled around twenty post office box numbers. Here mail for diverse organisations such as the British Afro-Asian Solidarity Campaign, The Friends of Afghanistan, No Intervention in Libya, Hands Off Ireland and Hands off Iraq were received and disseminated to the officials. Many of these are anonymous; however most openly advertised MPs as patrons.

. The overarching supporter for these organisations was the IADL. This provides a good example of how non-aligned progressive movements were drawn into the pro-Soviet orbit. The IADL was created and directly controlled by Moscow. The Haldane Society, the British subsidiary, was run firstly by Pritt, then by John Platts-Mills. This society aided the establishment of smaller, single-issue organisations that attracted a different calibre of member. Many Labour MPs supported the Anti-Apartheid cause; prominent members were Stan Newens and Bernie Grant. Grant, veteran former MP for Tower Hamlets, supported many black rights and anti racist causes, Newens, as a prominent figure within Liberation promoted many campaigns against US supported regimes in Latin America; particularly Pinochet's Chile. Equally many MPs, some of whom were Jewish, supported pro-Palestinian societies; these included Sydney Silverman, Ian Mikardo and in recent years Jeremy Corbyn and George Galloway. These MPs were more than likely to have been unaware of the extent of Soviet control the organisations had, or did not care provided the civil rights issue was publicised internationally and addressed within the respective nations. This was the case with most members, however, if the Soviet Union could have made explicit, and popularised, the perception of itself as an ally of this progressive cause, it was hoped that the dominant perception of the Soviet Union would change. This was the true reason for the Soviet Union supporting these organisations.

. Alongside these organisations were the truly independent peace movements who were constantly targeted by the WPC. This was largely successful. For example, Communists became prominent in CND during the 1980s. The CPGB had been a co-supporter of the Aldermaston marches since the 1950s, the Communists appeared as fellow pacifists, however, their interests were not solely pro-peace. Labour Action for Peace [LAP], retained a non-communist leadership, but also appeared to subscribe to the notion that the Soviet Union was pro-peace, reiterating this argument in many publications.[51] Members of the LAP, particularly Frank Allaun, were often found supporting the Soviet argument. They did not go as far as the WPC, however, appear to have been influenced by Soviet arguments.

These ideas were clearly recognised as a threat to British political stability by all parties in government. The Labour Party proscribed membership to the WPC in 1951, almost immediately after its inception. It also investigated anyone who had links to the WPC.[52] However, it was not necessary to be a member to be under the influence of such an organisation. Through subsidiaries, such as the British Peace Committee, myriad publications entered the country. They were sold in many left-wing bookshops, on peace rallies and marches, and were sent as trial copies to those who had previously shown an interest. Left-wing MPs were sent review copies, in the hope that their content would influence the arguments. The question is did this propaganda campaign influence them or simply reinforce their existent world views?

Those MPs interviewed do not recall any influence being drawn from pro-Soviet publications. They see their arguments as being a product of their own beliefs and experience. However the arguments of those who take up a greater part of this study, Konni Zilliacus, Frank Allaun and Stan Newens particularly, follow the tenet of WPC material to the letter. They did not openly support the Soviet Union, only world peace. But each argued that the Soviet Union had the greater propensity for negotiating peace while the United States was characterised as a dangerous and antagonistic force. This is a conundrum that can only be answered by the individuals themselves. It appears that they were influenced, in some way, by Soviet propaganda because they arrived at the conclusion that the Soviet Union was fervently pro-peace and the United States opposed these ideals. Moreover some were so keen to believe that they risked their careers, and political credibility, to defend Soviet policy.

Perhaps the most important front organisations were those that co-ordinated opposition to United States backed anti-democratic regimes. These specifically targeted MPs who had previously espoused sympathy with their particular cause. This can be best exemplified through the work of the League for Democracy in Greece. This had been established during the Second World War as an aid organisation under the Presidency of Compton Mackenzie, writer and humanist (1883-1972) with Pritt as Organising Secretary. Following the war activism increased as the British government supported the anti-Communist monarchist forces in the civil war and the League became a fervent opponent of this policy. Initially the League enjoyed substantial support from the parliamentary left-wing, claiming 80

members from the 1945-50 parliament,[53] this was largely lost, however, when
the Labour Party proscribed the league in 1950. The League did retain a cell of
support however and were constantly kept up to date on who was sympathetic.

     New life was breathed into the organisation in 1968. From the con-
clusion of the Civil War, and establishment of King Paul II as de jure
leader, there had existed a conflict between the civilian government and
the military. Papandreou, the nominal Social Democrat Prime Minister, attempted to gain control of his defence ministry. This prompted a coup led
by Colonel Papadopoulos. In response to these developments John Fraser,
MP for Norwood 1966-97, formed the parliamentary Greek Democratic Committee to exert pressure on the government to support Papandreous. Fraser
forged links with the League, using it as an adjunct. In a letter to the League's
Secretary, Diana Pym, Fraser listed all the MPs who had supported motions
calling for an investigation into the human rights record of the right wing
Greek government.[54] In 1973, following the abandonment of proscription
by the Labour Party, the 98 MPs Fraser listed were systematically approached
by Pym and Marion Sarafis, fellow administrator of the League. Each MP
was invited to join, and offered Vice Presidencies or other Executive
positions.[55] From this they gained 21 new members and a further forty-two
agreed to promote the Greek political situation as a special interest. They were
then prompted by letter when an issue of importance should be raised.[56]

     It is important to note who did join, and who put their names
forward as willing to argue the League's case. Most who joined had supported
other 'front' causes. Though this organisation did not specifically draw
MPs to the Communist cause the links with the Soviet Union were fairly
explicit. In 1946 the League incorporated Maritpress, a propagandist press
agency run by the Greek Communist Party. Pym shared an office with
Maritpress and therefore could brief members and sympathisers on the
Communist arguments. Pym also forged links to what Rose describes as
Matrix Organisations, those which co-ordinate covert activity internationally.[57] She was in constant contact with the Soviet Women's Anti-Fascist
Committee [SWAFC] and the Soviet Committee of Solidarity with Greek
Democrats [SCSGD]. In an undated letter to Lydia Petrova of the SWAFC it
is evident that Pym visited the Soviet Union on several occasions and participated on a 'joint action planning committee' with the SCSGD. Pym also
encouraged left-wing figures to visit and meet Soviet officials of these organisations. On 20 February 1973 she wrote to Sergei Smirnov of the SCSGD
to inform him that Alan Sapper, an influential Communist Union leader,[58]
was due to visit the Soviet Union and had an interest in Greek issues. She
told Smirnov that he should "meet him to discuss the international action
which you have been over-seeing." Pym also wanted Sapper to be taken to
the Greek exiles' community in Tashkent that the SCSGD had established.

Sapper was to become Chairman of the League in 1977, but had been involved in the organisation's activity since 1968. During the filming of Doctor Zhivago reports from Union members had indicated that the political situation was worsening, summary executions were taking place and non-Greek film workers felt unsafe. He spearheaded a Union-led blockade of Greece, established links with Greek dissidents and began a file listing those who were committing crimes against the Greek people. Sapper recalled that the only international support for the anti-fascist movement in Greece came from the Soviet Union. This led to much information being passed through Greek refugees in the Soviet Union to their supporters in Britain. He testified that this necessitated that clear links between the League and the Soviet Union were established and a joint programme of activity pursued.[59] The Soviet Union had established clear links with the Greek socialists thus were in a better position to co-ordinate the support campaign, this led the League's policy to be placed under Soviet control.

Pym did act as a conduit for Soviet instructions, particularly in the 1967-73 period. There are many letters that show links being established between the League and organisations such as the World Federation of Democratic Youth. The Vice President S Chakraborty, told Pym that "we should like solidarity to be expressed in the most diverse forms."[60] Pym sent literature to British youth organisations, Trade Unions, left-wing publications and sympathetic individuals. Much of this was produced in the Soviet Union and disseminated through the Bureau of Liaison with Organisations by Ivan Bachev. Letters from Bachev, in both English and Russian, exist in the League for Democracy in Greece Archive. Records show these were translated by the League, converted into pamphlets and sent out to other organisations. Copies of letters from Pym to local peace groups, Youth Federations, and Student Unions exist requesting that pamphlets be disseminated among their members. The pamphlets encouraged the reader to take action to support Greece. Pym did not inform any of the organisations where the material had originated.

There are no specific details of meetings with Soviet officials, however the tone of the letters, which shows a familiarity, indicates that Pym had met them on several occasions. This is also indicated by references to meetings in Moscow, London and across Europe in letters between Pym and several of the officials. It can also be inferred that these meetings were at the expense of the Soviet government. The League at no time had a mass membership and though no full accounts exist after Leslie Solley's departure as Honorary Treasurer, some time after the 1956 AGM, we can see it was not an affluent organisation. It was of course in the Soviet interest to encourage a good relationship between their domestic organisations and international counterparts. This allowed the Soviet Union greater policy control and afforded them a direct link to membership. The fact that this included several MPs, who also harboured sympathies in other areas of Soviet foreign policy, made the advantage greater.

These examples allow us to gain a snapshot of how some of the front organisations operated. Particularly in the case of the League for Democracy in Greece we see an organisation, founded on humanitarian concerns, become pro-Soviet due to a series of well placed individuals within its hierarchy and a Soviet campaign to establish itself at the head of the Greek anti-fascist movement. Evidence indicates that similar campaigns were undertaken with regard to the Anti-Apartheid and pro-Palestinian campaigns. Pritt was instrumental in ensuring the League adopted a pro-Soviet perspective when he became Vice President. Diana Pym, as secretary, acted as the main conduit of communication with the Soviet Union. This is similar to the role of the anonymous secretary of the Birmingham BSFS, therefore we can assume that similar methods were used in other organisations.

The front organisations were highly organised and effective, promoting a popular cause, while being backed covertly by the Soviet Union. We can observe how the process of courtship by the Soviet Union worked and how the organisation was able to encourage a number of individuals, in positions of influence, to support the organisations' cause. This could mean, at key times, also supporting the policy of the Soviet Union. The mechanisms for achieving this appear as simplicity itself, but are the product of a well organised propaganda machine. This was part of the process of drawing individuals towards the Soviet side in the ideological war.

The pro-Soviet strand within the British Labour Party were not a product of this campaign. They did enjoy contact with Soviet officials, reiterated Soviet arguments, visited the Soviet Union and were prominent members of front organisations. However they pursued these activities on the strength of personal beliefs. These were reinforced by the Soviet campaign, and efforts were made to maintain support at times when support was liable to weaken. The Birmingham BSFS engaged in frenetic activity in January 1969 to explain Soviet actions in Czechoslovakia. This included mailing the two local MPs sympathetic to the Soviet Union, Renee Short and William Wilson. These individuals were important to the Soviet Union and the campaign aimed to increase their number. This was largely a failure. However, the study of Soviet methods of gaining support allows us to understand how an alternative perception of the Soviet Union became popularised among a minority of individuals who held existing sympathies towards the Soviet model of peaceful socialism.

2

FROM EMANCIPATORY REVOLUTION TO GRAND ALLIANCE

The Traditions of pro-Sovietism

The ideological division of the world, synonymous with the Cold War, served to focus the activities of individuals who possessed a sentimental attachment to the ideals of Soviet Communism. However the arguments that were developed in defence of the model of 'actually existing socialism' were not developed purely as a counter balance to Western produced anti-Soviet propaganda. The pro-Soviet position was the public expression of the belief that ideological links existed between the Soviet 'socialist experiment' and the future of socialism as a political programme. This belief led British socialists to develop means to defend the Soviet Union on the basis that a common objective existed and that this could only be reached in a stable and interdependent world order.

The traditions of pro-Sovietism emerged as a result of the Russian revolutions in 1917 and a symbiotic relationship developed between British pro-Sovietism, and the pro-Soviet milieu's analysis of British socialism, and the Soviet Union which was to remain a permanent feature within this political strand. Evidence for this relationship can be found in the fact that pro-Sovietism became pronounced and then submerged in response to developments within the Soviet system and Soviet actions in foreign policy and as a reaction to failures with the British gradualist tradition of socialism. Clear breaks with the Soviet model were made in reaction to Stalin's purges and show trials, the Nazi-Soviet pact and the invasion of Hungary and Czechoslovakia, however some individuals were unable to make this break and were forced to excuse these actions. The individuals who maintained a pro-Soviet position held the viewpoint that elements of the Soviet system were built upon socialist principles that should be adopted by the British Labour Party. Thus the Soviet Union was employed as a hook on which to hang these individual's opposition to Labour's economic and foreign policies.

In order to understand the opposition to the post-1945 Cold War rationale it is necessary to place these pro-Soviet sentiments within a historical perspective. The traditions underpinning them mainly date back to the period immediately preceding the Second World War, specifically 1931-39. There was little lasting attachment to the revolutionary spirit of 1917 in Russia within the British Labour Party, nor was there any ideological sympathy for Soviet Communism during the 1920s. There were, however, contrasting views of the Soviet Union and the Communist International, therefore it is necessary to explain how British socialists greeted the societal changes in Russia and their perception of how this would effect the world order. This chapter covers the period 1917-1945, and charts the currents of support as they moved towards and away from the ideas emanating from the Soviet Union. During this period fervent opponents became ardent admirers, and erstwhile supporters turned their back upon the Communist ideal. A minority of those who inherited the pro-Soviet perspective of world politics were elected to the Labour benches of the 1945-50 parliament. Their election would mark the beginning of active parliamentary support for the Soviet Union within the Labour Party.

There are several existent studies of the relationship between the British Labour Party and the broader socialist movement and post-revolutionary Russia, subsequently referred to as the Soviet Union.[1] These characterise the period under focus here as one that set the scene for the anti-Sovietism of the Cold War. The Labour Party saw the Soviet Union as the antithesis of its socialist beliefs and recognised that contact was electorally damaging. This led to a division occurring in the British socialist movement between the British Socialist Party, which evolved into the CPGB, the Independent Labour Party [ILP] who were more tolerant of Soviet ideas, and the anti-Soviet Labour Party.[2] The Labour Party's mistrust of the Soviet Union emerged almost immediately after political power passed to the Russian Communists.[3] The ideological dichotomy is highlighted by the fact that the October 1917 revolution was perceived, with a zero-sum perspective, as either a triumph of the people over tyranny or as an act of violent repression. The PLP leadership universally subscribed to the latter. What is clear is that the two perspectives shared little ideological middle ground and thus no alliance between the PLP and the Communist International [Comintern] was ever seen as viable or attractive. This means that support for the Soviet Union was pursued at the dissident individual level.

The fact that, after 1922, there was an organised pro-Soviet political organisation within Britain, the CPGB, does not indicate the presence of a coherent pro-Soviet movement. Pro-Soviet sympathisers could not be so

easily compartmentalised. While the CPGB attracted those who believed in
key revolutionary ideals and became proactive within the politics of class
struggle, the party was perceived by the working class as operating from a
very narrow political perspective. As Laybourn and Murphy observe "the
CPGB was an immensely sectarian organisation [that] attempted to impose
what many would now see as inappropriate policies on the British political
tradition of compromise and radicalism."[4] Thus, for those who supported
the ideals of Soviet Communism but opposed Moscow's dominance over
CPGB policy, there was not always a clear choice of which political party to ally
with. Therefore, although the CPGB is an integral element of this story, the
level of support for the party only acts as a definer of the political mood of
the period. Membership of the party and the proximity between pro-Soviet
MPs arguments and the simultaneous position of the CPGB on an issue
can, however, be indicative of an individual's beliefs.

There were periods when CPGB activity did act as a focal point for
some degree of mass activity, for example the Popular Front period saw the
CPGB at the head of a popular campaign for an Soviet-led alliance against
fascism. Similarly the electoral success of the CPGB, and many left-wing
candidates in 1945, can be argued as the result of a shift leftwards and a
general pro-Soviet mood within British society. The final example would be
the opposition to nuclear weapons, which while not a Communist led movement, saw respect for the CPGB arguments increase among a section of the
British socialist movement. However, we do not find many individuals drifting between Communism and Labourism, due mainly to the opposition to
Communist ideas within the Labour Party. Individuals did leave the CPGB
to join the Labour Party however, in studying these cases, it is possible to
find individuals who made a break not only with the party but also the politics of the communism.[5] The lack of electoral credibility experienced by the
CPGB forced many who developed a pro-Soviet perspective to choose to
remain independent from the party, prior to 1945 many centred upon the
ILP, but there were also influential Labour members who exhibited pro-
Soviet sympathies.

The CPGB did promote the argument that there was significant middle
ground between Labourism and Communism. J T Murphy argued that a
'united front' programme calling for the creation of a socialist society, radical
welfare reforms, recognition of the rights of Trade Unions and a lasting
peace in Europe, should be adopted by all the left-wing political groups.[6]
Murphy argued that this would attract the "proletarian masses" to the party
"eventually liquidating the Labour Party."[7] Thus while shared objectives did
exist the Labour leadership maintained a permanent distance from the CPGB

and, after 1924, Labour actively obstructed Communist entryism. This is clearly evident from the creation of the proscription list in 1925, which defined the organisations that promoted pro-Communist causes as inimical to the rules of Labour Party membership.[8] However, this did not detract Labour members and theorists from supporting pro-Communist and pro-Soviet causes and discussing a shared socialist destiny. The Soviet Union provided proof, as Dell observes, that "socialism could be successful, because it was believed that at least economically it was successful."[9] This was the product of a certain series of historical developments, ones which would have ramifications on the perception of World War II and the post war world order.

What can be observed in the 1917-45 era is a short honeymoon, in which the February 1917 revolution was welcomed as a triumph of prole-tarian power, while the October 1917 revolution was viewed with uncer-tainty. This was followed by a protracted period when there was little pro-Soviet activity outside the CPGB. However after 1930 a distinct shift of ideas towards the Soviet economic model can be detected and support grew for the Soviet Union in opposition to the growth of fascism. The reasons for these shifts, as throughout the history of pro-Sovietism, were developments in domestic politics and the international arena. The only reason that pro-Sovietism can be described in terms of being a movement during certain periods, albeit a minority movement, particularly 1945-1987, is due to the relative constancy of the bi-polar antagonism. Prior to 1945 it was not strictly necessary to choose an ideological side, though the ideas surrounding the Popular Front, which gained support after Hitler rose to power in Germany, did argue that an ideological dichotomy was being de-veloped. Thus the history of the relationship between the British Labour movement and the Soviet Union tells us a great deal about the roots of the pro-Soviet movement, and can indicate why certain MPs chose the Soviet side.

The questions this chapter seeks to answer are what factors led to the development of pro-Soviet analyses, how were these arguments ex-pressed and what traditions were bequeathed to post-war socialist politics. This will be achieved by focusing upon key figures within the British La-bour movement who produced pro-Soviet analyses in response to interna-tional events. In focussing upon the arguments developed we see how at times, and around certain issues, pro-Sovietism became pronounced, only to wane in response to the events in the international arena. Therefore we will see that there was an initially favourable response to the Russian revolution-ary movement which cooled almost as rapidly as it grew. This led to a period of estrangement beyond the CPGB circles. However as parliamentary socialism failed in Britain and socialism came under attack in continental Europe, new models were sought and focus shifted, once again, toward the Soviet Union. This led to a group to actively protect the Soviet model of existent socialism. The activities of these individuals reached their climax during the Second World War as fascism and communism were perceived to be fighting over the future of Europe. The arguments developed during this period were to shape thinking for the next fifty years, and beyond, and ensure that pro-Sovietism was to remain a feature on the fringes of British labourism.

BRIEF HONEYMOON, QUICK DIVORCE: FEB 1917-AUG 1931

The limited organisational strength and cohesion of the pro-Soviet political strand is indicated by the fact that in periods of international stability pro-Soviet support was usually marginalised if not pacified entirely. This is what can be clearly seen in this period. Massive initial support for the revolution within the anti-war movement, members of which would later enter parliament, was followed by a degree of reservation, then complete rejection. This defined the relationship until the repercussions of the Wall Street Crash forced a Labour Prime Minister to cut benefits and reject socialism, be subsequently be abandoned by the majority of the Labour Party and head an all-party National government. The myth that MacDonald's "perfidy had caused the only reverse in Labour's otherwise relentless forward march"[10] became popularised. British socialism, underpinned by traditions of gradualism and reformism, had failed, only the revolutionary model was able to withstand the disaster that had beset capitalism. This led socialist intellectuals to view the Soviet economic and political model in a similar way to which the February 1917 revolution was greeted by many of the leaders of the British Socialist Movement. It is with this favourable reaction that this narrative must begin. In 1917 the peace movement and the Russian revolutionary movement forged ties that would reappear much later in their history. As Tsarism fell, socialists within Britain talked of worker's control and of forcing the governments of Europe to end the war and dissolve the 'ancient regime', arguments inspired directly by events in Russia.

The highpoint for this movement emerged during the summer of 1917 when an unofficial convention was held in Leeds. This 'Peace Convention' drew together the radical strands of British socialism with a view to determining the future. The Conference agenda, and the objectives and rhetoric of the delegates, was influenced by the example set by the events of February 1917 in Russia. British socialists argued that Russia was a role model for action and delegates proposed that they establish a vanguard to lead the workers and soldiers in some form of rebellion against government policy; particularly the continued prosecution of the war and the forced labour schemes in operation on the Clyde. The influence of events in the Soviet Union would be apparent among British socialists forty years later.

Those Leeds attendees who would later become Labour MPs did not retain their radicalism much beyond the end of 1918. The prime examples were future Prime Minister James Ramsay MacDonald and future Foreign Secretary Ernest Bevin. It could be argued that these two made a deep genuflection when adopting an anti-Soviet perspective. However, the rejection of the Russian model for political action was due to the development of the Soviet political form and the contact MacDonald and Bevin had with representatives of the Soviet government. What is indicative is the zeitgeist of this meeting and how the ideals filtered into British socialism.

Though the ideas of the Marxist-Leninism gained prominence in the speeches at this Convention, these socialists were not supporting Bolshevism per se. Their model for action was the revolutionary spirit of the Russian proletariat, a spirit that was embodied to a far greater extent by Kerensky than Lenin. Russian workers and peasants had fought for their rights in opposition to autocracy, as MacDonald stated in his message to the Russian people:

> with gratitude and admiration [The Convention] congratulates the Russian people upon a Revolution which has overthrown a tyranny that resisted the intellectual and social development of Russia.[11]

The gratitude and admiration is here awarded to the Russian people, the agency behind the February uprising; many socialists and historians would view the Bolshevik revolution as an opportunistic coup d'etat rather than the result of a mass-inspired revolt.

However activists at Leeds were to borrow their modus operandi directly from Leninism. Rather than just sending messages of admiration the Council created a quasi-revolutionary vanguard for Britain and agreed upon a strategy of direct action. The Russian proletariat was placed on a pedestal as the epitome of the European worker.[12] Sylvia Pankhurst, leading Suffragette, argued that the Provisional Committee of the United Socialist Council, the Convention's organising body, should follow the example set by the Russian workers, take action and assume political control. While the chief objective was ending the first World War, the 'great imperialist war', there were also hints that these socialists had a clear view of the society they aimed to establish. C Ammon, Labour MP for Camberwell North 1918-24 argued that a future government should:

> place itself in accord with the democracy in Russia by proclaiming its adherence to, and determination to carry into immediate effect, a charter of liberties establishing complete political rights for all men and women, unrestricted freedom of the press, freedom of speech, a general amnesty for political and religious prisoners, full rights of industrial and political association, and the release of labour from all forms of compulsion and restraint.[13]

This revolutionary rhetoric was a direct result of the Russian revolution; it offered to Western socialists a romanticised ideal of proletarian action. Importantly it also led to the identification of an iconic correlation between the oppressed proletariat and peasantry of Russia and their British counterparts. British socialists had equally suffered for their pacifist stance while Union leaders faced troops for demanding shorter working hours and wage increases. This led the proletarian leaders to equate their struggle directly with that of their Russian counterpart and wish to follow their lead. As Bevin stated, "I believe even in our country there will have to be the shedding of blood to attain the freedom we require."[14] Bevin had faced troops when opposing compulsory overtime; ILP leaders James Maxton and Fenner Brockway were imprisoned for conscientious objection; James Connolly had been executed for leading the Easter Rising in Dublin. These actions were equated with the executions of peasant farmers and striking dockworkers in the Luna shipyards; examples of oppression that had laid the foundations of Russian revolutionary tendencies. As Ammon intimated, perhaps Maxton, Brockway, Connolly and the other martyrs of the working class had planted the seed of revolution in Britain.

Labour MP for Sheffield Attercliffe, William Anderson, proposed the creation of a vanguard to infiltrate worker's and soldiers' organisations, undermine the government's authority and bring to bear the power of organised labour. This vanguard should "work strenuously for a peace made by the peoples of the various countries, and for the complete emancipation of international labour".[15] The vanguard was not designed with a purely parochial outlook, but should plant the seeds for an international socialist revolution. Reading the speeches delivered at this convention as exemplary of the spirit of 1917 it is little wonder that Trotsky and Lenin led the

Bolsheviks to power with the belief that much of Europe was about to follow in their path.

This said, it should be noted that insurrection and subversion were not the aims of every delegate to the Convention; nor did the Convention have a mass support among political groupings or Trade Unions, though it did attract 1,150 delegates representing the British Socialist Party, the Independent Labour Party, the Labour Party as well as the Fabian Society and the Socialist Women's Guild. The Convention did publicise the fact that there was a revolutionary undercurrent present in Britain, however. Equally it stimulated sympathisers of revolutionary socialist ideas to make their voices heard in support of Russia. Future Communist MP Willie Gallacher led Clydeside strikers in support of both the Provisional government and later the Bolsheviks, he later recalled: after February 1917 symbols of 'Free Russia' were "emblazoned on our banners".[16] Equally the embryonically communist British Socialist Party campaigned for support and recognition for the new Russian government. Such strands would filter into the ILP and Trade Union sponsored Hands Off Russia Movement, within which Ernest Bevin was a key activist. Hands Off Russia was created specifically in opposition to intervention into the Russian Civil War, an action that was later described as the establishment of bi-polarity.[17] However, this was the true extent of any British revolutionary spirit. The Leeds Convention cannot be viewed as the birth of pro-Sovietism but the refocusing of the radical traditions of British socialism. As Bullock argues convincingly, the arguments put forward at Leeds can be presented as "a preview of the British left between the wars, anarchical, utopian, already fascinated by and profoundly ignorant of the Russian experience."[18] This is reinforced by Miliband's appraisal of the event.

> The Leeds Convention had fortuitously brought together the revolutionaries and the constitutionalists. But the gulf between them remained as profound as it ever had been and the installation of the Bolshevik regime in November 1917 only served to widen that gulf.[19]

There were similar murmurs on the Labour benches in parliament, but here the real concern was for the progression of the war, in which Russia's role was seen as pivotal, not for the success or failure of the post-revolutionary regime in Russia. The fact that Kerensky followed his predecessor Prince Lvov and maintained Russia's presence in the war meant that he was respected by his western parliamentary counterparts. When Lenin deposed him, and sued for peace, he became anathema to the Allies. This was compounded by the perception that Lenin's government was founded on a 'dangerous' ideology that promoted global revolution.[20] The Labour leadership was indecisive over how to react to Lenin. Sections within the Unions appeared well disposed towards Bolshevism, however the broader movement soon became concerned by reports of oppression and tyranny and began to distance themselves. Equally Bolshevism was used increasingly to undermine the Labour Party through association with the socialist doctrine therefore, despite the existence of some latent sympathies, party conference decisions between 1918-22 ensured that any links with Bolshevism could not easily be inferred.

The anti-Bolshevik stance was reinforced by Kerensky's testimony to the 18th Annual Conference in 1918. He visited Britain to call upon the Labour Movement to help in the struggle against Leninism. In emotive phraseology he requested the support of his British comrades, arguing that:

> the most ruthless oppression is applied against the Democratic and Socialist Parties in Russia... comrades it is up to you... to settle the question whether it is, or not, possible to remain a calm spectator of that unheard of tragedy.[21]

Kerensky expected that MacDonald, his correspondent, would lead the British democratic socialists in support of the White forces backed by the Entente powers. In this matter he was mistaken. The broader socialist movement had no sympathy for interventionism and thus the power of the British worker was used to undermine the international anti-Communist.

In 1947 Ernest Bevin's greatest regret must have been his role in securing Bolshevik victory in the Russian Civil War. In 1918 Bevin stood as a better ally for future luminaries of the CPGB than Churchill as he threatened to call a general strike.[22] He established a Council of Action against intervention and argued eloquently, in his role as Union leader and Labour Party delegate, the case for protecting the Soviet Union:

> Czars have murdered thousands and we have not interfered. But if a people's revolution takes place we are called upon... to stamp out a terrible menace. That is a policy that Labour cannot idly stand by and see develop.[23]

This was a stance that pro-Soviet MPs would also adopt during the Cold War. Labour members argued that the 'people's revolution' should be protected from a hostile world and reinforced the statements made by the delegation sent to Russia in 1920. The delegation's report had claimed that the oppression detailed in the 'capitalist' press was a "perversion of the facts."[24] They would perceive, as did the ILP in 1922, that

Organised capitalism, lacking the bowels of compassion, sees in the natural horror that has overtaken Russia a means to bring about the defeat of a theory it hates and fears.[25]

While those who exhibited pro-Soviet sympathies, in the period immediately following the October revolution, would mainly alter their perceptions others would adopt their perspective of the Soviet Union. Therefore the historical context is crucial to understanding the activities and perspectives of those MPs who expressed pro-Soviet sympathies during the Cold War. In this initial period we see a growing perception that the Bolshevik regime was attempting to enact socialism while under threat from the reactionary forces of capitalism associated with the old order. Socialists opposed the aggression to the Leninist regime on principle, even those who doubted that Russia could progress to true socialism. John Clynes, Labour MP for Manchester Platting, argued in parliament that, though Lenin ruled as a dictator, it was not the right of Britain to intervene and that Russia should be allowed to choose its own political system, not have democracy imposed upon it.[26] These principles of non-aggression and non-intervention would be revived, particularly by Zilliacus, as a basis on which to attack Bevin himself.

Labour established a policy of neutrality towards the Lenin government. The MacDonald government did offer formal recognition, despite the dangers of association, and opened negotiations on the Tsarist debt. Official recognition encouraged the formation of a group of pro-Soviet activists within parliament. The Anglo-Russian Parliamentary Committee [ARPC] was established as a pro-Soviet pressure group by MPs and Trade Union leaders; this argued for the "the establishment of the friendliest diplomatic relations and the greatest possible development of trade between the Soviet Union and Great Britain."[27] Despite worsening relations members of this committee continued to argue the Soviet case in parliament. This activity waned as many members of the ARPC lost their seats after 1931 and subsequent Labour governments, regardless of existent sympathies within the party, found maintaining relations with the Soviet Union an untenable policy. The Soviet propaganda campaign, allegedly exploited by Conservative central office when producing the Zinoviev letter, damaged Labour's electoral credibility, though it is open to debate whether the incident was instrumental in the party losing the 1924 General Election.[28] Following this experience the official party organisation would keep contact to the minimum. It became the task of individual members to forge links if they felt inclined. This happened increasingly after 1945 however the model for this type of relationship would be forged during the 1930s, the period that would become known as the 'Red Decade'.

COLLAPSE OF FAITH: THE FAILURE OF DEMOCRATIC SOCIALISM AND THE RISE OF FASCISM

-    The economic depression following the Wall Street Crash of 1929, and the manner in which James Ramsay MacDonald, the Labour Prime Minister, addressed it, led many to doubt the parliamentary road to socialism. More importantly the failure of gradualist socialism, and the perceived betrayal of the party and the British proletariat by MacDonald, led some to view the Soviet Union and 'actually existing socialism' as a viable alternative. Amid western economic collapse stood the Soviet Union, prospering with a planned economy. Despite recognition of the failures in the political system many could not deny the comparative societal benefits of Soviet communism. Leading party members, trade union leaders and influential socialist intellectuals embarked upon visits, produced studies of the Soviet political and economic system and reached conclusions that favoured the adoption of Soviet not British socialist principles. MacDonald had stated that Communist methods could not be adopted because Soviet socialism was fundamentally opposed to British democracy. However, by introducing emergency measures that included cuts in unemployment benefit, the perception that MacDonald had chosen the interests of capital, particularly the bankers, over the working class became popularised.[29] Thus MacDonald himself provided the impetus for many to adopt a pro-Soviet stance. Thus, during the 1930s, many looked to the Soviet Union for inspiration in developing an alternative socialist theory of the role of the state.

-    It was not a new phenomenon for Westerners to visit the Soviet Union and produce favourable reports.[30] Throughout the 1920s intellectuals and writers were given guided tours, encouraged to publish their observations and were often paid generous advances for publication costs. While the Soviet Union encouraged these pro-Soviet propagandists to produce favourable accounts of Soviet society, during the 1930s a new scientific analysis was employed by British socialist theorists, particularly G D H Cole and Sydney Webb, that was not influenced by Agitprop. The Soviet Union was described as the epitome of how a socialist society could, and indeed should, work. The reason was not because of the perfection evident to visitors to the Soviet Union, but because British socialism had failed. The old struggle between Britain and the Soviet Union as the leaders of world socialism was over and it appeared, from the arguments promoted by many former Labour supporters, that Stalin had emerged as the victor. Jennie Lee, Labour

MP 1945-60 and wife of Aneurin Bevan, when recalling her experiences in the 1930s, asked "what sort of socialist movement had we in Britain?"[31] John Strachey, Labour MP for Aston 1919-31 and post-war Cabinet Minister, described the MacDonald group as "the deadliest enemy of the British workers."[32] More telling however, was Sidney Webb's conversion to Soviet Communism.

.   Despite being architect of the Labour Party constitution, Webb became disillusioned with the leadership. This led him to become perhaps the greatest exponent of the argument that the Soviet Union was socialist. This was highly influential due to his standing in the British socialist movement. It was of the Fabian Society, of which Webb was a founder, that Hugh Gaitskell stated "They are the people British socialists most respect."[33] Therefore Webb was ideally placed to be an agent of influence for the Soviet Union. Reading the Webbs work led some young socialists to join the CPGB. Eric Heffer recalled:

> I read it [Soviet Communism: A New Civilisation?] from cover to
> cover. It convinced me that Russia was socialist and that Stalin's con-
> stitution was genuinely democratic. The Webbs have a lot to answer
> for.[34]

Praise for their publication came from the highest echelons of the British communist movement. When reviewing the book for Labour Monthly, Dutt, then Vice Chairman of the CPGB, wrote that "[t]heir concrete picture will win conviction in many quarters where the current generalisations fail to reach."[35]

       We cannot quantify the numbers influenced by their work, Heffer's condemnation of the Webbs indicates that their writings did have an effect on British socialists, particularly those who wished to believe in the Soviet ideal. Therefore, while it is impossible to state categorically that the Webbs directly influenced any pro-Soviet MP, they represent one aspect of a range of pro-Soviet influences prevalent during the 1930s. This is important because it was during this period that many of the post-war pro-Soviet MPs became active within the socialist movement and developed their perspective on the world.

       The Webbs painted a view of the Soviet Union as the ideal of socialist life. This was an unprecedented genuflection for a couple whose previous work was founded upon the 'inevitability of gradualness'. Socialism, the gradualists' argued, was the inescapable conclusion of history. This necessitated a parliamentary socialist party that would erode the basis of capitalism through public ownership schemes and welfare reforms. Beatrice Webb wrote

in her diary that "My husband and I have always been against the Soviet
system, and have regarded it as a repetition of Russian autocracy."[36] It was
the reversal of socialist reforms by a Labour government that made Sydney
Webb doubt his own theory. His letters to Beatrice portray him as a defeated
man, however he was also searching for a new belief. It was George Bernard
Shaw who provided the impetus for Webb to search for his new belief in
Soviet Communism. Shaw had already joined the fellow travelling coterie,
making several visits to the Soviet Union. He was able to draw the Webbs
into accepting Soviet Communism as the reality of their socialist ideals.

In rejecting the parliamentary road to socialism Webb intimated that
attaining socialism might only be possible through "a terrific struggle on
clearly thought out lines."[37] This could be argued to indicate that Webb had
accepted the Leninist revolutionary doctrine, Shaw encouraged him to accept Stalinism also. Shaw achieved this by convincing Sydney Webb that
Stalin had adopted the Webbs gradualist theory. This allowed Webb to view
the Soviet Union from a fresh perspective. Beatrice recorded the conclusion
of Shaw's Summer School speech thus:

> It must be right! The paradox of the speech: the Russian Revolution
> was pure Fabianism, Lenin and Stalin had recognised the "inevitability
> of gradualness"! Also they had given up "workers' control" for the
> Webbs' conception of the three-fold state, citizens, consumers and
> producers organisations.[38]

Beatrice Webb had already shown an interest in the Soviet Union, being one
of the founders of the SCR, by 1932 Sydney Webb appeared to have developed the belief that the Soviet Union was an experiment that he could influence. Thus he was to visit the Soviet Union, be given a guided tour by
interpreter Griseli Barishnic, who would have been a highly trained and
loyal Stalinist, and ultimately be convinced to become a propagandist on
behalf of Stalin.

The ideas put forward by the Webbs, mainly in 'Soviet Communism:
A New Civilisation?',[39] were ones which must have played a role in encouraging
support for the Soviet Union and were to become a part of the British
socialist tradition. While many did not apologise for the excesses of Stalin as
Webb did, Webbs' description of Soviet society was one of a range of
influences that convinced many that socialism was possible and that it existed
in the Soviet Union. In constructing their positive analysis of the Soviet
Union the Webbs countered criticism of the system directly, particularly the
views of those who described the regime as undemocratic. They accepted the
fact that there was no legal opposition, but argued this was not necessary.

The soviets allowed much greater democracy than any system of public ballot. They described the Soviet policy formulation process as being:

> an upward stream of continuously generated power, through multi-form mass organisation, (through soviets, committees, etc) to be transferred at the apex into a downward stream of authoritative laws and decrees and directives.[40]

Thus, according to the Webb's analysis, the lower orders of society decided what they wanted and passed the power to implement legislation to the Politburo. The Webbs described Stalin, as did their contemporary Anna Louise Strong, as "the supreme combiner of wills".[41] As a leader Stalin arbitrated between opposing forces, but was unable to make a decision that opposed the will of the people. Their conclusion read:

> if by autocracy or dictatorship is meant government without prior discussion and debate, either by public opinion or in private session, the government of the [Soviet Union] is, in that sense, actually less of an autocracy or a dictatorship than many a parliamentary cabinet.[42]

The Webbs characterised the Soviet Union as being founded upon the will of the people displayed through a Periclean system of government. They admitted, though, that they did not see this system in action and that they had been unable to communicate with the ordinary Russian people to check the authenticity of the leadership's claims.[43] Therefore the eloquence of their guides, coupled with a desire to believe, led the Webbs to accept Soviet propaganda as reality. They concluded that the world was set on an ideological collision course; capitalism versus communism. The Webbs saw the United States as the capitalist bastion, the enemy of socialism, a conclusion that would be reached by many socialists during the Cold War. In choosing an ideological side the Webbs' argued that Communism offered the better life for its citizens, and therefore should be adopted as the model for a socialist state:[44]

> We hope to give a vision of the Communist alternative to decadent capitalism, planned production for community consumption with as much liberty and equality as is compatible with the continued progress of the human race in body and mind and social life.[45]

The Webbs harboured personal doubts as to the authenticity of their own claims regarding Soviet democracy and egalitarianism however. These are evident in Beatrice's diary, particularly regarding the purges and show trials. However these doubts were never intended for publication. To adver-

tise the contradictions between the ideal of Soviet society and the reality
would dispel the myth of true socialism. However these doubts do lead us
to question the conclusion that the Webbs had found "an alternative, 'new',
morality"[46] in the Soviet Union. Seymour-Jones puts the blame for the Webbs'
conversion to pro-Sovietism upon Sidney Webb, arguing that "it was a tragedy that she [Beatrice] ultimately allowed Sidney's insidious influence to corrupt her integrity and compromise her life's struggle."[47] While Sidney Webbs
role as publicist and active change agent was described "of great value"[48] by
Soviet Ambassador Ivan Maisky, he was not alone in his pro-Soviet writing.
As Kidd argues both Sidney and Beatrice argued separately that their own
collectivist socialist ideals, the basis for a moral community, were reflected in
the Soviet Constitution.[49] Doubts between the Soviet system, as described
by the Soviet Constitution, and the reality of purges and show trials were
voiced privately only. This private, almost moral, conflict is pervasive within
the arguments of many that were sympathetic to the Soviet political model.

The Webbs furthered their propagandist activities by holding seminars at their Bloomsbury home. Regular guests were Communists such as
Lytton Strachey and JBS Haldane, sympathisers such as Charles Trevelyan,
President of the SCR, and other interested parties such as the economist
John Maynard Keynes,[50] who likewise saw statism as appealing. These meetings were frequented by Soviet Ambassador Ivan Maisky, possibly talent
spotting sympathisers for a more active role within the pro-Soviet movement. In this context the allegation that the next generation of spies were
"Bloomsbury's children"[51] is possibly not too excessive. However a much
greater force was to encourage the socialist to adopt a pro-Soviet perspective.

In Britain socialism appeared to be defeated. The Labour party's parliamentary representation had been reduced substantially, the leadership "smashed... the gradualist ideology... seemed to be in ruins... [and]
the party's policy was confused."[52] George Lansbury attempted to create a
credible opposition to MacDonald's National Labour Party, which amounted
to no more than eleven ministers and a dozen backbenchers with no support from the Unions or affiliated societies, but lack of unity and his own
ill health caused Lansbury to fail. Thus in the 1931 Election non-National
government Labour Party candidates were returned in only fifty-two constituencies with Lansbury, Clement Attlee, then a virtual unknown, and Stafford Cripps as the most senior parliamentarians.[53] The worker's parliamentary voice became impotent for the best part of a decade. Despite condemna-
tions against CPGB entryist tactics by the TUC, within some Trade Unions
and many industrial communities Communism gained favour.[54] Not only

did the CPGB agents supply funds to strikers and their families, but also the Communist leaders spoke of issues that the Labour Party refused to raise. In tandem with other young socialists around the ILP, the CPGB were seen to be active in the worker's struggle, importantly the Labour Party was not seen in this light. Due to this extra-parliamentary activism support could be found for the formation of a Popular Front of socialists. This even found support among Labour's ranks as Europe saw the rise of, what Communists and many socialists argued to be, the most virulent form of capitalism; fascism.

Fascism rose out of the settlement following the First World War. The so-called mutilated peace allowed Mussolini to manoeuvre his way to power in Italy during the early 1920s, while Nazism flourished as the economic and political humiliation of Germany under the terms of the Treaty of Versailles led inevitably to socio-economic and political collapse.[55] Threats to stability, trends such as nationalism and the growth of the popularity of Bolshevism among the proletariat, became magnified with economic depression. This situation led those who sought security and strength to turn to "the most radical form of counter revolution."[56] Fascism took hold in countries that had been weakened following WWI, and where liberal social democracy was failing in the face of a Communist threat. This led the Stalinist analysis of the phenomenon to be widely supported among socialists. Fascism, he argued, stood as "the open terrorist dictatorship of the most reactionary, most chauvinistic and most imperialist elements of finance capital."[57] Fear that this phenomenon would spread, and that conservative governments such as the British National government would support these regimes, led socialists to support the formation of a left-wing, extra parliamentary coalition to organise opposition.

This was the ideal behind the formation of a popular or people's front[58] backed by G D H Cole, who published his supporting thesis in 1937. The Labour Party opposed the idea because it would be under "international control".[59] The National Executive (NEC) understood this to mean Soviet control, however, the party leadership faced strong dissent to their directive from an influential minority. This dissent came particularly from two young MPs sponsored by the National Union of Mineworkers S O Davies and Aneurin Bevan, but also the more urbane Stafford Cripps. These should not be dismissed as fellow travellers but, like Cole, they recognised the importance of forming a bulwark against fascism. Thus the movement found support among all sections of the British socialist movement.

The argument put forward was grounded squarely within socialist ideology. These individuals recognised that if fascism became the dominant ideology then socialism would become not only excluded from politics but also crushed. If a war were to take place in Europe, figures on the left as diverse as Emanuel Shinwell and Denis Pritt agreed that this would adopt the character of socialism versus fascism. Proof of this was provided when the Communist supported Spanish republican government forces fought a civil war against an army that was reinforced by Italian troops and the German Luftwaffe. Socialists who supported the creation of a popular front against war and fascism adopted the view that the force that would defend socialism was the Soviet Union. Cripps argued that Britain "should make it clear to the world that it will do everything possible to support the [Soviet Union] …[and]… any other socialist states."[60] In a speech at the 1935 Labour Conference he criticised the appeasement policy of the government for being based upon imperialistic self-interest and argued that this perspective would determine policy in any future war.[61]

Cole synthesised the mood most eloquently, stating his case for dissent and the purposes of the proposed front. He stated that the People's Front was not designed as an electoral rival to Labour, particularly as no General Election was imminent, but as a force of opposition to the Conservative dominated National government. He saw it as an international pressure group acting both domestically and within the League of Nations. While the term pressure group was not in common usage in the 1930s, it would probably have not held sufficient emotive strength for Cole. He used the term crusade, the raison d'être of which would be:

> to arouse and to unite democratic opinion upon issues which have to be faced at once… which, in international affairs, will insist on Great Britain taking the lead in a democratic movement to check fascist aggression and to prevent war, while here at home it will insist that the nation wage relentless warfare upon unnecessary poverty, upon unemployment in the depressed areas, and upon all monopolists who make men cheap and goods dear in the interests of higher profits.[62]

Such far-reaching ideals were to be dashed at the first hurdle. Though the Popular Front was established without Labour Party support, without Labour's participation it could not be described as a mass movement and was politically ineffectual. Furthermore, no international cohesion was attained; thus Cole's ideals were unrealised. However, they were not forgotten. The notion that socialists of the world should unite for international and domestic benefits was exhumed in 1945. At this point the international order was based upon United States, British and Soviet co-operation. The ideals expressed by Cole in 1937 appeared, in 1945, more tenable.

Labour's stance on international affairs damaged the party's credibility within the British socialist movement, a credibility that would not return until the final years of the Second World War. This was particularly clear following the response to the Spanish Civil War. Neutrality, the official policy, was described by one maverick backbencher as being akin to a "Christian declaring himself neutral in the struggle between God and the Devil."[63] Emanuel Shinwell, MacDonald opponent but no left-winger, recalled in his autobiography that:

> The disaster came because the Great Powers of the West preferred to see in Spain a dictatorial government of the right, rather than a legally elected body chosen by the people.[64]

Therefore, it was the Soviet Union that was accepted as the pro-socialist, anti-fascist bastion. This led to the wartime support invested by the British people in 'good old Uncle Joe Stalin'. More importantly, these arguments vested in the Soviet Union a crucial role in Europe's future. The twin notions that socialism was going to be victorious in war and that, allowed to develop unhindered, the Soviet Union could attain true socialism led to the development of theories for peace and stability in the post-war world. In 1939 pro-Soviet enthusiasm collapsed as a result of the Nazi-Soviet Pact. However the notion of Stalin's betrayal was forgotten as Hitler's forces invaded the Soviet Union under the auspices of Operation Barbarossa, and to an even greater extent when the German army was routed at Stalingrad. After 1942 it seems that a majority looked squarely at the Soviet Union as the force that would, to a much greater extent than the United States, determine victory and defeat and would determine the character of the post-war European political system.

THE SOCIALIST CHAMPION: WHO WON THE WAR ANYWAY?

As Hitler's forces turned against Soviet Russia Cripps, from his position in the British Embassy in Moscow, wrote to British Prime Minister Churchill that: "Russia is one of our fronts and must be regarded and treated as such."[65] Cripps encouraged British socialists to campaign for an alliance with the Soviet Union and, in agreement with Churchill, a propaganda unit was created to encourage the British people to support their new communist allies. The leader of this unit was John Platts-Mills, associate of D N Pritt, and Labour Party worker.[66] Public opinion indeed focussed on the Eastern

front; this is recalled by many of the pro-Soviet MPs who spent their formative years as young men in the forces. Mass observation reports describe
rallies and demonstrations, enjoying substantial support from the public,
being held calling for greater military aid to be awarded to the Soviet Union.[67]
Bevan, Davies and Willie Gallacher, Communist MP for West Fife, brought
this debate directly to parliament. Their fears were that the British government was happy for the Soviet Union to be crushed by Germany.

The most notable result of the propaganda campaign was the level
of public support for the Soviet war effort. Aid Committees were created
at the local level and fuel, medical supplies, blankets and clothes were collected for the beleaguered Russian people. The membership of the British
Soviet Friendship Society [BSFS], Russia Today and the SCR increased; funds
swelled, as did donations to the Joint Committee for Soviet Aid. Pro-Soviet
sympathies became not only legitimised but fashionable. Thus it appears as
no exaggeration when Labour MP Philip Noel-Baker told the House that:

> They [the British people] have been profoundly moved by events in
> Russia. Hour by hour, day by day, they can never forget the millions
> of men, women and children who are resisting, with self immolating
> heroism, the most powerful and cruel onslaught in the history of
> mankind. They want to share that ghastly Calvary. They are ready to
> take risks, grave risks for Russia.[68]

Those who called for a Second Front to be opened argued that the
leadership was abnegating their responsibilities despite Prime Minister
Churchill constant protestations that a pre-emptive strike, intended to draw
the war away from the Eastern Front, was untenable and potentially sui-
cidal. The failure of the British government to act led to increased pro-
Soviet activity that appeared to enjoy the support of a significant number
of the British population.

It can be argued that the mass support was an indicator of the fervency of anti-fascism rather than fanatical pro-Sovietism. Largely this is an
accurate conclusion evidenced by the fact that much of this enthusiasm was
to wane before the Red Army reached Berlin. However a degree of latent
support, established as a result of the Soviet contribution to the war effort,
remained a feature of the post-war pro-Soviet tradition and became exacerbated as a reaction to the pursuit of the anti-Soviet policies of containment
and rollback. For example figures like William Wilson and James Lamond
both recall the war years as influential to their political development. These
MPs revived the themes of these arguments, and the underlying reasons for

offering support to the Soviet Union, in parliament during the late 1970s and 1980s. Thus it was within the period prior to 1945 that the strong attachments exhibited during the Cold War were developed between members of the British left and the Soviet Communist system.

Part of this was a direct result of Popular Front activity. However following the front's collapse the organisation was superceded by the People's Convention. This was created in 1941 with the objective of creating a coalition in opposition to the war. Following the Soviet entry into the war the Convention shifted to opposing totalitarianism as represented by fascism and the National government in Britain.[69] The Convention established links with various aid committees which had been created to support strikers and their families and refocused their activities to collect aid for the Soviet Union. It also launched a campaign to unite the aid organisation with so-called ultra democratic political societies to establish a political agenda. This organisation, created by CPGB luminary Rajani Palme Dutt and organised by D N Pritt, promoted the overthrow of the Churchill-led National government and its replacement with a 'People's' government.[70] While this movement was a failure in political terms it did promote the pro-Soviet war effort among the British Trade Union members and established the 'Help for Russia' fund. The pamphlet The People's Convention Says argued that the munitions workers would increase production if the supplies were to be sent to the Soviet Union.[71] Thus evidence exists that the mood within Britain, to definite but unquantifiable degrees, was sympathetic to the Soviet Union.

The level of funds raised by Help for Russia is one indication of the level of public support for the Soviet war effort. This fund, administrated by the Trade Union Congress [TUC], raised £816,099 between August 1943 and October 1946. The Unions raised £121,082 of this figure but the joint committees, consisting of various locally organised societies, raised a total of £273,058 while the Co-operatives accrued £312,064. The amounts collected, at a time of national hardship, indicates that an empathic relationship existed between the British worker and their families and their Russian counterpart. This is reinforced by the fact that the British United Aid to China Fund, also administrated by the TUC, raised only £127,590, one sixth of the funds raised for Russia.[72] There are also indications that an alliance with the Soviet Union was seen as desirable, according to a 1944 Gallup Poll 76% of those asked wanted the co-operation between Britain and the Soviet Union to continue.[73] As Callaghan argued, the Soviet Union had emerged from the war as "a decisive force in the world."[74]

These public and political associations, created between the British people and the Soviet Union, developed a vision for the future. They argued, to varying extents, that the future of Britain and the Soviet Union were intrinsically interlinked. Rapprochement seemed likely, even between Labourites and Communists in domestic politics. Harry Pollitt, General Secretary of the CPGB, wrote to J S Middleton, Labour Party Secretary, asking for affiliation. He swore to "accept all the obligations of being affiliated to the Labour Party, and loyally… carry out all decisions reached at its annual conference."[75] Arguably these overtures were genuine. With the Comintern disbanded in 1943 the CPGB was nominally independent and therefore could no longer be perceived as a puppet of Moscow, though the degree of independence of the CPGB is a subject of debate.[76] Furthermore, beyond the highest echelons of government, it appeared that such an alliance would be quite normal given the international situation 1941-4. Churchill, and perhaps the Labour leaders Attlee and Bevin held the view that Stalin was only slightly less dangerous than Hitler, and saw the lesser threat as a symptom of geography more than intentions.[77] Despite these private views, as the conclusion of the war appeared inevitable, Stalin was perceived as the emerging victor and Soviet-style socialism was, albeit momentarily, the only way forward for Europe. As the editor of the Anglo-Soviet Journal argued in 1944, a time when the SCR's magazine was closest to boasting a mass readership: "we in Great Britain who sleep peacefully in our beds, who have almost forgotten we are at war, should, like the Soviet people, be grateful to Stalin."[78]

It was with this mood as a backdrop that socialist theorist G D H Cole produced his personal thesis on how the future of Britain and Europe should be organised. Cole cannot be described as being traditionally pro-Soviet, nor a Communist sympathiser. His roots lay in Guild Socialism, and though his thought and that of the Communists converged in the mid-1930s, his sights were set on domestic improvements not world revolution. But, like the Webbs, Cole had grown to despair of parliamentary socialism. Though he opposed centralism and statism he argued in 1942 that "A National Plan is [possible] when the government of a country holds in its hands the reins of economic power in every part of national life."[79] This led him to promote nationalisation as a necessary step towards socialism. He analysed aspects of Soviet political life and developed an argument for the transfer of those aspects that were appropriate to the circumstances in Britain. He recognised, as others failed to, that the Soviet Union was a totalitarian regime built upon fear, cruelty and persecution.[80] However he extolled the virtues of centralised economic planning while supplying his own caveat: "social control of the State and the means of production… is not by itself enough to ensure freedom in all its desirable forms."[81] He believed, like the Webbs, that Communism was fashioning a new civilisation and that the success of this project would enhance the perception of socialism as a social theory. However, despite inconsistencies in his arguments, Cole did not argue for Communist rule, or even the transplantation of Soviet society onto British democracy. He was a reformist and a gradualist, and wished to see reforms implemented that would guide Britain towards socialism in a form desirable to the nation's citizens. It is surprising, therefore, that it was he who was to publish a work which argued that Stalin should rule post-war Europe.

Cole's publication, Europe, Russia and the future was a classic in terms of Soviet propagandist material. It was also influential, the circulation of Left Book Club editions means that it would have reached an audience with a less informed perspective on the world than Cole. None of the pro-Soviet MPs interviewed cite Cole's work as the source of their inspiration however, his arguments, like those of the Webbs, are indicative of the zeitgeist of the age in which they were published. This was an age when many of the pro-Soviet MPs of the 1970s and 80s were young students, factory workers or soldiers, thus it can be utilised as an example of how the period 1942-5 shaped the thought of future generations of socialists.

While contemporary writers looked specifically at a new future, Cole used his present circumstances to develop a critique of the past. He argued for a Europe based upon co-operation and collectivisation, one that had a socialist basis rather than one in which nations competed for power, wealth and empire. It was with this end in mind that he wrote the following:

> I would much sooner see the Soviet Union, even with its policy unchanged, dominant over all Europe, including Great Britain, than see an attempt to restore the pre-war states to their futile and uncreative independence and their petty economic nationalism under capitalist domination. Better be ruled by Stalin than by the restrictive and monopolistic cliques who dominate Western capitalism. Nay more: much better be ruled by Stalin than by a pack of half-hearted and half-witted Social Democrats who do not believe in Socialism, but do still believe in the 'independence' of their separate, obsolete national states.[82]

Cole therefore argued that Europe would benefit more under Stalinism, and state economics governed from the centre, than under the socialism of MacDonald or Weimar's Chancellor Bruning.

The fact that Europe was to become a unified region should have made Cole's critique obsolete. However, it was because Europe, or at least Western Europe, was perceived to have unified only because of the Cold War that this critique gained followers. Cole wanted the creation of an amalgam of the Soviet command economy and parliamentary social democracy. In his words the appropriate elements of Soviet society would:

> become the instruments of a new and invigorated parliamentarism, of a 'liberal' socialism, and of a policy of tolerant democracy, they need not involve the creation of a totalitarian regime.[83]

Cole argued for a half way stance between gradualism and Communism. A socialist government should implement Stalin's economic model, but within the framework of the British democratic tradition. He did, however, have reservations regarding British democracy. He had seen the National government, like many on the left, as an undemocratic institution because it had not been elected by true mandate. That a government could be formed without the mandate of the people indicated, to Cole, that British democracy was flawed. This led him to support a more Periclean democratic ideal, one whose only exemplar existed in the Soviet constitution. When replying to a critic of his 1941 thesis, he adopted the following stance:

> I regard the Soviet system as much more democratic than parliamentarianism and I advocate it for a large part of Europe as the most appropriate way of bringing real democracy to power.[84]

Here Cole seems to raise a contradiction in his own work. He identified the Soviet Union, in separate tracts, as both totalitarian and democratic. This appears to be an attempt to reconcile the view that socialism must be democratic to be successful and his personal view that the Soviet Union had achieved elements of both while retaining a one-party authoritarian style of leadership.[85]

This analysis of Cole's position gives the impression that he subscribed to the same slavishly pro-Soviet perspective as the Webbs did in publications. He did not clarify whether his analysis was based upon the paper constitution or the practice in the Soviet Union. Therefore, once again it can be argued that he supplied some of the impetus to the pro-Soviet movement. Cole offered his support to the Soviet system on the grounds that key aspects of it were comparatively better, more democratic and more advanced than the British social democratic model, a perspective that would draw many to support the Soviet Union.

The inconsistencies were clarified a little in a later publication. In Great Britain in the Post-War World Cole argued that a United Socialist Europe should counteract United States capitalist influence. Here the Soviet Union is given the role of ideological guide, rather than that of dominant political force. Britain, he argued, must follow an individual course. However, this would be dependent upon "close economic and cultural relations with the United States."[86] This was seen as being particularly advantageous in light of Roosevelt's launch of the 'New Deal'. Cole had few fears of United States influence under Roosevelt, though this mild Atlanticism was short lived, arguing that if British industry became dominated by United States capitalism:

> It would not... be such a disaster for the British people as the retention of control by the heavily damaged monopoly capitalism of Great Britain... the continuance of this type of capitalism... would mean poverty and mass unemployment and the continued loss of markets and of productive power.[87]

The foreign policy of a post-war government prescribed by Cole must also ensure close working relations with "British Dominions and at the same time... build up relations equally with the Soviet Union and with the coming Socialist system of continental Europe."[88] Peace within the 'Dominions', Cole argued, could only be guaranteed through:

> unification under socialist control, and with an influential participation by the Soviet Union, which will be able to bring its own highly successful experience in the democratic handling of national problems to bear on the situation on the African continent.[89]

In this work Cole argued both the middle way, Bevanite, stance, while also promoting the Soviet Union as a progressive influence, an argument that would find popularity among the members of the post-war pro-Soviet strand.

It is important to note that the pro-Soviet sympathies, exhibited in Cole's wartime publications were also a feature of his Cold War tract *The Meaning of Marxism*. Here Cole argued that the Soviet Union had "solved the dilemma which capitalism had found insoluble [how to] ensure... that... every advance in technical efficiency shall be passed on to the consumers in the form of a rising standard of life." Cole argued that the Soviet system of "planned socialisation" provided a model for those nations that were "far ahead of Russia in their mastery of productive technique."[90] Like others he argued that the strict authoritarian nature of the Soviet political system was the result of external aggression which had prevented the Soviet Union from cleansing itself of its Tsarist political heritage, though he recognised that the lack of a liberal tradition had also restricted the development of democracy.[91]

Cole did extol the virtues of the Soviet socialist construction and argued that such a project would have been:

impracticable except under the auspices of the CPGB. The same was
true in 1945 over most of Eastern Europe; and anyone who denies
this is merely kicking against the pricks of social necessity.[92]

This appears to be a direct condemnation of the policy of containment and
the campaign against Communist parties in Western European elections.
He predicted that the "offensive-defensive" strategy of United States
capitalism would be met by a reciprocal "defensive-offensive" strategy from
Soviet Communism, a situation that would lead to "repeated deadlocks."[93]
While Cole's conclusion is accurate, it is interesting that he saw the Western
side of the ideological dichotomy as leading an offensive while the Soviet
Union was essentially pursuing a defensive strategy, a conclusion that many
on the left would return to throughout the Cold War. Cole stressed the
Third Way position, that a socialist system should be installed across Europe
while capitalism was weak due to the devastation of industry incurred during the Second World ar and he argued that British Labour should establish
a union with:

> like-minded collaborators in other countries to make possible the crea-
> tion of a group of Socialistic countries able to stand out against en-
> gulfment by either American capitalism or Soviet Communism, and
> so... preserve... what is valuable in the 'liberal' tradition.[94]

Cole's pro-Soviet arguments were supported and magnified by other
writers. Pollitt called for unity between socialist groups, both locally and
internationally. The Second World War had become a people's war, and
therefore must be followed by a 'socialist' people's peace.[95] While this did
not win Pollitt a seat in the House, it did win a degree of support for the
CPGB, particularly as it appeared increasingly that the post-war Labour
government was in the process of losing that very peace. Perhaps more
telling is the call for continued friendship by Mrs Clementine Churchill; the
liberal wife of the Prime Minister. She became personally involved in the Aid
to Russia Campaign, and established a Red Cross service dedicated to the
victims of German occupation. Not only did the pamphlet on her visit to
the Soviet Union paint a picture worthy of any fellow traveller; she also
expressed hope for the continued alliance. As she witnessed her husband
stand alongside Truman and Stalin she felt that she was "standing on the
edge of a vast, new and unexplored world."[96] That world was not only one
of co-operation with the Soviet Union, but, moreover a world at peace
living in harmony. She saw the grand alliance, as some called it, as the
backbone for this brave new world and, therefore, the major foreign policy

aim had to be to retain it at all costs. Though the costs were deemed too high for western governments, some Labour politicians did not lose their grasp of this dream.

Those individuals who retained these ideals would establish a minority bulwark against the Cold War, a small but vituperative group who became drawn towards the Soviet Union. The Soviet leadership and its agents exploited sympathisers, but despite this they retained a link to the Soviet political ideal, an attachment that led them to become disillusioned with domestic politics and the loose ideological basis of British labourism. Mazowar argues that this loss of faith in ideology happened immediately on witnessing the post Second World War settlement. This is true of the vast majority of those, like Bevan and Cripps, who were prominent before 1945. However, the next generation appeared to embrace the struggle with alacrity, without regard for their personal credibility or the electoral image of the party. It was only after 1989 that the minority studied here, and their comrades in the Unions, front organisations, Communist Parties and the broad pro-Soviet milieu became, in Mazowar's words, "apathetic, resigned and domesticated".[97]

3

KONNI ZILLIACUS
AND LABOUR'S ADVERSARIAL
VOICES FROM THE LEFT

The traditions of the 1930s popular front against war and fascism, the public support for the Soviet war effort during the Second World War and the ideal of continuing co-operation between the 'Big Three' after victory in Europe, were to shape the dissidents arguments during the 1945-50 Labour government. The majority of the studies of this period focus upon the leadership of the party and ignore the left-wing opposition to the developing Cold War.[1] This is due to the minimal effect that those MPs, who developed a pro-Soviet critique of the Cold War anti-Communist ethos, had upon party policy. There was no attempt at making a trade-off between the imperatives of international security and, what Koelble described as, the "rationalities for action"[2] of the ideologically motivated members. The Labour leadership developed a zero-sum perception of relations with the Soviet Union and therefore those who opposed party policy were believed, by some, to support the enemy. The leadership's anti-Soviet position was in direct opposition to the decisions of the 1944 party conference and the ideals expressed by Labour's 1945 General Election Manifesto. Furthermore the Cold War conflicted with the vision of the future asseverated in the campaign addresses of many of the newly elected left-wing Labour parliamentarians.

The 1945 Labour Party manifesto borrowed largely from the Beveridge report, despite a decision by the War Cabinet to make no commitment to implementing Beveridge's recommendations.[3] The manifesto also, against the judgement of the party's National Executive [NEC], pledged a future Labour government to a broad nationalisation programme. This programme was supported by a massive majority at the 1944 Annual Conference and had been campaigned for within parliament by ninety-seven Labour backbenchers. As Morgan has argued the 1945 Manifesto presented to the electorate a practical expression of the ideals and aspirations associated with the party constitution.[4] It also represented the practical ideals of many of those who entered parliament for the first time after the landslide victory. Particular stress was placed upon the necessity to retain the alliance between the three major powers. The Manifesto, personal election addresses and many influential theoretical analyses argued that "the consolidat[ion] in peace [of] the great war-time association of the British Commonwealth with the U.S.A. and the U.S.S.R"[5] was the only stable foundation for future peace. Such arguments were made prominent in a significant number of Labour candidates' personal election addresses.

While war was averted between the Soviet Union and the NATO alliance, stability was dependent upon the dangerous premise of mutually assured destruction. This was to become the socialist anathema after Hiroshima and Nagasaki. To the campaigners who had plotted a course through the pre-war peace movement, organisations such as the Union for Democratic Control or the People's Front, co-existence became an imperative. This led to some individuals adopting an oppositional position to the consensual Atlanticist, anti-Soviet policy. The position developed by a broad left backbench movement involved the argument that any alliance built on opposition to another nation or collective of nations was certain to lead to war. However, this current of thought involved much more than pacifism. Within this strand of thought a pro-Soviet analysis developed. This was fuelled firstly by pro-Soviet propaganda but secondly, and more importantly, by events taking place on the world stage. This pro-Soviet campaign was launched as a reaction to the development of an Anglo-American anti-Communist ethos that was based upon fear of Communist incursion, a fear many left-wingers argued was unfounded. The most vocal opponent of anti-Communism was Konni Zilliacus. He and a small group of Labour backbenchers persistently undermined Foreign Secretary Ernest Bevin's anti-Soviet stance by arguing for a policy of co-operation and co-existence with the Soviet Union. This ideal had been supported by Conference therefore, Zilliacus and his allies argued, it was the Labour Cabinet's duty to carry this policy forward.

The history of the inter-war Labour movement shaped the party that would enter government in 1945. This Labour government should not betray its principles, as was the perception of the MacDonald government. The Attlee government, armed with a significant electoral mandate, should create a socialist settlement for Britain. Evidence suggests that there was a belief on Labour's backbenches that socialism was finally victorious. One newly elected Labour MP, and ex-miner, rose to sing the Red Flag at the close of the first day of parliament. One observer recalled that this was met with delight by some Labour members and the Communist and ILP members but caused consternation among the Conservative opposition.[6]

The 1945 election campaign had focussed upon the values of socialism. Churchill argued that this would mean "totalitarianism and the abject worship of state" and societal control by some form of "Gestapo".[7] With the benefit of hindsight we can argue that Labour only had to treat such derision with contempt, capture the moral high ground, and run a responsible campaign built upon promises that the British people wanted keeping. This was achieved and Labour won a resounding victory.[8] As Thorpe argued, it is unlikely the British people wanted the creation of an idealistic or ideological state,[9] but societal change and welfare reform. These were key reforms that Labour were trusted to deliver. Thus a section of the left appear to have held expectations that went far beyond the aspirations of Labour's leadership and the electorate.

A minority on the left, such as E P Thompson, believed that Britain was on the cusp of a democratic revolution.[10] By the 1950s this minority argued that they had once again been betrayed. This betrayal myth resulted from the degree of high expectations. Labour had the majority to achieve socialism, but had accepted a consensus foreign and domestic programme. The left wingers immediately set about condemning the leadership.[11] The idealism waned almost immediately among the majority of Labour MPs, and it is debatable whether it ever enjoyed majoritarian support among Labour backbenchers, party members or the electorate. The largest block vote against the government's extension of conscription by Labour MPs could only muster seventy-two supporters.[12] The most organised oppositional force, the Bevanites, argued from a position consistent with Labour policy and traditions; radical idealism was the preserve of a minority whose most influential orator was the Gateshead MP Konni Zilliacus.

KONNI ZILLIACUS: THE REBEL WHO KNEW BEST?

Zilliacus' idealism was founded upon the notion that the world should co-exist without conflict, a theme which would be prominent in the peace movement that would form in 1960s Britain.[13] Throughout his writings on international relations during the 1930s and early 1940s there runs the theme of a socialist peace being the only desirable future. He places the blame for the First World War squarely on the shoulders of capitalists and imperialists, while the Second World War, he asserted, was created by intransigence on both sides of the political spectrum. He argued that the National Government of Britain had been driven by imperialist desires rather than any sense of, what is referred to by Michael Foot in his introduction to The Mirror of the Past as: "[t]he law of nations, respect for their neighbours, the moral conscience of mankind."[14] These factors were irrelevant in a world system based upon power politics. As Morgenthau argued in his analysis of international relations from the realist perspective; state interests ruled diplomatic relations.[15] Zilliacus wanted Europe to break from this tradition; firstly through the League of Nations and then later through new alliances built during the Second World War. The Treaty of Versailles, with its basis in the notion of crippling the losing nations, had led to a flawed peace. The settlement of 1945 would have to be different if a lasting peace were to be secured.

Zilliacus entered parliament as an expert in international affairs and hoped for a role in steering Britain and Europe towards a new future. However, he allied with a minority in the party which remained under constant attack from the leadership. Due to the party's large majority following the 1945 General Election it could afford to expel radical voices. This was to be the fate of Zilliacus and three colleagues. By 1950 he was disillusioned by the failure of the Labour government to oppose the Cold War, but not totally thwarted. However, his radicalism was sufficiently subdued and he was allowed to return to the Labour Party in 1952 and to stand for election in 1955. This minority, of whom Zilliacus was the most prolific and vocal representative, consisted of individuals who looked to a whole range of influences and external interests, all seeking an elusive and arguably illusory socialist peace. Jan Zilliacus remembered him as a man whose "knowledge was ahead of most people... [But who was] often damned for acting with the best intentions."[16] This was probably how he perceived himself.

His writings exhibit a belief that he knew best. This belief was based upon his experience as a member of the League of Nations Secretariat General's Information Section for twenty years 1919-1939. What he did not realise was how far his ideas were out of step with the mainstream beliefs of his party. He stated the following in his introduction to I Choose Peace:

> The MP's loyalty to his party should not and normally does not conflict with his loyalty to his constituents and his conscience... But he must also be ready, when the issue is grave enough, to stand and deliver on his conscience and judgement, even though that make him a rebel and an anarchist.[17]

Zilliacus decided that the government's foreign policy affected the future so gravely that he was willing to be a rebel, seemingly on the strength of his conscience, beliefs and experience. I Choose Peace, published just prior to his expulsion, stands as his major work on post-war foreign affairs. This represents a historical analysis of Anglo-Soviet relations from a pro-Soviet perspective and offered a template for the policy changes he saw necessary for the Labour Party to enact to secure a peaceful future. To assess his true beliefs it is necessary to analyse the central tenets of his arguments and critically assess the pejorative labels attached to him during his years on Labour's benches.

He has been accused of being a fellow traveller of the Communists in very vehement terms. Gaitskell's diaries describe him as being part of the, "lunatic fringe [of] pseudo-Communists."[18] This has led some to draw the conclusion that he was some form of agent of the Soviet Union. This chapter outlines his arguments and activities to assess the level of independence Zilliacus maintained from the Communist line. As comparative studies there will also be a study of his three co-expellees, Leslie Solley, John Platts-Mills and Lester Hutchinson. This will provide a picture of this period of government, the arguments and issues that became central to the pro-Soviet position and how their arguments were shaped by exogenous events. This chapter will characterise what led these four individuals to face expulsion rather than accept government policy and how they developed a tradition that evolved within the Labour Party as an undercurrent of the left-wing agenda. This five-year period witnessed cogent opposition from the backbenches over foreign policy and, within that opposition, the emergence of parliamentary pro-Sovietism.

THE ZILLIACUS PERSPECTIVE OF INTERNATIONAL AFFAIRS

Zilliacus' perspective of European affairs since the Russian Revolution characterised the world as enveloped in a struggle between capitalism and socialism or communism. He made no distinction between the latter two ideological paths. He argued that from the outset the capitalist world was frightened of communism, a fear that led firstly to intervention in the Russian Civil War and secondly to a policy of exclusion against the Soviet Union. Using the Memoirs of Consul-General in Moscow 1914-7 Sir Bruce Lockhart[19] as evidence, Zilliacus argued that these policies led to the harshness and perpetually violent element present in the Soviet regime. A paranoid fear of external forces infiltrating Soviet Russia had developed and therefore all non-Bolshevik elements had to be prevented from being able to damage the system. Thus he constructed an apology for the excesses of Stalinism. Notably, unlike Pritt and many propagandists within the CPGB, he recognised that the ideal and the reality of Soviet Communism did not equate to one another, but he was able to develop an excuse for the inconsistencies between fact and rhetoric. Zilliacus portrayed Russia as a struggling nation, permanently beset by hostility for effecting a transition from authoritarianism to a socialist or workers' democracy. This mirrored the argument put forward by Labour MPs and Trade Unionists in opposition to intervention in the Russian Civil War.[20]

In more damning terms Zilliacus argued that the intervention in Europe against Socialist and Communist groups, such as the German Spartacists, paved the way for Fascism. He quoted Lloyd George who had expressed fears that a Spartacist-led Germany could ally with Bolshevik Russia against the capitalist West. Zilliacus argued that this policy of intervention had aided the more reactionary groups to come to power. Had this not happened, a "social revolution, mostly under Social Democratic leadership"[21] would have occurred in Germany. He argues that had this policy been reversed then the Second World War may have been unnecessary as Hitler, and the Nazis, may never have gained power. Furthermore, had the intervention in Russia been successful, and Tsardom restored, then the alliances in the Second World War may have been substantially different. The authoritarian regimes of Hitler's Germany, Tsarist Russia, Hirohito's Japan, Mussolini's Italy and Francoist Spain would possibly have been too strong an enemy for Britain and the United States to handle. This analysis can be linked with the, then emerging, tradition of thought that viewed the Soviet Union as the decisive combatant in the Second World War.

Equally, he argued that when fascism did emerge the leaders of the capitalist group in parliament initially welcomed it. Zilliacus quoted Winston Churchill, who stated that Mussolini had: "provided the necessary antidote to the Russian poison,"[22] to provide the necessary evidence. Zilliacus argued that the belief that the fascists were people that could be dealt with, and that Communists were inherently untrustworthy, had led to the National Government's policy of appeasement. Baldwin and Chamberlain, in Zilliacus' opinion, understood the imperial aspirations of the fascists but not the socialist statism of the Soviet Union. Therefore, it was the Soviet Union that became isolated from European politics. Zilliacus argued, using evidence based on Conservative members' arguments, that this attitude remained unchanged.

Even after the German invasion of the Soviet Union, Zilliacus tells the reader, many still held the view that the Soviet Union was the true enemy, while the fascist opponent only needed their power and aspirations restricting. Zilliacus argued that Churchill believed that Hitler and Mussolini were "friends of yesterday that might have to be salvaged tomorrow."[23] Zilliacus' claim was that the Conservatives were naturally anti-Communist and thus pro-fascist; they declared war on Nazi Germany to reassert Britain's traditional superpower status, not to defeat an ideology. This analysis continued a trend developed within G D H Cole's arguments regarding the nature of future conflicts between capitalist states.[24] Cole believed that World War II was to be the definitive ideological battle,[25] and arguably Cole also recognised that this was not a perspective held by the Conservative Party. With this analysis as a foundation, the Soviet victory over fascism in war and the Labour defeat of the Conservatives were linked, by some radical socialists, to the ideal of a post-war socialist settlement.

Zilliacus argued that it was Soviet Russia that defeated Nazi Germany and therefore, had every right to ensure that Germany could never rise again to attack Russia. Thus he excused the Soviet Union for creating itself a 'sphere of influence' or 'buffer zone' in Eastern Europe.[26] The Soviet Union, as the bulwark of democratic socialism, had defeated imperialism and should now be the leader, or at least a significant partner, in the New World order. This was the conclusion that Cole had reached in 1942, but rejected by 1945.

Zilliacus accepted that the Soviet Union had tried to remain neutral, explaining that Stalin had not been certain in 1939 who would ally with whom in the forthcoming conflict. Therefore the non-aggression pact with Germany, Zilliacus argued, was totally rational. Stalin recognised Britain as an enemy, not an ally, even after the German invasion, a perception reinforced by Britain's reluctance to aid the Soviet Union. The suspicion of the West adopted by the Stalinist regime, Zilliacus argued, was proven correct in the post-war world. Once again Zilliacus saw intervention attempting to prevent the election of socialist or communist parties to government in Europe. Throughout the United States' sphere of influence the policy of containment, as outlined in the Truman Doctrine, dominated foreign policy. Zilliacus saw this as a zero-sum game that was certain to lead to a third World War.[27]

While Zilliacus rejected the Cold War rationale, and heavily criticised Atlanticism, he did not, however, slavishly support Stalin or Soviet Communism. Not only did he support Tito and the independence of communism from the CPSU and Cominform, but he was also able to criticise aspects of the Soviet system. These were not the actions of a Soviet agent or confirmed fellow traveller. However, it appears that he was able to excuse much of the harshness of the Soviet system. While accepting that the post-war Communist states were essentially police states, Zilliacus excused this by arguing that it was that same aggressive policy which had been pursued by the western capitalist world that, as he put it, "aggravate[d] the evil and choke[d] back the good."[28] He saw all the failings in the establishment of socialism in the Soviet Union as being the fault of, primarily, the suspicion and antagonism that was displayed towards the state by the capitalist world, the epitome of which was displayed by the emergence of Fascism. This point was stressed in an unpublished draft of a Fabian pamphlet written in 1939:

the Soviet Union is still remote from realising the civil liberties side of this [socialist] programme, and it is not likely to make much progress in this direction so long as we have not defeated the menace of fascism and war.[29]

Zilliacus refuted the argument that Communism was no more than 'Red Fascism' arguing that equality was the greatest acquisition of the Russian people. Denouncing reports of oppression he argued that all forms of discrimination, such as racism, sexism or class-ism, had been eradicated. He compared the melting pot of United States to the 'electric mixer' of Russia's one hundred and eighty nine races, ignoring the reality of anti-Semitic policies. While he believed that he was producing a balanced argument, in the end the sum of his argument is to blame, prior to the Second World War, Britain, and in the post war world, the United States. At no time does Zilliacus apportion any blame for the outbreak of Cold War upon the Soviet leadership.

His analysis of the events in Greece, Germany and Italy, all potential Cold War flashpoints, confirmed his opinion that there existed a new western imperialism. In all these nations United States forces had tried to prevent or contain the spread of Communism. Zilliacus criticised this heavily:

> Uncle Sam comes across thousands of miles of sea and land to squat on Uncle Joe's doorstep and calamity-howl about Soviet expansion. The whole thing would be comic if it were not so tragic.[30]

Here Zilliacus displays the hypocritical position that devalued the arguments of those who exhibited pro-Soviet sympathies and used the Soviet Union as a focus for their dissent to the Cold War rationale. The Soviet Union was allowed almost complete latitude of action in the name of protection and self-preservation while the West, particularly the United States, was not. In hindsight we can argue that the Cold War rationale was flawed, and that a more co-operative, peaceful future was ultimately more desirable. However, in hinging his opposition upon an apology for Soviet foreign policy Zilliacus devalued the main tenets of his argument and thus his alternative foreign policy programme.

Konni Zilliacus perceived that the world had two choices. The Cold War offered the maintenance of a balance of power through a protracted arms race. That would lead to reductions in domestic spending and inevitably to war. His alternative was to abandon containment and accommodate Russia in a socialist European union. Zilliacus stated that the creation of a United Socialist Europe would be impossible without the inclusion and co-operation of the Soviet Union,[31] an argument that had few supporters within Labour circles.

R W G Mackay, Labour MP for Hull North West 1945-51, predicted that a stable post war settlement necessitated the establishment of a socialist European Union. However, countering the arguments of Cole and Zilliacus, Mackay stated that the inclusion of Russia would be fatal to harmonious relations,[32] arguing: "war with Russia [may be] inevitable."[33] Bevanites similarly focused on Europe as being pivotal. The Europe Group, a broad left-wing coalition, argued that a non-aligned European Union should be created to counter the influence of both superpower blocs.[34] Zilliacus countered this argument stating that peace should be maintained through the United Nations. Rather than creating a neutral barrier, negotiation and conciliation should "lock the door on the third World War."[35] The UN should stand, not as a tool of the United States against the Communist states, but as a proper consultative body operating through the governance of treaties to ensure pacific settlements to all disputes.[36] This he argued would lead to world government. The drive towards co-existence should start with an end to hostilities both real and via propaganda, particularly between the various leaders of the socialist parties and nations, indicating the domestic feuds between Communists and the Labour Party and the stand-off between Britain and the Soviet Union. He argued that if the British Labour Party led the way in foreign affairs then detractors would naturally dwindle away. There would be opponents but compromise both nationally and internationally would create the right environment for change.

The 1945 manifesto of the Labour Party, Let us Face the Future, stated that:

> We must consolidate in peace the great wartime association of the British Commonwealth with the [United States] and the [Soviet Union]. Let it not be forgotten that in the years leading up to the war the Tories were so scared of Russia that they missed the chance to establish a partnership which might well have prevented war… an International Organisation capable of keeping the peace in years to come. If peace is to be protected we must plan and act."[37]

This was the notion that Zilliacus supported and actively campaigned for. He recognised that the Soviet Union must withdraw from Eastern Europe to an extent, but that Stalin needed certain assurances before that could happen. This could only be achieved through open, friendly negotiation, not by threat of force. It was the latter that had created the post-war situation.

Zilliacus accused Ernest Bevin, Foreign Secretary, of losing Britain all the goodwill that was present in Europe in 1945. Therefore, the first task he argued for was the replacement of Bevin, but not of the government. As he concluded:

> "It can only be done under Labour rule because the making of peace has become inseparable from the building of a Socialist Commonwealth."[38]

The question is why did Zilliacus, unlike Mackay or the Bevanites, call for Soviet inclusion. It appears that Zilliacus held either a genuine hope for a lasting peace or a greater fear of impending war. However he is often accused of more cynical motives for his writings. In answering this critique of Zilliacus it is important to remember that nowhere in his writings, up to 1949, can be found a criticism of Stalin or Lenin, only the argument that they had reacted in a defensive manner towards aggression. This has led opponents to question exactly what the role of Konni Zilliacus was, and by whom was he influenced?

INDEPENDENT SOCIALIST OR AGENT OF INFLUENCE

It is unsurprising that opponents accused Zilliacus of acting under Soviet influence. It is not difficult to locate circumstantial evidence to indicate that he was a Soviet-controlled agent of influence. This, more often than not, was presented not by his opponents but by Zilliacus himself. Zilliacus argued that the smear campaign against him was part of a strategy developed by a Labour right wing and Conservative coalition:

> they do not believe in the possibility or desirability of living at peace with the Socialist third of humanity, and denounce as a crypto-Communist and practically a traitor anyone who believes we can and should try to discover common ground between our purpose and interests and those of Eastern Europe and the Soviet Union and revolutionary China.[39]

Zilliacus recognised that he was a prime target for such accusations but readily provided his opponents with ammunition. It seems that he was daring his opponents to prove these allegations. Within his background, however, are clear links to Soviet society and indications that the sympathies evident in I Choose Peace were developed early in his life.

In the introduction to *A New Birth of Freedom* he provided a short biographical note.[40] He recalled that his father was a Finnish Bolshevik who fled Finland to escape Tsardom. Konni Zilliacus senior wrote on the Russian Revolutionary Movement, and was founder and leader of the proto-Bolshevist, Finnish 'Activist' Party. Therefore the young Konni, born Kobe Japan in 1894, lived through this period of revolution influenced by his father. His father's influence, to support the progressive, anti-imperialist forces, lived on in the writings of Zilliacus. The young Konni was taught, as he later recalled that:

> some day there was going to be a revolution in Russia, and this would be something great and good to which all liberal and civilised people looked forward.[41]

However, during his education at Yale, he was encouraged to adopt a more conservative approach towards impending revolution.

Prior to the start of the First World War Zilliacus joined the US Air Force and then became attached to British Intelligence. Here he made his first direct contact with revolutionary Russia. For around a year, during 1918 and 1919, Zilliacus worked on the British Intelligence mission in Siberia. His role in the mission was to keep data and transfer messages between the British government and the forces on the ground. This role meant that he was party to the secrets of the British Government and their attitudes to revolutionary Russia, the movement he had been brought up to support. In the House in 1948, during a heated debate with Churchill, Zilliacus revealed this fact and used it to show that Churchill's attitude to the Soviet Union had never changed. There are no records of this intelligence mission however we can probably assume that as he was willing to mention it in the House of Commons the details were accurate.

Perhaps more indicative of his sympathies is the fact that, while in Siberia, he married a Polish Revolutionary, Eugenia Nowicka. Archie Potts, Zilliacus' biographer, indicated that there is evidence to suggest that Nowicka was an exile in Siberia and that her parents were reasonably middle class and privileged. Whether the Nowicka family were exiles of Tsarism or Bolshevism is unknown though given the period under discussion the former is a more reasonable assumption. Regardless of this any links with the Leninist regime, or its ideological traditions, that she brought to the marriage remain unknown. Unfortunately, due to the failure of this marriage, he does not mention her in his publications or his unpublished autobiography.

Britain's role in the Russian Civil War was short lived, mainly due to the opposition of the Labour Party and the Trade Union Movement, a factor that led Zilliacus to join the party in 1919. In 1921 he began an eighteen year post working in the Information Section of the League of Nations in Geneva. His role for the League was, due to his linguistic abilities, to review Russian affairs, assessing the content in Russian papers and journals and receiving Soviet delegates. In this capacity he must have met most of the leading Bolsheviks. It is impossible to assess whether they were aware of his background or his sympathies with their movement. They would probably have researched his background and would have been aware who his father was. Whether he was ever approached and asked to work on their behalf at this time is unknown, but when researching how the Soviet network of this period worked, it would be hard to imagine that he was not. The son of a revolutionary, in a place of responsibility and influence, must have been viewed as a golden opportunity for Soviet agents. This raises the question of what led him to start publishing.

During the 1930s, using the pseudonym Vigilantes, Zilliacus began writing on foreign affairs. He concentrated on why the League of Nations was failing, why Europe was drifting into war and what should be done to end this situation. His major work of the period, Inquest on Peace, published in time for the 1935 British General Election, is specifically aimed at demanding an anti-Fascist policy emerge within the British socialist movement. At this time he also argued for Soviet inclusion into the League of Nations. His motives for this are open to speculation because it was at this time that he began to develop his pro-Soviet arguments. While Stalin was portraying himself as a peaceful man wishing to become part of the world order, Zilliacus wrote of inclusion of, and co-operation with, the Soviet Union. The question remains whether this was produced due to Zilliacus' personal feelings and beliefs, or whether he was influenced by Soviet propaganda and contact with representatives from the Soviet Union. Later writings are based on evidence collected from discussions with Soviet leaders. Therefore it is likely that it was during this period that he established links with leading Soviet officials and later explored these relationships to gain information about Soviet foreign policy aims. There is no evidence that he was ever encouraged to write on behalf of the Soviet Union and it remains doubtful that Zilliacus would have done so. Despite this, Moscow would have perceived him as a pro-Soviet change agent and arguably this was correct. Zilliacus was perfectly placed to attempt to alter the climate of opinion by producing favourable analyses of the Soviet Union and its foreign policy objectives. His profile would have been raised further when he became an unofficial advisor to the Labour Party.

During the 1930s Zilliacus was approached by Hugh Dalton to act as an advisor to the Labour Party on foreign affairs. This role allowed him to develop his interest in British politics and the Labour Party. During this period the CPGB were arguing for the creation of a popular front and many were arguing that the Soviet Union should be seen as an ally. Here he appears perfectly placed to act as a lever on those who doubted the motives of the Soviet Union in Europe, such as Arthur Henderson and Clement Attlee, with whom he worked closely. Hugh Dalton recalled that Zilliacus was under suspicion in 1932. In his diary he noted Henderson had told him "a strange tale of allegations that Zilly[42] is a Bolshevik agent and may have been having his correspondence tampered with."[43] He resolved to look into these allegations. In January 1932 Dalton stayed with Zilliacus in Geneva. Here he became aware that Zilliacus had Communist connections. Dalton accompanied Zilliacus to a meeting promoting the boycott of the 1936 Berlin Olympics. This was attended by Ernst Toller and Claud Cockburn, both journalists for the Daily Worker, and Edgar Mowrer, an expelled German Communist. Dalton recalled that the meeting agenda followed "very much the Soviet line."[44] No records of an investigation, if one took place, exist. Dalton himself makes no further reference to the allegations. We should suppose that, given the positions Zilliacus was to be elevated to, they remained unsubstantiated. However it is open to debate whether there was any truth in such allegations, or whether he was simply an easy target due to the open way in which he moved within Communist and pro-Soviet circles.

In 1939 Zilliacus resigned from his post at the League of Nations in disgust over the Munich Agreement, a move that was to bring him to Britain and the Labour Party. During the war Zilliacus held a Civil Service post in the Ministry of Information [MOI], working alongside many who supported the Soviet Union. Many of the celebrated Cambridge spies held posts within the Civil Service or the Intelligence agencies during the war and immediately after.[45] Whether any links were made between the veteran of diplomacy and the young communist idealists remains undocumented. However Zilliacus was again in a position where he was able to maintain links with the Communist world as a legitimate gatherer of governmental intelligence.

Whether there was an unofficial contact between Zilliacus and Soviet Russia during the period up to 1945 is unknown. Certainly he was sympathetic to the regime. Thus we can argue that following Nazi Germany's attack on the Soviet Union, and the development of a tripartite alliance, Zilliacus had confidence in the future. Due to Hitler's military miscalculation the mistrusted Stalin became 'good old Uncle Joe' and the Soviet Union became an ally. Moreover, the Labour Party had become a progressive movement advocating sweeping reforms, albeit on the back of a national consensus.

The only evidence that has been put forward implicating Zilliacus as an agent of the Soviet Union referred to his wartime post in the MOI. Nikolai Tolstoy quoted the letters of Viktor Kravchenko, one time Soviet diplomat who defected in 1944.[46] Kravchenko placed Zilliacus in Beirut as an Allied Officer with access to sensitive information on manoeuvres in the Caucasus. Tolstoy claimed that links already existed between Zilliacus and an agent called Rado, who was, according to information in the US National Archives of the FBI in Washington, a high level spy handler code-named Dora.[47] Tolstoy argued that this link was strengthened and that Zilliacus was part of a group in the East which other sources testify included Kim Philby and Jack Klugman. Potts refuted this completely, stating the only military role Zilliacus had was as a member of the Home Guard and that he did not leave the country during the war years, this information was corroborated by his widow.[48]

It could be argued that such clandestine activities would be concealed, particularly by his widow. However, this alleged role appears contrary to his earlier and later behaviour. Furthermore with figures like Philby and Klugman active in this area, what would be the need for Zilliacus to expose himself to suspicion if he was an agent. Equally, as a translator, it is highly unlikely that Zilliacus would have had access to "staff maps". Kravchenko claimed Zilliacus sent a grossly over-estimated figure of the troops to Stalin, a tactic which could have been a ruse organised by the Ministry of Information, for whom Zilliacus worked.

The only factor that gives the allegation weight is that Kravchenko named Zilliacus. Of all the possible targets, if there was no truth in the accusation, why name him? It may have been a trick of the memory, a name or face being confused, by a man writing ten years later with no documentary evidence to hand. Alternatively it may have been written for anti-Soviet propaganda purposes. However evidence suggests that this, along with many allegations against Zilliacus, is largely false. This refutation is reinforced by Oleg Gordievsky who believed that Kravchenko's allegation was based upon a misheard code name and that the person passing information to Moscow from Cairo was the CPGB member James Klugman. Gordievsky recalled that Kravchenko was not party to high level information and therefore was working from hearsay. Kravchenko may well have been a contact of Zilliacus legitimately in relation to the League of Nations work and so knew of him. As Gordievsky highlighted, everyone is given a code name to confuse listeners and "muddy the waters of understanding."[49]

It appears that Zilliacus acted in too obvious a way to have been any sort of reliable agent, particularly as a member of parliament, which is the period that is under scrutiny here. Whether he was under Soviet influence or not he did fulfil the role of a propagandist. Soviet articles published in Britain argued that the Soviet Union was acting defensively and that it was the Western Alliance that was the aggressive force. These arguments were constantly reinforced by the arguments of Zilliacus both in I Choose Peace and subsequent publications and in speeches to the Commons. It can even be argued that although his pro-Soviet sympathies were not slavish, this could also have been part of his role. He had to be someone that the British politicians and people would listen to. Cominform did not need another Dutt, or Harry Pollitt, who produced similar arguments, but were perceived as under the control of the Kremlin. Misguided Soviet officials may have assumed Zilliacus was influential and thus destined for higher positions in government.

THE MYTH OF THE CRYPTO-COMMUNISTS

For Soviet ideas to percolate into British politics what was necessary was a body of independent support within parliament. These semi-independent but Soviet influenced MPs would be able to explain that aspects of Soviet society had strayed from the socialist ideal, while not being too critical of Stalin, and blaming Western capitalist aggression where possible. These MPs could produce reasoned, well argued analyses that would attract those who sought an understanding of foreign affairs but who did

not possess many preconceived ideas. This would have been the perfect role
for someone like Zilliacus.

Chapman Pincher argued that the KGB did control certain members
of parliament, employing them to embarrass the Government by asking
questions "calculated to damage the interests of Britain or her allies."[50] He
also claims, albeit without substantiation that:

> Some of the MPs are even named, by their code-name, in KGB radio
> traffic. The late Konni Zilliacus was one of them, and Driberg was
> another. [To excuse his lack of evidence he stated] I greatly regret that
> at this stage, I am unable to name others who are still alive and shelter
> behind the libel laws, as it is difficult to induce any intelligence source
> to appear as a witness, as MI5 itself knows only too well.[51]

Henry Pelling reinforces this thesis arguing that several crypto-Communists
were elected to parliament in 1945,[52] suggesting that many of the left-wingers
were at least acting covertly on behalf of the CPGB. While Pelling avoids
naming any MP in particular he does allude to the fact that they had "all but
disappeared by 1951" suggesting those who were expelled were part of the
CPGB's Cadre Department.[53] This argument is based on Douglas Hyde's
recollection of receiving a call at the Morning Star office from a Communist
who "announced himself as the new Labour member for his constituency…
with a loud guffaw."[54] Hyde recalls that the "eight or nine cryptos"[55] were
soon to leave either the Communist Party or parliament:

> [s]ome… [came] to feel that the parliamentary way to socialism was
> the best… others became attracted by a political and parliamentary
> career… [o]thers… were subsequently… purged by the Labour Party
> itself and who, in the 1950 election, all lost their seats."[56]

While much of this is circumstantial evidence, Zilliacus did appear as
a witness for the defence of the Soviet Union at the Kravchenko libel trial in
1949. His case was that slave labour, as described in Kravchenko's I Chose
Freedom, was not practised in the Soviet Union.[57] This role indicates that
Zilliacus was acting on behalf of the Soviet Government, and Gordievsky
claimed that he was seen in Moscow as an asset of the KGB. However,
evidence suggests that he was not the 'Soviet stooge' Pincher would seem to
suggest. Many of his, more moderate, left-wing colleagues doubted the
leadership's view of him. Labour MP for Huddersfield, 1945-79, J P W
Mallalieu wrote: "[t]o be a secret agent, Zilly is too clumsy and much too
honest."[58]

It is equally indicative that Zilliacus rejected the Soviet model of
socialism, unlike figures like Pritt with whom he was categorised. In 1952
Zilliacus abandoned his support for the Soviet Union and focused upon

Tito's Yugoslavia as the new hope for the future of Communism and world peace. This was not a shift in thought that was particular to Zilliacus. Within the British-Yugoslav Association a split developed between the advocates of the Stalinist line, a group led by D N Pritt, and the more internationalist and democratic socialists such as Zilliacus and Peterborough MP 1945-50 Stanley Tiffany. It appears doubtful that those who found themselves able to break from the Cominform line were at any time under the influence of Stalin's agents. Zilliacus was a key player in breaking away from Pritt's influence, reinforcing his position as a non-aligned critic of the British government.

The only source of information on the private life and thoughts of Konni Zilliacus was his widow Jan. When she met Zilliacus actress Janet Harris was a Communist Party member though, due to her Hollywood upbringing, this was arguably a faddish attachment. Jan recalled that when she and Konni began their relationship Harry Pollitt, a close personal friend, told her she must leave the Communist Party; "give up on this and join the Labour Party, if not it will look bad on Zilly you know."[59] Pollitt was fully aware of the stigma attached to having CP links. Jan retained her strong socialist beliefs, seeing the ideas of Pollitt and Zilliacus as those to which she would personally subscribe, and admitted that their perspectives were not dissimilar. This gives the impression that Zilliacus was well disposed towards the CPGB and its leadership, particularly Pollitt.

However evidence appears to contradict the perspective that a benign relationship existed between Zilliacus and the CPGB. It appears that during the Second World War Zilliacus was indeed approached and invited to be, in Laski's words, "a member of the CP in the LP concealing his name."[60] Laski stated that Zilliacus refused. This does indicate that overtures were made and that MPs were encouraged to conceal their affiliation, thus acting secretly on behalf of the CPGB. The objective was to gain influence within government, however a further implication was that membership could be employed as a lever of control if the Soviet Union did not get the expected benefits from the relationship with the MP. There is no evidence to indicate that Zilliacus did, or would have considered, taking up such an opportunity. The fact that he openly discussed the incident with Laski reinforces the open, almost carefree, image that Zilliacus assumed. Equally he seems to have lacked the ideological commitment to belong to the CP, his objective was world peace not the predominance of one or the other side in an ideological war.

Jan accompanied her husband on nearly all of his visits to the Soviet Union. She told me that they were usually invited, particularly after Zilliacus presented a strong pro-Soviet argument in the House. This indicates that Soviet agents kept an eye on their verbose ally. She described these visits as very informal, possibly geared to impress the couple, but that the Zilliacuses were not impressionable people. Konni had no need for an interpreter, he discussed politics with the Soviet leaders, and she recalled that "he would argue and explain the Western point of view."[61] When asked if they ever tried to steer his literature she replied that they "wouldn't dare,"[62] that Zilliacus was too independent. He had real hope for the Communist bloc in the post war world, but became disillusioned with the foreign policy motives of the Soviet Union. This and no other reason led him to lend his support towards Tito. Following the death of Stalin, Zilliacus became a close friend of both Khrushchev and Tito and visited their dachas often. Jan recalls that Zill, as she called him, was never fully supportive of Stalinism. He recognised the truth behind the socialist façade63 but saw this as a poor excuse to start a third World War.

      -    Zilliacus argued that Stalin had no intentions for further expansion and felt that the fear of Communism, that existed to extremes in the United States, and to a lesser extent in Britain, was "ludicrous and unfounded."[64] He argued: "the Soviet Union d[id] not want war and Communism [wa]s a social challenge, not a military threat."[65] He saw the dominant rationale leading to the situation of permanent paranoia later synonymous with McCarthyism. Many of left opposed the investigations launched by the leadership into their activities. Jan recalled that Zilliacus was the subject of an MI5 investigation and had secretaries thrust upon him who would search through his papers when he was out of the office. Ambitious members of the party had to be careful in their associations and arguably Zilliacus was a particular victim of the anti-Communist ethos. In party circles he was suspected of being a 'Red',66 therefore, younger members who supported his stance, individuals such as Frank Allaun, found themselves tarred with a similar image. This attitude disgusted Zilliacus. He saw himself as being victimised due to his beliefs in peace and socialism.

      \   To Zilliacus these two ideals were inseparable. Socialism, he argued, represented the only way of achieving peace, co-operation and social equality. A stance that leads us to question why he supported the Soviet Union as it was clearly not socialist. Zilliacus argued that it was. The egalitarian society, state ownership and a non-aggressive foreign policy in the face of provocation, he eloquently argued, were fundamental to Soviet society. External pressure from the West and Stalin's response to this aggression had deformed the original blueprint, but the ethos remained and could still be rescued. This was the central argument of *A New Birth of Freedom*. The achievements of the society, which had had western Socialists and intellectuals gazing in awe since 1931, would act as the ideological glue of the system. Meanwhile, ideological dedication from the new leadership would cleanse it of the excesses of Stalinism and produce a more democratic political system, a socialist society rather than just a socialist economy. He recognised faults on both sides of the ideological spectrum and argued that the people could and would redress this eventually:

> The longing for freedom and equality can never be wholly extinguished in human hearts, nor can men indefinitely be deceived into believing they already possess freedom when in fact they do not. That is as true of the absence of economic and social democracy under capitalism as it is of the lack of political democracy under Communism.[67]

Zilliacus preferred the economic and social freedom that he saw represented under communism. That is obvious, though never openly stated. He wanted the Soviet Union to have a chance to develop, for the state bureaucracy to wither away, but argued that this was dependent upon the actions of external forces. He believed that the Soviet system represented the ideal for mankind's future relations; these should be founded on peaceful co-operation not the competitiveness of capitalism. This belief, amalgamated with his experience in foreign affairs, shaped Zilliacus' theories on international relations. His experiences indicated that one system emerged as the progressive alternative to capitalism. It is likely that contact with Soviet delegates, coupled with theories emerging from Britain and Western Europe, nurtured and reinforced his perception of the Soviet Union. This belief in Soviet society, and his deep fear of war, can be argued to have underpinned his attachment to pro-Sovietism and his motivations for acting as a propagandist of pro-Soviet and pro-Communist arguments.

THE TOTALITARIAN ELEMENT

During Labour's 1945-1950 term of office Zilliacus was not the sole proponent of the pro-Soviet analysis on international relations. His allies were among the amorphous group that Raymond Blackburn, Labour MP for Birmingham, King's Norton 1945-51, referred to, in a debate on the infamous 'Nenni telegram', as the "Totalitarian element of the Labour Party."[68] Blackburn called for their complete expulsion, a goal that was never fully achieved. However between April 1948 and July 1949 four MPs were expelled, and it is interesting to view the sources of opinion that they, particularly, should be expelled, while others such as Geoffrey Bing or Tom Driberg were to remain within the fold. Geoffrey Bing stated that the reason that he had not been earmarked for expulsion was that he had been "more adroit than they have been in not being put into a position where I had to declare myself."[69]

Though this is probably true for many of the potential expellees, to expel every opponent of Bevin's foreign policy would have been impossible, or at least extremely detrimental to party cohesion, Labour's parliamentary

majority and future electability. Examples had to be made in order to kerb
the left, particularly the Keep Left group who maintained a moderate anti-
Atlanticist position. Though Aneurin Bevan and Richard Crossman were
staunch opponents of Bevin, arguably it would have been political suicide
for the party to expel them because of their ability and popularity. Those
who would become examples to other left-wing dissidents were members
who the press had highlighted as being troublesome and for whom the
public, particularly Labour voters, had little support. This was largely achieved,
the key critics of the government all lost their seats in 1950, though the
electorate moved substantially away from Labour at the 1950 Election any-
way. So how and why did these four dissidents make themselves the targets
of the Labour Whip?

The Labour leadership was aware that a problem existed. It was the
task of Morgan Phillips, General Secretary, to find who were the main
proponents of the pro-Soviet perspective. D N Pritt criticised the process as
resembling the "McCarthyite witch-hunt" experienced by anti-Cold War
activists in the United States. The file that was created on the individuals,
known collectively as the 'Lost Sheep', was carefully compiled. Party members, in parliament and the constituencies, were employed to gather evidence and send it to Transport House. This evidence combined hearsay
records of speeches, press cuttings and even opinions of party members.

Hugh Dalton provided the damning piece of evidence against Zilliacus.
This was an article in The New Statesman and Nation called 'The Labour
Party's Dilemma', in which Zilliacus argued that the policy of intervention,
pursued by Britain and the United States, within other nations domestic
politics was "indefensible in terms of democracy."[70] Dalton footnotes this
article with the sarcastic comment "tell this to the Kremlin."[71] In an
accompanying letter, Dalton suggested a solution: "I feel we cannot, much
longer, avoid dealing with the author, as we did with Platts-Mills."[72]

A seventeen-page document was drawn up which contained evidence of Zilliacus' pro-Communist support. This was used to prove that
Zilliacus was unfit to be a Labour Party member. In defence of the party's
decision, Phillips wrote to one critic:

> they… used their positions and their prestige, as members of the
> British House of Commons, in a manner inimical to the work of the
> party and in support of policies which, time and time again, had been
> rejected by the Annual Party Conference.[73]

There are entries for all of the individuals expelled, and eighteen[74]
other possible candidates for expulsion. This shows there was a degree of
support for pro-Soviet ideas and that the party was keen to act against the
major proponents.

John Platts-Mills, the first to be expelled, plotted an unusual political course before standing as a Labour candidate in 1945. He was a New Zealander by birth, had spent time in the British Air Force, worked as a propagandist under Churchill during the war and had worked in the Yorkshire mines as a 'Bevin boy'. The latter had led him to have a close affinity with the British people, a quality that he recalled encouraged him to pursue a career in the Labour Party. In his opinion the higher echelons of the party were against him from the outset. He recalled that his election expenses were restricted to hinder his campaign, though this did not stop him selling himself, using billboard posters, as the 'People's John'.[75] His maiden speech 20 August 1945 should have been a warning to the front bench.

Despite his rough and candid style, Platts-Mills would endeavour to be as contentious and controversial as possible. His subject was Greece, cleverly quoting Churchill's speech of 16 August when he stated that "we must remould the relationships of all men, wherever they may dwell, in all nations."[76] Platts-Mills asked, therefore, why was Britain reinforcing a corrupt, fascistic regime in Greece and preventing free elections from taking place. Furthermore, he enquired, if the Government was so keen on ensuring the freedom and self-determination of a nation's peoples, why was India still under British rule. These were issues on which the Labour Government could guarantee support from the Tory opposition. The only voices to break the parliamentary consensus on foreign affairs were the intra-party left-wing and their independent allies, D N Pritt, Independent member for Hammersmith and Phil Piratin and Willie Gallacher, the Communist Party MPs for Mile End and West Fife respectively. Alongside the so-called 'Lost Sheep', these MPs used these and similar issues, highlighted as anti-socialist policies, as a stick to beat the front bench, particularly the hapless Ernest Bevin. This was a small, but formidable, group, eloquent and extremely critical of the Government's handling of foreign affairs.

In the House Platts-Mills, alongside Hugh Lester Hutchinson, Leslie J Solley and Konni Zilliacus, continually adopted an oppositional stance to the cross-bench consensus and took great pleasure in asking the most difficult questions of Ernest Bevin. It was not that the questions were unanswerable, but these were questions designed to cause the electorate and party members to doubt the socialist credentials of the Labour Party. Solley, supported by others on the Labour Left and the elected Communists, asked George Brown, speaking on the Greek situation, if "he was suggesting that we have supported democracy in Greece when we compelled the holding of elections without any working class party participation."[77] Equally, Hutchinson, in his maiden speech on 21 February 1946, stated that the Government, and particularly Bevin, was:

the unfortunate heir to the traditional policy of bolstering up reactionary monarchs and decaying regimes wherever we can find them. In that
policy I believe we can find the explanation for the antagonism between ourselves and Soviet Russia.[78]

The most notable factor that links these four individuals is that in
speeches on foreign policy, the Soviet Union's policy was referred to as the
positive alternative to the negative anti-Communist Cold War rationale.
Equally if there was a debate on the Soviet Union, or one of its client states,
at least one of their voices was heard opposing Bevin and promoting a pro-
Soviet line. It is not difficult to see why these individuals were singled out.
Others, highlighted by Schneer[79] as government opponents, were never so
vocal in the House, the medium receiving most attention in the press. This
reportage embarrassed the Labour Government greatly. The Times of the
period, throughout its political pages, highlights incidents where these
individuals publicly exposed the inconsistencies and failures in Labour's foreign
policy.

John Platts-Mills, culprit or victim of the 'Nenni Telegram' incident,[80]
was the first to be expelled for his opposition despite the fact that Zilliacus
was the most active in opposing government policy in the House and in his
independent writings. Perhaps the party believed it could control Zilliacus
with the threat of expulsion. Due to his wealth of experience in foreign
affairs many did argue that he was a "loaded gun that required careful handling"[81] indicating a desire to control Zilliacus, if possible, through the party
whip procedure. Equally the expulsion of Platts-Mills may have been an
attempt to break the group's apparent cohesion. This was arguably a pointless exercise. Platts-Mills recalled no true cohesion; he admitted that they met
for dinner from time to time and Jan Zilliacus recalled that Platts-Mills and
Hutchinson were regular houseguests. However their alliance was due to
their beliefs; they were friends due to their political stance, but did not act in
an organised manner. He provided the image of these four dissident MPs as
pragmatic opponents of the government motivated by their principles alone.
Jan argued that Zilliacus, despite being the most knowledgeable of the group,
would never have wanted to be a leader: "he had no ego whatsoever."[82] What
is evident is the ideological cohesion of the group; they spoke as a party
within a party, supported by the external pro-Soviet faction, the two
Communist MPs and D N Pritt. Thus the only course of action open for the
party leadership was to ensure that their pro-Soviet arguments could not be
interpreted as representing party policy.

Their unity on the international situation is evident from parliamentary debates recorded in Hansard. Zilliacus stated that the Conservatives'
desire to make an issue of the Russian war crime trials of eleven Poles, all

suspected of 'Fifth Column' activities, was "not unconnected with their desire to stir up trouble between us an the Soviet Union."[83] Platts-Mills described Conservative foreign policy, and by implication that of Bevin, as being along:

> familiar lines, a complete absence of any clear policy that will make toward world peace and break down the existing difficulties; the same veiled abuse of the Soviet Union running through it.[84]

Arguing that the policy of interventionism in the political arrangements of other nations was flawed, Platts-Mills asked pertinently "[if] the French people were to decide to have a left-wing Government… should [we] then invade France to prevent it."[85] Leslie Solley, in sealing his fate, stated on 14 May 1948, five days before his expulsion, that

> we are not faced with the line up of the so-called anti-democracies on the one hand and the so-called democracies on the other. It is a line up of, on the one hand the warmongers who are substantially the capitalists, and on the other hand the non-warmongers who are substantially the anti-capitalists. [He argued] Let us join the anti-capitalists and we shall win peace for the peoples of the world.[86]

These arguments could have come straight from the writings of Zilliacus, whether in the 1930s or the post war period. The style of delivery shows Zilliacus as the most eloquent member of the group. Not surprisingly, all members of this elite minority showed a greater vituperativeness towards the Government following their expulsion, none more so than Platts-Mills. In his unpublished autobiography he recalled:

> This one man [himself] hurled himself at Ernie Bevin like a clenched fist whenever he appeared… to be acting… more abjectly servile than usual to United States foreign policy. This was only about once a day.[87]

The reasons for this appear two-fold, Platts-Mills opposition to the Cold War ethos and his open, deep dislike of Bevin. Platts-Mills described Bevin as bigoted, anti Semitic, and horrible.[88] However, Platts-Mills major concern was that an anti-Communist propaganda campaign had been initiated in order to prepare the British people for a war against the Soviet Union.

THE PRO-SOVIET PROPAGANDIST

If Hyde's recollection is correct, and there were crypto-Communists within the 1945-50 Labour government, John Platts-Mills appears one of the most likely candidates for such a role. However he himself tells a different story. His first official connection with the Soviet Union was when working for Churchill during the Second World War. He was singled out to lead a nondescript team of propagandists, whose task was to change public opinion.

> Churchill said he had been teaching the British since 1918 that the Russians were un-Christian, they ate their babies… If the British people went on thinking that there would be no war effort, because the only war effort could be in favour of Russia.[89]

Stafford Cripps, then British Ambassador to Moscow suggested Platts-Mills for this task in 1941. The question is why? Platts Mills was an apprentice barrister and part-time worker for the Labour Party, in the role of secretary of St Philips Ward. However, he was also a member of the SCR, a Labour Party proscribed organisation. He also had close links with members of the International Brigade, the People's Convention and the Popular Front Movement. It is possible that, during their association in the latter campaign, Cripps learned of his sympathies. Platts-Mills had also enlisted to fight in Spain, but was refused because he was married with a child.[90] Equally he had been prominent during the 1930s in prosecuting cases against fascists and defending their Communist opponents following street fights.[91] These activities brought him to the attention of the fore-runner to the Haldane Society: The League of Socialist Lawyers, then chaired by Frank Soskice and presided over by Cripps. His new found credibility allowed him to be found a new role under Churchill himself.

Platts-Mills recalled that he was very successful as a pro-Soviet propagandist, this led Churchill to dismiss him and encourage him to take work in the South Yorkshire coal mines as a Bevin boy. However, Platts-Mills role as a change agent was to be revitalised when he became a Member of Parliament. This role was not founded upon a desire to support the Soviet union per se; his opposition to Bevin was founded on the belief that the government's scheme of rearming Germany was part of a Churchillian plan to start a new war:

> Churchill conceived the idea, and this is not made up on my part, this is direct information from the horse's mouth as it were. He made up the idea that the Labour Government being in power and he being in opposition, but Bevin and Attlee so worshipping him, Churchill, that they would do what he suggested, and he should get the Labour Party leaders to get Germany rearmed, set her again on Russia. This time not having to fight us as well, but with us as a neutral with America and France providing the arms and money, then Germany would beat Russia at last… It was the most monstrous thing really.[92]

This was his rationale for opposing the party. He and his colleagues shared the view that Labour foreign policy was tied to Churchill and a scheme that would lead to an unjust war. Platts-Mills did not share Zilliacus' total opposition to war, but opposed the anti-Communist and anti-Russian ethos of the Cold War.

Platts-Mills equally opposed the hypocrisy that underlined Churchill's plan. Under Churchill's instruction Platts-Mills had spent two years turning the British people towards the Soviet Union. British workers had been producing 'Tanks for Joe', tanks in support of the Soviet war effort. To Platts-Mills it appeared that these same workers were now being called upon to produce 'Tanks for Germany', 'Tanks against Joe'. This he argued was wrong:

> I thought the best thing was to go on making the same propaganda as I had been making during the war under Churchill's instruction, making people think what good chaps the Russians were.[93]

He recalls this as the true reason for his expulsion.

He visited Russia several times, leading exchange visits of war heroes. He describes the individuals he met there as wonderful people, not the barbarians that pre-war propaganda had led him to expect. This led him to the conclusion that "Joe Stalin can't have been so horrible as they fought for him, made sacrifices for him, as they did."[94] Future Labour Prime Minister James Callaghan accompanied Platts-Mills on one visit designed for young people who had been active during the Second World War. Callaghan was then Vice-Chairman of the Parliamentary Defence and Services Committee. These recollections tell us of the British delegation drinking heavily with their Russian counterparts. Callaghan recalled that "we were heavily indoctrinated with propaganda during our visit and I daresay it had more effect on some than on others."[95] We can assume that the aim was to turn individuals like Callaghan, in a position of relative influence and power, into Soviet sympathisers. One fellow visitor, Captain Harry Ree, who represented the Army, was regarded by the Soviets as a spy after his visit, though Lord Callaghan cast doubt on the authenticity of the claim. Platts-Mills was possibly already seen as an asset, particularly given his role in organising visits to the Soviet Union.

Upon his return to post war London, John Platts Mills found himself a new post, as junior partner in the law firm run by D N Pritt. It is more than likely that they had already enjoyed some contact through the SCR and other wartime pro-Soviet organisations. Platts Mills became a member of the International Association of Democratic Lawyers [IADL],96 of which Pritt was President. This, as well as his link with the SCR, a Communist front organisation that Pritt also chaired, makes the two appear intrinsically linked in their pro-Soviet activities. It is unknown whether Platts-Mills' association with Pritt shaped his political perspective or whether he was drawn to Pritt because of existent pro-Soviet sympathies. Pritt was seen as an active OGPU agent during the 1930s, it is possible that he also recruited sympathetic young intellectuals to front organisations and then encouraged them to participate in further activities at a later date, depending on their position in British society. It is equally possible that Platts-Mills was influenced by both peers and alumni of Balliol College, Oxford University. These included past pupils R P Dutt, Theodore Rothstein and Tom Wintringham, and current pro-Communist students like Marxist historian Christopher Hill. Pritt was also an Oxford fellow though not at Balliol College. Koch indicated that pro-Soviet agents operated in the Universities during the 1920s recruiting sympathisers for more active roles, it is possible that Platts-Mills was referred to Pritt for 'further political education'.[97]

◄   Platts Mills's contemporaries included fellow Labour MP Denis Healey. Healey admitted joining the Communist Party due to the influence of contemporaries,[98] but resigned due to the CPGB's analysis of the Second World War. Many others refused to break their links with the Soviet ideal they had supported during their youth. Platts-Mills, however, refuted the notion that he was ever a CPGB member, however his activities indicate that he was, arguably, a Communist in all but name. Platts-Mills stressed that his sympathies were with the Russian people but not the Soviet leadership. As for being a fellow traveller and a follower of the Communists in parliament, he admitted that they were friends, going as far as on one occasion to become involved in a fist fight in the Commons Tea Rooms. This was with the Conservative MP for Brighton "a real Fascist"[99] in defence of Phil Piratin,[100] but "as far as me following the Communist line, they followed our line rather than our following their line."[101]

◄   Free from the shackles of Labour Party membership Platts-Mills continued his support of the Soviet Union through his membership of the IADL and the SCR. Since 1989 he has been the President of the SCR, and spent many years on the Executive Committee, particularly as Vice President alongside the Presidents D N Pritt and Hugh Jenkins. During the 1960s he was involved in IADL work, investigating former Nazi judges, US intervention in Vietnam and in Iraq and was prominent in the establishment of a bureau to investigate US war crimes which was based in Postdam. After Pritt's death Platts-Mills became the figurehead of many of the pro-Soviet organisations formally controlled by Pritt. Equally letters between him and Ivor Montague, the pro-Communist journalist and filmmaker, show that Platts-Mills was instrumental in Montague being awarded the Lenin Prize for Peace in 1959. He must therefore have had some degree of influence in Moscow.[102] The very innocent letters show that the two men were obviously old friends rather than fellow conspirators. However, they were in a position by the late 1950s to be open about their sympathies.

    Platts-Mills also wrote for the SCR's publication, the Anglo Soviet Journal, which was a medium for pro-Soviet propaganda. These articles give some indications of his true beliefs: "the Soviet people work because they have confidence both in what is happening today and in the future… there is no mistaking their enthusiasm for the regime."[103] Platts-Mills believed that the Russian people controlled their own political destiny. They had chosen to live under Communism because of the benefits experienced in a 'true socialist society'. He argued that they had changed the political regime previously by revolution therefore, if Stalin was so unpopular, why had they not operated once more as the vehicle for societal change. He appeared to refute evidence that indicated that the Soviet system was unsocialist, supporting a Journal which, on Stalin's death, printed a eulogy, written by Pritt, for the late dictator:

> Thank you, Joseph Stalin, for the cultural human development, for the conscious purposeful humanism that you have brought to the lives of all who have eyes to see, minds to understand, and hearts to rejoice.[104]

Though Platts-Mills does not display the same devout Stalinism of this eulogy, he argued that there was nothing wrong with Stalin on the basis of the love the Russian people had for him. He argues that the death of Stalin led to the 1989 collapse: "it all went wrong after that."[105]

    Platts-Mills heavily criticised the changes in the beliefs of his erstwhile colleague, going as far as to allude that Zilliacus' change of beliefs was a cynical ploy to gain re-election; a sin none of the others in the group committed. It is obvious that the Communist MPs had a greater respect for Platts-Mills than his Labour colleagues did. This is shown not only by their support for him in the House. In Willie Gallacher's memoirs of the period he described Platts-Mills as "the most indomitable and courageous Member of the House of Commons."[106]

    Whether Platts-Mills' pro-Soviet beliefs came from contact with the Russians or their agents, or the impact of his experiences, is hard to establish with any degree of exactitude. He insisted that he believed in what he was doing, firstly for Churchill, then for the Soviet Union. He opposed a policy that he saw would lead to an unjust war, and a process through which an entire nation's people had become demonised. Platts-Mills had little care for the concerns of governments only the interests of the people, albeit the people of Soviet Russia. He identified the people he met during his time in the coal mines with the Russian people; "good people who wanted peace and prosperity"[107] his objective was to ensure that the British government would not stand in their way.

* The 1930s, as several historians have argued, was the "golden age for Communism in Britain."[108] Labour was seen to be impotent in creating social inequality. The alternative was revolutionary socialism. These ideas appealed to many middle-class intellectuals. Some saw themselves as Lenin-like figures, leading the way by producing revolutionary material, a role consistent with Roberts' characterisation of R P Dutt.[109] Those who stood on the fringes such as Platts-Mills were more independent, but maintained clear support for the Soviet ideal. These figures operated within parameters determined by a pro-Soviet campaign centrally controlled by Cominform agents. They produced the same arguments, kept an appearance of independence, but were careful not to denounce the model of 'actually existing socialism'. Not all were as prominent as Platts Mills, some kept their alliances with the front organisations reasonably secret, Julius Silverman for example. Beatrice Webb coined the phrase "Mild mannered desperadoes"[110] because of their backgrounds. These were middle-class intellectuals who would become influential in later life however Webb observed that in their youth they would yearn to overthrow the system in which they were destined to prosper. What Webb did not foresee was that this also made them ideal subjects for Soviet recruitment.

There was no reason for figures like Platts Mills to be CPGB members. Their role as non-aligned progressive and influential socialists was important to Cominform's objectives. Their promotion of the Soviet Union as a socialist state, the progressive alternative to United States capitalism, and their condemnation of the United States as the 'aggressive superpower' reached a wider audience than openly Communist pamphleteers. Locating supporters for these arguments within parliament and using their positions to further the goals of the Soviet Union were the roles ascribed to them. Platts-Mills assumed this role with enthusiasm and, in later life his only regret was that his ideals crumbled before his eyes. He argued, almost tearfully, that "socialism has no chance anymore, they [the anti-Soviet western leaders] destroyed it".[111] The British affiliate of the IADL, the Haldane Society of Socialist Lawyers, carries on its work with Platts Mills as President. Through this organisation pro-Soviet policy lines are maintained despite the collapse of the focus for these activities. The Haldane Society acted as an umbrella for organisations that offered support to Cuba against the United States, and exposed the injustices prevalent in the dictatorships supported by the United States to contain Communism. Recently the society has supported campaigns in support of Libya, Argentina during the Falklands Conflict and currently Iraq. The fight seems to be continuing long after the ideological struggle is lost. Platts-Mills' pro-Soviet network is now a poorly funded source of permanent dissent.[112]

THE ADVOCATE OF TOTALITARIANISM AND THE
CAMPAIGNER FOR DEMOCRACY

Hugh Lester Hutchinson equally had a history of Communist connections. His mother, Mary Knight, was a founder of the CPGB. Hutchinson
himself was arrested by the British Government in India in 1932 while
investigating the arrest of prominent CPGB members on the charge of
"conspiracy to deprive the King-Emperor of sovereignty over British India."[113] This episode, the Meerut Conspiracy Trial, was an attempt by the
Colonial Office to quell the rising tide of Indian Communism. The conspiracy involved British Communists actively supporting the Indian Communist Party by providing funding and tactical advice. Key activists were
British Indians Shapurji Saklatvala, Rajani Palme Dutt and M N Roy, all of
whom were members of the CPGB. Callaghan argued that the Indian Communist movement was mainly controlled from Britain and orchestrated by
Rajani Palme Dutt,[114] despite claiming Indian independence as its chief objective and enjoying some support from Mahatma Gandhi. Non-Indian British
Communists were also prominent agitators and this was the accusation levelled against the thirty-one militants arrested in March 1929.

His experiences in Meerut encouraged Hutchinson to place the
question of colonial rule and the issue of imperialism high on his agenda as
a Labour MP. However there exists no evidence that Hutchinson took an
active part in the conspiracy or that he had any contact with the chief
conspirators in Meerut, Ben Bradley and Philip Spratt, or with the CPGB. It
is also unclear if he acted under Communist Party control. Branson
maintained that he was acting on behalf of a Trade Union, members of
which were among those imprisoned.[115] It should also be noted that, following the division of the Labour Party after the MacDonald-Lansbury split,
the Lansbury-led Labour Party argued in favour of the release of the Meerut
conspirators. An official 1933 publication argued that the arrests, which had
been approved by Ramsay MacDonald in his role as Prime Minister in 1929,
and subsequent sentences of up to twelve years were "indefensible."[116] This
indicates that Hutchinson was not acting in opposition to the Labour Party
or that his pre-war activities can be used as evidence that he was a Communist
plant as Pelling argued was the case with many of the pro-Soviet radicals.[117]
Equally he does not appear to have sought a career within politics and, unlike
Platts-Mills, did not continue his work within the extra-parliamentary pro-
Soviet network. Following his expulsion from the Labour Party Hutchinson
returned to teaching, and drifted into obscurity, retaining no links with his
previous colleagues. However, Morgan Phillips was certainly satisfied with
the conclusion that "he is undoubtedly a Communist in everything but
name."[118]

Phillips was probably correct. In his one published article on post-war political ideology Hutchinson defines himself as a revolutionary socialist in the communist tradition. This short article for Left, April 1946, is written as a rebuttal of previous articles calling for the creation of a Third Force. This stance, Hutchinson argued, was motivated by a hatred of Stalinism and as such ignored the realities of post-war Europe. This reality, that the Soviet Union was the decisive political force in post-war Europe, Hutchinson argued, should not be rejected simply because of opposition to Communism. The Bolshevik revolution was successful, Hutchinson argued, because it had created a socialist state. The Bolshevik example, set in Russia in 1917, had been seized by many Eastern European nations therefore, he argued, Soviet Communism represented the political future for Europe. Hutchinson accepted the brutality of the regime stating that "there is a profound difference... between Utopian and Marxian Socialism."[119] Marxism, to Hutchinson, was the highest form of socialism, the ideology destined to replace capitalism, but its success depended upon resolute action from the socialist movement. Parliamentary democracy, Hutchinson argued, was a sham that defended the self-serving capitalist class only. However, it did provide the opportunity for a socialist group to seize the power of the state. On achieving this, as Labour had in 1945, the state must be "smashed" and replaced by a state organ "created of Socialists by Socialists... the rights of man can only be obtained in a classless society, which can only be intro-duced by stern and dictatorial methods."[120] The spread of this type of so-cialism Hutchinson saw was inevitable and ultimately desirable. As radical socialism was established across the world an alliance of these regimes would be established to protect them from the twin horrors of United States impe-rialism and war.

Hutchinson never argued that Britain, or indeed Europe, should ally with the Soviet Union, though this is implicit in such terms as "socialist unity" and his argument for establishing an anti-United States socialist alliance. Marxism and the Post-War World was, however, a clear message to the socialist movement in Britain, particularly the Labour Party, to fulfil its historical destiny and accept that the world was heading towards a socialist revolution. To Hutchinson, Labour should have been the catalyst not the opponent:

> It is high time that we re-instated Marxism as the political theory of British Socialism, and thus do our part in speedily completing the Revolution, before worse horrors than we have already undergone are upon us.[121]

This was not a tenable role for the Labour Party. Hutchinson appears to have entered parliament in the belief that this government would tear away the structures of the old society and create a new socialist state. His methodology for this was the creation of a proletarian dictatorship. This was neither labourism nor gradualism; these were Communist ideals and were inimical to the principles which guided Labour's political thought.

Hutchinson sealed his fate while on an extensive lecture tour of the United States. The Soviet Monitor, 29 April 1949, quoted his denunciation of the Marshall Plan and the North Atlantic Treaty as "instruments of war."[122] He is quoted as arguing that the true purpose of Marshall Aid was to tie the economies of Western Europ inexorably to the United States. With the economy under Americancontrol, so domestic and foreign policy would be subordinated too. British capitulation to United States foreign policy, he argued, was "turning this country into an aircraft carrier for the designs of American imperialism."[123] Hutchinson was arguably from a similar school of thought as Zilliacus, but a more radical variant. He was clearly the mostideologically radical of those expelled and it is unsurprising that he never returned to the party.

Leslie Solley appears as the enigma of this group. His career in oppositional politics centred upon one issue in foreign affairs, Greece, and his publications, either alone or with fellow Labour MPs Norman Dodds[124] and Stanley Tiffany, opposed British Governmental intervention in the Greek political situation. Solley's analysis argued that a semi-fascist monarchist group was being allowed to take control of the Greek Government rather than the Social Democrats. This policy, Solley argued, had begun under Churchill's War Cabinet and had been opposed by many in the Labour Party. A Labour government had been expected to change policy toward Greece but had refused to consider the alternatives. Solley argued that a Labour government should break from the Conservative traditional foreign policy.

Solley stands out in comparison to his fellow expellees due to the lack of consistent, direct support of the Soviet Union. In *Greece: The Facts* he argued that there were very few Communists in Greece, only several groups of progressive Socialists who have the support of the people, but who, due to British intervention, were being persecuted by the forces of authoritarian reaction. Though he supported the views of Zilliacus in parliament, he cannot be described as a fellow traveller, more a staunch democrat wanting his party to practise what many of the front bench had preached prior to taking office. He does argue against capitalism, which does tie him to the Communist line but he did not argue for an alliance with the Soviet Union, though he had no fear of Soviet influence in international affairs.

The main tenet of his publications on Greece is the futility of the British Government's policies which entailed an interventionist stance based on a fear of phobic proportions. The anti-Communist foreign policy, under-pinned by a fear of Soviet expansionism, was being practised, he claimed, to the detriment of the socialist principles on which he had been elected. Like

Platts-Mills and Hutchinson, Solley also left politics following his expulsion. Equally Solley did not believe he was doing anything either disloyal or immoral. In his own defence, following the Nenni Telegram incident, he wrote to Morgan Phillips stating that he was unaware that the Nennists had been proscribed by the NEC. He did not agree with this decision, but assured Phillips that "I shall certainly confine such disagreements to what is permitted by the party constitution."[125]

After Hutchinson, Platts-Mills and Solley joined with Pritt in forming the Labour Independent Group [LIG], and standing as independent 'true socialists' in the 1950 General Election, all three lost their seats. They were never to return to parliament. Their objective was to influence their colleagues, and the British public, and chane the perception of the Soviet Union and consequently government policy towards the Communist bloc. Their tactics, and the effect of these upon the party, can be seen in reports of the Foreign Affairs Group of which Zilliacus, Platts-Mills and Solley were members. Zilliacus was selected because of his experience, Platts-Mills and Solley chose to join in order to influence the Labour government's foreign policy. Solley used the group to prpagate the opinions, based on his role as Honorary Treasurer and chief parliamentary voice, of the League for Democracy in Greece. The aim of the Foreign Affairs Group, headed by Bevin, was to act as a think-tank aiding policy formulation. but, due to the inclusion of these individuals, as junior Civil Servant Kenneth Younger recalled, "[it] was reduced to a very angry and virtually impotent body."[126] This represents a snapshot of the effect of this element's presence within the Labour Party. It was this effect, and the embarrassment they caused the party and its leadership, that led to a campaign being spearheaded against them. They represented a strand of the British socialist tradition that was inimical to the tradition of the Labour Party and incompatible given the developments in international relations. Only Zilliacus was welcomed back, though some argued that this was due to a significant shift in his thinking.

FROM GATESHEAD TO GORTON: A GENUFLECTIVE JOURNEY

It can be argued that the Labour Party had little choice in expelling the man who was described by his Conservative opponent in the 1950 Election as "[t]he Communist member for Gateshead."[127] Zilliacus and his fellow expellees were fighting for an Election pledge that Ernest Bevin could no longer deliver due to the realities of the post-war international order. Denis Healey, Labour's International Secretary 1945-51, explained in his autobiography that the governmental perception of the Soviet Union was based upon fear. He recalled that:

I believed that Stalin's behaviour showed he was bent on the military conquest of Western Europe. I now think we were all mistaken. We took too seriously the Leninist rhetoric pouring out of Moscow.[128]

With hindsight it appears that Healey agreed with Zilliacus' analysis that the Labour gvernment was suffering from 'Forrestalitis'. Zilliacus argued that their anti-communism was akin to that of James Forrestal, the US Secretary of State who had a mental breakdown after convincing himself that "the Russians were coming."[129] Zilliacus' obsession was the reverse: he was convinced that it was the United States who were dragging Britain into a crippling arms race and subsequent Third World War.

Zilliacus argued that the result of this policy would be the reversal of Labour's social reform programme and could lead to a Third World War. As both sides had armed themselves with nuclear weaponry Zilliacus, and many of his allies within the peace movement, feared that this would lead to the destruction of civilisation. These arguments would remain central to Zilliacus' analysis of international relations. However, during his absence from parliament and the party, he did appear to reject his attachment to the Soviet Union as the focus of his dissent. John Platts-Mills described this as "a deep genuflection"[130] though this represents his reiteration of the Stalinist critique of Zilliacus following his condemnation in the Slansky trial.

However, Zilliacus' position did shift over the three-year period 1949-52, and it is useful to consider why this shift occurred. Zilliacus did not expect to be expelled.[131] He may, therefore, have reappraised and adjusted his arguments to match broader trends in the party. Whatever the motivating force during the early 1950s, the focus of his criticism fundamentally altered. This adjustment allowed Zilliacus to see that both the United States and the Soviet Union were guilty of causing and exacerbating the East-West tensions. On the strength of this conclusion Zilliacus chose to champion a new cause, that of Yugoslavia, the first independent Communist state.

The reorientation of Zilliacus' analysis was first introduced in a pamphlet written around 1950.[132] In Tito v Stalin: Yugoslavia and the Cold War he supported Tito's refusal to suborn his state to Moscow. Zilliacus criticised as unwarranted the verbal attacks made against the Tito regime, quoting Khrushchev's speech on the occasion of Stalin's seventieth Birthday, which referred to the Yugoslav leadership as a:

> gang of murderers and spies which has completed the transition from nationalism to Fascism, which has turned into a direct agent of imperialism and become its tool in the fight against socialism and democracy.[133]

Zilliacus treated this condemnation with contempt. From this point of departure he puts forward a dual argument. The first point is that if the West can come to terms with Tito, accept him as a both Communist and as a co-operative, peaceful leader of an equally co-operative and peaceful nation, then this could represent the first step towards the rapprochement of capitalism and communism. His second point for debate was that, as the Soviet Union had categorised Yugoslavia as an enemy and the West had offered no assurances for the security of the Titoist regime, why had the Soviet Union not annexed Yugoslavia. Any subsequent threat of reprisals would not be an issue as Stalin would have recogised the unwillingness of the West to start a war in defence of a Communist state. Annexation, Zilliacus argued, was the action to be expected of an imperialist, expansionist power but Stalin had not taken this route. Thus Zilliacus was attempting to demnstrate that not all Communists were as uncooperative as Stalin while maintaining his criticism of the Anglo-American containment policy.

This revised argument was probably designed to redefine Zilliacus as an analyst of international relations independent from Sovietinfluence. It is true that the Soviet Union was not criticised in this pamphlet but, importantly, neither was it supported. This gave clear signals to the Labour leadership that Zilliacus was in a process of ideological reformation. The pamphlet also shows a degree of support for Titoist politics a theme that would continue in later works by Zilliacus.[134] What this pamphlet achieved, however, was it placed a clear gulf between Zilliacus and the Stalinist regime, one that would be pronounced until after the death of Stalin and Khrushchev's denunciation.

This revision did leave Zilliacus politically isolated. In the introduction to *A New Birth of Freedom*, he described his shock at being openly criticised in the Soviet Press, and described as an "attorney of Fascism."[135]   This stemmed from his support of the Titoist regime, which equally led to Zilliacus to become ideologically separated from his allies in the LIG. His condemnation by Cominform, in November 1952, as an agent of imperialism, who had worked with Titoist agents in Yugoslavia and Czechoslovakia,[136] propelled him back toward the Labour Party but did not guarantee him immediate re-selection as a parliamentary candidate. Gallacher highlighted the rift between Zilliacus and the nominal leader of the LIG Pritt. He recalled that:

However hard Pritt and others... Platts-Mills, Solley and Lester Hutchinson... tried, they found it more and more difficult to work with Zilliacus. His case, in his opinion, was a very special case. He was the man who was fighting Bevin's foreign policy. [Though they] had given a good account of themselves in foreign affairs debates, … only his own speeches counted with Zilliacus.[137]

This seems to indicate that Zilliacus also distanced himself from Platts-Mills and Pritt because he believed that they were too slavishly pro-Soviet.

The situation in which Zilliacus found himself, alienated within domestic politics and denounced by his erstwhile left-wing colleagues in parliament and the Soviet Union, appears to have allowed him to be more openly critical of Stalinism. His most telling criticism of Stalinism is in his analysis of Tito's policy of neutrality. In his biography of Tito he argued that, in splitting away from Cominform, Tito was:

defending the all-important principle that the relations between So- cialist states should be based on equality, mutual respect for each oth- er's national independence and non-interference in each other's inter- nal affairs.[138]

However, he was unable to reconcile himself to the fact that there was anything inherently wrong with the political and economic framework of the Soviet State. On viewing the state in the post-Stalinist era he noted the presence of the "evils of tyranny, oppression and the Police State"[139] but explained that these were a direct result of the western attitude to the Soviet Union. He did accept that there were unsocialist aspects and that both sides were "using ideologies to mask their national interests."[140] Zilliacus hoped that with the death of the two major Cold War Warriors, Truman and Stalin, a new era of co-operation could begin. His hopes were con- stantly dashed. His ultimate dreams were lodged with the British Labour Party who he believed "with… courage… could lead mankind out of the valley of the shadow of death in which we are wandering."[141] However, for the majority of his time as MP for Manchester Gorton, the Labour Party was confined to opposition so unable to effect the changes he called for.

Whether the motive for his reformation was disillusionment with Soviet policy or a desire to return to the ranks and spread his ideas from within, the result was his return to the Labour Party fold. He was readmitted as a member in February 1952, stood for the seat of Manchester Gorton at the 1955 Election, and took his seat as Labour candidate there until his death on 6 July 1967. The Labour Whip was withdrawn once again between May 1961 and March 1963 due to his persistent dissent over the party's support of United States foreign policy in Vietnam. Zilliacus continued to criticise the bullying tactics of the United States which, pitted against the weak countries of the Caribbean, South East Asia and Latin America, were distasteful and provoked war with the Soviet Union.[142] When criticising the actions and beliefs of US President John F Kennedy he quoted Ruskin, English social critic of the Nineteenth Century, who stated that there was "no more dangerous a snare… set by the fiends of human frailty than the belief that our enemies are also the enemies of God."[143] This would have been his analysis of all the conflicts the United States waged under the aegis of containment and rollback. The mindset of the Cold War, in his eyes, had taken the shape of a religious crusade. Zilliacus' concern was to keep Britain from being infected by the all-consuming passion to destroy Communism. His alternative was to pursue a policy of accommodation.

The theme of his final work was *Labour's Crisis: Its Nature, Causes and Cure*.[144] Here Zilliacus linked his interpretation of world politics with a more traditional Bevanite perspective. The policy of containing Communism, he argued, involved spending plans that threatened the domestic social reform programme conceived by the Attlee government. This position was largely consensual across Labour's left-wing.[145] The Conservatives, he argued, had little care for social welfare and had no ideological reasons for breaking with the traditional anti-Soviet policy. Labour did and should. This did not represent a 'deep genuflection' of Zilliacus' previos analysis however, this less radical stance does indicate that he instituted a reformation of his patterns of thought. It is difficult to determine how or why this gradual process of reformation took place. It is possible that this was a reaction to the investigations that were taking place and an indication that he was attempting to disassociate himself from pro-Sovietism. However it seems unlike Zilliacus to bend in the face of adversity. A more plausible interpretation is that this was Zilliacus making an attempt to reach a reasoned conclusion, one that appeared tenable as East-West relations improved.[146] He maintained that accommodation with the Soviet Union should be pursued, though he used George Kennan's arguments as evidence rather than the arguments of the Soviet leadership.[147] This gave him the appearance of being non-aligned and led Watson to the conclusion that this 'alternative centrality' was the real Zilliacus.[148]

We can conclude that this alternative analysis of the Cold War was the result of Zilliacus's acceptance of Tito over Stalin and his initial acceptance of Khrushchev, coupled with his continual maintenance of distance between himself and Soviet Communism after 1950. Zilliacus was never an ideological communist; his arguments hinged upon developing an alternative to Cold War. His last published work highlights this perhaps better than any other. The party did not contain any figure as profoundly anti-Soviet as Bevin thus Zilliacus believed that, as Wilson attempted to develop channels of communication between London and Moscow, rapprochement had become a distinct possibility.[149]

Zilliacus was equally developing a tradition of analysis that would later be espoused by his supporters Frank Allaun and Stan Newens. He argued that the Wilson Government had betrayed the electorate by enforcing wage freezes to pay for a foreign policy that was tied to the Johnson administration in the United States. He argued that this was the result of a policy tradition set by Churchill and enacted by Bevin, which had subsequently enslave the Labour administration. He talked of the "disgraceful policy"[150] whereby a Labour government was supporting the war in Vietnam, an issue that caused uncompromising dissent on the Labour backbenches. is conclusion was that Labour must make a stand for socialist principles, purge the party of the policies of earlier governments and start afresh with socialism. The United Nations should stand as the arbiter of international disputes and the sole agent of protecton against aggression, ending Western reliance upon NATO. Those nations who could not afford to support the foreign policy of the Johnson administration and maintain troops overseas, he argued, should remove them and plough the released capital back into domestic public services.

This is Zilliacus as a principled democratic socialist. In this short pamphlet he tied together many of the loose ends of his thinking. The Soviet Union is referred to as a "fellow member" of the United Nations. Neither a shining example of society; nor an excuse to incur the cost of an arms race. Here, with the benefit of hindsight, his arguments make a great deal of sense. The revelations of the state of the Soviet economy that emerged following the collapse in 1989 showed that, given the opportunity, the Soviet Union may have willingly curbed escalation.[151] However, with the United States and her supporters opposing it, constantly improving and innovating their destructive capability, there was no chance of this. The result was the collapse, not only of the Soviet state, but also of the free provision of certain forms of health care, an issue that had led Wilson to resign from the Cabinet in 1948. Heavy defence spending equally led to cut backs in welfare spending, wage freezes and civil unrest which marked British history during the 1970s, all of which were predicted by Zilliacus. Whether this pamphlet represents his ultimate beliefs is a moot point. What it does represent is his last words on the inconsistencies between the party's policy and its declared objectives.[152] Whether he flirted with Communism or not is unknown. His proclamations of innocence are arguably expected, but he did oppose the Communist Party,[153] or at least he appeared to. Whether this was to convince the Labour Party of his right to membership, is uncertain. It should be noted though that he never acted like a man whose beliefs had been bought.

OLD TRADITIONS WITH A NEW IMPERATIVE

Zilliacus' arguments encapsulated the collision of traditions of thought that occurred as world war drifted towards Cold War. His analysis of the

Soviet Union was a more realistic, though not unsympathetic, analysis than that of the Webbs. Clearly he did not argue for a Europe dominated by Stalinist politics but claimed that the ideal of Soviet Communism, rather than the disfigured reality, was an experiment that needed to develop without aggressive intervention. While Platts-Mills and Hutchinson argued that there was something inherently superior in the Soviet political model, Zilliacus can be seen to hesitate on this point. He could see the potential for a more socialist system within the Soviet Union but at no time did he argue that this system had been established. The fact that he focused upon Yugoslavia as an alternative indicates he was seeking a model, not however to attempt to prove that socialist theory could be transformed into a tenable political programme. The ultimate objective for Zilliacus was to prevent war. He and Leslie Solley argued that the Soviet Union was not expansionist but that Stalin was only pursuing a protectionist policy due to the aggressive stance that had been adopted by the non-Communist nations towards the Bolshevik regime since October 1917. In recognising that the West's leaders would never trust Stalin, Zilliacus attempted to utilise Tito as a Communist leader that did not pose a threat. If Tito could be perceived as a leader with whom the West could co-operate then future leaders of the Soviet Union could be perceived in a similar way and a policy of co-existence pursued. This ideal was fundamental to Zilliacus' arguments and underpinned his attempt to draft an alternative foreign policy for the British Labour Party. Zilliacus' alternative programme set the agenda for the pro-Soviet milieu and featured prominently in the publications of members of the pro-Soviet left. Not only those produced by Frank Allaun and Stan Newens, who recalled being influenced by Zilliacus, but also in arguments produced by figures like James Lamond and Renee Short who took a more radical and pro-active course of opposition to the Cold War ethos.

The debate on the role of Zilliacus has featured in many studies of left-wing activism during the 1945-50 period. Many group the four expellees together under the label of crypto-Communist. Others, however, do recognise the importance of Zilliacus in his own right. Meehan recognised him as an experienced analyst of foreign policy but concluded that he was "very influential and definitely harmful to Labour's interests.[154] An extensive study of Zilliacus by Sharon Ferguson argued that he was committed to Britain, and to the Labour Party especially. Ferguson's analysis appears correct when focussing upon Zilliacus' analysis of the Labour Party as the agent capable of implementing a policy of co-existence, however, this conclusion appears precarious when we consider his statements that express commitment to the success of the Soviet Union. Evidence for this can be particularly found in quotes in the press from his trips to the Soviet Union, or from speeches given at Soviet sponsored events,[155] where he wished the Soviet Union success in both domestic and foreign policy. There is also Potts' perspective, that Zilliacus was an internationalist and so lacked any nationalist tendencies. Evidence to reinforce this claim can be found in his advocating world peace through the United Nations. While this perspective is equally plausible he did argue that Britain was a key player. This however can be understood within the context of the era in which he was a practitioner in international affairs. Britain's pre-war role as leader of an Empire and sole superpower gave it immense power and influence within international relations.

Zilliacus opposed Britain allowing itself to be eclipsed by the United States, arguing instead that the Attlee government should have pursued a new 'Pax Britannia'. Britain, he argued, should have been re-established as the guarantor of stability and peace, the role adopted in the Nineteenth Century. This may have been unrealistic, however a trend can be observed within left-wing thought that placed Britain as a moral guide within the international community. This trend is clearly shown within the arguments for unilateral nuclear disarmament.[156] The fact that Labour pursued a policy advocated by Churchill, who Zilliacus described as "that senile Walter Mitty of anti-Communist carnage",[157] was to enrage many sections of the left of the party. Few were to make as definitive a stand as Zilliacus or would develop the prolonged programme of opposition as pursued by Platts-Mills. Nevertheless Zilliacus defined a tradition for opposition within the Labour Party.

Dan Watson placed Zilliacus as the precursor of a current that would be popularised within the left-wing groups across Europe when he characterised him as a "premature Eurocommunist."[158] This is a conclusion that deserves some consideration. Eurocommunism was an adaptation of Marxist-Leninism that rejected the revolutionary model of societal change because of the conclusion that this would inevitably lead to a bureaucratic dictatorship.[159] It was recognised that "to achieve socialism in the industrialised countries [required] the consensus of a large majority of the population."[160] This meant that the only viable route for socialists was the parliamentary route, effecting a "democratic transition to socialism engineered through the political institutions of advanced capitalism."[161] Boggs argued that this redefinition of the aims of European Communists, particularly within the Partito Communista Italiano [PCI], was instrumental in gaining popularity for these ideas, a trend that gained impetus when subscribed to by the Spanish Communist Party after the death of Franco.[162] Togliatti, the leader of the PCI, argued that the movement should act while the opportunity presented itself. During the period of détente, at a time when the United States was seen as impotent after the defeat in Vietnam, he argued that, in the late 1970s: "there [wa]s a chance of escaping an immediate military intervention on the part of [Communis's] international enemies."[163]

Carrillo, the key theorist of Spanish Eurocommunism, stressed there was an ideological link between Eurocommunism and the Soviet model. He argued that, should the movement have widespread success, the Soviet Union, finding a more co-operative political system emerging in Western Europe, would "make progress in transforming [Soviet society] into a real working people's democracy."[164] This supports the claim that there was a link between the ideals of Eurocommunism and the thought of Zilliacus.

Zilliacus did believe in working class unity, and could foresee circumstances under which the CPGB would be admitted to the Labour Party, though he agreed that this would have to be under terms set by the Labour Party.[165] This gives some credence to Watson's hypothesis. The point of contention remains, was he premature in these beliefs or was he influenced by a theory that emerged during his lifetime. The root of Eurocommunism, Watson argued, were the late 1960s and 1970s, placing it in the context of the radical movements of 1968. However Carrillo argued that his influences were the independent socialist regimes of Tito and Dubcek.166 Boggs, on the other hand, agreed that Tito was a practical example but cites Pietro Nenni as the first exponent of Eurocommunism as a political theory.[167] Zilliacus built up a firm friendship with both these figures, sharing several platforms with Nenni while campaigning for the 'Partisans for Peace'. Thus Zilliacus may well have absorbed these influences into his political philosophy.

Zilliacus' obvious belief in democratic socialism would have meant that there was much to attract him to a strategy that, in Togliatti's reworking of Nenni's theory, argued for plotting a gradualist route towards a democratic dictatorship of the proletariat.[168] Furthermore the agency prescribed as the organisation that must drive forward this programme was one built upon working-class unity. Togliatti argued that the only body capable of this were the Trade Unions, while Mandel, using vaguer language, discussed a "union of progressive forces."[169] This reinforced the faith Zilliacus placed in the Labour Party, the one organisation built upon working class unity and the British Trade Union movement, while reviving the ideal of the 'people's front'. As friend and fellow Labour MP Mervyn Jones recalled, Zilliacus believed in the practicability of an "alliance with communists against capitalists", Jones stated that: "No enemies to the Left was always his watchword."[170]

Zilliacus' belief in left-wing unity was seldom reciprocated. Communist MP, Willie Gallacher described Zilliacus' faith in the Labour Party and the democratic route to socialism as his 'Achilles heel'. Gallacher argued that, in rejecting revolutionary tendencies and accepting the parliamentary route to power, Zilliacus allowed his opponents in the Labour Party to ignore him as he "constituted no danger to their power and privileges."[171] Despite this critique, this combination of theoretical and practical models that collide within the work of Zilliacus places him in a unique position. His analysis not only reflected the political culture of Britain and the trends of pre-war socialism, but he also embraced radical trends emerging from post-fascist Europe. Eurocommunist ideas were by no means a central theme of all his analyses and, within some publications and speeches, he did appear to be a greater exponent of traditional pro-Soviet and pro-Communist ideals. However, it is important to note that Eurocommunists did not reject the Soviet ideal. Within the Eurocommunist literature runs a debate of whether it was, as Zilliacus argued, the hostile capitalist world that had disfigured the Marxist-Leninist society, or whether Stalinism had emerged, as Trotsky argued, as an anti-revolutionary despot. It was in reaction to the histories of Italy, and later Spain, that the notion of dictatorship of the proletariat was rejected[172] a shift that allowed Eurocommunism to be compatible with the traditions of British labourism.

Zilliacus' attachment to the ideas of Tito and Nenni, and thus the analysis which he developed, can also be perceived as an aspect of the Anglo-Marxist tradition.[173] The parliamentary path was the only route available within the British political system. While this frustrated many left-wingers who, like Hutchinson, were keen to alter the societal structure, it was also a reality which had to be accepted and accommodated. Zilliacus argued that national traditions did matter. He observed that to defend itself the Soviet leadership had reverted to the authoritarian traditions of Tsarist rule in order to maintain order. This had caused the sharp contrast between authoritarian leadership and a socialist economic system. Zilliacus equally maintained that Bolshevism was particular to Tsarist Russia and could not be exported. He wrote: "to me the Russian Revolution has always seemed too Russian to spread except to countries that missed the French Revolution."[174]

Zilliacus arguably saw the Soviet Union, in the same way as Churchill, "a riddle wrapped in mystery inside an enigma."[175] It was a vast and barbaric nation, and the Russia revolutionary spirit mirrored this. He attempted to encourage the capitalist world to come to terms with this new civilisation, put an end to unfounded fears, and establish a peace based on co-operation between capitalism and communism. This would, he argued, benefit all the peoples of the world. These beliefs are the constant theme of his work. Admittedly his work evidences a perception of Britain as a pivotal power, and a belief in the Labour Party, but his perspective was one of an internationalist. While he is often accused of acting as an agent of influence, it appears that this was strictly on his own terms. He argued that he had never been a Communist; that would have been "a disgraceful thing."[176] Jan described him as finding the description of him as a fellow traveller of the

Communist party as humorous. She said he would laugh and shout "Nonsense, they are my fellow travellers."[177] Zilliacus was a free agent with clear beliefs by which he stood despite the consequences. Neither expulsion from the Labour Party or to be branded as a fascist by Pravda deterred him:

> If I am a rebel on these matters, I am not the first, and I shall not be the last, to stand on his own conscience for what he believes to be right, in spite of what everybody has said against him.[178]

Zilliacus was the chief exponent of the pro-Soviet alternative during the 1945-50 government and, to a greater extent than his co-expellees, develoed the framework of analysis that would be used by those who were to inherit this tradition. Within his arguments we find the traditions of the 1920s and 30s encapsulated within the anti-Cold War framework of analysis. This tradition would become embedded within the arguments of left-wing organisations within the party. The first of these was Victory for Socialism which would extend the ideas of Zilliacus through to a new generation of left-wingers. These individuals would develop new ways, within prliament and at the extra-parliamentary level, of furthering the campaign designed to change the climate of opinion. His ideas would bridge the gulf between parliamentary left-wing traditions and the pro-Soviet front organistion network co-ordinated by Pritt and Platts-Mills. Therefore within this period, which witnessed the drawing of sharp, ideological battle lines, divisions between right and left would develop within the Labour Party. Though the division can be simplistically defined within a spectrum running from the pragmatic realism of the leadership to the ideological idealism of those who would constitute the left, there are many different perspectives that are apparent on both sides of this dichotomy. Some of those who can be placed into the category of 'ideological idealist' would adopt the pro-Soviet position and attempt to act as change agents in the Zilliacus mould.

4

VICTORY FOR SOCIALISM:

Developing a pro-Soviet alternative to the Cold War rationale

The Attlee government was hailed as "perhaps amongst the most effective of any British government"[1] and whose achievements are almost universally regarded as formidable.[2] Despite having made "a significant contribution towards the lives of the people who supported it, and indeed of many others"[3] Labour was, in 1951, consigned to thirteen years on the opposition benches. The legacy of the 1945-51 government for the party became a double-edged sword;[4] the welfare state became both an emblem and a millstone for each Labour government after 1951.[5] Spending plans in the domestic sphere became untenable, particularly alongside a high spending defence policy. Equally as the post-war boom began to slow, the battle between left-wing idealism and the leaderships' pragmatic approach was exacerbated as revisionists reconsidered the objectives of state ownership and full employment and abandoned key elements of the Keynesian project. The gulf between the left and the leadership, emerging with the Ministerial resignations in 1947 and the backbench rebellions over foreign policy, was crystallised in the parliament of 1945-51. However the battle for control over party policy became increased as the leadership pursued an anti-left campaign while the left developed a coherent organisational strategy with the reformation, in 1958, of Victory for Socialism.

The Attlee Cabinet, many of whose members had been anti-MacDonald rebels during the 1930s, were physically and mentally exhausted by the General Election of 1951. The Conservatives inherited the benefits of Labour's domestic reforms and the post-war economic boom. It was only an out of touch Conservative Prime Minister, standing impotent as the economy drifted toward recession, that allowed Labour, in 1964, to stand as the force of modernisation, the party 'in touch' with British society and the changing nature of economic imperatives.[6] Clear internal battle lines had, by this point, been drawn within the party, though the left-wing were more reticent in attacking the Wilson government's revisionist socialism than Gaitskell, Wilson's predecessor or Home's Conservative government.[7] However, a minority led a sustained campaign against the Labour party's support for the Cold War rationale. The international bipolar dichotomy had developed a zero-sum nature, dividing the world into two ideological power blocs that were perceived to be preparing for war. This led to an increasingly organised programme of attack to be launched by those who opposed the Cold War rationale.

The centrist and Atlanticist section of the party controlled policy formulation, and until the end of the 1960s they enjoyed a clear majority on the National Executive but an increasingly narrowing majority within Conference. Control was maintained through continued attempts to undermine and suppress the left. Hugh Gaitskell, party leader from December 1955 until his death in 1963, became a hate figure for the left coming under attack at Conference and through the left-wing press.[8] To counter the left's moral stance on defence policy and the party's proposed spending plans, Gaitskell, along with George Brown, Roy Jenkins and William Rodgers, sponsored the formation of the Campaign for Democratic Socialism [CDS]. The rationale of the group was to argue that the left-wing agenda was opposed to democracy, supported Stalinism and was the antithesis of the ideals and ethos of the Labour Party.[9] The group's magazine Campaign, edited by Rodgers, launched a smear campaign against the left, particularly highlighting weaknesses on defence policy, and constantly criticised the left's nominal leader Aneurin Bevan.[10]

Left-wing activists were, however, successful at gaining support within the constituencies, dominated the agenda of Tribune and Reynolds News, and used the Morning Star as a platform. The period 1957-62 witnessed bitter disputes at Conference, with the leadership finding widespread opposition from the party. The fact that opinion within Conference had begun to shift leftwards was of greatest concern for Gaitskell. The strength of support for unilateral nuclear disarmament was a particular embarrassment to a leader who had publicly pledged himself to the nuclear defence policy launched by Bevin.[11] Gaitskell's left-wing opponents attacked him on the basis that he was anti-Socialist, a campaign some argued to be designed to undermine support for him as party leader.[12] In reality this was nothing more than a reaction to Gaitskell's perceived right-wing stance on foreign and security policy. As Keohane argues, Gaitskell, like Attlee previously, held the belief that socialist values and principles should be adhered to but "contended that power and force were inescapable realities of international politics which could not be wished away by fidelity to socialist norms."[13] It was this pragmatic approach to politics that caused a rift between the leadership and the left. Under ideal circumstances Gaitskell and his left opponents would arguably have enjoyed significant common ground, however the circumstances were not ideal for the development of a socialist foreign policy. Gaitskell recognised this while the left refused to do so. The factor that allowed Gaitskell to retain control over policy was the incoherence of the left's campaign. There remained deep divisions over policy objectives, the opposition was incoherently stage-managed and, because of this, the left was impotent in changing party policy. Indicative of this was Bevan's debacle over unilateralism at the 1957 party conference. Foot argued that Bevan's ambitions for office, particularly the position of Foreign Secretary in a Gaitskell-led government, had led him to support multilateralism.[14] The strongest criticism came from Bevan's colleagues at the Tribune newspaper and his rejection of unilateralism led the left to seek a new focus.

The Bevanites, as they later became known, had developed a broad left-wing manifesto espoused by Bevan and voiced through the Tribune newspaper. Domestically they demanded the completion of the nationalisation programme and espoused the establishment of a workers' democracy. In foreign policy they opposed German re-armament, adopted an anti-Atlanticist stance and opposed the rhetorical anti-Communism of the post-war British governments.[15] A degree of cohesion and organisation existed, as Peggy Duff has recalled.[16] Within the Bevanite movement existed a strategy to increase left-wing representation in the house. Duff, Tribune circulation manager, organised a group of prospective parliamentary candidates whom she referred to as the 'Second XI'.[17] These included Hugh Jenkins, Stan Newens and Renee Short. Trade Unions were encouraged to adopt them and pay election expenses. Equally constituencies were encouraged to short list 'Second XI' members in preference to centre-right candidates. This was combated by the NEC's candidate approval procedure, which placed approved candidates on the 'B list', a procedure which excluded Jo Richardson, secretary of Victory for Socialism, from being adopted because she refused to sign an undertaking not to criticise Gaitskell.[18]

The hostilities over prospective candidates are indicative of the battle between left and right for control over party policy. There were several attempts by the Elections Sub-Committee of the NEC to block the left-wing's choice from being adopted. In each case that came under scrutiny a dossier was produced, compiled by the party's National Agent Sara Barker, detailing the 'misdeeds' of the left-wingers. Heated discussions took place regarding the acceptance of Frank Allaun "as doubt had been expressed about his full acceptance of Labour Party policy".[19] Other cases to attract attention were Tom Braddock, Bernard Floud, and Sam Goldberg, all of whom had Communist connections and during the late 1950s failed the approval procedure, and Ernie Roberts and Zilliacus who would eventually be approved. Left-wingers within the NEC constantly opposed this practice; Mikardo, a campaigner for intra-party democracy who accused the party leadership of adopting 'authoritarian' practices, informed CLPs that they could not and would not be bound by the selection committee's decisions. The eventual success of the left's campaign can be measured by the steady left-wing trajectory experienced by the party from the late 1950s which culminated during the 1980s.

• The intense anti-left activity by the party leadership caused the left to become increasingly organised. However the collapse of Bevanism, or at least Bevan's move away from the Bevanite tradition, meant a new organisation was required to step into the breach. As Anne Swingler recalled: "the left followed Bevan, but when he abandoned them they needed someone else to get things done."[20] Stephen Swingler, using Tribune as a platform for his arguments, filled this void and reformed Victory for Socialism. This organisation allowed the left to regroup, establish an alternative manifesto and promote left-wing ideas through the constituencies. This alternative Labour programme would be spearheaded by a group of Labour left-wingers with existent pro-Soviet sympathies. Moreover as the international situation worsened defence issues became of paramount significance to the left. The fear expressed through the pages of Tribune was that the anti-Soviet foreign policy, and reliance on nuclear defence, would result in the mutual annihilation of mankind. Victory for Socialism's defence policy formulators attached a pro-Soviet critique to their analysis of these international developments.

The launching of a campaign to alter the governmental world view became a strategic imperative as, during the 1950s, the Cold War dynamic adopted a zero-sum character. As Scott argued, "the idea that communism was a monolithic political entity controlled from Moscow became an enduring American fixation."[21] The policy of containment developed a new impetus, rollback; promoted as a moral response to Stalinism by US Secretary of State John Foster Dulles. He described containment as "negative, futile and immoral" arguing that the East should not be sacrificed to Communism "to gain time for the West."[22] The adoption of rollback meant that there would be a determined response to the spread of Communism, not only restricting advancement but also taking active measures to reverse the tide. In practice this new trajectory led United States forces to face Soviet weaponry in Korea, Vietnam and Cambodia. Proxy wars were fought between many Third World nations and the Cuban missile crisis brought the world to the brink of nuclear war. The left united in opposition to the anti-Communist foreign policy and the proliferation of nuclear weapons as a deterrent against Soviet incursion and demanded that negotiations replace military aggression. Though not all the proponents of these arguments solely criticised the United States and defended the Soviet Union, Victory for

Socialism arguments promoted the idea that the United States was the aggressor despite the realities of Soviet foreign policy.

It is clear that the Soviet leadership were not purely pursuing co-existence in the face of hostility. Khrushchev pursued a foreign policy of arming the enemies of the United States, undermining US hegemony and openly provoking the United States leadership. However the fact that Khrushchev backed down when faced with the threat of a nuclear exchange allowed him to adopt the image of having saved mankind, so nurturing support among left-wing groups. Soviet support for third world nations or rebel movements, during conflicts with the United States or United States backed forces, Soviet propaganda argued, was offered in order to defend democracy in the struggle against US imperialism. The explanation provided by Soviet propaganda filtered into the arguments of the pro-Soviet strand within the Labour Party. It should not be assumed, however, that purely progressive ideals and protectionism underpinned Soviet foreign policy. Khrushchev clearly recognised the threat which Cuba's proximity posed to the United States mainland and saw an opportunity to reduce United States' superiority in the arms race. Soviet defence minister Malinovsky argued that Cuba gave the Politburo the opportunity to "place one of our hedgehogs down the Americans' trousers."[23] Presidium minutes indicate Cuba was a strategic rather than an ideological ally; used, rather than protected, to improve the Soviet bargaining position.[24] This was, however, disguised heavily by Soviet propaganda. What is indicative is that those who were members of Victory for Socialism appear readier to accept the Soviet arguments than those put forward by Britain or the United States.

As the international dichotomy became zero-sum, the left-wing found themselves isolated, rudderless and impotent within the Labour Party. Equally fresh perspectives had developed within the 'New Left' intellectual strand that focused upon Third World influences of non-aligned socialism.[25] This revitalised internationalism, the inter-war socialist aspirations and the concerns voiced by the anti-nuclear socialist movement all filtered into Victory for Socialism's alternative programme. The alternatives put forward by Victory for Socialism indicate both a collision of differing left-wing positions and a sympathy for the pro-Soviet analysis in opposition to Atlanticism. They were to create a self-perpetuating meta-narrative. These Labour MPs had a clear vision of how the nations of the world should interact and how the people of the world should live and argued that this could only be achieved under socialism. This became synonymous with the ideal of 'actually existing socialism', as embodied by the Soviet Union. Thus an argument developed in which the Soviet Union was placed upon a pedestal as the model for the future. This was not specifically Soviet socialism in the form in which it existed at that time. Many, like Frank Allaun, did hope for political democratisation to complement the existent socialist economy. However, this could only be achieved within an atmosphere of co-operation and co-existence. Thus within the alternative socialist manifesto, which was promoted in various forms between 1960 and 1983,26 a pro-Soviet slant to foreign and defence policy developed. This was the legacy of the Victory for Socialism tradition.

VICTORY FOR SOCIALISM AS A PRO-SOVIET AGENT FOR CHANGE

    . Victory for Socialism was originally formed in 1951 with then prospective Labour candidate, later a Minister under Wilson, Hugh Jenkins as the chairman. It had little effect on party policy, and was to peter out as other similar groups had before. However, in 1958, the name and the idea were to be resurrected by Stephen Swingler and other like-minded individuals on the left of the Labour Party. The new group was open to Labour Party members only and would amalgamate the broad left-wing ideals of pacifism and humanism, revitalising many of the ideals of the Union for Democratic Control. The members were influenced heavily by the Bevanite tradition; they were Third Way-ers, internationalists and confirmed socialists. Victory for Socialism did not stand as a pro-Soviet group, however the group was steered by individuals who expressed their criticism of party policy using a pro-Soviet analysis. These individuals argued against the Cold War, NATO and nuclear weapons and for rapprochement and co-existence with the Communist bloc. The individuals who dominated the policy of the group were the most prominent advocates of these arguments. For example Konni Zilliacus, who became Victory for Socialism's Foreign and Commonwealth Secretary by unanimous mandate,[27] was to develop the defence policy programme advocated by Victory for Socialism.[28] His appointment ensured that Victory for Socialism's alternative defence strategy was broadly sympathetic to the Soviet Union, describing the Soviet nuclear arsenal as necessary on protectionist grounds due to the aggressively anti-Soviet stance maintained by the NATO alliance.

    - Zilliacus' biographer Archie Potts argued that following his expulsion Zilliacus was a spent force. However, Jan Zilliacus recalled that when he returned to the party he did have supporters, a group she referred to as the 'Zill boys'.[29] This consisted of the Foreign and Commonwealth Group within Victory for Socialism which included Frank Allaun and Stan Newens. Frank Allaun, fellow entrant into parliament in 1955 in the neighbouring seat of Salford East, had been integral to the campaign to reinstall Zilliacus as an MP. Through Victory for Socialism, and later through Labour Action for Peace, the analysis of Zilliacus was to live on.

The rejuvenated Victory for Socialism group was formally established in February 1958. Stephen Swingler, Chairman of the group set out the agenda in an article in *Tribune* stating that members should encourage "fresh discussion about the application of Socialist principles, and above all, inspire renewed faith in the power of democratic action."[30] As with those accused of being fellow travellers in the 1945-50 government, this organisation was received with a similar mixture of fear and distaste. It included many of those MPs who had orbited the Zilliacus group of the earlier period, including Swingler himself, Geoffrey Bing, Tom Braddock, Emrys Hughes, Ian Mikardo, Julius Silverman, Sidney Silverman and William Warbey. Bing himself was a self-confessed "fellow traveller of Zilliacus."[31] However, younger, soon to be highly prominent, faces were recruited also. They included Frank Allaun, Judith Hart, Stan Newens and Renee Short: some of whom would be prominent advocates of the pro-Soviet perspective.

Victory for Socialism promoted a pro-Soviet perspective of the Cold War among the Trade Unions, constituency Labour parties [CLPs] and the ordinary membership. It is impossible to calculate the effect of this, however, given that certain key left-wing ideals, particularly unilateralism, were to gain prominence during the 1970s and 80s, it can be argued that this was, in no small part, a result of the activity of Victory for Socialism.

Furthermore Victory for Socialism also provided the left with a network of supporters on which activists could call. Stan Newens recalled that through Victory for Socialism and Tribune, MPs knew who they could rely upon to support them over certain issues.[32] Thus when statements were made to the press, questions submitted to Ministers or meetings arranged to debate policy issues, invitations were made to like-minded MPs to join the campaign. Examples of this can be seen on the letters pages of The Times. One example was a letter, written by William Wilson calling for full relations to be established with Communist Albania.[33] The signatories included Wilson, James Lamond, Ernie Roberts, and Stan Newens. Thus from connections made through left-wing groupings Wilson was able to add weight to his argument by inviting like-minded MPs to sign the letter. Therefore we can assume that, as a result of Victory for Socialism, after the 1960s the pro-Soviet left-wingers were acting as a much more cohesive unit.

This chapter focuses on two individuals; the man who resurrected Victory for Socialism, Stephen Swingler, and the key activist within the anti-nuclear and pacifist element within the Labour Party, Frank Allaun. These two politicians represent the strands that converged into the alternative manifesto put forward by Victory for Socialism. Swingler's perspective was rooted within the Communist traditions of the 1930s. His analysis of the Cold War was largely drawn from a Marxist-Leninist perspective. Allaun, despite gaining a political education during the 1930s, and having campaigned alongside Communists, brought the UDC tradition of pacifist socialism to Victory for Socialism. His arguments achieved greater longevity despite being built upon the Zilliacus perspective of international relations. Prior to analysing the roles and ideals of these two individuals it is useful to outline the Victory for Socialism position on defence policy and provide some detail of the origins.

A SOCIALIST DEFENCE POLICY: DESIGNED BY MOSCOW?

For the broad Labour left the greatest anathema was the initiative to develop an 'independent British nuclear deterrent'. Their opposition was based upon two premises. Firstly failures on the part of the British nuclear weapons programme had forced Britain to purchase a defence system from the United States, the left argued that this would mean that British defence would be ultimately under United States control. This countered Gaitskell's position that Britain's nuclear capability would secure "influence and prestige and a measure of independence vis-à-vis the United States."[34] Figures including Harold Davies argued that the existence of nuclear weapons in Britain would make the nation a target that lacked independent means for activating its defences, thus it was argued that the weaponry was a pointless acquisition. The second premise, put forward by the pacifist left who dominated Victory for Socialism, rejected the nuclear deterrent completely. The nuclear deterrent was described as anti-socialist. Allaun argued that no socialist could envisage using weapons of mass destruction. There were equally arguments that described nuclear weapons as too expensive, thus detrimental to domestic socialist policies. [35]

These debates had been a feature within the Labour Party since 1945. Ernest Bevin had argued that nuclear weapon were highly desirable on nationalist grounds. Bevin stated "We have got to have this thing whatever it costs. We've got to have the bloody Union jack on top of it."[36] Due to the divisive nature of the nuclear deterrent initial plans were made in secret and without recourse to any level of the party. When the plans were made public they did appeal to the 'little Englander' section of parliament and country, but not to the internationalist element of Labour. The left argued that nuclear weapons were undesirable and the antithesis of the ideals of socialism. After the failure of the Blue Streak project[37] the plan to develop a independent deterrent were shelved. This allowed the left to argue that Britain, as a non-nuclear power, should act as a model for European nations. However plans by the Conservatives, firstly under Macmillan then Home, to buy Skybolt from the United States brought the issue of Britain as a nuclear power back into the limelight. The left feared that, should this transaction be ratified, Britain would become a dependent satellite of the United States, therefore backbench activism increased.

The proposal for a British nuclear deterrent was put forward in Defence White Papers firstly in 1957, and then in 1964. These argued that the keystone of British defence was the prevention of war. The Conservatives expressed the fear that "there is at present no means of providing adequate protection for the people of this country against the consequences of nuclear attack."[38] The solution offered by the then Foreign Secretary, Alec Douglas-Home, was to develop, or buy, a nuclear weapons system. Allaun, when criticising the appointment of Home, described him as "so anti-Soviet as to be unsuitable for the post."[39] Zilliacus ridiculed the logic of Home's argument:

> The Americans and Russians may be deterred by the deterrent, … but not John Bull, we may have only a tiny nuclear force, no modern means of delivery, and an impossibly vulnerable territory compared to the giant [Soviet Union], but we shan't yield to Soviet nuclear blackmail. It is for them to yield to ours.[40]

Zilliacus was not alone in raising his voice in opposition. Benn Levy and Harold Davies, both left-wing Labour MPs, though by no means pro-Soviet, were equally vocal in their opposition. In his undated pamphlet, Bull's Eye Island, Davies argued that one or two strikes would be enough to devastate Britain. The resulting nuclear fall-out would be sufficient to wipe out the entire population. Davies called the Conservative defence policy "spineless [and] servile [to] American brinkmanship."[41] Levy reiterated much of Davies' and Zilliacus' arguments, as did many on the left. Harry Pollitt, General Secretary of the CPGB, wrote extensively on the subject, Tribune brimmed with anti-nuclear articles, and the Independent Labour Party joined in the castigation of the policy. Still it went ahead. The socialist movement, Labourist and Communist, found this one issue, opposition to the presence of nuclear weapons on British soil, became a policy around which it could unite.[42] The main argument was based on a combination of socialist ideals, pacifism and fear of war. Foot put it most succinctly in *Tribune*, writing in criticism of Aneurin Bevan proselytising his position to supporting the H-bomb:

> I remain unconvinced that the possession of a few bombs which can never be used except as an act of national suicide and which as long as we produce them will impose enormous burdens on our economy, will assist in making Britain's voice more powerful in the world… [On the other hand] Britain's readiness to renounce the weapon… could capture the imagination of millions of people in many lands.[43]

This was a core belief among many left-wing socialists. The advocates of this position would continually make their voice heard and eventually stamp their mark on official party policy.

The conflict between right and left in the party was deepened by the issue of nuclear weapons. Hugh Gaitskell supported the nuclear deterrent and was largely Bevinite in his approach to foreign and defence policy. Until 1957 Nye Bevan was seen as the champion of the left-wing cause, but, at the Brighton Conference Bevan recanted his erstwhile beliefs in favour of nuclear weapons. Bevan motives are the subject of much debate. Foot argued that he had been persuaded during discussions with Gaitskell and Durham miners leader Sam Watson. Bevan, Foot assumed, was led to recognise that the issue was not a vote winner, and to gain election the party leadership had to be seen to be united and responsible.[44] With hindsight it appears unrealistic to believe that the party would alter its policy once in power, Bevan may have believed that this could happen.

It does appear that his opposition to unilateralism was a sharp U-turn in his thinking. Indicatively, none of his colleagues believed he was sincere. They argued that he had been influenced either by the party hierarchy, his recent visit to the Soviet Union and meeting with Khrushchev or, as the New Statesman wrote, that he was simply hungry for power in a forthcoming Labour government.[45] For Bevan the act was a sad epitaph; he was to die prior to the next General Election. David Coates writes of this genuflection: "the perennial dilemma of the Labour Left MP, of needing a Labour government and a position within it if he was not to be totally impotent, but having to pay a high price."[46] This was not a dilemma for individuals like Zilliacus, Mikardo or Allaun. These radical MPs maintained their resolve in remaining independent voices of opposition to the party line.

Despite Bevan's change of heart, the 1960 Conference accepted unilateralism as the policy of the Labour Party. The factor that changed party policy was the Union vote. Frank Cousins, speaking for the Transport and General Workers [TGWU], put forward the common sense argument against non-proliferation:

> If we have the right to possess the nuclear weapons, then every other country in the world has that same right. And if they have the right, how do we ever get into that atmosphere of avoiding the accidental drift into war?[47]

This was also the position of the Communist Party and it was argued that the emergence of unilateralism was due to CPGB influence within the Unions, CND and the broader peace and unilateralist movement. The Soviet Union did not want every nation who supported the United States to have missiles directed at the Communist bloc, and encouraged its supporters abroad to support the anti-nuclear campaign, a line which the CPGB followed loyally. The Communist's support for unilateralism led many on the left, including Frank Cousins, to be accused of being a member of the CPGB. In Cousin's case, as with the case of many of the leadership's opponents, these allegations were usually pursued by those he opposed the most vituperatively, Arthur Deakin, his predecessor at the TGWU, and Gaitskell himself. Dorril and Ramsay claim that these allegations were unfounded.[48] Determining the origins of the unilateralist position are problematic, the policy was promoted and supported by a broad section of the British left. Arguing that unilateralism benefited the Soviet Union was a convenient method for undermining the chief proponents, as was linking together "pacifists, unilateralists and fellow travellers."[49] However, it is difficult to sustain the argument that unilateralism was a position developed by individuals with pro-Soviet sympathies. The arguments presented by the left were logical and in keeping with the traditions of the peace movement that emerged during the First World War, there is scant evidence to suggest that these MPs were loyally reproducing arguments originating in Moscow. However, it suited Gaitskell to label the unilateralist defence policy as inspired by Soviet propaganda.

The proximity of the left's position and the official line of the CPGB adds weight to the view that the unilateralist position, adopted in 1980, was 'tailor made for Moscow'.[50] A critique of the party that gained prominence within the popular press. In reality however it was a policy that had the support of a broad range of individuals emerging from disparate socialist traditions. The supporters of the 'socialist foreign policy' included Marxists, Trotskyists and the pro-Soviet left, many of whom became prominent members of the NEC as the party was drawn to a more left-wing political stance. However, their influence was negligible when the party was in power. As Taylor observed, "CND and the Labour left failed to hold the Labour Party to the unilateralist policy of the 1960 Conference."[51] This failure led many to adopt extra-parliamentary methods to attempt to achieve their goals. Victory for Socialism members carried out a dual role that would survive into the 1970s during the period of détente. While pursuing extra-parliamentary activity they campaigned for a change to Labour's foreign and defence policy. They offered an alternative view of East-West relations and promoted the ideas emanating from Moscow. This group represented the only true organisation that espoused the pro-Soviet perspective. This was due, in no small part, to the individuals who drafted the policies that the group advocated.

THE LAST LOST SHEEP

Stephen Swingler was lucky, it appears, not to have been expelled with Zilliacus and Solley in 1948. On Morgan Phillips' list of possible expellees there are five ticks, one by the name of each of those expelled plus two others outspoken MP for Mitcham and author of the satirical 'The Importance of being Ernest Bevin', Herschel Austin and Swingler. Next to the latter is a question mark. Why was it that he had been earmarked for expulsion? Phillips selected MPs who were prominent dissidents, but who did not have any significant popularity within the party. Not all on this list could be expelled; the most vocal were chosen because of the attention they generated for their arguments. Swingler was not one of the most high profile advocates of the pro-Soviet position during the 1945-50 period, though he was suspected of being a Communist Party member. In many ways the high point of his leftist activity was from 1958 to 1964. However, the radical socialist perspective he brought to parliament originated in the traditions of the Communism of the 1930s.

Within the pages of his 1939 publication, *Political Thought since the French Revolution*, Swingler's support for Soviet ideology was made transparent. Swingler argued that the Communist State was the ultimate form of emancipation of political thought and practice. Covertly referring to the British Labour government of 1929-31 he discussed the failure to "translate real political desires into social activity and to achieve success."[52] He argued that democratic politicians sublimate themselves and their country to dogmatic controversies, which are used as a shield for their inability, or indeed lack of enthusiasm, to implement revolutionary change. This, he argued, was not the case in the Soviet Union.

The achievements of the Russian revolution, Swingler argued, were real, emancipatory, and had to be safeguarded, firstly from outside, but importantly also from dissent within. The Stalin-Trotsky dichotomy over the creation of socialism in one country he saw as being thoroughly de-bated and resolved. Thus he excused the treason trials as necessary to combat attempts to subvert the principles of the revolution:

[T]o demand freedom for Trotskyism in the [Soviet Union] or fur-ther discussion of the issue is merely stupid... The controversy over theory has been settled in practice and further discussion can in no way aid action; therefore to demand the right to free discussion of the issues, as people have done over the Moscow trials, is to demand the right to obstruct and constrain, the right to negate freedom.[53]

He explained the lack of understanding of the purges and trials in Britain as being the result of the political commentators and analysts: "find[ing] it difficult to understand that political discussion should be directed towards practical change, having made in parliament a positive virtue of obstruction.[54] This shows that his sympathies, at this time, lay entirely with revolutionary socialism and the Marxist theory of the inevitable collapse and supercession of capitalism. It is unclear what he envisaged for Britain as this work is historical not prescriptive. However, in his work we see the tradition of the Leeds Convention of June 1917. A belief in the concept of change as emanating from the Soviet Union: this belief was translated, to an extent, into the arguments Swingler put forward during his parliamentary career.

Swingler, while at New College, Oxford, had joined the Young Communist League, and later the CPGB itself. Oxford was a significant breeding ground for Communist sympathies. However, by no means should this be seen as a life-long association. Many young politicised people joined the radical left, only to 'grow out of it', or more equally grow disillusioned with the slavish support for Soviet policy and the prescribed role of the Communist International. The Swingler family were all left-wingers, his father was a friend of the 'Red Dean' Hewlett Johnson, the communist Dean of Canterbury, who would attend dinner parties and deliver a pro-Soviet sermon to the avid audience. Stephen's brother, Randall, was a lifelong Communist Party member and celebrated poet. Therefore, that influence constantly surrounded him.[55] However in 1938 Swingler and his wife Anne decided to join the Labour Party. Anne recalled that:

> we went to live in North Staffordshire. There, I joined the Labour Party and he joined the Labour Party. The reason was that it was just so obvious, in that area there was a very small, tiny Communist party but we wanted to be effective, we wanted to make change and so we joined the Labour Party.[56]

Anne Swingler had also been politically educated within Communist circles. During the 1930s she worked for the Labour Research Department [LRD], which was dominated by members of the CPGB like Noreen Branson and was proscribed by the PLP. Therefore, Anne's political education was imbibed with a clear pro-Soviet slant. Anne admitted that she did not realise the implications of this until much later. Anne recalled that Stephen was initially reluctant to stand as an MP. He already had a career as a teacher. It was only when he realised that no one else would stand for Labour in the constituency of Stafford in 1938, and that it was unlikely the Labour Party could unseat the Conservatives, that he allowed his name to be put forward as the prospective candidate. War intervened, public opinion changed and Swingler was to come to office in 1945 with a massive majority, all of which was lost by 1950. It is possible that he retained his Communist Party membership during this period: Anne Swingler hinted that this was the case.[57]

It is significant that he returned to Oxford in 1939 to lecture, rather than being drafted. In 1939 the Communist Party analysis, as propagated by Stalin, was that the war was a further imperialist excursion by Great Britain and Germany and therefore Swingler chose not to join the army. More significantly, and consistent with the Communist line, he enlisted into the army in 1941, being posted to the Royal Armoured Corps in 1942. Bill Alexander, International Brigade stalwart and CPGB member was at Sandhurst with Swingler. Alexander recalled that Swingler indeed saw the British motives for declaring war as protectionist and imperialist. However, he did not recall if Swingler's attitude changed, Swingler was posted to Europe while Alexander went to North Africa.[58]

It is unknown when Stephen Swingler's membership of the CPGB expired. It is possible that due to the disorganisation of the CPGB membership files in the immediate post-war period, his membership was never formally cancelled. Whether Swingler was, or was not, a Communist member while a Labour politician is immaterial. What is important is that in his younger days he forged associations with Communists, and was therefore influenced by them. These associations were retained. Anne still dines with the former leadership of the London Communist Party, friends she has retained since her time at the Labour Research Department. Stephen Swingler's private life was spent within the far-left milieu and this influence arguably spilled over into his political arguments. Once in parliament he followed the anti-Atlanticist line, though, to a much lesser extent than many of his left-wing colleagues. At this time Swingler's pro-Soviet activism was strictly extra-parliamentary.

Stephen Swingler bore no hostility towards the Soviet Union. Like Platts-Mills he enjoyed friendly and informal visits to the Eastern bloc in the early post-war period, once getting drunk and falling into the River Volga.[59] However, it is not unusual for a Member of Parliament to be the guest of a foreign country. What is important is the mindset of individuals such as Swingler; they did not, and in many ways could not, accept the Russian, Czech or any of the peoples of Eastern Europe, as their enemy.

Vladimir Shaposhnikov, a one-time official in the Ukraine region of the Soviet Union, recalled that this was common among socialist politicians. As a Soviet official he found it easier to deal with 'right-wing' governmental representatives, as with them the agenda was strictly business. Socialists would want to discuss political theory and offered their own opinions on the Soviet system. They treated their Russian counterparts as slightly disenfranchised siblings; people recognised as having similar beliefs, but ones that had been led astray.[60] Conversely, Stan Newens found that such discussions were almost impossible to enter.[61]

However, this attitude towards the Soviet socialist model goes some way to explain the great hope that existed within the work of individuals such as Swingler and many within the vanguard of Victory for Socialism. Their objective was the establishment of socialism and success relied heavily upon the Soviet Union. The basic premise of the Swinglers' beliefs was firstly, that the Soviet Union had a socialist economic framework and secondly that the Soviet Union would be able to evolve and become democratic, allowing political freedom to complement public ownership. This belief was central to the pro-Soviet mindset. It led many individuals within the pro-Soviet milieu to ignore the flaws in the Soviet socialist model, this would cause them to question their faith. Anne's faith was, by 1968, eroded completely. She recalled that "I and millions like me, were led astray into believing Russian Communism could change itself into a reasonable democracy."[62]

Alongside their beliefs in the Soviet Union there was also one tie to the Communist world that the Swinglers were unable to break. This was the link with Czechoslovakia. The Swinglers and Barnett Stross, who was condemned posthumously as a spy by Josef Frolik, took in Czech refugees from the Nazi invasion in 1937. This led the Swinglers and Stross to have a lifelong association with the mining town of Lidice. Stephen Swingler and Stross jointly formed the Anglo-Czech Parliamentary Committee, sat on the Executive of the Anglo-Czech Friendship Society and raised money for the rebuilding of Lidice under the auspices of the Lidice Shall Live Campaign. Barnett Stross was the prime organiser of both the societies and of the handing over of money collected. This left him open to suspicion and accusation. It was only when Swingler was made Minister of Transport by Harold Wilson that he was forced to break his most obvious links. At the time he was investigated, and felt compelled to deny his membership of the CPGB. His cabinet position meant that Swingler was unable to attend the celebrations marking the anniversary of the freeing of Czechoslovakia held in 1968. Anne was the sole representative due to the death of Stross in 1966. She cut the ribbon to the garden of remembrance flanked by sombre, austere Communists who, she recalled, were aware that they had become very unpopular. It is unknown what Swingler's reaction was to the Czechoslovakian invasion by the Soviet Union in 1968. He died months later. Anne recalled that this was the point of no return for her. Following that incident she rejected the ideals of the Soviet Union completely.[63]

The heritage of Swingler was that he and his left-wing comrades of the immediate post-war period created a movement that would maintain opposition to the Cold War. Though Stephen died due to a combination of overwork and heavy drinking in 1969, Zilliacus's beliefs, matched with Swingler's less narrow-minded style, were adopted as the way forward. Victory for Socialism was the first vehicle to be used to establish a cohesive left-wing programme. The Tribune Group would supercede this though it became fraught with divisions over perceptions of the Soviet Union, policy towards the European Community and the position on Palestine.[64] The individuals who pursued the pro-Soviet perspective on international relations found that they were constantly the subjects of accusations and investigations. The suspicion surrounding them, as with Swingler and Zilliacus, was that they were really Moscow's agents attempting to influence and indoctrinate the party and the public. It is a fact that this was their role, but it is doubtful that it was at Moscow's behest. Their desire to act as agents for change appears to have developed out of their personal beliefs rather than under the influence of persuasive envoys for the Communist powers.

Nuclear weapons became the first issue around which Swingler, Victory for Socialism and the pro-Soviet strand became united. The notion of mutually assured destruction, or MAD, which constituted the assurance that neither side of the bi-polar stand off would attack the other, was in direct opposition to the beliefs of certain sections of British Socialism. Their intention, as put forward in the party's 1983 Election Manifesto, nineteen years after the dissolution of Victory for Socialism, was to "draw back from the nuclear abyss."[65] The left, which would dominate the party by 1983, opposed the Cold War rationale on the grounds that it offered no prospect for co-operation. The left argued that efforts should be made to accommodate the Soviet Union's needs; the Cold War rationale, which relied upon a military stand-off, they argued, was a dangerous policy. The occurrence of crises, such as the Berlin blockade in 1948 and Cuba in 1962, only exacerbated the fears of the pacifist wing of the party. This led the left to develop a coherent oppositional strategy. Equally they were encouraged to believe that the greater threat came from the West not the East. Khrushchev spoke of weapons control, co-operation and disarmament. The United States offered no sign of supporting any form of rapprochement. Eisenhower's 1955 Christmas message to the peoples of Eastern Europe was clearly provocative, stating that he recognised the trials suffered under Soviet rule and offered hope that right would win in the end.[66] Though these sentiments were probably sincerely appreciated by those under Soviet military rule, it made any form of co-operation seem very distant.

This led many to view the Soviet Union as the only potential peace-maker; the Soviet leadership wrote of peaceful co-existence, while the NATO leaders spoke of containment and rollback. This perspective was constantly promoted by Victory for Socialism and many pacifists were then drawn into supporting the Soviet Union in opposition to the United States and to opposing the British government's support for the Cold War. Those who adopted this strand of thought believed that the Soviet Union was pro-peace but was hindered by the antagonistic capitalist world. The pro-Soviet MPs steadfastly promoted this position in parliament and within the Labour Party. The common language shared by peace movement literature and pro-Soviet propaganda led many who supported the Campaign for Nuclear Disarmament, opposed US foreign policy and defended the Soviet Union to be accused of spying, particularly between 1950 and 1970 when Britain was suffering a mild form of McCarthyism. This, however, did not dampen the activists' spirits. The chief points of contention between the left and the party were the support for the United States, acceptance of the nuclear deterrent and subscription to the anti-Communist rationale. The alternative programme and independent foreign policy, established by Victory for Socialism, was based upon the principles of co-operation, co-existence and unilateral nuclear disarmament. This would become official party policy, facilitated by a leftwards shift by the leadership of the National Executive, as the young left-wingers prominent in Victory for Socialism during the 1950s found themselves promoted to areas of greater influence. One of the major forces behind establishing this programme as party policy was Frank Allaun, whose single dedication made him the leader, by default, of Labour Action for Peace, an organisation that incorporated the ideals of pacifism with the pro-Soviet perspective. It was Allaun's adherence to this perspective that led him to be considered an asset by the Soviet Union.

ZILLIACUS' SUCCESSOR

• Frank Allaun, Labour MP for Salford East 1955-83, appears to have been greatly influenced by Konni Zilliacus. Allaun recalled that he "knew and liked him well."[67] Equally he had the highest respect for Zilliacus' ability and knowledge. He stated that Zilliacus "knew more about foreign policy than any other MP in Parliament."[68] This belief must have added a great deal of weight to the arguments of Zilliacus. Allaun fought to get Zilliacus nominated as Labour candidate for the Manchester Gorton constituency where Allaun was active within the local Labour Party and where he worked as a journalist.[69] They worked alongside one another to develop Victory for Socialism's alternative foreign policy and Allaun was to inherit the tradition of seeking peace and co-operation in the international political arena. A deep fear of nuclear war was integral to Allaun's analysis, as war was, he argued, the logical outcome of the Cold War bipolar stand-off.

• Allaun's perspective on Soviet foreign policy led him to stand on the far left-wing of the Labour Party, leading some to describe him as a fellow traveller. He was even denounced by *The Sun* newspaper as a traitor, during his vociferous opposition to the British government going to war with Argentina over the Falklands, though this scarcly bothered Allaun.[70] It is extremely questionable as to how far such accusations were deserved. In his writings he was not slavish to the Soviet leadership and he followed a broadly independent course, remaining critical of the oppressive nature of the Soviet regime. However, Allaun showed that he retained a belief that there was an inherently socialist element to the Soviet Union, and this belief led him to argue that the Soviet Union posed little threat to the world. According to Allaun's analysis, the Soviet Union emerged as the best and only hope for a peaceful conclusion to the Cold War, an argument founded on the premise: "I was convinced – as I am today – that the [Soviet] people and their government did not want war."[71]

    Allaun argued that this perception was proven conclusively: "First and most important of [Gorbachev's] achievements, in my view, is his uni-lateral action in ending the Cold War, which nearly became the nuclear and final battle.[72] He described Gorbachev as leading "the struggle for peace"[73] a description he attached to no other Soviet leader, despite the propaganda they produced to prove their worth.[74] He stated that Gorbachev:

> has given me hope in a cruel age… It was he who ended the East-West Cold War, fought with weapons of mass destruction on both sides, when he announced… that he would withdraw 800 planes, 8,000 tanks and 500,000 troops from the Russian frontier… Gorbachev forced the other nations to follow suit.[75]

    In an article for the *Morning Star*, reviewing Gorbachev's *Memoirs*, Allaun recognised the need in the Soviet Union for free elections and the formation of a parliamentary democracy. However, he criticised Gorbachev's economic reforms because they were founded on the premise that the Bolsheviks' model of planning was a failure.[76] Allaun argued that the 'new' market economy established in Russia created greater economic hardship for the people. He maintained that Gorbachev should have introduced a system that retained a command economy combined with the reformist programme of glasnost, or openness, of the political system. He remained highly critical of the system that supplanted Communism:

> I accept that glasnost, or freedom of speech, media and political parties, is welcomed by the Russian people. But it has been perestroika, or reconstruction, which has ruined the country… the truth is that the Russian people were far, far better off then than they are today.[77]

Allaun, therefore, welcomed the democratisation of Russian politics and the opportunity this presented for rapprochement between East and West, but he unequivocally opposed the policy of economic privatisation pursued by Gorbachev. Allaun's fight for peace was ultimately successful but at the expense of socialism. Peace was achieved between East and West, but the price for this was that the Soviet Union, and all it had stood for, had collapsed. The contradictions within the Soviet experiment were laid bare. Gorbachev exposed the faults in a manner that Khrushchev could not have envisaged when denouncing Stalin. Socialists like Allaun attached their hopes of a global socialist revolution to the success of the Soviet Union, in some democratised form, therefore he and his allies had to face a very difficult conclusion in the light of the events of 1989. As he stated "I do believe that the collapse of the Soviet Union has set back hopes of a socialist world, at least for a time."[78] This shows that Allaun saw an ideological link between democratic socialism and the Soviet model and that he believed that they shared a common destiny. It is necessary, therefore to investigate fully the intellectual development Frank Allaun underwent in pursuit of a socialist future based on peaceful co-existence, and how his pro-Soviet sympathies shaped his perceptions of the world.

Allaun had visited the Soviet Union during the 1930s. He recalled saving for many years so he could see "socialism in practice", so this was obviously the fulfilment of a burning desire. His visit was sufficient to convince him that there was a great deal of potential for socialism in Stalinism, though his desire to visit indicates that he was already sympathetic to the ideals of the Soviet Union. This belief was based upon a conviction that it stood as a viable socialist alternative to capitalism. Allaun accepted the faults with the Soviet system but saw that the underlying ideology was worthy of protection and emulation. However, he did not argue that Communism should be transplanted into British political society. Allaun argued that a socialist system must be established by "a democratically elected government."[79] Like many commentators he accepted that the political circumstances in Russia in 1917 and those that existed concurrently and subsequently across Europe were significantly different. Britain could, and indeed should, become socialist through the democratic process without resorting to violent means.

The second belief he held is that both the people, and more importantly the government, of the Soviet Union did not want war. Moreover, Allaun argued, the Soviet leadership were prepared to act to prevent a war. He believed that in the Russian psyche was a deep fear of war and, had it not been for Hitler's invasion, the Soviet Union would have remained neutral during the Second World War. Allaun employed this argument to explain the Nazi-Soviet Pact and Soviet actions during the post-war settlement.

In all references to the Soviet Union he omits to mention the coercive actions of the Soviet leadership to their own people and the nations annexed after 1945. As with many of the pro-Soviet left-wing he is able to ignore these inconsistencies on the grounds that there was, within in the Communist system, a socialist ideal which would emerge given the correct circumstances. Therefore, Frank Allaun appears to have subscribed to the same world view as his erstwhile friend and colleague Konni Zilliacus. These views are apparent from Allaun's early published writings and are consistent with the principles of the groups Allaun was active in.

Aside from the peace movement Allaun's other concern was to improve the housing of the poorest in Britain, a mission on which he was joined periodically by the CPGB. The 'bathrooms not bombs' campaign became a key policy to gain membership for the CPGB amongst the disaffected and disadvantaged and was to be utilised as a focus for anti-Cold War activity particularly in the Greater Manchester area. Allaun saw that public service issues and arms reduction were policies that could be promoted simultaneously: "for the less spent on the military the more money there would be for housing."[80] He argued that a socialist government should allocate a greater proportion of the budget to domestic spending and stated that defence was "the only sphere in which the government can cut [spending] without hurting ordinary working people."[81] He argued, as a constituency MP, for raising the standards of housing in Salford, calling for the provision of baths, hot water and inside toilets, all of which were considered luxuries to many Mancunians in the 1960s. To Allaun these policies seem to be argued from the heart, not for cynical reasons. This focus also made him a more rounded constituency representative than Zilliacus could ever be. Allaun, however, was also a member of the party at the right time, a time when he could progress into the Labour hierarchy gaining some, albeit limited, influence.

As with many of his left-wing colleagues on the NEC, he was seen as too out of step with the leadership to be given a Cabinet post, particularly as a spokesperson on foreign affairs. However his popularity, and the support for his ideas, within the party is evidenced by the fact that he was elected to the NEC annually from 1967-1983, and became Deputy Chairman and Chairman of the Party 1977-9. His highest Cabinet position, however, was as Parliamentary Private Secretary to Anthony Greenwood, Secretary of State for the Colonies for six months from October 1964; a position from which he resigned as a protest against Wilson's support of the US bombing campaign in Vietnam. This was the end of any ambitions he may have had for greater influence. Like radicals before him he was to be a voice from the sidelines, marginalised but never silenced. This did not bother Allaun, who stated in his memoirs that he "prefer[ed] the freedom of the Back Benches."[82]

      The main vehicle for his criticism, apart from parliamentary speeches, was the press, particularly the organ of the CPGB, *The Morning Star*. Though he had other links to Communist inspired organisations, this was his strongest association with the revolutionary left during his parliamentary career. Within his formative years, however, he was educated into radical socialism. He frequented the Left Book Club Library in Manchester which was run during the 1930s by Marjorie Pollitt, the mother of CPGB General Secretary Harry Pollitt. He recalled the "enjoyable political debates" when he joined Communists and Socialists alike in sending condolences to Pollitt on his mother's death.[83] Allaun appears to have shared many ideals with Harry Pollitt. Both saw themselves as fighters for the working class and, during the 1930s, put forward very similar arguments. Allaun had little sympathy for the CPGB organisation, but he did not see Communists as enemies. Allaun also worked closely with Eva Reckitt, who formed the radical socialist book chain Collets, organising an exhibition in Manchester which Reckitt was to move to London under the title 'An Exhibition of Books, Posters and Cartoons showing the Struggle of Six Generations of Workers for Peace, Freedom and Democracy'. This advertised the role of the Soviet Union in the international workers' struggle, promoting aspects of Soviet society and policy that Soviet propaganda highlighted to gain the support of individuals like Allaun; those with a keen socialist perspective who were dissatisfied with Western policy.

      It was the peace movement that became Allaun's raison d'être. He was made honorary secretary of the Manchester Anti-War Council at the age of nineteen, an organisation he described as tiny compared with what he would become part of in later life.[84] The radical writers of his youth, Upton Sinclair, Jack London and Robert Tressall heavily influenced him and he developed his grasp of economic theory through reading Das Kapital. His initial career was as a journalist, firstly as a Town Hall correspondent in Manchester, then as foreign affairs correspondent for the Daily Herald, before becoming the Editor of Labour's Northern Voice in 1951. From here the transition to active politics was reasonably painless though, as he recalled, filled with foreboding. Though he admitted he became quite at home on the backbenches.

      Allaun enjoyed longstanding links with left-wing socialist organisations. He joined the Union for Democratic Control [UDC] in 1922 and was prominent in the Movement for Colonial Freedom. On joining the Labour Party he became part firstly of Victory for Socialism, then Labour Action for Peace and began a career of dedicated activism within the party. He also joined the Campaign for Nuclear Disarmament, [CND] and helped

form a parliamentary branch among Labour backbenchers. His dissent, like
Zilliacus', was based on the fact that Britain was tied to the United States and
dominated by an anti-Communist rationale. He saw this as being both
dangerous, and ultimately false, and was seldom reluctant to put forward
this view. "The whole of my object was really to influence the Labour Party,
to make the party the 'peace party'."[85] Zilliacus, Allaun and the wider
disarmament movement maintained the view that the Labour Party was
"the natural vehicle for bringing CND policy into effect."[86]

The organisations that he allied himself to, during his pre-parlia-
mentary career, reflect his fundamental political stance. Strong continuity
can be found between the ideas of the UDC and the stance adopted by
LAP and CND. The UDC was a liberal, pacifist organisation established by
Liberal Charles Trevelyan, on 5 August 1915, as a reaction to the failure of
negotiations aimed at ending the First World War.[87] The central tenets of the
organisation were that territory should not be annexed without the consent
of the populace, foreign policy should be governed by democratic mandate,
international conflicts must be settled through arbitration and armaments
should be limited to the level of absolute necessity. It also believed that state
compliance should be monitored and enforced by an international
organisation with the power to settle disputes through negotiation. The
intellectuals drawn to this organisation were to include those who later
circulated around both the Society for Cultural Relations with the Soviet
Union [SCR] and CND. These figures held an internationalist outlook and
put forward alternatives to bipolarity and war. These traditions of anti-war,
anti-bloc and pro-UN ideas are prominent throughout the arguments of
Allaun and, although he followed a pro-Soviet perspective, evidence suggests
that his perspective was developed independently through influences acquired
early in his life.

Allaun was attracted to Victory for Socialism because the group
advocated a programme to "lay the foundations of socialism and lasting
peace".[88] His membership meant that he was working alongside like-minded
individuals among whom he could attain a position of influence. He was
immediately posted to the Executive Council and was elected to the Foreign and Commonwealth Policy Group chaired by Zilliacus. His first publication as an MP was for the Salford Reporter, in which he wrote that only the
Labour Party had the ideological foundations that could avert war.[89] Like his
leftist predecessors in the 1945-50 government he opposed the fervent anti-
Communist propaganda. In a speech to a formative group of individuals,
who later became Labour Action for Peace, he argued that:

> there seems to be developing the idea that the only good Russian was
> a dead one. I have not come here to defend the Russian government,

but I warn you to be on your guard against this day-to-day propaganda against the Russians.[90]

This speech is important in the fact that it displays a central theme of Allaun's perspective. He argued that the Cold War ethos drove the world towards the edge of a nuclear volcano.[91] One provocative move by either side could plunge the world into an inferno. He accepted that there were faults on both sides but, to Allaun, the evidence indicated that it was the hawkishness of the West that was leading the world closer and closer to being engulfed in the metaphorical lava.

This fear, for Allaun and many of those of the same mind, was at its height in the 1960s. Firstly in Cuba, then in Vietnam, the United States leadership was pursuing an active policy of the 'rollback' of Communism. The pro-peace organisations, many of which were Moscow supported, fed upon these hot spots in the cold conflict. Other organisations such as CND and LAP fell into line with the arguments promoted by Soviet propaganda. LAP literature constantly criticised the United States as the aggressor, arguing that the United States was the nation that would plunge the world into a nuclear abyss. Thus Allaun was to discover the futility of remaining non-aligned within an atmosphere of bipolarity.[92]

Allaun personally criticised the prosecution of the Vietnam War at every possible occasion. He feared that the war would spread and escalate, and hinted on occasions that the United States leadership did not share his fear but rather that a large-scale conflict was part of their agenda. The rhetoric of 'rollback' advocated the eradication of Communism, Allaun argued that the Vietnam conflict was a precursor to war with China and the Soviet Union. Though this seems implausible, it was an element of the zeitgeist of the 1960s. The fear of nuclear war kept thousands marching on Aldermaston every year. Socialists like Allaun marched alongside men of the cloth such as CND leader Bruce Kent and members of the Communist Party, all united under the banner of nuclear disarmament. This was a non-aligned movement, but Soviet propaganda attempted to influence the European peace movement. This propaganda campaign was designed to convince the members that, like them, the Soviet Union supported peace and disarmament and that it was the aggressive stance maintained by the West that prolonged hostilities. However, as Zilliacus observed in 1958, the mass movement was not one that was slavish to Communism, but that: "a great and growing number of people in Europe and in the United States is more afraid of the risks of the arms race... than of Communist aggression."[93] Therefore, many of the pro-peace lobby became supportive of the pro-Soviet arguments in the hope that if these could reach a wider audience, and alter public opinion to oppose the Cold War rationale, there was a chance of peace rather than increasing hostility.

Allaun, despite his perception of US foreign policy objectives, attempted to maintain a non-aligned pro-peace position. He described the LAP, of which he was President from 1965, as being "neither for the Russian nor the [United States] government, but for peace and friendship between the two."[94] To achieve this goal many of his allies were to attempt to alter the public and governmental perception of the Soviet Union. This went beyond merely declaring themselves in opposition to the belief that the Soviet Union was aggressive and imperialist. Allaun avoided displaying overt support for the Soviet Union but, despite this, he won few friends among the party's hierarchy and there were several attempts to oust him for abstaining on principle during votes on foreign policy.[95] Allaun refused to accept that there was anything whatsoever wrong in his actions. His aim was to help safeguard the future of mankind. He possessed the same ill-founded hope in the Labour Party as Zilliacus, seeing it as the only vehicle that could achieve peace. His self-proclaimed mission was to "deflect [the party] and steer it onto a safe course."[96] He was not without supporters, among them Ian Mikardo, who joined him in criticising the party over not following the promises written in the 1966 Election Manifesto.

The Manifesto described the Vietnam war as "cruel", talked of seeking agreements on "nuclear-free zones" and "verified international disarmament", and espoused establishing greater contact with Eastern Europe and reaching understandings with the Soviet Union and China.[97] Instead Wilson supported the United States in Vietnam and the rearmament of West Germany as a bulwark against the East. Allaun criticised both courses of action and stated that a rearmed Germany was exactly what "the Russian leaders fear most, and who can blame them."[98] This should not be viewed as evidence of anti-Germanic tendencies, but as an example of Allaun's opposition to any move that could provoke crisis and lead to what he dreaded most, nuclear war.

Allaun did recognise that, on both sides of the bipolar stand-off, fear reigned supreme. Both the White House and the Kremlin feared lagging behind in the arms race and thus leaving themselves open to attack. This fear was passed down to the satellites of both states, so perpetuating the arms race. Allaun argued that the "ordinary men and women should call a halt to this madness."[99] He recognised that, in reality, neither side was prepared to push the world into the nuclear volcano and that the nuclear deterrent had been developed purely for defensive purposes. The problem was establishing an atmosphere in which both sides could recognise this, agree to make reductions, and so make the world a safer place. The United States remained the chief bogey; Allaun recognised that the 'gap' in nuclear capability was false and that the Soviet Union was not superior. He argued that the 'gap' was a propagandist's ploy, whipping up fear to make the ordinary person support arms spending in the name of their own defence.[100] He stated that "the warhawks are trying to convince us that we are militarily inferior and that Russia is about to attack."[101]

While the public was led to support the Cold War, Allaun argued that in the long term nothing was being achieved. Both the international and domestic situations were in stagnation. Allaun argued that "those responsible for whipping up anti-Soviet hysteria are guilty of bringing war closer."[102] Equally the people endured cuts in public services due to the burden of spending while Britain suffered the ignominy of losing any independence that was possible in the post-war world. Britain had become, he argued, no more than a United States base, without any power over the nuclear arsenal but responsible for its presence. He equally argued that the capitalist ethos of profit, preponderant in the West, had gained hold of the armaments business; thus giving it a self-perpetuating force. Allaun argued that this was not the case under Communism, "there are no people in Russia making a packet out of armaments as there are in this country and [the United States]."[103]

The ultimate fear Allaun held was that the presence of nuclear weapons made Britain a 'sitting duck' should the Kremlin wish to make one last desperate gesture. In many ways it could be argued that he would have supported any nation had they promised a conclusion to mutually assured destruction. However his belief in Soviet socialism, a belief reinforced by Soviet propaganda, led him to argue that Soviet foreign policy was motivated by protectionism. Therefore his objective was to alter the perception of the Soviet Union, so averting war and calling a halt to the self-perpetuating nuclear arms race. These objectives underpinned the unilateralist policy that he promoted through the party's National Executive. Whether he was also motivated by a desire to protect the socialist economic system established in the Soviet Union is difficult to ascertain. However this was the objective of others who supported his stance and allied with him in the LAP.

THE VICTORY FOR SOCIALISM VISION

Swingler told the 1959 Labour Conference that:

> Only if we are clear that the aim of the party is to achieve a classless society can we get our supporters actively and enthusiastically to go out into the highways and byways and tell the truth about the nationalised industries, and tell the truth that full employment is only secure and total disarmament only possible if we have in fact a planned economy in Britain. That is the clear bold policy we need to adopt. If

this Executive gets immediately on with the job of declaring such a clear and bold policy for peace, ... colonial freedom, an unequivocal policy for a planned economy for a society of equal citizens in Britain, then we can go out into the highways and byways and we shall win.[104]

This was the political raison d'être of Swingler and his allies within Victory for Socialism. Throughout the CLPs meetings were organised, all advertising keynote speakers, such as Allaun, Newens and Zilliacus, who were prominent opponents of the Cold War rationale. The objective of these meetings was to encourage a broad support for a 'socialist' programme within the Labour Party. Key to Labour implementing this programme was for the party, once in government, to seize control of the British economy and the means of production, an economic model argued to be successful due in part to the example of the Soviet Union. While many of the speakers did not make this link explicit, a significant number of Victory for Socialism spokespersons did. Many of those who became prominent pro-Soviet activists during the period of détente, and critics of the Thatcherite foreign policy during the Second Cold War, figures like James Lamond and Renee Short, metaphorically 'cut their teeth' within Victory for Socialism.

The group's ideals were a continuation of those that had been promoted by Hutchinson, Platts-Mills, Solley and Zilliacus during the 1945-50 parliament. Equally indicative is that key tenets of the Victory for Socialism programme, particularly the opposition to the Anglo-American special relationship and prioritisation of NATO over the United Nations, have outlived the Cold War. This shows that these issues held, and to a limited extent still hold, great significance for a section of the British Labour Party. Throughout the Cold War the ghost of Zilliacus continued to haunt debates on foreign and defence policy. The peace movement, which existed on the fringes of the party's left-wing, ensured that input into government was maintained and its supporters within parliament persisted in promoting their often unpopular arguments.

The anti-Cold War campaign gained a new impetus during the 1980s, initially due to increased bipolar tensions. Western hawkishness fuelled Eastern European paranoia, increasing the possibility of a nuclear exchange. However the pro-Soviet strand saw their influence eroded as a new thaw beame visible within the Soviet political system while a greater impetus towards agreement over disarmament developed. The two dreams of many on the left, rapprochement and disarmament, were perceived to be heading for fruition, and once again the change agent was the Soviet leadership. The Soviet Union was implementing democratisation and openness and spearheading talks on disarmament. This was the ultimate objective that many on the left had been focused upon; therefore the campaign gained a

new clarity of purpose. Both Houses witnessed heated debates on the official attitude towards Gorbachev, particularly as public opinion embraced him
and traditionally anti-Soviet world leaders openly courted him. 'Gorby fever'
allowed the pro-Soviet left to glimpse their last chance of hope for peace and
socialism just before it, as all others before, slipped from their grasp.

Prior to this, albeit for a short period, the dreams of the exponents
of the Victory for Socialism vision seemed to be close to becoming a reality. Détente, ushered in by Labour Prime Minister Harold Wilson signing
the Helsinki Accord alongside Soviet leader Leonid Bezhnev, brought a fresh
chance for rapprochement between the Communist bloc and the West. This
led, during the 1970s, to a resurgence of extra-parliamentary pro-Soviet activity.
Many of Victory for Socialism's prominent activists adopted a key role in
those front organisations that established political and cultural links between
Britain and the Soviet Union and encouraged an atmosphere of understanding
to develop between Communism and Capitalism. This was to be the legacy
of Victory for Socialism. Under this organisation's co-ordination, three
objectives were crystallised as a blueprint for activism, maintaining and
strengthening peace, pursuing disarmament and fostering trust.

This consistent programme was aided by the network created by
Swingler. The CLPs had shifted leftwards and were dominated by individuals that sought to alter the centrist position of the party. They included
Trotskyists and Communists, often working side by side with little knowledge
of, or little regard for, their clear ideological differences. To these MPs the
ends justified the partnerships forged en route. By 1983 this mixture of left-
wing influences did steer the party into a leftward trajectory. The Labour Party
manifesto, famously derided as the 'longest suicide note in history' by Gerald
Kaufman, appears to have been an updated re-working of the Victory for
Socialism manifesto written by Swingler in 1958. Swingler had tapped into a
powerful force within the party, a force that increasingly demanded that the
party should strive towards the establishment of a socialist economy and a
socialist foreign policy.

The history of how these ideas developed within Labour's left-wing
to become the socialist alternative to the consensual party line is equally the
history of a slow upward trajectory of left-wingers of various backgrounds
and ideological traditions to positions of influence within the party. While
privately they disagreed with one another's political beliefs, often clearly divided
between 'Trots' and 'Stalinists', they also supported one another in the battle
with the party's leadership. Left-wingers reached positions of power within
the Unions, the NEC and the parliamentary party hierarchy. This was not a
programme designed by the pro-Soviet MPs in a party dominated by their
number, but one developed due to a growth in opposition to the inter-party
consensus on domestic and foreign policy among a broad left-wing section

of party membership.[105] However the British electorate rejected in totality the Labour left-wing socialist alternative, which became official policy in 1983 and represented the collision of intra-party ideological traditions. Thus the Victory for Socialism success story is a hollow one. The dominance over policy enjoyed briefly by this coalition of left traditions led not to the establishment of socialism but, to a protracted review process, a purge of radical elements from the party and a redrawing of the tenets of abour Party policy.[106]

5
BENEATH DÉTENTE

Victory for Socialism concentrated upon altering Labour Party foreign policy from the bottom up, attempting to gain a significant level of influence over Conference and the CLPs. The chief objective was to steer the party into positioning Britain as a pacific influence over world affairs, thus reducing the chance of war. This meant ending the transatlantic special relationship, opening cordial diplomatic relations with the Soviet Union and encouraging the formation of a non-aligned bloc that would reject the anti-Communist Cold War ethos. Due to the party's traditions of pacifism, anti-imperialism and humanism, Labour was perceived as the perfect vehicle to promote this internationalist programme. The party, however, maintained a consensual anti-Soviet, Atlanticist position, and avoided offering the overtures to the Soviet Union that the left demanded. Despite this the left of the party, and in particular the pro-Soviet strand, began to feel empowered by developments in international relations. These developments were the result of the rise of a more moderate President to the White House in 1968 and significant shifts in British foreign policy after the 1966 spending review.[1]

After 1969 United States President Richard Nixon made efforts to end the war in Vietnam, began Strategic Arms Limitation Talks [SALT] with the Soviet Union and opened relations with China.[2] The Wilson government had already reduced commitments in foreign policy, withdrawing British forces from East of Suez,[3] Harold Wilson also put some pressure on the United States government to open relations with the Communist countries.[4] It is doubtful that British concerns had any influence over United States foreign policy, as Jones argued the Wilson government did not have the kudos of their Conservative predecessors.[5] However, as the 1960s drew to a close it was apparent that the groundwork had been laid for a thaw in East-West relations. Underpinning this perception was the development of what became known as the Helsinki process.

The Helsinki process was particularly favoured by the left-wing because it excluded the United States. Therefore both the adherents to the Bevanite 'Third Camp' tradition, as well as those who supported the pro-Soviet position and opposed United States influence over Western Europe, could unite around this objective. They hoped for the supercession of NATO, which had been weakened by French withdrawal, and for the Warsaw Pact to become moribund. This was not to happen, instead the summits were fruitless due to the continuing mistrust shown by both sides. This was highlighted when severe difficulties were experienced when Western European members demanded access to Communist bloc nations in order to verify that human rights standards were improving and, more fundamentally important, that missile capabilities were being reduced in line with the SALT process. The demands made by Western governments were continually greater than the Soviet government were prepared to offer. A particular example was the demand that the future of Germany be determined by 'the free decision of the German people'.[6] Furthermore, due to United States non-participation, the Helsinki talks was unable to alter relations between the superpowers. Thus the Helsinki process was powerless to prevent the collapse of détente.[7]

However the Helsinki process represented the ideals that the Labour left-wing, and particularly the pro-Soviet strand, had been campaigning for since 1945. These were the avoidance of conflict through negotiation, the development of interdependence through freedom of movement and cultural exchange, co-operation in the fields of science and technology and glasnost within the Warsaw Pact nations.[8] These commitments, laid down by the West, were mirrored in the Brezhnev Doctrine outlined in the Declaration of Prague, 25th January 1972.[9] Left-wing idealists hoped that finally capitalist and communist nations had finally found principles around which they could find agreement.

This led to a fundamental change in the behaviour of the pro-Soviet MPs. Primarily they focussed upon ensuring that the Helsinki process remained on track. Labour backbenchers constantly called on successive British governments to strengthen East-West relations, consider both sides of arguments and allow concessions in the name of world peace. However, a mixture of enthusiastic commitment and morbid scepticism characterised both parties' official response to the developments. Aside from those who already exhibited pro-Soviet sympathies no British politicians completely trusted the motives of the Soviet leadership, a factor that acted as a constant obstacle to success of the Helsinki process, particularly after the 1979 General Election.

Beneath the high politics of international relations the pro-Soviet MPs became involved in more open forms of pro-Soviet activity in order to institutionalise détente. MPs helped establish trading links between East and West, promoted co-existence based on evidence gathered through contact with Communist bloc leaders, subscribed to pro-Soviet organisations and openly promoted pro-Soviet arguments in the House of Commons. This chapter focuses on three Labour MPs whose activities are indicative of the pro-Soviet left's response to the improved East-West relations during the détente period, a period when contact was encouraged between Britain and the Warsaw Pact nations in an attempt to draw the Communist leaders into the international community.[10]

Each of the three cases pursued a different form of pro-Soviet activity, and their level of pro-Soviet sympathy and their objectives also differed quantitatively. The first case, Stan Newens, developed a highly supportive analysis of the ideals of one Communist leader to encourage a deeper understanding of Communist politics and promote the creation of sustainable links between Britain and the Communist bloc. Unlike Zilliacus, who pursued a similar tactic using both Khrushchev and Tito, Stan Newens chose to use Romanian leader Nicolae Ceausescu as an exemplar of a fundamental shift in the foreign policy objectives of the Soviet camp. In promoting these arguments Newens developed a rationale for complete rapprochement with the Communist bloc and argued that détente necessitated a fundamental change in East-West relations. The second case, Ian Mikardo, attempted to develop East-West understanding through unofficial trading links between British companies and industry within the Communist bloc. Mikardo created a public limited company, Ian Mikardo plc, which was solely devoted to matching supply and demand between British businesses and their counterparts in the Soviet sphere. The links Mikardo established were intended to encourage a degree of economic interdependence as well as allowing the exchange of cultural and political ideas. The third and final case is Renee Short. Short is indicative of MPs who actively furthered the objectives of Soviet front organisations which allowed close personal relationships to develop between British MPs and representatives of the Communist bloc. These activities will show how détente was viewed as liberating, not only for the future of foreign and defence policy, but also for allowing a broader base of understanding to develop between the people of Britain and their Communist peers. These activities were encouraged by the development of détente, but promoted the broad aims of the pro-Soviet tradition. These objectives can be defined as ending the Cold War through rapprochement and establishing a new climate of opinion. This climate would be based upon co-operation and co-existence between the Soviet Union and Western society.

NO ENEMIES TO THE LEFT

The broad left-wing consensus that had been created by Victory for Socialism believed the anti-Soviet climate of opinion might become a feature of the past with the emergence of East-West détente. The pro-Soviet left-wingers now became determined to maintain East-West relations, increase Anglo-Soviet communication and ensure that a more positive image of the Communist leadership was projected within Western polities and society. This led some individuals to construct an alternative characterisation of the Communist bloc leadership. This was a task that was encouraged by the Communist propaganda departments and many left-wing MPs were invited to study the policies of the Communist states. A central objective of the Brezhnev Doctrine was to encourage those within democratic socialist groupings and the peace movement to believe that the Soviet leadership shared their objectives.[11] Therefore when attempting to attract influential individuals the favourite tool employed by Cominform was to project an image of the Communist leader that fitted with the ideology of those who were being invited. Thus Nicolae Ceausescu, the Romanian Communist leader, was characterised as carrying the revolution forward and encouraging the development of personal freedom within a statist economic system.

Stan Newens was not specifically pro-Soviet. Like many of his colleagues, he opposed the Cold War rationale and the dominance of the United States' zero-sum anti-Soviet perspective over British foreign policy. He also shared Allaun's deep fear of the consequences of a protracted arms race and reliance upon the nuclear deterrent. Therefore his tradition of dissent was one shared by many within the left of the Labour Party and is not an indicator of pro-Soviet sympathies. Newens argued that he was not sympathetic to the Soviet regime whatsoever; his objective was to end the Cold War by encouraging East and West to open channels of communication and develop mutual understanding. He defended his actions by stressing that he, Zilliacus, and many others including Allaun and Norman Atkinson, Labour MP for Tottenham 1964-87, openly criticised the Soviet Union as much as America. However, what is clear is that his perception of the Soviet Union differed from the perception held by the Labour Party leadership. Newens believed that the Communist bloc was approachable and willing to negotiate, while the United States was completely hostile to peaceful overtures. Equally he also argued that there were aspects of the Soviet society that were socialist, following the tradition established by G D H Cole and the Webbs.[12] This places Newens on the cusp of the pro-Soviet left. Studying his patterns of thought it is possible to learn why the left was able to establish a broad alliance despite its members differing perceptions of the world.

Stan Newens was elected to parliament in 1964, and remained a Labour MP until February 1983, when he lost his Harlow seat. Throughout his
career as an MP, and as the candidate for Harlow prior to becoming MEP
for the London Central ward in 1984, he was active in left-wing groups within
the Labour Party. His membership of the Eastern Area Group of Labour
MPs, which focused upon improving relations with the troubled South-East
Asia, as well as the more broadly-based left wing organisations: Tribune
Group, the Foreign Affairs Group, Labour Action for Peace, Liberation, and
the Movement for Colonial Freedom is an indicator of his interests; international relations, peace and humanitarian concerns. He was also actively involved with the London Co-operative Society, a diligent member of the
National Union of Teachers and an advocate of workers' rights. However, it
was his internationalist stance that dominated his political agenda. Newens'
recalled he gained his internationalist perspective at an early age. In 1948, as
an eighteen-year-old Sixth Form Student, he was taken to the House of
Commons to watch a political debate. Here he was introduced to the Zilliacus
perspective of the Cold War:

> Ernest Bevin spoke and I thought he was putting things across rea-
> sonably, then I saw a chap get up from the back benches, with buck-
> teeth sticking out, if it had been these days he would have had them
> fixed with a brace, but well, he had a great pile of books and a bald
> head shining. I watched him go through this pile of books, and I was
> sitting there as a neutral, and absolutely tear apart the logic of what
> Bevin had put over.[13]

Newens was deeply impressed and the experience convinced him to join the
Labour Party. He accepted that he was: "very much influenced by Konni
Zilliacus, as far as my attitude to foreign affairs was concerned."[14]

     Newens's supplementary political education was in Trotskyism; ini-
tially as a member of the Revolutionary Communist Party [RCP], then as a
member of Socialist Outlook and columnist for the Trotskyist magazine
Socialist Review.[15] He worked alongside activist Tony Cliff, as well as future
parliamentary colleagues Eric Heffer and Sid Bidwell. As a member of these
organisations he helped organise anti-Suez demonstrations, pro-Cuban
marches and many meetings opposing the Vietnam War, an issue that would
become of special interest once he had taken his seat in the House. It was
from these groups that the slogan "Neither Washington nor Moscow; but
International Socialism" emerged. Newens believed in this ideal and argued
that Britain should stand as a non-aligned socialist nation. His analysis of
the failure of Labour was that it had not created a socialist society, but instead
had accepted capitalism.[16] The strategy he prescribed was to "rule out pro-

posals for accepting capitalism. ... and provide a comprehensive alternative to the increasingly crisis-ridden conditions of our times."[17] He argued that Labour should present a manifesto that pledged to extend the nationalisation programme, create industrial democracy and institute non-profit related economic planning measures. This is representative of the Marxist-Trotskyite position adopted by a section of the Labour left-wing.

Despite the retention of his radical socialist ideals, Newens moved away from the revolutionary groups during the late 1950s. In 1958 he was adopted as parliamentary candidate by Harrow CLP and found a niche in Victory for Socialism. "I was not interested in a Trotskyist sectarian organisation... I was interested in a ginger group within the [Labour] party."[18] He became Organising Secretary and helped develop the alternative, socialist foreign policy alongside his erstwhile hero Zilliacus. Newens established himself as a prominent speaker at anti-Apartheid, anti-Vietnam War and pro-Cuba rallies and was led to show a degree of support to these causes' greatest ally: "the Soviet Union supported the struggle in South Africa, in Cuba and in Vietnam... the materials were instrumental to the[ir] just struggle."[19] However, he did not believe that the Soviet Union was simply reacting to aggression from the US, he saw aggressive policies enacted by both sides. He deplored Soviet actions in Hungary and in Czechoslovakia, and it was his opposition to Soviet 'imperialism' that drew him towards Communist Romania rather than the Soviet Union. However, he also intimated that it was the Soviet Union that was avoiding escalation in the Cold War.

Cuba was a perfect example, Newens argued, of how the Soviet leadership had actively averted war. Khrushchev halted the Cuban missile crisis, preventing escalation, while also ensuring that the Castro regime was protected from future United States interventionism. Had the roles been reversed the United States would not have acquiesced in the face of a Soviet military threat. This allowed Khrushchev to seize the moral highground and become a symbolic hero for protecting the revolution which Newens and many on the left, including Allaun, Atkinson, Driberg, Mikardo and future leader Michael Foot, supported wholeheartedly. Newens argued that this perception was reinforced by the fact that the Soviet Union did not threaten the United States with retaliation over Vietnam, a time when the United States leadership believed they were vulnerable and lagged behind in the nuclear arms race. This brought Stan Newens to the conclusion that Nikita Khrushchev was "an extremely bold and great figure".[20] However he did not argue that Britain should ally with the Soviet Union.

Newens supported the creation of a Socialist Europe as a Third Camp. The aim was to exclude the United States from determining Europe's future. He outlined this argument in 1970: "As much as I condemn the Russian intervention in Czechoslovakia, this is no excuse for our agreeing to fall in behind the American proposals for Western Europe."[21] This 'camp' could include Eastern European nations, such as the independent Communist Yugoslavia and Albania and would stand as a socialist bulwark against both poles. With this objective in mind he forged links with Romania, and Ceausescu.

Zilliacus had cultivated Tito, and it appears that Newens attempted to do the same to the Romanian leader. The Romanian Embassy invited Newens after his expression of interest in the policies of Ceausescu and he had established cordial relations with representatives of Romania in London. Newens drew up a list of highly searching questions and submitted them to the Romanian Embassy. These were refused so Newens decided not to visit. However the Romanian government insisted he should go; his questions were allowed and Newens was flown to Budapest. Newens recalled that he was concerned when he was given his own apartment, in case blackmail was attempted. To prevent being compromised he spent the nights with a chair propped under his door handle, but he found that he was safe. Ceausescu appeared willing to talk openly to Newens and allowed him to criticise the lack of democracy and failings in agrarian policy that were apparent. The point Ceausescu wished to stress was that Romania was independent of Moscow and that the Romanian government wanted to forge greater links with the West. Ceausescu, therefore, tried to link himself to a movement now emerging within the world order. This movement would become known as Eurocommunism and was perceived by those who followed the Zilliacus tradition as the fully developed form of socialism.[22] Eurocommunism also, it appears, appealed to Stan Newens. Newens concluded that Romania was "the model of a Communist country which is both socialist and fully independent."[23] Newens also argued that Ceausescu had developed a socialist foreign policy. Newens quoted the latter to this effect: "as a socialist country we lay special stress on co-operation with all socialist states... based on the principles of peaceful co-existence."[24]

This was not a new programme developed by Ceausescu; this was his way of advocating the Brezhnev doctrine. This argued that all CPSU allies were independent of Moscow, and worked from a socialist perspective in all policy arenas. The Warsaw Pact was only established to guarantee the 'socialist' nations peace and prosperity under the Soviet security umbrella. This was offered to all nations who allied with Cominform, and was only necessary because of the aggressive policy of rollback.[25] Despite this rhetoric Cominform was a rigid structure designed to control the political and economic life of the Communist bloc. However Ceausescu did show a degree of independence despite his adherence to Brezhnev's line. His was the sole voice in the Warsaw Pact to criticise the Soviet invasion of Czechoslovakia and in 1967, against the Soviet line, Ceausescu established diplomatic relations with West Germany.

Equally he refused Moscow's orders to sever ties with Israel during the Six
Day War. However Ceausescu, as Meier observed, "walked a fine line". He
gave the appearance of being independent while maintaining doctrinal purity
at home.[26] This could have been the role Brezhnev ascribed to Ceausescu to
enable him to gain support from the West. It appears therefore that Newens
unwittingly became a pro-Communist propagandist. Cominform wanted a
British MP to produce pro-Ceausescu propaganda and Newens was available,
sympathetic and willing. This was a trap that the Soviet Union prepared for
many left-wing MPs. These MPs beliefs set them apart from their colleagues
because they yearned for a world based upon peaceful co-existence and did
not mistrust Communists on principle. All that Cominform had to do was
project the right image and the sympathetic MP could be convinced that the
Communist leaders shared their ideals.

The plausibility of Ceausescu, and the beliefs of Newens, converge in
the pamphlet Talking with Nicolae Ceausescu and the preceding book entitled
Nicolae Ceausescu. These works argued that Ceausescu believed in "respect
for the rights of all peoples to self-determination."[27] The international
community, he argued, should enforce "abstention from maintaining troops
on the territory of other states without their agreement... and non-
intervention in the internal affairs of other states."[28] The global rationale
should be one of co-operation, particularly in "scientific and cultural matters".[29] These were central tenets of many of Labour's left-wing and frequently promoted in their arguments in the House of Commons and various newspaper articles.

The rebirth of independence and freedom from Moscow in Eastern Europe, Newens argued, could lead to a New World order. He argued
that Ceausescu presented:

> an overwhelming case for Britain to adopt an independent foreign
> policy. This would... bring us closer to countries like Rumania and
> would accelerate the development of the demand for the withdrawal
> of troops on both sides and ultimately the winding up of both mili-
> tary blocs.[30]

This, Newens believed, was only tenable under a Labour government.
However, he argued, this would mean that:

> A future British Labour government... [must] face the question of
> attempting to justify the foreign policy which Labour has been pre-
> pared to accept of practically uncritical support of the United States
> since the beginning of the Cold War.[31]

The real lesson that should be learned from Ceausescu, he argued, was the
ability to be independent from the superpowers.

This was a common theme of New Left arguments, though these steered away from Eastern European examples.[32] Newens had to maintain a focus on Eastern Europe due to the twin objectives of his work, developing a model of existing socialism and establishing a climate of understanding between East and West. He believed that both objectives were achievable by advertising the advancements of Ceausescu's Romania and highlighting the desire of Ceausescu to establish links to Western socialist groups. Newens' paramount objective was for the British Labour Party to adopt an internationalist perspective in world affairs and to this end he argued, on the publication of his book of Ceausescu's writings, that if the British government was to learn from the Romanian example, a socialist foreign policy could develop.[33] Newens became vilified for this work, particularly given the later revelations regarding the reality of life under Ceausescu. Anne Swingler called Newens "utterly reprehensible"[34], others were more forgiving; Frank Allaun stated "I guess we were all a little blind to the faults of these people now and then."[35] His failure to recognise the inconsistencies between rhetoric and reality indicate that his publications on Romania show a marked naivety and are evidence of Newens' deep desire to believe that Communism was evolving away from the Stalinist model.

Brezhnev attempted to persuade the world that he was a benevolent, almost democratic, socialist. Largely, this failed. Those who hoped that the Communist political system would evolve, but were suspicious of Brezhnev himself, attached their hopes to the leaders of the Soviet satellite states, or independent Communists like Cuba's Fidel Castro, as the model for a future socialist society. While not debating the degree of independence of either Ceausescu or indeed Tito of Yugoslavia, it should be noted that both nations were to retain membership of Cominform and became loyal exponents of the Brezhnev Doctrine. Their perceived independence was often employed to prove that, despite contrary evidence, the Warsaw Pact was not an empire and that the Soviet Union was no longer holding the bloc together through force. However, independence from the Soviet Union was impossible within the Warsaw Pact. However, Newens stubbornly retained his belief in Ceausescu:

> I very much defend what I did. I think Ceausescu was used as a scape-goat. I don't think Ceausescu, well the system there, was at all as bad as under Stalin. They rehabilitated people... [but] It was not a democracy and I would be very critical of it in that respect.[36]

The underlying reason for Stan Newens' support of Ceausescu was his opposition to United States foreign policy, an opposition that continued in his critique of the Gulf War and subsequent treatment of Iraq. Influenced by the arguments contained in I Choose Peace, he agreed with Zilliacus that it was the support offered to the White Army and subsequent isolation of the Soviet Union that led to the harshness of the regime. Newens saw the Russian revolution as the:

> greatest emancipatory movement of this century. [the Western allies] helped impose the conditions which made for the toughest and most inhumane people to come to the top.[37]

He argued that the Cold War was a continuation of this anti-Communist policy. Containment was the political expression of the United States leadership's desire to dominate the post-war world order: "the United States is totally intolerant of any other way than one which is based on a free enterprise system dominated by the United States."[38] This perpetuated the harsh style of the Communist regimes and forced any would-be independent socialist state to ally with the Soviet Union to enjoy the protection of her nuclear umbrella. He argued that this situation occurred throughout Latin America where the United States aided military dictators such as General Pinochet to gain power.

Newens pursued a career in opposition to United States interventionism. He formed 'Liberation', under the auspices of Fenner Brockway's 'Movement for Colonial Freedom', in order to publicise the United States oppression of socialist groups in Latin America. Newens and his left-wing colleagues made many references to these issues in the House but they were unable to alter the Atlanticist stance of the leadership. Newens argued that the international situation became far more dangerous with the end of the Cold War as, without a counter balance to American hegemony, the United States administration had a free hand to pursue her own interests. This was of great concern to Newens, particularly when the American people elected as President individuals "with the intellectual virtuosity of Reagan... or somebody like Clinton."[39]

These arguments were first introduced in Newens' pamphlet The Case Against NATO. This argued that NATO was a "potential death-trap"[40] for the nations of Europe. Agreeing with the arguments of Allaun and others, Newens stated that the correct alternative was to get all parties to the negotiating table. Only through inclusive negotiations could an agreement be reached that would ensure "an overall European guarantee against aggression by any European power and the withdrawal of foreign troops from all European countries."[41] Effectively this would mean the removal of troops under the flags of either NATO or the Warsaw Pact; Newens stressed that peacekeeping forces should be international and put in place under UN auspices. He argued that NATO was a tool of United States foreign policy and that all independent, socialist nations should withdraw from it. The basis for this argument was that no socialist, or indeed humanitarian, government could "remain a member of an international alliance which seeks to uphold exploitative systems, [they] must take an independent stand in international affairs."[42]

Arguably Stan Newens did not include the Warsaw Pact in this analysis. The Pact, in his analysis, was a purely defensive union necessitated by United States aggression. Thus, if NATO were disbanded then the Warsaw Pact could automatically be superceded by the OSCE. In Newens' analysis the United States administration was significantly flawed, had little or no regard for upholding the UN Charter, or indeed the International Declaration of Human Rights and had forced the socialist nations to adopt a bunker mentality. United States political culture, Newens argued, was fundamentally anti-socialist and therefore could not be expected to promote humanitarian values, only the ethos of competitiveness. This analysis indicates that Newens held an underlying belief that the existence of a socialist economic strategy in the Soviet Union automatically made the Soviet political and economic model more attractive. To Newens, the basis of a society must be to ensure:

> at least that you don't have people who are denied the basic needs for a satisfactory life, food, shelter, clothing and education… the Americans are against creating such a society, their administration is against creating such a society, despite paying lip service to such things.[43]

It was, therefore, the United States capitalist system that Stan Newens condemned unequivocally as exploitative. He perceived that there were socialist aspects to the Soviet Union, and was sympathetic to the ideal of a state-controlled economy. Thus he actively attempted to protect the ideal of the Soviet economic model.

This can be understood in terms of his political ideology. Newens was a fervent supporter of Clause IV of the Labour Party constitution, the abandonment of which led him to resign as an MEP in 1999. He accepted that there were elements in the Soviet Union that were not socialist and observed that the "deplorable practise of using the workers as slave labour"[44] was largely responsible for the high rate of growth. However, he supported Frank Allaun's argument that Gorbachev made a "fundamental mistake"[45] in implanting capitalism into Russia. Capitalism, Newens argued, destabilised society by removing all restraints and allowed those people who had amassed a small fortune through the black market under Brezhnev to become the new ruling class. Unlike Allaun, Newens did explain that Gorbachev had little choice but to establish capitalism in Russia, that was the penance for losing the Cold War. Newens reserved very high praise for Gorbachev, because it was he who had ended the Cold War, but criticised him for dismantling the Soviet system. The Soviet economic model was quantitatively advanced in comparison to Western capitalism. His rationale for this position echoed elements of RCP doctrine, which maintained that socialism could not be reduced purely to 'capitalism with a human face'. A socialist state could only be established after changing the ownership of the means of production. For Newens it had to be the state not, as he put it, the 158 millionaires.[46] This ideal had existed in the Soviet Union and he, like Allaun, opposed the introduction of capitalism.

Newens followed the traditions of democratic socialism, though he was influenced by Trotskyism rather than the Fabian gradualist doctrine which underpinned the Labour Party's ethos. His philosophy espoused command economics, humanitarianism, internationalism and pacifism, ideals which were fundamental to the arguments of Zilliacus, Allaun and many of the Tribunites. Equally like Zilliacus, his greatest influence, Newens refused to abandon his beliefs, even retaining his analysis of Ceausescu despite the weight of contrary evidence. However unlike Allaun and Zilliacus, Newens did find some of his ideals fulfilled and in Europe found his Third Camp. Newens maintained that only a socialist alliance of European nations could act as a counter to bipolarity, a position that led to a rift between the majority of Tribunites and Newens, Sid Bidwell, Eric Heffer and Robert Edwards. They argued that such a community would automatically adopt socialist principles and would encourage a broad alliance to develop that would naturally include many of the Communist bloc nations. This position set him apart from the Communists, and indeed the majority of the Labour left, who opposed the EU because they perceived that it stood as a capitalist club. He and the three other pro-Europe Tribunites often clashed with the rest of the Group, but now sees himself vindicated. In his view the EEC was instrumental in preventing East-West conflict during the 1970s and 1980s and, since 1990, has acted as a vehicle for greater international co-operation. As a Socialist European Group pamphlet argued: "It neither aspires to hegemony nor directs its efforts towards conflict or confrontation. This sets it apart from the two superpowers."[47]

In his political career Newens displayed, like Zilliacus, a great strength of idealism. His work during the early 1970s bears many of the hallmarks of pro-Sovietism, though he denies this. Newens argued that he was independent from all ideological groups, particularly the Communist Party, and maintained a non-aligned stance on the Cold War. The label pro-Soviet was an insult, one directed against him, and many of his allies on the Labour left, because the "anti-Socialists", in parliament and the media, could not counter their arguments.[48] The centrist Labour leadership aimed to control and undermine the left-wing's position in the party, the fact that there was a body of ideas on which they and the Communists sometimes agreed was, therefore, convenient. Newens maintained his stance despite this, as did many others, his objective was to steer the party towards adopting a socialist agenda.

The ethos of public ownership, alluded to in the wording of Clause IV, held great symbolic significance to a section of the Labour left-wing. The reticence of a Labour government to seize the 'means of production' and establish state control caused constant divisions between the leadership and the left. This encouraged some critics to attempt to show the potential benefits of a state-controlled economy, to achieve this however a practical example was necessary. Newens refused to employ the Soviet Union as many of his allies did, despite admiring aspects of the Soviet economic system. However he was encouraged to see Romania as the practical expression of his political objectives. This led him to develop a pro-Communist critique of Labour's policy. This was coupled with an analysis of foreign policy that had a clear pro-Soviet slant. He opposed the policy of the United States and the dominance of United States policy over Western Europe. Thus he became rhetorically supportive of the Soviet Union due to the zero-sum nature of the Cold War. He argued that, at times, a side had to be chosen and he found himself unable to support any aspect of United States policy. This set him apart from many critics of United States foreign policy among Labour's backbench groupings. Figures like Tony Benn and Eric Heffer put forward strong anti-Atlanticist arguments, however they avoided adopting a pro-Soviet position. Newens could not remain non-aligned and explained that there were clear reasons for his defence of the Soviet Union. His support for Cuba and Vietnam, both during and after the conflicts with the United States, indicates that he supported revolutionary socialist movements on the grounds that they were striving to establish a socialist society. The fact that the only force to defend these movements was the Soviet Union meant that Newens was drawn into the pro-Soviet orbit believing, in the words of former American Communist Ronald Radosh, that: "[t]o engage in anti-Soviet remarks served only one purpose: to detract from the fight against U.S. imperialism."[49]

Newens chief objective, however, was to establish a climate of understanding between capitalism and communism, as only within a stable world order could defence spending be cut, nuclear arms eradicated and socialism established. Adopting the methodology employed by Zilliacus, during a period of improving East-West relations, Newens attempted to put Ceausescu forward as the Communist leader who exemplified the ideals of détente. Ceausescu became Newens' model for future socialists and the exemplar of a leader with which open relations should be established. While the attempt failed, it indicates the importance the ideals of peace and socialism held to Newens. In attempting to further his objectives he appears to have devalued his arguments, by attaching his position to the policy of Ceausescu, he only succeeded in serving the Soviet leadership as a propagandist. His actions, however, should be recognised as a product of the international atmosphere. Stan Newens was not alone in attempting to ensure that the atmosphere of co-operation and co-existence became sustainable. Many of his colleagues within the pro-Soviet milieu attempted to establish less official structural links between the West and the Communist bloc.

TRADING WITH THE ENEMY

The dictum that underpinned the Cold War rationale enforced the view that any contact, which could have beneficial effects for the Soviet system, was inherently wrong. There is evidence to substantiate this perspective, particularly given that there was a political undercurrent to all contacts with representatives of the Communist governments. However it is also worth putting forward the hypothesis that, within this atmosphere of economic and cultural cross-fertilisation, capitalism was also introduced to the Soviet elite. Thus while the Soviet Union attempted to gain an ideological foothold in Western societies, it is also possible that some aspects of the Western liberal tradition also gained support among the influential elite that was to rise to the highest echelons of Soviet, and post-Communist, politics. Furthermore it should not be assumed that those who entered into the development of trading links between East and West were acting with ideological motivations. International trade is a highly lucrative business venture and therefore some of those involved will definitely have been driven purely by the opportunity to increase their profit margins. This is the context in which trading with the Communist bloc should be understood when studied outside the confines of the Cold war rationale.

Rudi Sternberg, an entrepreneur of East German extraction, was the first to recognise that there were profitable business opportunities going untapped. His success was so great that in early 1961 he was able to organise a Trade Fair in Leipzig with the support of the British Council for the Promotion of International Trade [BCPIT].[50] The BCPIT was established to promote the ideas of international equality through the free movement of trade and money. However it was described as having been "initiated by the World Peace Council, one of the principal agencies of international communism"[51] in a 1960 statement by the President of the Board of Trade. Dorril and Ramsay doubt the authenticity of this allegation, arguing that this was just another MI5 smear campaign.[52]

•   The 1961 Leipzig Trade Fair was supported by several British MPs. A cross party backbench committee was formed to promote East-West Trade, though indicatively only the left-wing members were prominent advocates of establishing trade links with the Communist bloc and subsequently faced allegations of acting as agents for the Soviet Union. Ian Mikardo became the prime mover in this organisation, assisted by Jo Richardson, his personal secretary, secretary to VfS, and future Labour MP, also prominent were Arthur

Lewis and Leslie Plummer.[53] Plummer was a close friend of Harold Wilson, a link that caused Wilson to be investigated by MI5 during the 1970s. A further three MPs can be identified as influential members of the East-West Trade Parliamentary Group, Robert Maxwell, Will Owen and John Stonehouse. Josef Frolik accused both of the latter two Labour MPs of spying on behalf of the StB. Owen was found guilty and Stonehouse was acquitted only to infer his guilt by later actions. All these MPs faced similar problems in legitimising their actions, particularly Robert Maxwell, Labour MP 1964-70 and later press baron. As Haines indicated, it was enough for Maxwell to be an émigré and Jewish,[54] as was Mikardo. Mikardo admitted that his background influenced his political career, whilst Maxwell was far more reticent regarding his past and much of his career.

Criticism of East-West trade came from the world of business, the British intelligence and security agencies and from the Labour Party leadership. Trading with the enemy was also an area of dispute between Britain and the USA during the early 1960s. The Macmillan government, acting as a precursor to Mikardo, had stressed that trade "was a way of easing international tension" and argued that US critics of British trade policy "did not appreciate Britain's [economic] needs".55 In a statement to the United States Ambassador, Foreign Office attaché Sir Patrick Reilly reminded his counterparts in the United States State Department that "HMG was under very great internal pressure to increase trade with the Soviets."[56] Reilly did not elucidate who was applying this pressure, however the cross-bench East-West Trade Parliamentary Group did include several influential Conservative MPs. John F Kennedy relaxed many regulations on East-West trade but did maintain that no American ally should supply material that would aid the Soviet arms industry. Particular concerns were raised in 1967 during the negotiation of an Anglo-Soviet contract for the supply of North Sea Oil. This contract, the United States State Department argued, would mean "the UK will have achieved almost perfect score of opposition to us in NATO on [East-West] issues."[57] Despite this governmental debate on trading with the Soviet bloc, the left-wingers who encouraged trade faced strong criticism for their unilateral action and were often accused of acting as vehicles for pro-Sovietism.

Desmond Donnelly, a staunch Gaitskellite, argued that "MPs should not accept Communist hospitality in the present state of international relations". He pursued his critique of left-wing activists by stating that "I have also felt deeply at the sight of British MPs being used as vehicles for Communist propaganda such as the East German campaign for recognition."[58] Donnelly linked two very different arguments in this criticism of these figures. Those who chose to argue the cause of recognition for the German Democratic Republic [GDR], for example, did not necessarily also encourage the establishment of trading links with the GDR. Some argued that official recognition was a necessary step towards East-West rapprochement. However, the most prominent voice in support of the GDR was that of Renee Short, who also championed trade expansion. Therefore these two issues became intrinsically linked. Official recognition of the GDR ended the debates over the German question and enabled the establishment of trading links. However rapprochement was not the objective of all the advocates of establishing trading links. Sternberg was an opportunist and arguably so were many of his colleagues. However, East-West trade became part of a movement for establishing and maintaining structural contact between Britain and the Communist bloc. This was pursued extensively during the détente era. The objective was to develop an atmosphere of trust by establishing mutually beneficial economic links between East and West. This would establish an interdependent structure that could prevent the Cold War rationale from becoming dominant once again.

It is important to provide some detail of how the trading networks were established. The chief task was introducing producers to markets. British businesses which produced goods that were in short supply in the Eastern bloc were identified. Introductions took place, and exchange visits encouraged. This allowed a working relationship to develop between trading partners.[59] The involvement of organisations such as the BSFS and the SCR indicates that it was not a purely economic venture. The records of the Birmingham branch show that there was a constant flow of Russian workers, trade unionists and officials visiting businesses in Birmingham. These visits were a feature of the expanding trade links between the West Midlands and the Soviet Union. The Birmingham BSFS provided platforms for those who visited from the Communist bloc to deliver presentations to their British counterparts. These events focussed on worker's rights, international socialism and co-operation in the peace campaign.[60] While there is no evidence that this increased pro-Soviet activity within these areas, it is clear that this was the intention. Furthermore, the funding of strikes through CPGB links was also strengthened by this contact, as it represented the ideal of international workers' co-operation. Exchange visits among workers and guided tours increased during the industrial unrest of the 1970s, and went some way to gaining funding for strikers in Britain.[61] This then was the undercurrent to non-governmental East-West trade, and goes some way to explain why it was viewed with such hostility.

It appears that political infiltration was the central objective of Cominform. The Soviet government offered substantial profits to Western companies that signed contracts to supply their markets. Particularly high profit margins were given to those companies that allowed further contact between Soviet representatives and their employees.[62] This contact involved allowing Soviet diplomats to visit and facilitating their lecturing tours of Britain.[63] British businessmen were also treated to all-expenses paid visits to the Soviet Union. These visits were organised through Progressive Tours and designed to show visitors the benefits of a communist society. It is difficult to gauge what effect, if any, these visits had. Equally it is difficult to ascertain the number of businessmen who became involved in East-West trading. Risks existed for those who did visit the Soviet Union frequently. There was the opportunity for blackmail, or more simply businessmen could be offered other ways of increasing profits, such as importing propaganda. It was these risks, which were dwelt upon by the opponents of East-West trade, that cast suspicion on Mikardo's trading network.

It is implausible to argue that those who argued for increases in East-West trade were aware of Cominform's objectives for encouraging the establishment of trading links. However those who pursued these activities cannot have been unaware of the oppositions' arguments. This begs the question of whether the supporters of increased East-West trade decided to ignore these allegations as erroneous, part of anti-Communist irrationality, or that they were aware of the risks but did not see them as an obstacle worthy of serious consideration. The latter argument is most plausible given the potential benefits of selling goods to the Communist bloc. The alternative thesis is that figures like Mikardo knew exactly what they were doing and willingly supported the Soviet Union by aiding the Communist bloc economically and allowing Cominform agents access to the British economy and society. This question is highly pertinent when studying figures who simultaneously expressed a sympathetic attitude to the Soviet Union. Ian Mikardo, the man responsible for encouraging extensive trading links to develop during the détente period, is evaluated as an example of an individual who actively pursued trading links with the Communist bloc specifically. Therefore an examination of his arguments and perspectives can shed some light upon the question of motives.

THE REBEL OF ZION

Ian Mikardo was born of Russo-Jewish refugees into the East End of London. His parents originated from Podolia in the Western Ukraine region of Russia, and were among many Jews who left Tsarist Russia to escape the pogroms. Their intended destination was America, but unscrupulous 'travel operators' took them to the nearest ship and stowed them in the hull. Finding the comparative safety of the Jewish community in London would have been a relief for Moshe and Bluma Mikardo. However, it was a harsh environment for a young boy, who could speak only Yiddish, to grow up in. In his autobiography Mikardo recalled being bullied by British children for being Jewish and by young Jews for not speaking English properly. He recalled feeling a strong sense of isolation and estrangement from the society in which he lived: "Those who go through that harrowing experience become either haters themselves or internationalists, and I had the good fortune to come out of it right side up."[64] This internationalism made him an ideal member of the Labour left whom he joined in 1945. His close friends in the House were Zilliacus, Leslie Solley and Sydney Silverman, all of whom would have shared his experiences as children. He also had close ties with the Swinglers. Anne recalled him being a true social-ist who saw no one as an enemy.[65] Beyond the political education he gained within the Jewish Community, and through the Marxist Zionist party Poale Zion which had links to the Labour Party, he also worked on Oswald Mosley's magazine Action. Mikardo shared Mosley's ideal of a centralised, state economy, though this association ended when Mosley turned to Fascism.

Mikardo entered the House as MP for Reading in 1945. Like many of his contemporary debutantes he possessed "the euphoric romantic belief that we were about to break out of the constraints of past practice and create a brave new world."[66] This feeling was to lead him to forge close ties with the left-wing. Mikardo launched oppositional motions against Bevin and shared Platts-Mills perception of the Foreign Secretary as anti-Semitic and closed-minded.[67] Mikardo was not as prominent dissident as those classified as the party's Lost Sheep, leading him to be accused by Zilliacus of "pulling his punches".[68] He allied with the Keep Left group of Bevanites, supported the Crossman Amendment, but avoided the sensitive telegrams. However Mikardo did oppose the Cold War on principle and argued that there was a personal aspect to Bevin's anti-Communism. Mikardo recalled that in 1937, the Transport and General Workers' Union [TGWU] leader and prominent CPGB member, Bert Papworth had thwarted Bevin by holding a strike calling for a shorter working day to coincide with the coronation of George VI. Mikardo argued that on meeting Molotov, Bevin "saw behind the full moon face of the Communist Foreign Minister the more rugged features of the communist Bert Papworth, and said to himself 'Lest We Forget'."[69] Mikardo believed that Bevin's attitude was a serious obstacle to co-operation between Britain and the Soviet Union and, like many of the pro-Soviet MPs, Mikardo argued that the Cold War, and its "sterile anti-Communism",[70] was an illogical course for Britain.

Initially he, and like minded rebels, hoped Bevin and Attlee could be convinced of the error of their policy. This ideal faded fast and was replaced by, firstly dogged defiance, and then a more personal crusade. Mikardo, unlike Bevan and others, was never silenced. He expressed his opposition without invoking the Soviet Union, in contrast to Stan Newens and Renee Short. However was as opposed to the Cold War as any of his pro-Soviet colleagues. Quietly, and often using the nom de plume Sagittarius, he argued for a "democratic and socialist alternative to an otherwise inevitable conflict."[71]

Mikardo moved in left-wing circles for his entire political career, pre-ferring the independence he enjoyed as a lifelong backbencher. He was a member of both Keep Left and Victory for Socialism and had input into the One Way Only pamphlet which critically examined the myth that the Soviet Union was preparing to attack. Mikardo argued that this was ludicrous as the Soviet Government lacked both the: "will and capacity for an invasion of the West."[72] Mikardo reiterated this argument when drafting the Labour Party pamphlet *Sense about Defence*,[73] the document that became party policy from 1980 to 1983.

Mikardo was a key left-wing activist on the Labour NEC. He cam-paigned for allowing the CLPs to choose their own candidates, a move that ensured a greater influx of left-wing candidates, particularly those selected as Second XI members and former Victory for Socialism activists, during the 1970s and 80s.[74] Furthermore, Mikardo was no stranger to writing policy documents, however he maintained a centre-left position in these publica-tions.[75] From his writings it is possible to gain a picture of his political posi-tion. In 1948 he published a personal manifesto detailing his prescribed party programme for the second term of office. In this he talked of estab-lishing 'economic integration' with Europe and the development of "trade with Eastern Europe".[76] While at this time the Soviet sphere was only be-coming established it is clear that his objective was some form of economic rapprochement.

Mikardo's centre-left position, and avoidance of pro-Soviet arguments, indicates that he made attempts to ensure that he was not perceived as a fellow traveller. His name was once attached to the list of supporters of the British Peace Committee [BPC], which was allied to the World Peace Council, [WPC] and reputedly a Soviet front organisation. Morgan Phillips, when investigating 'illegal' associations of party members, wrote to Mikardo asking for an explanation, making it clear that membership of such an organisation was not conducive to Labour Party membership. In reply Mikardo assured Phillips that "I have never been associated with the activities of this body."[77] Arguably, despite not being a member of the BPC, his arguments did follow the general tenets of the organisation. Mikardo maintained the stance that Britain should adopt a pro-peace policy towards the Soviet Union and declare itself independent from United States dictates. He sponsored the Committee for European Security and Co-operation [CESC] which, though not ostensibly a front organisation, was chaired by Gordon Schaffer, BSFS and CPGB executive member. This organisation was a key exponent of the pro-Helsinki perspective and maintained support for Soviet arguments on arms control and verification. Mikardo, as a recognised expert in Russian affairs, pursued numerous Soviet links and as International Secretary of the Labour Party, represented the party at various conferences. This allowed Mikardo to

pursue a pro-peace agenda on the international stage. He was a strong advocate
of East-West negotiations and asked, at 1973 CESC conference, if there was
a price too high to ensure a peaceful future.[78]

In his autobiography he recalled having links with at least one member of the WPC, Ilya Ehrenburg, a colleague on East-West Round Table
meetings. At these meetings British and Soviet delegates discussed world
issues in an open forum. The underlying agenda, Mikardo freely admits, was
to open discourse beneath governmental level on both sides. Representing
the Labour Party, though not in an official capacity, were Mikardo, Konni
Zilliacus and John Mendelson, MP for Penistone 1959-78. The latter two
Mikardo described as the most active members, due to them being "well
informed on all complexities and nuances of international politics".[79] He
admitted though that from these events a friendship between him and the
Ehrenburgs grew and that he and his wife Mary often visited their dacha in
Chechov.

Mikardo also made a stand against the 'witch hunting' of 'Reds' in
the Labour Party. He particularly fought the opposition to the endorsement
of Zilliacus, Allaun and sitting Stockport South MP Ernie Roberts as
parliamentary candidates.[80] His protest was, as he put it, that "my friends,
and doubtless myself as well, [are] being spied on as though we were crimi-
nals."[81] It is doubtful that this stand was motivated simply by self-interest.
Mikardo had input into the Tribune Group pamphlet *Party or Puppet*, which
called for greater democratisation of the candidate selection procedure[82] and
he constantly opposed the dictatorial tactics of the Gaitskell leadership. The
main thrust of his alternative, dubbed the 'Mikardo doctrine', was to allow
the CLPs, which were usually more left leaning than the party leadership, to
have responsibility for candidate selection.[83] This exemplifies the campaign,
which he launched from within Victory for Socialism, for greater power to be
bestowed upon the grassroots level of the Labour Party. However there were
also personal motivations for this campaign and it appears that it was the
campaign against his friend Zilliacus that encouraged Mikardo to lead
opposition against the dictates of Transport House.

Zilliacus was a close friend of Ian Mikardo.[84] They had faced racist
slurs together due to their names being 'non-English'.[85] Therefore it would
not be unexpected for Mikardo to show solidarity for a friend and colleague,
particularly one for whom he had a deep respect. He described Zilliacus as
"polyglot and encyclopaedic... sometimes among us but never totally with
us",[86] which appears to sum up Mikardo's opinion of Zilliacus reasonably
succinctly. Mikardo respected Zilliacus' knowledge and experience of foreign
affairs. He also respected Zilliacus' determination in standing for what he
believed in. However, Mikardo was not in total agreement with Zilliacus'
sympathetic perspective of the Soviet Union. They were colleagues and friends

but it is unlikely that they were fellow agents as Gordievsky would have us believe.[87]

. Ideologically Mikardo stood for a middle way in international affairs and was not pro-Soviet. Like Newens he maintained a staunch anti-American position and opposed the institutionalisation of the Cold War because it had turned the "[British] Foreign Office into a subsidiary and subordinate branch of the State Department".[88] This was a perspective he shared with many of his colleagues within Victory for Socialism. He was a staunch supporter of left-wing causes, speaking out against nuclear weapons, Britain's support for the Vietnam conflict and US interventionism in Latin America, particularly Cuba, El Salvador and Nicaragua. He also congratulated Ho Chi Minh on his victory over the French colonial forces; crowing in his memoirs "Ere long they were to outdo that feat of defeating a Great Power by defeating a Superpower."[89] Mikardo also promoted greater privatisation and state control over the economy. This indicates that, in essence, he did not fit with the Atlanticist dominated, revisionist party of which he was an elected member.

. In his autobiography he described his involvement in East-West trading as being based upon good business sense: "The one market in which British exporters were furthest behind their competitors from other countries was the Soviet bloc."[90] He conducted wide research both in Eastern Europe and among British businessmen and it was in Britain that he found the greatest obstacles. Those who accepted the anti-Soviet propaganda had a variety of "silly reasons"[91] for avoiding association with the Soviet Union and "were convinced by bogey tales in the tabloids that if they went on a business visit to Eastern Europe all sorts of horrendous things could happen to them."[92] Mikardo strove to alter these perceptions. He held seminars explaining how British businessmen could understand the political instruments and markets of a Communist country. These dealt with the mechanics of economic planning, how it could be analysed to make sense in capitalist terms and how these plans could be translated into a list of requirements that could be met by British industry. Importantly he also educated them in the language they should use when dealing with the Soviet industrialist. These seminars were extremely successful. Mikardo, as the East-West liaison, acted as a broker within the Communist market on behalf of many British public and private sector companies and at least one colonial trade development council. Jo Richardson was employed, within Ian Mikardo plc, as co-ordinator and maintained links with parties from both sides of the Iron Curtain. He recalled that "it was full of interest and challenge, and in the course of it we made a lot of friends and had a lot of fun."[93]

He freely admitted his contact with Communist officials but highlighted that these were not always cordial. One occasion he recalled was an experience during a visit to Hungary. He was introduced to a group of Polish Jews by his "unsmiling and rigidly Stalinist"94 interpreter. He began asking questions about what he considered the normal aspects of traditional Jewish life, activities that remained part of his own life. These questions, he was to realise, were not the questions that an English politician should be asking. This was made apparent when he heard one say to another in Yiddish, "This Englishman is by no means a gullible fool." Advantageously his knowledge of Yiddish enabled him to ask what made them think he would be a gullible fool. Once the surprise abated, the conversation was continued in Yiddish; the interpreter, probably a KGB agent employed to govern the conversation, was completely excluded.[95]

   •   He and Jo Richardson maintained Mikardo's trading network until 1977, when Ian Mikardo plc was folded. He does not give a reason for the cessation, however their age, and Richardson's failing health, were the most probable causes. While the trading network potentially benefited the Soviet government it is doubtful that this was Mikardo's intention. He maintained a critical view of the Soviet political system and, though he expressed some sympathy for the economic model, highlighted the inconsistencies between Soviet rhetoric and the reality of life under Communism. He witnessed at first hand the acute shortage of consumer goods in the Muscovite shops and was aware from his research that this shortage was deliberately created by the Government. Equally he recognised that there were vast inequalities between the living standards of the masses and of the apparatchiks, and argued that this was in stark contrast to the image projected by Soviet propaganda. More importantly he argued that the General Secretary was an unelected dictator and often argued that the Soviet society could never become socialist unless it was democratised. Therefore he supported many of the key tenets of the anti-Soviet position.

   However, he did not see the Soviet Union as a threat to Britain and argued that there was little enmity in the Soviet Union towards the West. Mikardo's role, therefore, was as a conduit of understanding between the Communist East and the Capitalist West, though we can argue that the Soviet Union saw him as facilitating a unidirectional channel of propaganda and influence. It seems that he saw the Soviet attempts to penetrate British society as having little significance and worth the risk if co-existence could be nurtured. Ironically it seems possible that Mikardo, in introducing capitalists to the Soviet Union, unwittingly introduced capitalism to the Soviet system. The quality of goods produced under capitalism were seen as far superior to Soviet-produced goods and the living standards experienced by many of the apparatchiks who visited Britain caused some to doubt in the Communist system.[96]

Mikardo enjoyed a degree of influence within the Soviet Union, and was seen as a non-aligned East-West expert within the British political system. This is indicated by the fact that, in July 1985 he advised Gorbachev during his visit to Britain. This was with the approval of both British Prime Minister Margaret Thatcher and the Soviet government. Mikardo produced a paper for Gorbachev on the effect of his glasnost and perestroika programmes on the East-West relationship and recalled that this paper was "studied and appreciated by [the] foreign ministries of both countries."[97] Therefore, during the final years of the Cold War, Mikardo attempted, arguably successfully, to act as a bridge across the ideological divide.

This was Mikardo's chief objective. He revelled in this image and maintained that he represented neither American capitalism nor Soviet Communism. Thus he attempted to position himself as a cultural bridge between East and West and described the trading network as "a little candle lighting up one corner of a dark world".[98] The ideal of establishing some form of mutually beneficial contact between the Soviet Union and Britain does not appear to be an unusual objective among the left-wing that opposed the Cold War rationale. Mikardo, like many of his left-wing colleagues, followed the rationale that if the British government refused to end East-West hostilities, then he would attempt, at non-governmental level, to plant the seeds of peaceful co-existence.

During the period of détente this activity can be seen as symptomatic of, and contiguous to, the changing international atmosphere. The trading links established were small but highly important aspects of the new climate of understanding that was developing at the governmental level. While the activity and the links established were not confined purely to the period identified as that of détente, they symbolised the kind of future these Labour left-wingers desired. Their ideal world order was one where the Western capitalist accommodated, co-existed with and learned to understand the Communist. Mikardo was a highly successful businessman, well educated in the capitalist world. He argued for economic planning and state control, as practised in the Soviet Union, and promoted the perception that the Soviet Union was not an imperialist and expansionist power but merely practising a policy of protectionism. This analysis was used to explain why the Soviet leadership saw that the degree of control over the Russian people and the citizens of its satellites was necessary.

Mikardo appears to have hoped that as détente developed, alongside interlinkages at the non-governmental level, this 'bunker mentality' would be relaxed. This was espoused by the Brezhnev doctrine, and later expressed in terms of glasnost and perestroika. Mikardo supported these initiatives and attempted to alter the climate of opinion towards the Soviet Union to accommodate these changes. This was the mission pursued by many within this political strand. The pro-Soviet left particularly, and many within the broad left of the Labour Party, supported the ideals of the Brezhnev doctrine and hoped that the Soviet Union could develop in line with that ideal. Importantly they recognised that this could not be achieved in an atmosphere of hostility. Therefore some MPs undermined the Cold War rationale by actively attempting to improve East-West relations. Détente offered the perfect opportunity for this and Mikardo seized this moment with alacrity, creating sustainable trading links between East and West. The international atmosphere was to thwart his hopes and the objective he had worked towards was to fail in the face of renewed and invigorated anti-Communism. This meant that the campaign would be forced exclusively into the extra-parliamentary sphere, a level at which extensive links were developed by many of Mikardo's left-wing colleagues during the period of détente.

'RED RENEE'

While Mikardo, assisted by fellow left-wingers in the East-West Trade Parliamentary Group, was responsible for the creation of trading links, others on the Labour benches were constantly striving to create a more favourable environment for the success of their efforts. Several of these MPs were accused of acting as agents at some stage or another. This is particularly the case with Will Owen, who faced espionage charges in 1971, and Arthur Bax, who also allegedly worked for the Czech Embassy. Bax was a prominent advocate of establishing East-West trade links. However, evidence suggests that this was only one aspect of his pro-Soviet activities. Pincher stated that as a result of a conversation with Lord George Brown, who at the time was Deputy leader of the Labour Party, Brown testified that Bax had admitted passing on information regarding the party and its members.[99] This appears to indicate that those MPs who advocated East-West trade, and were frequent visitors to the Soviet Union, were seen as confidential contacts of the KGB regardless of whether they ever ran 'errands' or not.

There is no evidence whatsoever to suggest that either Ian Mikardo or Renee Short were agents or contacts. However they were probably perceived as assets by their Soviet contacts, particularly Renee Short who appears to have been a devout pro-Soviet sympathiser and activist, more so than Mikardo. At present Short's papers are inaccessible and she is unwilling to discuss this issue, so a picture of her pro-Soviet activities can only be created by looking at her scant writings in the press and the affiliations she pursued during her political life. This dearth of information on Short is unfortunate as her involvement in pro-Soviet organisations and her constant pursuit of pro-Soviet objectives, indicates that she was a key figure within the pro-Soviet strand and would have been viewed as an important asset by the British political observers in Moscow.

＞   During her parliamentary career Short served as Vice Chairperson of the Parliamentary East-West Trade Group, Chairperson of both the British-GDR Parliamentary Group and the British-Soviet Parliamentary Group, and President of the British-Romanian Friendship Association. She was also listed as a sponsor for the League for Democracy in Greece and the CESC. Evidence indicates that she joined other similar organisations without holding an executive post, she was frequent speaker at BSFS events as well as a variety of conferences that supported the Soviet policy line.[100] It is equally apparent from the causes that she espoused in the House that Short willingly promoted arguments which furthered the aims of the Soviet Union, particularly trade, rapprochement, and nuclear disarmament. Short was probably a clearer case of a fellow traveller, if we were to employ this definition, than many of the left-wingers who pursued pro-Soviet activities during the détente era. Her arguments transcend those of Zilliacus and Allaun, though the latter supported her on a number of issues. She would have been aware that her consistently pro-Soviet stance was unpopular, however opposition did not deter her in the slightest.

＞   Short collected allies throughout her career. James Lamond cited her as an influence[101] and during debates when she was prominent she gained support from most of the figures identified as having sympathies with the Soviet bloc. However Short stands out within this group because she maintained a explicit pro-Soviet perspective and on every occasion upon which she contributed to a debate on an issue that would effect the Soviet Union or her allies she argued the pro-Soviet case.

It is significant that those who viewed her with highest regard were within the pro-Soviet coterie while those in mainstream politics saw her, at the very least, as radical. Former Labour MP Nigel Spearing, on hearing her name, laughed saying "ah yes Red Renee".[102] In contrast, Philip Crees, Chairman of the Birmingham BSFS 1966-94, described her as "one of the more progressive types."[103] Audrey Wise, a fellow Coventry MP 1974-2000 and Short's replacement on the NEC as Womens' Section representative, recalled her as: "a good friend and devout supporter of the oppressed in Britain and abroad. She spoke common sense... We sometimes followed different causes but I miss her support."[104] Equally indicative is the lack of recognition she received within the Transport and General Worker's Union [TGWU] and its monthly paper The Record. Given that this voiced the moderate stance of leader Jack Jones, alongside the Union's sponsored MPs George Brown, Arthur Creech-Jones and John Silkin, it seems unsurprising that no room could be found for the opinion of Renee Short. The only clear link between Short and the TGWU is that the Union paid her election expenses.

It should be noted that Renee Short was not however a single-issue MP. In fact during her career she promoted many domestic causes. These were social issues, particularly those which concerned women. Her only major publications dealt with the condition of long-term prisoners and women and children's health issues. Alongside her pro-Soviet affiliations she was also President of the Nursery Schools Association and Action for the Newborn from 1988, a member of the British Medical Association, the Campaign for Nursery Education and the Women's National Cancer Control Campaign, acting as Vice President of the latter. We can, there-fore, view her as an active campaigner on behalf of many causes and she used her parliamentary role as a promotional platform for them all. To gain an insight into her broader ideals it is useful to study some of the causes to which she lent her name. Short was a champion of the pro-Abortion lobby, sponsoring the 1967 Abortion Act. Equally she was scandalised by the lack of representation for women in parliament and admits "harangu[ing] meetings on this issue."[105] Equally, her publication on the rights for long-term prisoners argued for greater stress on rehabilitation, stating that family contact should be maintained through conjugal visits and that prisoners needed educating in order that they be equipped to cope on their return to society.[106] This provides the picture of Short as a staunch egalitarian and campaigner on behalf of minorities and the socially excluded.

However, she often used the Soviet Union as a comparative case study for her arguments. For example in the course of the work on prison-ers she stated that "British prisons had been shown to be unconstructive and less humane than those in other more progressive countries.107 Though this inference is somewhat veiled, on other occasions the com-parison between British and Soviet society was made much more explicit. To ascertain the basis of her pro-Sovietism, we need to look at the pro-Soviet causes Short pursued and the content of her arguments, which changed little over her years in parliament. This will generate some conclusions as to the nature and background of Renee Short's sympathies.

From her arrival in parliament in 1964, the chief objective of Short's argument was to encourage co-existence between East and West. How-ever, unlike many of her left-wing colleagues, Short did not promote rap-prochement from a pacifist stance. Short's position was that the peoples of Eastern Europe were not the 'evil Communists' that anti-Soviet propa-ganda inferred but that they sought co-operation and a cessation to the atmosphere of mistrust. Short opposed any policy that could damage the fragile East-West relations, arguing for the greatest possible gains to the Soviet side attainable from successively anti-Communist governments of either political colour. She gained some minor achievements as a member of Labour's NEC. However, NEC policy directives were seldom adopted by

Labour when in power and therefore Short took her campaign directly to the House.

, It is unknown when she joined the British-GDR Friendship Society, however James Lamond recalled that, when he entered parliament in 1970, Short was already a key figure within many of the parliamentary friendship groups. It is clear that the GDR was of special interest to her and Short opposed moves to encourage defection. On the 6th December 1965 she revealed that a letter from one of the West German Embassy staff in Nicosia had been passed to a group of East German artists. This stated, in Short's words, that "if these people did not wish to return to what the writer called the "Soviet Occupation Zone" of Germany they could go to the British, French, American or German Embassies for help."[108] Before she was able to give her account of the ramifications of such actions, the Speaker interrupted Short. This led her to put a similar question forward for written answer seven days later. Her question asked what measures were being made to improve relations between the UK and the GDR. The beleaguered Walter Padley[109] gave her a one-word reply: "None."[110] This did not deter her.

The issue of official recognition for the GDR was constantly high on her agenda. Criticising her own Secretary of State for Foreign Affairs, George Brown, for not following his resolution of the 1961 Conference, she called the absence of recognition "ridiculous", arguing that the ruling rationale forced the Government to "pay lip service to what the West Germans say about East Germany."[111] This criticism was employed particularly when arguing for an increase in trade with the GDR. Short argued that this would be enhanced by a visit from Herr Soelle, East German Minister for Foreign Trade. A visit prevented due to the political status of the GDR. The British Government, she argued, "should not allow political prejudices to interfere with our trade."[112] Short also argued that it was the FDR government that had ensured that the GDR remained excluded in order to enhance West German economic interests. Britain, she argued, was "hamstrung by the idiotic Hallstein doctrine and... over-conscientious in keeping to its rules".[113] The doctrine did not stop the FDR trading British made goods with the GDR and enjoying the profits, she argued. The Labour Government's intransigence over this issue was anathema to everything Short believed in. She stated that the policy: "prevent[ed] peace-loving friends from East Germany coming here".[114] It is interesting that she made no reply to George Brown's rebuttal "what inhibits peace-loving friends from East Germany coming here more than the existence of the Wall for which they are responsible."[115]

Short reiterated these pro-GDR arguments on several occasions. Support came from Will Owen and Arthur Lewis. Owen was a champion of East-West trade throughout his parliamentary career and he also involved himself first hand. Therefore, it is arguable that Owen, like Mikardo, had an interest in receiving governmental sanction and, where possible, enhancing conditions to further profit. It appears that Short pursued this issue purely in the name of improving relations between Britain and the Soviet bloc.

An early example of her campaign to improve relations with the Soviet bloc was Short's interest in the impending visit of Alexei Kosygin, Soviet Prime Minister. Short encouraged the Prime Minister Harold Wilson to speed up the process stating that:

> we on these benches and the majority of people in this country long passionately for progress on two aspects on which we are fully committed, namely a nuclear-free Europe and a non-proliferation treaty.[116]

This argument is similar to those of the Zilliacus tradition, which argued that every effort should be made to get Soviet representatives to the negotiating table and, once there, to make every effort to accommodate them. Short, however, seems to have taken this activism one stage further by actively taking part in encouraging contact between the British and their East European counterparts. It can be argued that her objective was to alter the perception of the Soviet world; what Pat Litherland described as putting "the cardboard Russians back in 3D."[117]

Short also keenly opposed the entry of Britain into the Common Market; this, she argued, would create a further bloc that excluded the Soviet Union:

> the major problem which faces us is not whether to go into the Common Market but to get a settlement of the political issues which divide Europe, an agreement on the frontiers between the two Germanys and a security conference between East and West. This cannot be done without the Soviet Union.[118]

Her analysis of each issue agreed unequivocally with that of the Soviet Union and its allies. No matter what issue she addressed, Short exhibited either devout support or a notable silence. Her silence, on Czechoslovakia for example, was striking because, despite the fact that her ideals should have led her to oppose the actions of the Soviet leadership, she refused to denounce the Soviet Union. This does raise the question of what led Short, a democratic socialist, to support a nation whose political and foreign policy objectives appeared to be opposed to every principle her party stood for. Short, like many sympathisers of Communist regimes, held the belief that "[a]ny criticism of Russia, any candid discussion of Soviet problems... was to aid the Revolution's enemies."[119]

The roots of Short's pro-Soviet perspective remain a matter for speculation as there is little recorded detail on her political ideas. Short produced one report for the NEC entitled 'Socialist Philosophy'. This un-published article encouraged moves towards worker's control, state plan-ning and greater social equality. This gives the impression that she held some Marxist tendencies. This is reinforced by her recommendation to the party that Labour should "carry out socialist policies and not allow itself to be swayed by the interests of free enterprise".[120] In this document she ap-pears to have fitted with the Bennite tradition, but, unlike Benn, her pro-Soviet sympathies guided her perception of foreign affairs. Short was also a prominent campaigner for sexual equality, and was a tireless campaigner for child-care facilities to be made available in the workplace. With Audrey Wise, she argued that the House of Commons should recognise that women MPs had family commitments and should set working hours in a way compatible with women's lifestyles.[121] Short also devoted a significant amount of time to the pro-Abortion campaign, and argued that women were entitled to equal pay and equal opportunities in the workplace, while being recognised as having different needs. It is for this work that many of her colleagues like to remember her.

It is difficult to define Renee Short's personal principles, and how the pro-Soviet perspective fitted into her philosophy. Her speeches and scant writings show a belief in social equality through proletarian control. How-ever, she did not elucidate what form of government she favoured. It ap-pears that she held a belief in the Labour Party as a working class representa-tive, and maintained that the party could adopt a pivotal role in ending the Cold War, a view she shared with many of her colleagues within the pro-Soviet left. This was an illusory ideal that often made her appear estranged from the Labour Party's broad church of traditions. Despite this Short did enjoy a degree of influence within the party; having a seat on the NEC from 1970 to 1981. However, she exerted little real influence over policy. Throughout her career Short worked consistently with a dual agenda and was instrumental in promoting the arguments of the Soviet Union in the House and within the party. She expressed her pro-Soviet arguments in such a way that indicates that they were ideals to which she herself was firmly committed.

From her position of limited power, Short did her best to ensure that organisations within the pro-Soviet orbit were able to recruit party members. To this end Short led a campaign within the NEC to end the policy of proscription. She highlighted that two organisations, the Labour Research Department [LRD] and the Medical Aid Committee for Vietnam [MACV], enjoyed substantial support among party members. Short cam-paigned for de-proscription of the MACV by using the LRD as an example of the inconsistency between rules and reality. Her proposal was that the rules either required tightening or that proscription should be officially abolished. In an Organisational Sub-Committee meeting of 6th December

1971 Short revealed the scale of membership shared by the Labour Party and the LRD and asked what should be done. Subsequent investigation found that the majority of Trade Unions were affiliated to the LRD therefore expulsion, the prescribed response, could not be pursued. At the Sub-Committee meeting 7th February 1972 it was decided that proscripion of the LRD was no longer tenable. The following year Short, as Vice Chair of the NEC, demanded that the whole list of proscribed organisations be put forward for review. The report found that many Union leaders and left-wing MPs were ineligible for membership. The only viable cnclusion remained to abandon proscription.[122]

While this conclusion was common sense the fact that the issue was raised by Short, a veteran of at least five of these organisations, is important. In essence she appears to have advertised her pro-Soviet affiliations and dared the party to dismiss her. Short had a strong position as Women's Section representative on the NEC and enjoyed the support of a majority of an Executive that included Driberg as chair, Allaun, Joan Maynard, Mikardo and Jo Richardson. Furthermore Trade Union leaders such as Ken Gill, General Secretary of the Technical and Support Section [TASS] of the AEUW, Ron Hayward and Alex Kitson, both of the TGWU, also supported various proscribed organisations and shared Short's pro-Soviet sympathies. Mikardo also supported the motion on the grounds that a socialist party should not fight totalitarianism by restricting the political affiliations of its members. Therefore at the 1973 Conference, a broad left-wing consensus emerged in favour of Short's motion.

- The abandonment of proscription quantitatively increased the membership of various pro-Soviet organisations. The pro-Soviet left-wingers were now able to affiliate and pursue the aims of pro-Soviet organisations without fear of the sort of reprisals that Zilliacus and Platts-Mills had faced. Following this decision James Lamond became Vice President of the World Peace Council [WPC], the parliamentarian membership of the League for Democracy in Greece increased exponentially and William Wilson became President of the British-Soviet Friendship Society. Despite the Home Office's fear of such organisations, there were no harmful effects to national security. The MPs who chose to support organisations like the WPC were a minority and the organisation did not gain any significant influence. However it did give these organisations a degree of credibility and lent their events a higher profile. This was, arguably, Short's objective when campaigning against proscription.

The fact that she did not hide her affiliations shows that Short saw nothing covert, or subversive, about her activities. In fact there appears, as with James Lamond, a sense of pride in her stance and the activities that were associated with pro-Sovietism. Short appears to have subscribed to the notion of 'no enemies to the left' and lived by this principle. This is indicated by the fact that when Labour Monthly published eulogies to Rajani Palme Dutt, out of all the Labour MPs who contributed, hers was the most affectionate. Julius Silverman and Fenner Brockway, both of whom were left-wingers who pursued similar arguments to Short, praised Dutt's devotion to duty but highlighted the different courses they had chosen. Short appears not to have perceived any difference. Short believed that she and Dutt were engaged in the same struggle:

> It is always sad when a devoted socialist and a staunch comrade dies. Raji's whole life was dedicated to the struggle for a better society for all working people, wherever they lived, whatever their race or religion. He was a fiery, determined speaker, a man of passion and conviction as I remember him.[123]

    In furthering her campaigns for racial and sexual equality and proletarian economic control she pursued every route available to her. Her methodology was close to Dutt's as Short also lent her support to the Soviet Union because her leaders espoused socialist principles. It is unfortunate that we do not know more about her influences, however arguably her strand of thought was infused with the idealistic principles inherent in the work of the Webbs and G D H Cole. She perceived the Soviet Union as a socialist nation and maintained that Communist society was governed with a socialist ethos, this perception had been established through several guided tours of Communist bloc nations: "[m]y visits to the Soviet Union extend over many years from the late 1950s and early 1960s and they have shown me how warm hearted the Soviet people are".[124]

    Short published several favourable reports following her visits. Combining her interest in child welfare she researched the education system in the Soviet Union and published her findings in the Guardian newspaper. Though she did not observe anything radically different from the domestic educational system it is obvious that she was highly impressed. She particularly highlighted the "real attempt to inculcate social and moral responsibility at every level."[125] In Soviet schools, older, more able students provided assistance to their younger peers she told the reader. This, she argued, helped to create a society founded upon collective responsibility where: "the strong must help the weak."[126] She refused to accept that the reality of Soviet society was markedly different to the model shown to visitors as it appears that Short, as an individual who needed to believe in the existence of a socialist society, could not accept these notions.

    Equally it was the Soviet Union, she argued, that had defeated fascism, and so should be recognised as a worthy anti-imperialist ally of the British Labour Party.[127] Short opposed the post-war vilification of the Soviet

Union and attempted to change public perceptions of, and governmental policy towards, Communism. Her methodology was to encourage the development of cultural links as these "between young people, are among the best ways of pursuing a fruitful and friendly policy."[128] As Short openly stated, she actively pursued this goal through "voluntary organisations."[129] Opponents of Communism classified these organisations as fronts for Soviet policy but this was not the view held by those who opposed the Cold War rationale. Short did oppose that rationale and acted accordingly. It appears that her activities were aimed towards the ultimate goal of co-existence, a goal that was anathema to most of her parliamentary colleagues. This did not deter her from her mission and she actively enlisted like-minded individuals to her cause.

It is likely that she was viewed by Soviet diplomats as an asset, and possibly an agent. How she viewed herself is unknown. Short's goal, like Dutt's, was to create a socialist society in Britain and help establish an international order based upon peaceful co-existence. Her affiliations appear to be the product of a degree of idealism and can, in some cases, appear highly questionable given her position within the Labour Party. This illustrates the fact that the pro-Soviet perspective was developed by individuals whose perceptions differed from the opinions that were popularised during the Cold War era. Short held the perception that the Soviet Union was not an enemy but a beleaguered nation isolated by an antagonistic world order. She and others offered their support to the Communist bloc, despite the perceptions of others and with little regard for the reality of life under Communism. Her ultimate ojective was to alter the prevailing climate of opinion. She hoped that her position of influence would enable her, in tandem with her colleagues in parliament and the pro-Soviet organisations, to establish sustainable links that would ensure that Communism was understood and that the Soviet Union was drawn out of isolation and into the world order.

DÉTENTE FROM BELOW

The three MPs studied in this chapter characterise the types of activity that developed alongside détente. These activities can be broadly defined as firstly, promoting the new policy directives being introduced within the Warsaw Pact nations and thus encouraging political leaders to adjust their perceptions of the Communist bloc, secondly, the creation of institutions that reflected the thaw in governmental relations and lastly, expanding the work of organisations which pursued cultural and political East-West links. Pursuing these objectives shows that there was an iconic link between these individual's ideas and the Soviet model of socialism, whether that was in the current form or an abstract version. These MPs believed wholeheartedly in the process of establishing bipolar communication and devoted a large proportion of their career activities to furthering this process. Mikardo presciently described this as lighting a candle. Thee MPs held the view that they were instrumental players on the front line of the defence of humanity, acting to avoid war and pursue interdependence through cultural and economic links and the exchange of political ideas.

It is equally important to note that each of these three cases possessed differing political beliefs. While it appears that Short was quite devoutly pro-Soviet, both Mikardo and Newens were critical of the regime and refused to offer unequivocal support for the Soviet socialist model. Therefore it is useful to explore why these three became prominent within the pro-Soviet milieu during the détente era. Stan Newens' ideas developed from a Trotskyist analysis. His ideal, however, was a global socialist revolution by democratic means. During the Cold War this was impossible and, according to Newens' analysis, the nation that opposed socialism to the greatest extent was the United States, not only because it stood as the capitalist bastion but because it was pursuing a foreign policy that acted against socialist regimes. Détente offered the opportunity for an independent course that would threaten United States hegemony over the non-Communist sphere of influence. While Newens harboured deep mistrust of the Soviet leadership he had some sympathies for the economic system and he argued that this must be married to a democratic political system and an open society. This, he argued, had been achieved in Romania. Thus Newens was drawn towards the ideas emanating from the Communist bloc because he opposed American influence over Europe and supported the ideals of the socialist state. As was the case with many socialists who rejected the Soviet model, but sought a practical model for their ideals, Newens was drawn into supporting an alternative revolutionary state after Ceausescu had proclaimed that he shared Newens' values. As Hayden and Lynd found in various Communist states, "we call ourselves in some sense revolutionaries. So do they. After all, we identify with the poor and oppressed. So do they."[130] Ceausescu promoted socialism, peace and co-operation. Newens was led to believe that Ceausescu was independent from Cominform's ideological and political control and that he represented the model for future Communist leaders. Romania was not the only focus Newens' arguments. He also supported Castro's Cuba, Ho Chi Minh's Vietnam and Ortega's El Salvador. Therefore he appears to have been constantly in search of a socialist model throughout his career. The models he supported all shared certain characteristics; they were in conflict with the United States and they espoused revolutionary socialist credentials. Ironically it was in the European Union that he would eventually find his political ideal, after apparently losing faith in revolutionary socialism completely.

In contrast, Ian Mikardo, who also supported the ideal of the socialist society, had little sympathy for revolutionary doctrines. In his case part of
his sympathetic outlook was due to racial solidarity. As was the case with
Julius Silverman, a lifelong supporter of the SCR and Vice-President 1987-
94, his roots were in the Russian Jewish community. Mikardo had supported
the ideals of the 1917 revolutions and developed an analysis of Soviet history similar to that of Zilliacus. Mikardo recognised that the leadership was
driven by a bunker mentality, but he rejected the thesis that there were socialist aspects to the Soviet model. His aim was to draw the two opposing
ideologies together, establish some framework for co-operation and build
the foundations for an interdependent future. This would negate the need
for anti-Soviet propaganda and anti-Russian attitudes in Western society,
lead to a reduction in defence spending and reduce the chances of war. Mikardo
saw himself as a conduit of understanding between the two contrasting
economic and political systems, not as an agent for one side or the other.
This was a position that Newens also attempted, unsuccessfully, to carve out
for himself.

Renee Short appears the most profoundly pro-Soviet of these cases
and her activities and arguments are more consistent with Platts-Mills's
approach to opposing the Cold War. Her objectives were the establishment
of a socialist society based upon sexual and racial equality, public ownership and workers' control, none of which was tenable in the Cold War
atmosphere. The vehicle for establishing this society was the Labour Party
and, from her position on the NEC, Short attempted to alter the party's
political objectives while also attempting to establish an atmosphere of
bipolar co-operation and co-existence. Her vehicles for achieving the latter
goal were the 'voluntary organisations', which espoused the establishment
of cultural links and encouraged contact between East and West at the
individual level. Through her role within these organisations she would be
invited to visit Eastern Europe and encouraged to provide reports on her
visit. The 'guided tour' she received would have helped to convince her
that the Soviet Union did indeed represent the model for her political objectives and encouraged her to protect the regime from her anti-Communist enemies.

While the motivations of these three MPs vary, their objectives were
similar and their methods had a similar result. They shared the objective of
wanting to alter the anti-Communist climate of opinion and sought to institutionalise détente within British political and economic life. The result
would be that the pro-Soviet cause gained some prominence, though among
a minority, and that some Labour left-winger's socialist ideals became linked
to the future of the Soviet Union. This was not the result Stan Newens or
Ian Mikardo wanted to achieve. Their support for the Soviet Union, pursued

through extra-parliamentary activities became linked to their arguments for socialism. Therefore pro-Soviet activities, and their concomitant arguments for establishing East-West links, became established as a tradition within the Labour Party's ethos. This tradition had gained prominence among the pro-Soviet left-wing during the 1945-50 parliament and continued as a tradition within Victory for Socialism. It was this link, which was perceived as fundamental by some on the left, hat led to the development of a campaign to protect the Soviet Union.

During the period of détente British socialists explored new ways of undermining the Cold War rationale. These methods would be the way forward as the stakes were raised once again during the Second Cold War. As détente collapsed, and a renewed ideological determination emerged in the United States and the Soviet Union, pro-Soviet activity took on a renewed impetus. The links that were established under détente survived into the next decade and would be exploited by the pro-Soviet sympathisers, and their Soviet contacts, to encourage deeper forms of pro-Soviet activity. Within the period characterised as the second Cold War the McCarthy-style fears and allegations became almost an acknowledged truism. A minority of Labour MPs promoted Soviet policy within the British parliament and on the world stage. They became apologists for the aggressive foreign policy of the Soviet Union and, more importantly, exchanged political information with their Soviet counterparts. Equally party policy reflected a complete rejection of the anti-Soviet rationale and mirrored the arguments of the pro-Soviet tradition. Perhaps for a brief period the pro-Soviet MPs were happy within their own party; however they were so far from attaining real political influence that extra-parliamentary activity became the only avenue through which they could pursue their goals.

6
RAISING THE STAKES

The Second Cold War

Détente had offered the left-wing, and in particular the pro-Soviet strand, the opportunity for co-existence to develop between the communist and capitalist blocs. However, by the end of the 1970s, the international atmosphere reverted to one of bi-polar hostility. As Cox outlined, this was the result of the Soviet Union "on the march"[1] and a United States Presidency renewing its resolve to contain communism and exploit the weaknesses of an increasingly overstretched Soviet imperialism.[2] The United States increased anti-Communist intervention in Latin America while the Soviet Union declared military rule in Poland and established a puppet government in Afghanistan.[3] This led to the period 1979-87 being referred to as the Second Cold War.[4] The hawkish New Right alliance of Reagan and Thatcher abandoned the reconciliatory stance of their predecessors; a policy that both leaders argued had left a void in Western security of which the Soviet leadership had taken advantage.[5] Soviet actions were used by the United States and British governments to prove that the New Right anti-Communist defence policy was the correct course and western propaganda characterised the Soviet Union as an 'evil empire' and the Cold War as an 'irreconcilable conflict'.[6] A decisive war seemed inevitable.

In Britain the collapse of détente led to the re-emergence of a deep fear of nuclear war[7] and an increase in anti-Cold War activism among the pro-Soviet left-wingers. However the lack of influence over British policy meant that their objectives were limited to influencing opinion and establishing interdependent East-West links beneath governmental level. The internationalist's agenda involved attempting to encourage co-existence between the Soviet Union and the West through non-governmental activity. Various pro-Soviet cultural organisations attempted to maintain unofficial dialogue and create an atmosphere of mutual understanding between Britain and the Soviet Union. The central aim was to limit the deterioration of East-West relations further and to prevent the outbreak of war.[8] The increased hostilities, coupled with a need to counter the official antagonism, meant that the attraction of organisations that were disposed to preventing conflict and promoting co-existence increased. The pro-Soviet left attempted to gain wider support among Labour Party members, alter aspects of the party policy and lead the attack against the Thatcher-Reagan alliance in parliament. These MPs publicised, but failed to popularise, the pro-Soviet analysis of international developments. This increased activism was facilitated by the Labour Party's leftward shift which led the pro-Soviet left-wingers to feel that they were no longer polarised from the majority.

At Labour Party Conferences the left-wing Trade Unions held a considerable level of influence. This led to what Shaw described as the "paralysis of leadership."[9] This was exacerbated by constitutional reforms within the party, spearheaded by the Campaign for Labour Party Democracy [CLPD], which were designed to redistribute power away from the PLP and award it to the rank and file.[10] These reforms gave power to a left-wing dominated NEC and a broadly left-wing Union leadership. The power of the left-wing over the parliamentary party is the subject of some debate, but the fact that the left agenda became party policy and that this was diametrically opposed to the stance of the Callaghan-Healey leadership is indisputable.

Thorpe highlighted the importance of the Trade Unions in shifting the party's stance. He argued that in supporting the constitutional reforms the Union leaders aimed to pay Callaghan back for his conservative responses to the 1978-9 economic crisis.[11]This should not be understood, however, as the left-winger's 'fit of pique'. The left-wing fight for control was a coherent and organised attempt to ensure that the party leadership adhered to 'socialist principles' and that no future leader could betray the party by allying with the forces of capitalism. This could only be achieved by giving control to the workers, the party rank and file, and forcing the leaders to act as spokespersons for their agenda. Between 1980 and 1983 this was almost achieved. Alan Sapper recalled that the left-wing Trade Union grouping, which was given the title of the Labour Co-ordinating Committee, could virtually set the agenda of the party. The left-winger's agenda was determined in meetings between left-wing Union leaders and their colleagues in parliament. The alliance of left-wingers in the parliamentary party, the NEC and at Conference ensured that the left was able to control the party manifesto and policy of the PLP, though this was not entirely driven by the Unions as Sapper claimed.[12] The centre-right of the party was unable to retain its traditionally dominant role over policy and accepted as leader Michael Foot, Tribunite and anti-nuclear campaigner. Arguably, whoever had become leader following Callaghan's resignation in 1980 would have had little choice but to accept unilateralism, this was one of the policies that the left had been attempting to force onto the agenda since the 1950s.

The left-wing of the late 1970s and 1980s have often been compartmentalised into hard and soft divisions.[13] This characterisation is somewhat awkwardly defined as being between the Bennite hard left, which would include the pro-Soviet strand, and the soft left characterised by Foot.[14] This is a largely erroneous description. Seyd has characterised Labour's left as:

> [M]ore than a set of political attitudes: it is also a distinct culture, a way of life and an approach to politics… someone from the Labour left is an 'outsider' who does not mix easily with the political establishment… The term 'comrade' is part of the language… The singing of 'The Red Flag' is symbolic…[15]

More importantly the left was not cohesive and largely avoided developing a serious alternative to the party's centrist position. Equally there was never an alternative left-wing leader waiting in the wings to take control of the party. The perceived contest between left and right for the deputy leadership in 1980 is a myth, left-wing support, and even that of the pro-Soviet fringe, was divided between Benn and John Silkin.[16] The left included a wide range of traditions, ideals and perspectives but lacked a clear, alternative agenda.

Despite this lack of unity and purpose the left was able to ally in support of the agenda adopted by the party at the 1980 Conference. This alliance was built around broad socialist objectives. Key issues included a neutralist stance on the Cold War, unilateral nuclear disarmament and the alternative economic strategy,[17] though debates raged within NEC policy subgroupings which were often extremely heated and highly divisive. Publicly, however, the appearance prevailed that the left was united, had a common body of ideals which had been translated into a Manifesto and had a leader. This perception was enhanced by the left's consensus of opposition to the Thatcher government's political agenda. A particular theme around which the left built this consensus was anti-Americanism. This allowed the promotion of a foreign and defence policy that could be accused of being pro-Soviet and that would mirror aspects of the programme put forward by the CPGB.[18] The consensus on this anti-American, neutralist stance is evident in the many articles written by profoundly anti-Soviet left-wingers during this period.

-   Anti-Americanism had been a tradition of Bevanism and a feature of Tribune articles and editorials, however during the second Cold War anti-Americanism reached paranoiac proportions. Tony Benn, Eric Heffer and Stan Newens were particular critics of Atlanticism and accused the Thatcher government of subservience on several occasions. Benn described the 'independent nuclear deterrent' as a tool of the United States that acted as a "ball and chain limiting [Britain's] capacity to play a more positive role in the world."[19] His fear of United States objectives was far more expansive:

> They are trying to transform the troublesome natives of Britain… into the subjects of a new imperialism… represented by the sort of federal Europe they would like to see created.[20]

While many left-wingers' fears were not expressed in such dramatic terms there was consistent opposition to deepening the 'special relationship' and a fear that Britain had become a subordinate partner, or, in Allaun's terms, a stooge in foreign and defence matters. Synthesising the mood eloquently, Ken Livingstone observed that: "US intelligence had managed to… achieve an almost complete dominance at the Ministry of Defence".[21]

The left-wing agenda therefore tied together a rejection of monetarism and Atlanticism. But, beyond these key tenets, divisions over policy alternatives were prevalent. Equally the left-wing's oppositional stance to Thatcherism attained a consensus across Labour's backbenches and at Conference, but it failed to gain mass support among the electorate.[22] Crushing defeats both in parliament and in elections made it clear that the parliamentary road for change was closed to the left, possibly forever.

This chapter is a study of the last battle waged by the pro-Soviet strand of the Labour Party. The MPs who acted as the frontline of opposition to the renewed policy of roll-back developed a much closer working relationship with the Soviet Union than their predecessors. This involved becoming a conduit of understanding, attempting to build personal bridges between the opposing political systems and developing common ground from which co-existence could develop. The highpoint for MPs establishing themselves in the role of conduit was the period of the Second Cold War, though the relationships that were established were founded upon structures that had been put in place since 1947 and which had been strengthened particularly during the decade of détente. However the increased requirement to act as an Anglo-Soviet bridge was necessitated by developments in East-West relations. The perceived thaw, during the 1970s, had led to the adoption of deeper pro-Soviet links, arguably underpinned by the belief that such activity would become a natural concomitant of rapprochement and co-existence. However, with these institutional links in place, as détente collapsed, they became an effective tool to utilise against a resurgent anti-Soviet rationale.

FRONT ORGANISATION ACTIVITY WITHIN THE LABOUR PARTY

The main conduit for developing links between British MPs and the Soviet Union was the network of front organisations. This Communist-sponsored activism was not a phenomenon solely of the 1980s. Since the establishment of the Popular Front in the 1930s, MPs sympathetic to the Soviet Union had become involved in deeper forms of pro-Soviet activity. This course of action had previously led to expulsion. Members of such organisations were seen as promoting the CPGB line and, as such, would attempt to subvert the policies of the PLP. The traditional solution to Communist entryism was proscription: this was now only a tenable, although ineffective, weapon against the Trotskyist Militant group.[23]

The Labour Party had proscribed any organisation that had Communist links, employed members of the Communist Party or was supportive of Soviet arguments and policy. It is fairly easy for these to be identified; the leadership of the front organisations usually consisted of the same individuals, their objectives were supportive of Soviet policy, and they were usually affiliated to one of the umbrella or matrix organisations such as the IADL that were under a more direct form of Communist control. Proscription stemmed Communist entryism throughout the period from 1927 until 1973. By this time so many organisations had been established that control over pro-Soviet affiliations had slipped away from the Labour Party. Furthermore many left-wingers were sympathetic to the ideals of these groups. The League for Democracy in Greece attracted 24 new members from the PLP and a further 43 Labour MPs listed Greek politics as being "of special interest" following the League's 1974 recruitment drive. Many of those who offered support; Frank Allaun, Tom Driberg, Michael Foot, Eric Heffer, Joan Lestor and Renee Short, were influential members of the NEC. Short also enjoyed significant support from Communist Union leaders Ken Cameron, Ken Gill, Bert Ramelson, Jimmy Reid, Alan Sapper, Hugh Scanlon and Arthur Scargill who put forward the claim about affiliation to the LRD after a meeting of the Liaison Committee for the Defence of Trade Unions.[24] This meant that it became a simple process to abolish the proscription policy.

The abolition of proscription allowed MPs to join and openly promote front organisations, and meant the organisations were able to recruit within parliament. However recruitment would not have been easy had the organisations not had existing supporters within the Labour Party. John Fraser, who drew up a list of MPs who were sympathetic to the aims of the League for Democracy in Greece, can be described as a supporter of the aims of the organisation; though Fraser avoided becoming involved further in pro-Soviet activity. There were others who would definitely have been regarded as friends of the Soviet Union, using Gordievsky's definition. MPs did share information with Soviet agents regarding the party and they discussed politics and developed personal relationships with members of the Soviet Embassy. However, these individuals should not be classified as acting as spies, agents or traitors. This is evident from their motives. The pro-Soviet Labour

MPs were not ordinary career politicians, they focussed on a higher ideal and ignored the consequences of their actions and how history would damn them for pursuing an internationalist agenda.

This was particularly the case with those who not only joined front organisations, but who took higher executive posts, promoted the organisations' cause in the House and took on extra tasks on behalf of these organisations. We now know that two MPs did this by their own admission. To have a former Member of Parliament admit acting as an agent of influence on behalf of a front organisation, discuss the role they played and place it within the context of the period provides a much better picture of an individual who would normally be written off as an agent. Neither Gordievsky, Pincher or Crozier examined the motives behind pro-Soviet activity; they saw the world in black and white while there are, in the words of Clement Attlee, infinite "shades of grey"[25] between right and wrong. We can argue that these figures were acting in the way they believed to be best and some have argued, with hindsight, that they did prevent escalation of the Cold War. For example William Wilson hinted that the existence of organisations like the BSFS, with a membership that included members of the political elite, showed the Soviet Union that it was not entirely isolated. Thus despite fears of a pre-emptive strike by NATO forces, the Soviet Union was able to discuss these fears and have them allayed by individuals with input into the political decision-making process. While this clearly over-exaggerates the importance of Wilson and the BSFS, it does explain Wilson's personal perception of his role.

Furthermore some of the arguments espoused by pro-Soviet delegates in the House have been proven correct. The arguments of those who recognised a decreasing threat from the Communist bloc and a genuine desire for rapprochement were validated by the Gorbachev overtures that initiated the end of the arms race. Volkogonov testified that ending the arms race was an aim expressed by the Politburo during the early 1980s, the obstacle was that unilateral arms reductions equated to surrender.[26] The fact that figures like Wilson had close contact with members of the Soviet Embassy and representatives of the Soviet government meant that they may well have had a more accurate picture of Soviet policy aims. We could classify this as pure propaganda designed to influence, however it is also possible that the Soviet Union was not always, metaphorically, 'crying wolf'. The individuals studied here believed in the integrity of their Soviet contacts, though some did hold reservations. They appeared to have been attempting, in Mikardo's terminology, to light a candle in a dark corner of the world[27] by extending the hand of friendship to the falsely demonised Russian. They equally hoped that if they could establish sufficient personal links between the peoples of the two nations the Russian people would not agree to initiate a nuclear attack on Britain despite the relationship of the two governments.[28]

With these ideals in mind pro-Soviet MPs became senior officials of front organisations. This led them to work on behalf of that organisation both in parliament and upon the world stage. This activity will be studied through personal admissions where possible. It cannot be achieved in the case of every individual involved; however we can gain a snapshot of their beliefs by studying those on whom evidence is available. Front sponsored activities are best viewed through the activities of James Lamond and William Wilson and to a lesser extent Ron Brown and Alex Kitson. If we employ the fellow traveller metaphor we can argue that these four left-wing figures travelled a further stage in the metaphorical Moscow bound car and hypothesise that they chose to remain seated until the very end of the journey. This poses the question were the motives of these individuals different to those previously studied and if so how? This question will be answered using their own rationale for their behaviour and an assessment of their complicity in working alongside the Soviet Union. In particular it needs to be assessed whether they offered unquestionable support for the Soviet regime and how they rationalised their role in light of the collapse of Soviet Communism.

PEACE AND INTERNATIONALISM: THE ALTERNATIVE PERSPECTIVE

For those individuals who enjoyed close contact with the Soviet Union the abandonment of détente, and return to the expansionist policy synonymous with the late 1940s, could be called a consequence of Western distrust. Brown told the anti-Communists that: "the more you try and fracture the alliance of socialist nations the more they will need to increase their defences."[29] Soviet propaganda reinforced this perception, arguing that the United States was determined to break up the Warsaw Pact using the procedure of détente. One story was that the FBI was funding Solidarity, the independent Polish Trade Union led by Lech Walesa.[30] Therefore, the Soviet Union had been placed under immense pressure to retain ideological hegemony over her sphere of influence, particularly if NATO was planning to actively pursue rollback in Europe. The Soviet strategy, developed during the détente era, was to elicit information regarding the intentions of NATO policy makers. After 1980 the Soviet Union grew concerned that NATO was contemplating a pre-emptive nuclear strike. To allay these fears Andropov launched Operation RYAN,[31] which entailed heightening defences and increasing intelligence-gathering measures. Diplomats who had contacts in the House increased the frequency of meetings and strengthened relationships with all sympathetic MPs. They also focussed on gaining material on specific policy areas and attempting to gain information that would enable the Soviet Union to gain control over key figures within government. The Soviet intention was to prevent attack or, at least, to be able to respond when an attack came. The Soviet leadership's failure to achieve this, compounded with the development of the SDI early warning system by the United States, led to an unassailable loss of parity and to Gorbachev's co-operation in ending the arms race.

The combination of fear of war due to increased international tension, and the Soviet drive for increased contact caused an exponential increase in peace activism. Anti-nuclear arguments were fervently propounded in the House by many of the surviving peace campaigners such as Frank Allaun, but more notably by newer allies such as James Lamond, many of whom had a more pronounced pro-Soviet viewpoint. The increasing divide between anti-Soviet Atlanticists and the moderate anti-Cold War activists led debates in parliament to adopt a zero-sum character. The all or nothing perspective allowed the pro-Soviet arguments to gain a degree of legitimacy as the official oppositional stance.

Hansard shows that James Lamond, pro-Soviet MP and Vice-President of the World Peace Council, was a more prominent opponent of Thatcher's foreign and defence policy 1981-85 than Shadow Foreign Secretary Peter Shore. Lamond was widely reported as a critic of the government, particularly in *The Times*, *The Daily Telegraph* and *The Sun*. The latter referred to him as 'a raving commie', 'a traitor' and 'the man from Moscow', one article claimed that the 'red invasion had started' and that Lamond, and 'members of the Labour shadow government', represented 'the shock troops'.[32] More importantly Lamond's position was reported as being representative of Labour's stance. This allowed the pro-Soviet position to become associated with the party and thus damaging to the party's image.

On consecutive dates both Houses of Parliament, firstly the Lords then the Commons, heard debates on the question of East-West relations after Gorbachev became leader of the Soviet Union. The majority of voices who spoke on the subject in either House expressed the traditional anti-Soviet position despite the change of leadership. The message of the opening statement to the House of Lords, delivered by Alec Douglas Home, Lord Home of the Hirsel, on 23 April 1985, asked whether Britain could realistically expect policy to change even if the Soviet leadership had. Gorbachev was still a man who subscribed to the Bolshevik ideology. Lord 'Manny' Shinwell, former Labour Defence Minister, stated, in support of Home's argument, that either the Soviet Union's ideological basis altered significantly or war may be eventually unavoidable. However, there were dissident voices. Baroness Gaitskell, widow of former Labour leader Hugh Gaitskell, reminded the House that "there was a time in fairly recent years when we were both allies… What have they done to us that we have not done to them?"[33] There was also the voice of seasoned left-wing campaigner, and President of the SCR, Baron Jenkins of Putney who accused his old adversary Home of "falsification of the facts"[34] when documenting the background to current East-West relations. Home's key tenet had been that mistrust was logical as statements made by the Soviet government promising one course were usually followed by contradictory actions. Jenkins refuted this stance.

Lord Orr-Ewing highlighted that the existence of MPs who expressed a sympathetic perspective of the Soviet Union, and who held prominent roles within the Soviet controlled peace movement, corroborated the notion that the Soviet Union was untrustworthy. He listed two MPs and seven Union officials who belonged to the British Peace Assembly, which he referred to as an "organ of Soviet foreign policy".[35] Orr-Ewing stated that the activity of such organisations undermined the worldwide efforts that were underway to negotiate disarmament. He used this platform to deliver a message both to the Soviet Union and the British electorate:

> The message to Russia is: your sincerity would be less suspect if you stopped training people from the free world to create dissent in their own countries and to destroy their own institutions. The message to Britons is: study the form of those who seek your votes.[36]

This message, mainly directed at the constituencies of parliamentarians such as James Lamond, Renee Short and William Wilson, was aimed specifically at undermining the ideas of rapprochement. Orr-Ewing used previous and current Soviet policy as the benchmark against which to gauge the level of trust that could be awarded the Soviet Union.

The majority of Lord's speeches supported this argument and this was echoed in the Commons the following day. Orr-Ewing pursued his attacks on the left stating that they were based on a long-term research project. Evidence was contained in a thick, pink, dog-eared file which he waved at those accused, stating: "it's all in here. It's a measure of the information that this file is so thick".[37] Such was the quality and quantity of this research that Blake Baker based two articles in the Daily Telegraph of the same month upon the Orr-Ewing file. Baker named several Trade Unionists and Labour MPs who were associated with Communist controlled organisations.[38]

The attitude of the governmental majority did not dampen the ardour of those who had devoted their political lives to the peace movement. Their activities increased particularly in opposition to the mistrust shown initially to the Gorbachev regime. The emphasis awarded to the pro-Soviet position was utilised by those who were prominent in the pro-Soviet peace network to heighten their attack on the dominant anti-Soviet policy. Those who believed that peace was an international issue largely led this attack. They argued that the British peace movements were too parochial and that questions regarding the future of mankind should be handled at the international level. WPC literature argued that the UN could not act in this capacity because it was under United States control. Therefore the WPC and affiliate bodies had been created to fill this void.

Konni Zilliacus had maintained this argument when calling for a strong, independent United Nations. Arguing that only through negotiations between all the powers could peace be attained and maintained. This perspective led him to attend the World Congress of Intellectuals in Wroclaw, Poland in August 1948. This one-day event witnessed a gathering of intellectuals from almost every nation in a town that clearly bore the scars of war. These intellectuals had one mission in mind, ensuring World War could not recur. The Conference decided that an organisation needed to be created to actively prevent war through open and inclusive meetings that awarded equal status to all participant nations, the organisation that was created was the World Peace Council. Unfortunately what these intellectuals either refused, or failed, to recognise was that they were, in joining this organisation, becoming part of the pro-Soviet orbit. However, many did attempt to excuse themselves for this oversight. Pablo Picasso, the Spanish representative, who witnessed and painted for posterity the devastation of Guernica by the German *Luftwaffe*, happily admitted "I am unfit for politics".[39]

There were equally those in the movement that should have known better. Konni Zilliacus in particular, given his experience of international politics. However, from their recollections they seem to have become blinded by the rhetoric. The concept of representatives of each nation sitting down to discuss peace, rather than oil prices or other capitalist concerns, had a very real allure and attracted some internationalist Labour MPs. Following the abandonment of proscription these MPs were allowed to join organisations suspected of Communist affiliation. One backbench MP with previous links to pro-Sovietism and the TGWU representative on the NEC were asked to join the WPC: they were James Lamond and Alex Kitson.

THE TRADE UNIONS AND PRO-SOVIETISM

Prior to studying the activities of James Lamond and his contemporaries in the WPC it is useful to explore one source of Lamond's pro-Soviet stance, his experiences within the Trade Unions. The factor of Union influence on a sponsored MP is largely ignored in studies of the left-wing. This section seeks to explore how a pro-Soviet dominated Trade Union had a tendency to adopt pro-Soviet parliamentary candidates and encouraged them to act, not only on Union interests but, to pursue an internationalist agenda with a pro-Soviet perspective. This is explored using the case of TASS members Ron Brown, James Lamond and Ernie Ross.

    • McIlroy and Campbell's recent study of the Liaison Committee for the Defence of Trade Unions shows the clear link that existed between the Communist Party and British Trade Unionism.[40] Prominent members of the CPGB who held important positions within the Unions or were influential activists maintained this link: of particular note are Baruch (Bert) Ramelson of the London Trades Council and the CPGB Industrial Department, Ken Gill, Chairman of the Technical Administrative and Supervisory section [TASS] of the Amalgamated Union of Engineering Workers [AUEW] and Reg Birch, official of the Union of Construction, Allied Trades and Technicians [UCATT]. These individuals ensured that the Communist line was injected into the policy of the Union and therefore the Labour Party. Ramelson claimed, in 1973, that:

> We [the Communists] can float an idea early in the year and it can become official Labour policy by the autumn. A few years ago we were on our own but not anymore.[41]

The allies Ramelson spoke of were the Union leaders Harold Wilson alluded to when he spoke of a "tightly knit group of politically motivated men."[42] Fears existed within the party that Union militancy would undermine government policy and damage the economy. It remains debatable whether the 'winter of discontent' was solely the responsibility of Trade Union activism and even more scepticism should be shown towards allegations that the Communist Union leaders were attempting to gain control of the Labour Party. The argument put forward in this section is that we can recognise that there was greater CPGB influence within those Unions which adhered to the unilateralist position. This is not a universal concomitant, however it is notable that certain Unions, that adopted CPGB members as their officials, promoted the left-wing agenda and sponsored MPs who held a similar stance.

    • The relevant example used here is that of TASS. TASS sponsored Ron Brown, James Lamond and Ernie Ross, along with Joe Ashton and Albert Booth. The first three MPs were prominent exponents of the pro-Soviet line, particularly Brown and Lamond and all three held offices in recognised front organisations. Before outlining the careers of these MPs this section will focus on how TASS and its predecessors put forward the pro-Soviet argument through its publications and encouraged its MPs to do the same. This shows a clear link between the political stance of a Union and the MP sponsored by that Union.

    The political stance held by TASS generally followed a pro-Soviet line of analysis, a tradition that can be recognised in the union's predecessors the

Association of Engineering and Shipbuilding Draughtsman [AESD] and the Draughtsmen's and Allied Technicians' Association [DATA]. These were independent Unions prior to the merger that formed the AUEW, however TASS was able to retain ideological and political independence. This was important for the Union as its views were not consistent with those of the AUEW that was led for many years by individuals who subscribed to New Left ideas rather than those of the CPGB. The ideological position maintained by TASS was made clear during the late 1950s and early 1960s in the publications of the AESD and DATA.

Articles in the AESD newspaper *The Draughtsman* provided a clear pro-Soviet analysis for the readership. These contained three main themes, the advanced status and influential role of Trade Unions in the Soviet Union, the need to recognise the Soviet Union and Warsaw Pact allies as proletarian states and partners in the socialist struggle and the need to protest against the arms race and concurrent anti-Communist foreign policy.[43] *DATA News*, emerging with the change of Union title in August 1961, adopted a similar political message. The paper supported Cuba, the Lidice Shall Live Campaign, and ran anti-Atlanticist, anti-NATO and anti-EEC articles. DATA also ran summer schools that educated the members in the pro-Soviet analysis. The 1963 Summer School advertised speakers from the World Peace Council, the Soviet Trades Council and the United Nations Association. The advertisement placed in *DATA News* called for all members to attend who wished to understand their role in world affairs.[44] Guided tours of Communist states were also advertised continually in the newspaper.[45]

The descendants of *Data News*, *TASS Journal* and after 1979 *TASS News and Journal*, continued this pro-Soviet tone. During the 1970s articles called for increased trade with the Eastern bloc and the building of fraternal links between TASS members and their Communist counterparts. Barry Seager's Presidential address argued that "the world has become a better place"[46] while Ken Gill warned against being fooled by the "clever reformists" in the Labour Party who distracted the workers from their international mission.[47] They also promoted the anti-American analysis of conflicts in Africa, South America and the Middle East.

The pro-Soviet arguments were exacerbated as détente collapsed and anti-Communism re-emerged. Des Starrs called for a united campaign for peace and détente to be led by the workers.[48] Gill, writing as representative of the All-Britain Peace Liaison Group, an affiliate of the International Liaison Forum of Peace Forces a Soviet-controlled umbrella organisation, called for "strong condemnation by delegates of the anti-Soviet cold war campaign which is being whipped up once again".[49] The 1979 TASS Conference led a campaign for members to ensure trading links with Eastern Europe be established or maintained. Starrs stated:

Conference recognises the growing opportunities being presented by
the planned economies of the socialist countries to British engineering firms to develop trade, and their failure to respond.[50]

Special issues of the *TASS News and Journal* promoted the campaign for peace
and disarmament. Frank Allaun, James Lamond and Ernie Ross made
contributions. Ross argued in 1980 that British foreign policy was not based
upon common sense but on the policies of Ernest Bevin whose interests
had not been to "defend Britain, but rather to defend the interests of the
US."[51] The 1981 TASS Conference mirrored the major tenets of the Labour
Party's 1983 Manifesto, and the following year Alexander Sobotin, Soviet
representative to the World Parliament for Peace, was invited to present the
Soviet case for disarmament.

This pro-Soviet line forced the Union into an oppositional stance
to the Labour Party for much of its history. This had been clearly stated by
the DATA representative council to be a necessary course of action:

To have a voice within the organisational machinery of the Labour
Party is insufficient as a means of strengthening the effectiveness of
the Union, but whilst continuing to fulfil our responsibilities as an
affiliated Union to the Labour Party, we must cease as an Executive to
attempt to keep our political action confined to our responsibilities to
the [Labour Party] and divorced from our industrial interests when, in
fact, the sphere of industrial and political activity is indistinguish-
able.[52]

This statement clearly expressed the desire to enter into industrial
activity on an independent basis, without consultation with the TUC or the
Labour Party, and to act against the party if necessary. While this was not
unusual for a Trade Union it also set the agenda for the TASS sponsored
MPs. The 1972 TASS representative council Conference report stated that
sponsored MPs should fulfil two criteria. Firstly they should reflect Union
policy and maintain full liaison and affiliations consistent with that policy
and secondly offer political and industrial leadership when promoting the
Union's policy.[53] The following year the union also called for the Labour
Party to "withdraw all bans and proscriptions preventing socialists who pay
political levy becoming individual members in addition to other political
affiliations."[54] It went on to state that "such affiliations were necessary to
furthering the Union policy."[55] This statement clearly links the promotion of
Union policy and the affiliation of their MPs to front organisations.

The five TASS sponsored MPs should not all be considered as pro-
Soviet. Joe Ashton and Albert Booth retained a degree of reticence in foreign
policy debates. Booth, though named as a member of the British Peace

Council, did not display the same type of commitment as Lamond. Ernie Ross avoided making pro-Soviet statements, but maintained an anti-American stance. James Lamond was seen as the greatest asset to the Union, a factor highlighted by the concerted drive to secure a seat for him.

Lamond had held executive posts in AESD and DATA branches. After nineteen years of active membership he became Chairman of the No1 Divisional Council and Chair of the Industrial and Political Committee. Letters between Jim Forsyth, Secretary of the Scotland Central Branch of DATA, and central office show there was a fear that DATA policy was being suborned in favour of the Labour Party line. Forsyth refuted this, stating that: "Lamond is a man of high principles and staunch credentials in the Union".[56] Forsyth's backing of Lamond saw him nominated for over twenty seats between 1963 and 1970. It is clear that there were ideological differences between Lamond and many of the CLPs. After failure to be nominated for Clackmannan and E Stirlingshire, the former seat of Emrys Hughes, Lamond informed Forsyth that the panel "didn't seem to agree with me".[57] Lamond recalled that he and the selection panel disagreed over policy.[58] In 1968 seven different constituencies were approached to adopt Lamond as candidate, he found success in Oldham West. Gill personally congratulated Lamond on his re-election in 1974 telling him in a letter: "I know you will do your best to express the views and objectives of TASS". He and Ross won similar public praise in 1980 from Gill: "on major questions like the fight against war hysteria [they] have been determined, loyal and radical in defence of TASS policies".[59] Clearly the ideas of Lamond and TASS were identical and his affiliation to the World Peace Council was encouraged.

This was not the normative relationship between pro-Soviet MPs and the sponsoring Union. For example Newens and Short were given little attention from the NUT and TGWU respectively. Allaun used many Union papers as a platform for his 'Bathrooms not Bombs' argument but avoided a clearly pro-Soviet line. In other cases the resident pro-Soviet was used as a representative under specific circumstances. Pro-Soviet TGWU representative on the Labour Party NEC, Alex Kitson, was the TGWU's representative on peace and security issues. Answering a personal invitation to the 'Prevent War-Build Peace' Conference organised by the CESC, Jack Jones, General Secretary of the TGWU, replied: "you will, of course, be aware that it is customary for Brother Kitson to represent this Union in connection with these matters."[60] This implies that Kitson was the Unions nominated representative and that CPGB and BSFS executive member, and Conference organiser, Gordon Schaffer should have been aware of this arrangement.

From this evidence we can build a picture of the relationship between Lamond and TASS. However, given that there were other Unions which were led by Communist Party members, we should assume that this type of relationship was common and that MPs and sponsoring Unions had some form of ideological consensus over policy. Evidence for this is difficult to locate, however, Alan Sapper, leader of the Association of Cinematograph, Television and Allied Technicians [ACTT], encouraged the affiliation of the Union, and individual members, to various front organisations. As Chairman of the League for Democracy in Greece, Sapper encouraged the promotion of the Greek democrat's cause through the media and for members of the Union to join the League: 'to promote the plight of the Greek democrats to their British counterparts'.[61] This encouraged his members to become involved in pro-Soviet political activism. The sole MP sponsored by the ACTT, Hugh Jenkins, was Chairman of the SCR for a short period showing that pro-Soviet ideas did seem to have held sway over the Union and their MP. Of course a larger sample of Unions and sponsored MPs is required to offer solid conclusions regarding this relationship. However, the pro-Soviet line maintained by DATA was one of the influences which governed the career of James Lamond and his relationship with the Communist leaders does provide some indicators of the broader picture of the relationship between the pro-Soviet Trade Union and their sponsored MP.

There were also clear lines of communication between left-wing Union leaders. A steering group was created within the TUC to co-ordinate with the left-wing MPs in parliament. At Labour Co-ordinating Committee [LCC] meetings a relevant MP would be called to discuss strategy and a coherent challenge to PLP policy was developed. Sapper recalled that when a particular issue was due for debate within the TUC, the NEC or either Houses of Parliament, left-wingers with a particular interest in the specific issue would be invited to an LCC meeting to discuss what the left's response should be. Sapper indicated that there were representatives who were recognised as the sympathetic expert on most issues. For example, Trade Union legislation was the special interest of TASS MP Joe Ashton, housing was seen as Frank Allaun's speciality and on foreign affairs and disarmament the LCC had a wide choice but favourites were Allaun, Lamond, Newens, Ross and Short. The relationship between the left-wing Trade Unions and their supporters in parliament developed during the 1970s but reached its peak during the 1980s when, "the challenge was greatest".[62]

The activity of the LCC adds weight to the notion that there was a coherent strategy to promote a left-wing agenda. This should not, however, be regarded as a strategy orchestrated by the CPGB. The Labour Party left-wing was alienated from policy making at the parliamentary level. The parliamentary party leadership constantly reversed conference and NEC decisions. As the left increased in numbers they could exert greater influence and mount a credible opposition to the consensual politics of the Labour

Party. It was in these circumstances that leftist Union leaders and MPs were able to develop a political strategy that was an expression of their core ideals. The success in promoting this agenda is a reflection of the influence of the left during the 1980s and was a result of the perceived danger that the disintegration of East-West relations invoked.

JAMES LAMOND AND THE SOVIET MOVEMENT FOR WORLD PEACE

James Lamond and Alex Kitson, his ally on the WPC, had similar political influences. These were gained through the Trade Unions, Lamond in TASS and Kitson from the Communist Scottish miners' leader Abe Moffat. Kitson displayed a more Marxist outlook and was an open admirer of Soviet society. He visited every year from the 1950s to the 1980s. After every visit he extolled the benefits of the planned, communist economy. Following his visit in 1977 he reported that:

I am pleased to visit a country where the situation differs from that in my own, where there is no unemployment and one can see a consistent rise in the standard of living of common workers.[63]

In making a statement such as this it would appear that he fell victim to the guided tour and had succumbed to the fake statistics produced by Soviet propaganda.

On the occasion of his visit, from the 5th to 11th November 1977, he received much criticism from the British media because of his controversial perspective of the Soviet Union. However he stated that his analysis had been proven during visits which spanned 23 years.[64] He had particular admiration for the progress made in housing, education and health. His compatriots on the left rallied to his support, though Allaun reminded Kitson's critics that Kitson's was a comparative perspective. This was an accurate account of his argument. Kitson compared the Soviet Union during the 1970s with the same country he had visited after the devastation inflicted upon it during the German invasion. Thus he argued that the level of progress attained, given the circumstances in the Soviet Union after 1942, vastly outstripped the achievements of post-war British governments. His main supporters were Frank Allaun and Norman Atkinson who opposed his dismissal from the NEC. Kitson maintained his support for the Soviet regime and admitted receiving gifts from the Soviet Union, one of which was from Brezhnev personally.[65]

However Kitson admitted that there were faults with the Soviet system. He argued the cause of Jewish dissidents in the Soviet Union and joined Tony Benn and Frank Allaun in their opposition to the continuing trials of

Czech dissidents in 1980. These contradictions in the Soviet Union he happily discussed with his contacts, particularly the case of the Jewish dissidents. He recalled telling a Kremlin official: "if these people want to leave,
for Christ's sake let them go".[66] Furthermore he supported NATO but argued for reform of the military alliance from within. Therefore we can recognise Kitson as a political actor who held very complex and often contrasting perspectives of the world. He described himself as a democratic socialist, distinguishing himself from the Social Democrats who led the Labour
Party.[67] He believed in the ideological basis of the party as defined in the
wording of Clause IV of the Constitution. This led him to support the Soviet system because of the benefits of "complete economic planning".[68] His
support for the Soviet economic model encouraged him to seek greater links
with representatives of the Soviet Union and her allies arguing: "I'd sooner
have colleagues in the Communist Party than in the Conservative Party any
day."[69]

    Though he was a member of the WPC, at the same time as being on
the NEC of the Labour Party, he was not the most vocal proponent of the
Soviet foreign policy line. His argument, in his own words, was based on the
advanced nature of Soviet society:

> They had no unemployment… they had a genuinely free health serv-
> ice; and… they had made more industrial progress in 60 years than we
> had made since the Industrial Revolution.[70]

Thus Kitson appears to have held reservations. James Lamond, in contrast,
focussed on the pacifistic nature of Communists, refusing to become involved in debates on Soviet politics. He was to become Vice-President of
the WPC under Romesh Chandra, and provided a good account of his
motivation for joining the organisation.

    James Lamond was taken on many visits of the Soviet Union while
an official of TASS. Lamond recalled that he was already a pacifist, having
witnessed the human cost of the Second World War. He equally admitted
that he believed that the Soviet Union had tipped the balance in that conflict and so deserved inclusion in the decision-making process surrounding
the post-war international settlement. However, one experience, when visiting the Soviet Union with the Scottish Trades Council in the 1960s, touched
him deeply. Neither the achievements of the Five-Year Plans, the superfi-
cial equality, or the leaders' rhetoric made Lamond pro-Soviet, it was the
desire for peace among the common Russian citizen. As he argued in the
House on 7 April 1987:

No-one can visit the Soviet Union without being impressed by the desire of the ordinary people for peace and friendship with the world and in particular the west. There is no anti-American or anti-British feeling there. Their concern for peace stems from the suffering they went through in what they refer to as the 'Great Patriotic War'... This desire for peace did not begin with the arrival of... Gorbachev... it has been there certainly as long as I have been visiting that country, and it is very deep rooted and sincere.[71]

The conclusion to the argument he developed was that "the danger the Soviet Union represented to us was grossly exaggerated."[72] In fact he was willing to argue that the perceived threat was mythical, created by the British and United States' governments to expand markets for their arms industry. The arms race, Lamond argued, was independent of developments in East-West relations:

If the Soviet Union disappeared as an enemy and there was subsequent pressure on the United States, Britain and other countries to reduce the amount spent on defence, a fresh enemy would have to be found.[73]

Like Stan Newens he predicted that this enemy would be found in the Muslim world and arguably was proven correct by the US-Iraqi conflict.

It was an ex-pilot, a veteran of the Battle of Stalingrad, who convinced him of the pacifistic nature of the ordinary Russian. He met the former airman, "blind and disfigured", in a sanatorium in the Crimea. For some reason they were introduced and the pilot spoke to Lamond. With an understanding of Soviet methods we can conclude that it is highly likely that this encounter was staged for Lamond's benefit. However this was not apparent to Lamond. Lamond recalled the airman telling him:

I know that you're very sorry to see me like this, but don't think of that. Just do one thing for me, go home and work to make sure that nothing like this ever happens to anyone else.[74]

Lamond did just this. He joined the WPC, established an affiliate body, the British Peace Assembly, and helped establish a Scottish branch of CND. In Lamond's opinion the WPC was the only organisation which fought for peace at the international level. He believed implicitly in the aims that had been laid down twenty years earlier by Frederic Joliot-Curie and was convinced that they were being followed to the letter by the organisation. The urge to spread these beliefs led him to parliament, with the encouragement of the TASS organisation, using the Labour Party as a vehicle for his ideas.

Once elected Lamond allied himself with the Anglo-Soviet Parliamentary Group. He recalled that Renee Short and Robert Edwards dominated this grouping. He also developed an independent role by founding 'Parliamentarians for Peace' which included many of the Anglo-Soviet Friendship lobby as well as individuals from across the left-wing including Bob Cryer, Alex Kitson and Ernie Ross. He also joined Labour Action for Peace, chaired by Ron Huzzard and Frank Allaun. We see, therefore that he migrated almost immediately towards the like-minded individuals on the left of the party. His strong association with the pro-Soviet left is mirrored in the debates in which he took part. Here we see him supported by the pro-Soviet TASS sponsored MPs Ron Brown and Ernie Ross and unilateralists and pro-Soviet peace activists like Frank Allaun, Norman Atkinson, Stan Newens and Renee Short. His highest office was as PPS to Stan Orme in the Ministry for Social Security, but he was forced to resign because of his pro-Soviet affiliations. He recalled that Orme, a staunch left-winger, was willing to stand by him but Lamond resigned to protect his colleague. Lamond's pro-Soviet affiliations were to cause him to come under constant attack. However, he was always more than willing to defend himself and the WPC.

Lamond refused to accept that there was a clear financial link between the WPC and the Soviet Union. As he stated on 25 April 1985, when defending his Vice Presidency:

> I am proud of it, and I would not deny it for a moment. However, I do deny the allegation that the World Peace Council is financed by the Soviet Union… If anybody can prove to me that money for the World Peace Council comes from the government of the Soviet Union, or from any other government, I shall resign immediately from it.[75]

His protestations were not accepted by the House, and have been proven wrong since the end of the Cold War. As his protagonist, Conservative Andrew Mackay, retorted: "It is for honourable members to decide whom they wish to believe."[76] All Lamond later admitted is that the organisation was definitely "pro-Soviet".[77] But he maintained that the WPC was not, to his knowledge, dependent upon Moscow finances. It is plausible that he was not aware of the extent of Soviet influence over the WPC. The organisation attempted to maintain an aura of independence, therefore any Soviet funding took a convoluted route to its coffers. Members such as Lamond were prized by the WPC and so were protected from some of the realities of the organisation. As Lamond admitted he possessed one of the greatest assets the WPC could ask for, a British passport.

Lamond recalled that members were selected to join by the Council. He believed that he was given the "honour" of an offer of membership because he had an air of respectability. He had sat on Aberdeen City Council

1959-1971 and had served simultaneously as Lord Provost and Mayor of the city in 1971. However, he recognised that the greatest asset he could offer was his ability to travel freely on the WPC's behalf. Chandra, the WPC President, was restricted because of his Communist affiliations. Equally, Alex Kitson had been refused entry to the United States because he was a frequent visitor to Cuba. Lamond was able to represent the WPC on the international stage without constraint. He refuted the claim that this meant he acted as a Soviet agent, because he denied that the WPC was a tool of Soviet foreign policy. Lamond argued that he acted with the best intentions, and we can conclude that he was blinded by the ideal of world peace that the WPC literature promoted and that the annual conferences appeared to engender. He admitted acting as advisor when an affiliate body was created in Afghanistan at some point prior to what he referred to as "the alleged Soviet invasion".[78] While his aim was to provide international support for the anti-American movement in Afghanistan, it is possible to claim that Lamond established an organisation within Afghanistan that would ensure the nation remained within the Soviet sphere of influence. What Lamond did not realise was that the Afghanistan Peace Council [APC] would subsumed into Babrak Karmal's foreign ministry after the Soviet supported coup installed Karmal as Afghan leader.

Lamond could not resolve the inconsistencies between his beliefs and the reality of the Cold War ideological battle. To accept that there was truth in the anti-Soviet position would mean accepting that his activities were wrong. He stood as an open and tireless campaigner for the WPC and contributed several supportive articles for *Labour Monthly*. Equally he was always open with his constituents and advertised his allegiances on all election campaign flyers. None of this harmed his electoral prospects whatsoever and he remained unashamed of his actions and proud of his beliefs. His arguments fitted well with the stance adopted by the left of the Labour Party during the years in opposition to the Thatcher government. He particularly focused on the opportunities for rapprochement that were presented by Gorbachev's reforms. At every opportunity he argued for greater relations to be established with the Soviet Union, whether they be at the national or cultural level. On the 25th April 1985 Lamond, supported by Norman Atkinson, accused Thatcher of only offering "frigidity"[79] in return for the Soviet overtures. Lamond argued that if negotiations were genuinely open then there would be a greater potential for success. He opposed the Cold War constantly and argued vociferously against the arms race. He argued that there were hidden victims of the Cold War that neither side publicised, particularly within the African states where proxy wars were fought by both superpowers:

> Perhaps it has kept the peace in Europe for forty years... but the victims of the nuclear arms race, the casualties of the hidden, secret war

of starvation, sickness and depravation, are the 800 million people in the Third World."[80]

Highlighting the tragic consequences of the Cold War and presenting an alternative to the people of the world, Lamond argued, was the mission of the WPC. It did not support the Soviet Union slavishly, but promoted peace. However he could not absolve himself of the mindset that the West was an aggressive force and that the Soviet Union was acting only in reaction to Western aggression.

Despite the benefits of hindsight Lamond remained unable to explain the contradictions between his actions and beliefs. He could only view the world through a zero-sum prism and, in his opinion, the Soviet Union was the side that best represented his ideals. This perception was developed through his experience of the propaganda produced during the Second World War that showed both the Soviet hardship and the dedication of the Red Army in defeating Nazism. His education within Communist dominated Unions reinforced this belief; he was then taken to the Soviet Union for the final lesson. It is possible that he was selected as potentially susceptible to the scenario of the blind airman, particularly because of his pacifist outlook. Lamond acted on convictions and, therefore, it seems doubtful that he accepted money for his actions, though the Soviet Union could possibly claim otherwise. His travel expenses would definitely be seen as a wage and though the amounts paid are unknown we know that he travelled widely on behalf of the WPC.

Lamond toured America in 1978 assessing the public's attitude to the SALT II talks.[81] The following year he was the British representative on a WPC delegation to Vietnam and Kampuchea 12-23 October 1979. His report, published in *Labour Monthly*,[82] followed the pro-Soviet, anti-China line to the letter. This position had to be maintained because these visits were funded by the WPC and, therefore, by the Soviet Union. Soviet officials dominated the membership of the WPC and set the agenda for officials and delivered payments. Lamond would have been viewed as an agent of influence on behalf of the Soviet Union, however he refuted these claims. By maintaining the belief that the WPC was independent of the Soviet Union he could also insist that he was an independent peace activist who "devoted nearly forty years of my life to promoting peace at the international level."[83] While he accepted that the movement failed he, like Stan Newens, attributed the blame for this failure directly against the United States.

What we do not know is how much contact he enjoyed with Soviet officials and how far he was convinced by them to run errands, publish sympathetic articles, and raise key issues in the House. From his unrepentant analysis of his position on the Cold War it appears that he would not have been hostile to such approaches and, disagreeing with the ruling rationale that defined the Soviet Union as an enemy, may well have agreed to put forward the Soviet case. This was not a traitorous act in his eyes, but the only course he could follow and remain true to his ideals. He stated that money was of no interest to him. If it had been, he may well have been more ambitious in his political career. Instead he chose the course of an independent within the broad church of the Labour Party. He was not alone in this and enjoyed membership of the party at a time when it shared his principles to a certain degree. However, after 1985 as the party lurched back towards the right and Atlanticism re-emerged, he and many of his allies were deselected.

Lamond saw himself, as did Zilliacus, as a sane man in an insane world and attempted to highlight the errors in the policy of consecutive British governments. In parliament and through WPC and BPC meetings and publications he tried to change the climate of opinion. The fact that the majority of this activity took place at the extra-parliamentary level, under the auspices of organisations identified as under Soviet control, led him to come under constant attack from the anti-Soviet majority. The criticisms levelled against him and his supporters did not detract him from his mission. He recognised that he worked with a different rationale, one that the anti-Soviet Atlanticists could never accept, his ideas were as alien to them as the dominant Cold War rationale was to him.

WILLIAM WILSON: THE CONFIDENTIAL CONTACT

Brian Crozier alleged that certain left-wing MPs were, in KGB terminology, confidential contacts of the Soviet Embassy, an accusation that has never been proven unequivocally. In fact such allegations led Crozier to withdraw one publication after the threat of libel action by Joan Lestor. Oleg Gordievsky identified other contacts whom he personally handled while in London. Once again these allegations remained unsubstantiated and are denied as ridiculous by those accused. This type of activity is inherently secret. No written evidence of meetings exists, the only way that the claims that such activities took place can be verified is by an admission from someone who was a contact of the Soviet Embassy. William Wilson, MP for Coventry South 1964-74 and Coventry South East 1974-83, admitted just this. Through his activities in pro-Soviet friendship societies and campaigns for recognition of the GDR and in support of the extension of trading links to Eastern Europe, Wilson became a close friend of a representative of the Soviet Embassy. Wilson admitted that this friendship was not purely innocent. He was aware that his friend in the Embassy wanted information and willingly discussed British politics and the Labour Party with him. However, Wilson should not be classified as a spy. The topics they discussed were what Gordievsky referred to as 'daily tittle-tattle', material that was available in the

news media. The content of the discussions and the quality of the information was unimportant to the Soviet Union, there were others in Western
nations that would obtain state secrets on their behalf. The role of a contact
in parliament was initially just to talk freely about current affairs. However,
had conflict broken out between East and West, which was the fear of the
Politburo, a contact who was close to the decision-making process may provide information that would be important.

William Wilson's role was as a conduit of understanding. He enabled
the Soviet leadership to interpret British politics and the imperatives of
decision-making from the perspective of someone who worked within the
British parliament. It is useful to elucidate the background, influences and
ideological motivations of Wilson to discern why an MP would be willing to
enter into this type of relationship. In building this prosopography we are
able to assess the nature of the relationship and the importance of this link,
as an aspect of Wilson's political agenda and in pursuing his objectives as a
change agent.

Wilson was born into a politically active, Trade Unionist family in
Coventry in 1913. An early hero was Richard [Dick] Wallhead, who was a
conscientious objector during the First World War. During the 1918 'Khaki'
Election Wilson recalled his house became the committee room for the local
Labour Party. He also recalled the plight of his father who, due to his
involvement in the Engineers' lock-out in 1922, was black-balled from the
steel works for over a year. The young Wilson was forced into work to help
keep his family. Therefore we see that he was introduced to socialist ideals
from an early age. It was these ideals that would draw him into politics.

Wilson's belief in the role of the Trade Unions as working class
representatives was a central theme of his domestic political theory. He
argued that the left-wing in Britain should develop a "unity of purpose".[84]
This would replace the uneasy relationship between the party and the Trade
Unions that characterised the 1970s, and should not be limited to establishing a corporate relationship with the Unions. Wilson argued that the Labour
Party in government should build an agenda around the desires of the working class, therefore promoting Conference and the NEC to the position of
determining policy and reducing the power of the leadership of the PLP.
Wilson's hope was that the Labour Party would be the vehicle for societal
change. He described capitalism as an anathema to socialism and argued for
economic reform of a radical nature. Capitalism, he argued was a "profit-
making, poverty-making, war-making, anti-democratic system of society",[85]
therefore it should be supplanted by a state-owned system founded upon
working class control. This was a belief imbibed during his early life and it
remained central to his objectives as a Labour politician. Alongside this
belief Wilson campaigned for complete social equality and completed many

studies for the party on race relations and social exclusion. The fact that his ideals were thwarted, as they were for many on the left of the party, led him to look for inspiration to the East and the Soviet Union.

Though he worked during the 1920s as an engineer's labourer, his involvement in the local Labour Party led him to be suggested for the job of clerk for a local socialist solicitor. He did not supply the name of this solicitor but indicated that through this job he was able to take his legal exams and passed at the bar in 1939. Notably it was not until 1941, when the Communist analysis of the war changed, that Wilson joined the army. He did not comment on why this decision was delayed, but it can be inferred that he became involved in more radical socialist activities during the 1930s. During his army service he pinned his hopes upon the success of the Russian front, a perspective encouraged by the socialist movement in Coventry. After the war Coventry was twinned firstly with Stalingrad and later with Dresden. The association with the latter led Wilson to join the British-GDR Friendship Society. He recalled that this gained him friends when he was to enter parliament in 1964.

During the 1950s he stood repeatedly for parliament, becoming the candidate for Warwick and Leamington. This was the staunchly Conservative seat of Prime Minister Anthony Eden, and was not to fall to Labour until after Eden's resignation. Wilson moved home in 1962, was adopted by Coventry South CLP and elected to parliament in 1964. His background led him to the left-wing of the party, particularly the Tribune Group. However it was through other alliances that he pursued his pro-Soviet agenda. When he joined the parliamentary branch of the British-GDR Friendship Society he found most of the members were also members of the BSFS; thus he joined also. Their number included Renee Short, James Lamond and Stan Thorne, Labour MP for Preston 1974-87. However the majority of his early BSFS activity was at the local level. Wilson was active in twinning Coventry with Volgograd and he led several exchange visits to the Soviet Union.

As with Philip Crees, Wilson's pro-Soviet support was nurtured during the 1930s when he was an active opponent of fascism. This led many to view the Soviet Union as the bastion of anti-fascism, a perspective that was reinforced as the Eastern Front became pivotal in determining the outcome of the conflict. Crees argued that the Soviet Union had "done more to defeat the Germans than we had".[86] This should have allowed the Soviet Union a major role in determining the shape of Europe's future. Individuals with these beliefs joined many friendship organisations on the grounds that the people of the Communist nations were not enemies. However, Crees, with the benefit of hindsight, exhibited doubts regarding the Soviet and Eastern European leadership. "We were never critical enough of these people"[87] he recalled when talking of his relationship with Ceausescu as a member of the

British-Romanian Friendship Society. Wilson exhibited similar doubts in interview but, like many others, found himself unable to be critical in a zero-sum world.

In the House Wilson remained particularly quiet in comparison to his aforementioned allies. The only pro-Communist causes he pursued were the recognition of North Korea, the campaign for admission of that nation to the UN in 1974 and 1977 and the increase of trade with Albania in 1980. It appears that his role was not as a pro-Soviet activist in parliament. This makes it difficult to determine the core of his ideals at this time. However he did write for *The Morning Star*, as did many left-wingers, and from these articles we can get a picture of where his sympathies lay. The central campaign he extolled was for the recognition of the GDR. Following a visit during February 1967 he outlined his argument. Wilson focussed upon economic stability, he observed that the "people are well dressed, there are more cars on the road and an increased variety and quantity of goods in the shops."[88] It was from this argument that he developed a theory outlining why it was important for Britain to trade with the GDR, and reminded his opponents that while the FDR blocked recognition it was one of the GDR's major European trading partners.[89]

Wilson also discussed the threat posed by the Soviet Union, arguing that he "was satisfied that the desire for peace... is a genuine aspiration".[90] However he was not prominent within the peace movement. The only campaign he supported that pursued rapprochement was the recognition of the GDR as a *de jure* government. He called this essential, not only so Britain could enjoy the benefits of an economic relationship with the GDR but also, "to secure real peace in Europe."[91] As he later reiterated, Europe as a continent, not defined by blocs, should be made into the "continent of peace and friendship".[92] It appears that, in his own small way, this is the ideal that Wilson attempted to make a reality.

Following the 1975 Disarmament Conference, held in Helsinki, it was expected that arms spending would be reduced. The maintenance of a high defence budget led those left-wingers, who believed that the Communist regimes and their populace had purely pacifistic intentions, to be highly critical of governmental policy and act in opposition to anti-Communism through extra-parliamentary activity. In parliament Wilson acted in a supporting capacity only, the most vocal critic of government policy was his BSFS colleague Stan Thorne. In September 1975 Thorne visited the Soviet Union on an exploratory visit. Reporting to the *Morning Star* Thorne described "the great desire for peace among the Soviet people."[93] Thorne led calls for a reduction in arms spending on the strength of the Helsinki agreement and thus the development of a 'socialist budget'. The failure of this campaign led the left within the party and Conference to revolt against leader

Z. While the majority argued for increases in domestic spending other left-wingers opposed Labour's defence spending because it was a concomitant of a policy that maintained that the Soviet Union was an aggressor. The left argued that the party's domestic policy was anti-socialist, particularly following the adherence to Crosland's revisionist socialism by the parliamentary leadership. The pro-Soviet left-wingers, particularly figures such as Thorne and Wilson, developed a critique of the party that identified the anti-Soviet policy with an anti-socialist attitude.

Thorne argued that the Labour Party could not accept that the Soviet Union was willing to seek rapprochement because that would mean the party leaders would have to deal with Communism as an ideological threat rather than as a purely military adversary. Thorne called for his allies to apply the maximum pressure upon the Western governments: "that we may realise the high aims of the Helsinki Conference."[94] The number who adopted this stance were too few to apply any significant pressure, therefore some pro-Soviet left-wingers made greater efforts to develop personal contacts with Soviet representatives in oder to encourage co-existence.

As Wilson observed the Helsinki process reduced to a series of lengthy conferences that concluded in stalemate, he became extremely disillusioned with the commitment of the Western governments to détente. Wilson argued that this was the fault of Western leaders who opposed Communism on principle and refused to believe that Soviet approaches were genuine because of a deep fear of the Communist ideology. This had led, in Wilson's opinion, to the West, and particularly the United States, reinforcing the perception that Communism was "evil… [not] about people power".[95] It was in this climate of increased bi-polar hostility that William Wilson developed a relationship with one "staff member of the Embassy."[96]

When interviewed, Wilson recalled his contact to be a "diplomat".[97] He met this diplomat at the first BSFS Annual Dinner he attended, he recalled that he was friendly and interested in his work. Following this meeting Wilson was to receive invitations to "Embassy dos" which enabled the diplomat to talk with him further. Wilson is not specific as to when this relationship began, however we know that Wilson became Chairman of the BSFS in 1977 and, therefore, it is reasonable to assume that this relationship was established prior to this appointment.

The relationship between Wilson and the diplomat became more intimate after 1977. Wilson was often invited to lunch at the Diplomat's expense at which he was encouraged to "discuss the British political situation and who in British politics were likely to be favourable to the Soviet Union."[98] This he recalled was not a passing interest but the underlying reason for the meetings. Therefore we know that Wilson was aware of the purpose of these meetings and entered into the relationship voluntarily. He

recalled that at an meeting in 1979 they discussed the result of the forthcoming
General Election. Wilson predicted that the next government would be
Conservative and would survive for ten years due to North Sea oil revenue.
While he admitted that his economic analysis was flawed, his prediction was
correct. Therefore, he argued, "they thought I knew my stuff so kept in
touch".[99] This means that he must have been aware he was being used as a
conduit for information; the kind to which the Soviet Union did not readily
have access.

    Wilson's rationalisation of this relationship bears all the hallmarks
of a view with hindsight. While he recalled that his initial rationale was that
the Soviet diplomat simply wanted to attain a different perspective on the
British political scene, the nature of which a Russian may not understand,
Wilson also recognised that more cynical motives existed.[100] The diplomat
used their friendship to gain information on British politics and to ascertain
which MPs would be responsive to Soviet overtures. Wilson did not carry
out any introductions, but did give the diplomat information on who would
be sympathetic and how to contact them. He also relayed messages and
invitations between the diplomat and other contacts. This he rationalised as
the diplomat simply "doing his job" and knew that he had to report to his
superiors. Therefore Wilson saw it important to supply good information
in order to establish a relationship.[101] Despite this Wilson believed that there
was a bond between the two men. When Wilson visited Moscow he usually
stayed with this diplomat. It is possible therefore that the two men did have
a close personal bond beyond the agent-contact relationship. The fundamental
motivation for Wilson was that he did not see the Soviet Union as a threat to
Britain therefore, to him, there was nothing wrong in his actions. Furthermore, while a body of friends existed the British people could not be dehu-
manised within the Soviet Union and war would be less likely. To Wilson he
was simply extending the hand of friendship and, as he stated, "I didn't tell
them anything they didn't already know."[102]

    From information supplied by Oleg Gordievsky the diplomat can be
identified as Anatoly Maisko who, as Cultural Attaché in London, oversaw
the friendship societies. Maisko was not a KGB officer but can be defined as
a "co-optee", a KGB-trained diplomat who operated with a dual brief.
Gordievsky recalled that Maisko was a man with similar ideas to himself,
someone that had become disillusioned with Communism and played out
his role to the minimum. His relationship with Wilson was utilised to pro-
long Maisko's appointment in London. Wilson was his personally cultivated
contact but, as Maisko's KGB case officer, Gordievsky was well placed to
observe that there was "very little flesh" to the relationship. Due to
Gordievsky's similar disenchantment he did not press Maisko's to obtain
more sensitive information or encourage Wilson to run errands that would

compromise him. Instead Gordievsky allowed them to "chat as friends rather than act as the traitor he wanted to be."[103] Reading between the lines it is possible to accept that, as Wilson admitted, his role had little insignificance. In fact Wilson possibly saw himself as more important than he actually was.

This is possibly the case with many of the MPs that Gordievsky is aware were 'confidential contacts' but with whom he had no personal dealings. He recalled a similar case with Alf Lomas MEP[104] who had been cultivated by Bogdanov, the amanuensis of Brockway's latter days. The order from the Centre was to encourage all sympathetic MEPs to heckle Ronald Reagan when he addressed the European parliament at Strasbourg. Bogdanov passed the idea on to Lomas, who complied encouraging his left-wing colleagues to join in. Bogdanov was able to claim a great success, however we can hypothesise that Lomas would have taken part in any demonstration against Reagan and the United States. Fellow MEP Stan Newens would have agreed with the principle of the demonstration and, arguably, others would also have seen this as 'good fun' and so joined in semi-independently. This alternative interpretation of the event proposes that just because the Soviet 'friend' suggested an action does not mean it was automatically complied with. Equally compliance cannot be used as a measure of the extent of Soviet control exerted over these figures. This reinforces the alternative perspective of agents of influence. Though confidential contacts existed, it appears that none of the MPs were either slavish or blind supporters but individuals who acted according to their own ideologically-driven agendas.[105]

This argument is reinforced by the fact that Wilson was aware of the faults of the Soviet Union. He was a frequent visitor and was given freedom of movement. He saw that standards of living were lower than they should have been and blamed this upon mismanagement. Wilson argued that the Soviet Union had all the resources necessary for creating socialism in one country, but the totalitarian nature of the Stalinist model of governance had acted as an obstacle to socialist achievements. In Wilson's words, the Soviet leadership and people had "lost their inspiration."[106] Wilson made no excuses for this, but remained unable to divorce his socialist aspirations for Britain from the success of the Soviet system. To denounce the Soviet model would mean rejecting existing socialism, so Wilson preferred to ignore the faults in his public statements on the Soviet Union and provided help where possible. He stated that the failure of the Soviet leadership to achieve a socialist society was not just a domestic failure; they failed socialists the world over. The ideological link he believed existed between the Soviet Union and the global socialist movement led Wilson to desire success for the Soviet Union and, therefore, he "didn't mind helping it a bit".[107]

Like Philip Crees, he recognised that the Soviet relationship with the BSFS was purely political. The purpose of the organisation was to gain supporters in high places. This was made evident during celebrations of the 75th Anniversary of the Russian Revolution. Wilson attended events on the basis that if he, or another MP, did not then neither would a representative of the Soviet Embassy. However, this did not dampen his spirits. Wilson believed in the fundamental basis of the BSFS:

> Without doubt in my mind the real driving force was that by support-ing the Soviet Union the cry of 'workers of the world unite' would be realised upon the economic success of the Soviet Union.[108]

The membership consisted of individuals who "had hoped the Revolution would succeed or were grateful to the Red Army or wanted the Cold War to end."[109] These ideals were consistent with Wilson's motivations and beliefs.

Wilson grew up in the shadow of the Russian Revolution as the great socialist achievement, one in which exploited workers like his father had sought inspiration. Furthermore Soviet aid to striking workers would have reinforced the link between the workers struggle and Communist Russia. Wilson's experience of the war, as with Lamond and Short, imbibed him with the perspective of the Soviet Union as the saviour of Europe and, like many of his contemporaries, he viewed the ensuing Cold War as an anathema to everything he believed in.

The important aspect of Wilson's mindset is his perception of the nature of Soviet society. Like Cole and the Webbs, he believed in the socialist basis of that society. Equally he recognised that it was a project under development and this led him to attempt to aid its success. Arguably he became an agent of the Soviet Union. However his relationship with Maisko was founded upon neither traitorous or self-seeking ideals. Wilson's belief in international socialism, not the paramount parochial realism, motivated him to act in opposition to government policy and the normative negative perspective of the Soviet Union. He believed that the world needed a so-cialist nation to act as a model and, though fundamentally flawed, the clos-est practical example of his model of socialism was the Soviet Union. This led Wilson to support the Soviet regime. To reject the model would mean denouncing his own ideals, a shift he was still unable to make in 1999.

We can therefore characterise Wilson as a man whose activities were motivated by deep-seated socialist ideals. He believed in worker's equality and argued that greater political power should be vested in the producing class. The ideal was not to be realised in this country or under the political system within which he worked. Therefore he protected the one nation that aspired to the same principles as he did. He was not alone in pursuing this idealised and self-ordained role. To interpret his activity we should look at one further example of an individual who acted as a contact and assess the fundamental basis of his motivation, thus testing the hypothesis established by the Wilson case.

THE WILD MAN OF LEITH

Ron Brown, MP for Edinburgh Leith 1979-92, had what can be described as a colourful parliamentary career. His political trajectory was founded upon a radical socialist agenda fighting for workers' control. Brown had been sacked in 1972 for leading an electricians strike in support of the miners. Furthermore, as a councillor in Lothian he was suspended for voting against spending cuts proposed by his own party. Therefore, Brown can be categorised as being of a similar vein to Wilson, Kitson and Lamond as far as political roots are concerned. His opposition to capitalism and Conservatism led Brown to throw eggs at Prime Minister Margaret Thatcher on the occasion of her visit to Glasgow in 1982, and to wield and drop the mace while opposing the introduction of poll tax in Scotland in 1985. However, it was his internationalist ideals, alongside events in his private life, which led to his deselection.

Brown's internationalism was guided by his pro-Soviet sympathies and his admiration for existing socialist systems. He enjoyed close links with Libyan leader Muammar Gaddafi and made frequent visits without the sanction of party leader Foot. Gaddafi was a Soviet ally and laid claim to socialist credentials and Brown's support for him was one aspect of his role in supporting the working class struggle. Brown obtained money from Gaddafi to fund the striking miners in 1984; an activity shared by Mick Welsh[110] and John Platts-Mills. Milne's account of the affair found Platts-Mills as the most active in obtaining funds from both the Soviet bloc and Libya and ensuring it reached the NUM's Warsaw bank account.[111] This shows that there was a degree of cohesion between the parliamentary and the extra-parliamentary pro-Soviet left at times of keen struggle. This should not be seen as unusual. Brown was a keen working class activist; Platts-Mills, a veteran of the British pro-Soviet left-wing, had already shown his colours during his career as a QC. That they were allied in support of the miners is not particularly striking, particularly as Brown had already been active as a member of the pro-Soviet coterie.

The only voice from the Labour benches on the Afghanistan conflict came from Ron Brown. He had established links with the Soviet sponsored government led by Babrak Karmal, and had been a guest of Karmal in early 1981 during a mission sponsored by the Soviet Embassy.[112] His actions during this visit gained him much press coverage, particularly when, accompanied by Bob Litherland, MP for Manchester Central 1979-97, Brown unwisely posed in front of a monument in the shape of a tank after writing in *Labour Monthly* that he had seen no tanks in the country. The media ignored his work in procuring the release of Pinder Wilson, a British national taken hostage in Afghanistan during the conflict, this was not part of the received image of the 'loony left' which Brown personified.[113] Brown pursued a pro-Karmal position after his return and argued in parliament that the Karmal regime should be recognised. Recognition, Brown argued, would reassure Karmal that the Western world was not antagonistic towards him. Karmal, Brown claimed, was willing to extend the hand of friendship: "we are talking about world peace, does that not matter, or does militarism cloud every mind in the House?"[114]

Brown produced an 'eyewitness report' for *Labour Monthly*[115] following his visit. He reported that Karmal had told him that Western hostility towards his regime, formally established in April 1978, forced him to "seek aid from the USSR".[116] The previous President Hafizzulah Amin, whose coup had overturned the revolutionary People's Democratic Party government in July 1979, had been a CIA agent, Brown argued, who had been employed to undermine the popularity of the revolutionary party. Therefore the Soviet army with public backing had executed Amin. The Soviet occupying force now remained to keep the regime secure from further attack from the West and would leave only "when the border areas were guaranteed from interference".[117] Brown claimed that he saw none of the warfare that the Western media described. He also saw no sign of rebels and described Afghanistan's capital Jalalabad as "quiet and peaceful."[118] He argued that to have been duped into this perception would have taken "a cast of thousands and the biggest Hollywood set ever. And quite frankly this would have turned Cecil B de Mille into an amateur in comparison".[119] This means that either the Western governments had initiated a gigantic conspiracy campaign or Ron Brown, despite his protestations, was either duped or was lying. The question is if he was lying, why; and for what?

Brown argued that to the West, and particularly to the Thatcher government, the 'red bogey' was a convenient tool. It justified arms spending and an aggressive foreign policy. He argued that this was the real reason for Western refusal to recognise the Karmal government. The alternative, Brown argued, would mean admitting that the Soviet Union was not acting in a hostile manner, an admission that would force the British government to review its anti-Soviet defence policy. This analysis of British policy determinants, and his sympathy for the Soviet model of socialism, led Brown to develop a relationship with an agent of the Soviet Union.

In his autobiography *Next Step Execution* Gordievsky revealed that Brown was a willing, but incomprehensible, contact that he had inherited.[120] It is unclear what Brown's role was in relation to the KGB, or how he was recruited. Brown's private life suggested he lacked moral standards and self-control. This made him the perfect target for the KGB, notwithstanding his personal beliefs. It also could explain how he came to the conclusion that the Soviet forces in Afghanistan were living in harmony with majoritarian support. This was the picture that the Soviet government attempted to supply to the West. Could he therefore have acted as a propagandist on their behalf? Without forming conclusions based upon circumstantial evidence, it is indicative that Brown became a trade agent for Communist North Korea, acting as a conduit between British companies, such as the Virgin Trading Company and Highland Distillers, and the Stalinist regime.[121] Therefore he maintained a role as an agent working for a Communist power, possibly due to his ideological links with the dogma of that society. This also appears to have been the motivation for his pro-Soviet activity that is under examination here.

Brown's only attempt to explain his stance was made through letters to *The Scotsman*. From these scant statements it appears that he, like Platts-Mills before him, was attempting to redress a balance. He stated that the right wing used the Soviet Union as a "bogeyman" which was "conjure[d] up… to divert attention from the real issues in this country."[122] This he believed should be redressed by the Labour Party which should recognise that it could not create socialism in a vacuum, but must ally with other progressive forces both national and international.[123] This meant adopting the Soviet economic model of planning, one which Brown reminded readers was not only a Communist theory but also one that had been proposed by Nye Bevan in the late 1940s.[124] His disappointment lay in the fact that the Labour leadership had abandoned socialist principles to gain office and subsequently built a consensus in parliament on both domestic and foreign policy. Labour, he argued, must be authoritative in policy making when in power and their policy should be constrained only by the principles of socialism and the demands of the Trade Unions, not the forces of capitalism. The principles he promoted were those laid down by Sydney Webb in 1922 when he authored the Constitution, Brown invoked the symbolic significance of the words of Clause IV arguing that worker's control of the means of production was fundamental to establishing a socialist state.[125] Here we can see how Brown's thinking led him to support the Soviet Union as a socialist model and how this mindset led him to become a confidential contact of the Embassy's diplomats.

Brown believed that the Soviet Union was socialist and argued that the Anglo-American anti-Sovietism was part of a strategy of deception founded upon the self-interest of the capitalist class. It was this anti-Communist campaign, Brown argued, that was posing the greater threat to world peace as it opposed the creation of socialist nations, ones that were non-competitive so would actively avert war. The perception of the West as anti-socialist highlights Brown's belief that the Cold War was zero-sum. He argued that if the Soviet Union lost the Cold War, and was forced to adopt capitalism, then a socialist future would be unattainable. It seems, therefore, that Brown, like Wilson, was prepared to aid the Soviet Union in order to ensure the survival of the 'socialist superpower' and its ideology.

In a letter to *The Times* Brown defended his relationship with Gordievsky. He denied ever acting as an agent. Gordievsky, he recalled, was someone he had known as a "newspaper man who claimed he wanted to brief the Soviet reformers, including a rising star called Gorbachev, about the realities of British life."[126] The information imparted was trivial, Brown argued: "[Gordievsky] could have got it from the Beano".[127] Gordievsky had led him to believe the Politburo desired "better understanding of the situation in this country" telling Brown that the Soviet goal was establishing a "mutual purpose and camaraderie."[128] Brown's attitude is tinged with bitterness towards Gordievsky, possibly as a traitor to the Soviet Union but, mainly because he revealed his relationship with Brown. Perhaps presciently Brown recalled:

> I have now to ask myself was the information for British Intelligence? It was always Labour figures Gordievsky wanted to know about. The information was more valuable to the Tories than it would have been to the KGB.[129]

This demonstrates the risk in pursuing this type of contact. The KGB operatives held a zero-sum perception of the world, there were no friendly contacts, only potential spies and traitors. Brown's perspective was that he was personally contributing to the creation of a new rapprochement, this perspective was not shared by the security and intelligence services of either side.

FRIENDSHIP: FOR THE COMMON WEAL OR ANTI-DEMOCRATIC TRAITORS?

There are no key differences between the motivations of these individuals and those studied in chapters covering previous periods. There is some evidence that Brown and Wilson held a more radical outlook, one similar to Renee Short's, while Lamond seemed to argue from a position similar to that adopted by Ian Mikardo and Konni Zilliacus. Arguably Brown's stance was influenced by his role as a Trade Union activist and his lack of an intellectual, socialist perspective. He perceived the world as black and white, socialist or anti-socialist, and could not see the nuances between differing systems and regimes as other left-wingers did. This zero-sum opinion of the world was one that was shared by many who held pro-Soviet sympathies. The perception they held was that the Cold War was a zero-sum ideological conflict and evidence indicates that they also held the belief that the future of socialism was intrinsically linked to the survival of the Soviet Union. Perhaps it is accurate to argue that they perceived the second phase of the arms race as being decisive. Equally, they realised that their influence within the party had reached its watershed. This does not, however, necessarily set them apart from their predecessors.

What is clear is that, like their predecessors, they believed that they were acting with the best intentions and on behalf of humanity as a whole. They created a linkage between the ideals of peace and co-existence and the goal of attaining a socialist future. They were not slavish to Moscow, or supportive of Washington or London, but held the rather exaggerated view that their constituency was the future generations of the world. They wished all children, of all nations, creeds and political systems, to be born into a world founded upon peace and socialism, not capitalism and competition. Many of their left-wing colleagues, such as Tony Benn, also promoted these ideals, however these figures avoided linking their socialist doctrine with the Soviet communist model. The pro-Soviet position, held by figures like Brown, Lamond and Wilson, led them to argue for an end to the bi-polar antagonism and the pursuit of co-operation and understanding. This would allow the Soviet Union to introduce democracy to the state economy. This would be the fruition of the dream that the majority of the non-Communist, pro-Soviet left shared, and the objective they worked for despite broad hostility to such ideas.

The pro-Soviet left-wingers were unable to achieve this through the lobby or from the backbenches in parliament. These figures therefore adopted a more individual approach; one of personal contact and rapprochement at the personal, rather than governmental, level. The motivation for this is largely identical to those which drove Zilliacus to establish a relationship with Khrushchev and Tito, his aim was to act as a conduit between the two leaders and their western counterparts. These figures acted in opposition to the policies of their party and ultimately the law of the nation. They appear not to have recognised the legitimacy of these policies and concomitant laws due to the fervency of their opposition. They could not view the Soviet Union as an enemy and thus co-operated with organisations that attempted to change the ruling rationale. By no means was this a new phenomenon. Laski argued in *Tribune* in 1937 that "are we not all, as socialists, friends of the Soviet Union, even if we are also critics."[130] In the zero-sum world of bipolarity criticism was no longer an option for many. Therefore they acted in the only way they believed to be correct. They refused to accept defeat by majority decision. Instead they chose to work as activists on the fringes of politics.

This led some to support the notion of totalitarianism, in the form of a commitment to establishing socialism through strict control of the economy of a nation. This was seldom made explicit, however a tradition

existed for a minority of left-wingers to argue that only by seizing full control
of society could the groundwork for a socialist state be established. These
socialists had experienced the defeat of their ideals from time immemorial.
The only success in establishing socialism had been made by the Soviet
leadership and only achieved by removing political opponents, ending
democracy and ruling by force. Marx after all had hinted at this by extolling
the notion of a dictatorship of the proletariat. Thus some were led to accept
totalitarianism as a route towards socialism and supported and defended the
Soviet Union and her allies because of the system they had created. They had
accepted the necessity of harsh means to attain the ends they required and
were willing to support the Soviet Union in comparison to the ineffectuality
of western democratic socialism. These figures retained democratic socialist
credentials, and supported the ethos of that creed, but they had also become
disillusioned with Labour governments that rejected socialist principles and
accepted the constraints of capitalism. This was the conundrum they faced
when arguing their causes in parliament. They knew they would not be taken
seriously, that the majority either would not or could not effect change,
however they stood by their personal principles and dreamt of becoming
influential. They acted independently and supported the cause of a foreign
nation purely on the grounds that its ethos was closer to their own than that
of the British government, or indeed, the Labour Party.

THE END OF PARLIAMENTARY PRO-SOVIETISM
In 1989 the focus for pro-Sovietism collapsed, however by this time
pro-Soviet influences had been exorcised from the Labour Party. The NEC,
accurately described by Richard Crossman as the 'battering-ram of
change',[131] was to lose this power under the Kinnock initiated organisational reforms. The only oppositional force to these reforms was what Shaw
described as the 'hard left'. This group should not be characterised as being
pro-Soviet, nor should it be assumed that all pro-Soviet MPs belonged exclusively within the hard left To group the left together in this way disguises
the nuances within its traditions. However an agenda was developed, based
upon democratic socialist principles, which was spported by the majority of
those who harboured pro-Soviet sympathies. Neil Kinnock, as party leader
1983-92, led an attack on those individuals who, as Hattersley put it, made up
the "illegitimate left" who were "cuckooing in Labour's nest".[132] There were
continual attempts to introduce one member, one vote [OMOV] between
1984 and 1993 in order to reduce the power of the constituency based activist.
The introduction of OMOV for elections to the NEC eroded the power of
the left-wing and reduced the influence of Communist Trade Union leaders
like Ken Gill and Alan Sapper. A clear concomitant of the reform procedure
is that, as TUC President 1985-6, Gill had little opportunity to reverse the

rightward shifting balance of power. This was Kinnock's chief objective.[133]
Responding to a report produced by Geoff Bish, Labour Research Secretary,[134]
Kinnock strove to ensure that the leadership's hands were not tied by
manifesto commitments drawn up by the left-wing and that the Cabinet
regained control over party policy, candidate selection and communications.
This was to be achieved by the 1992 General Election.[135]

The battle over candidate reselection resulted in the pro-Soviet MPs
losing their parliamentary seats. Pro-Soviet ideas were unpopular within
Militant, the left-wing group that had become influential within many of
the staunch Labour constituencies. This resulted in William Wilson resign-
ing rather than face an unsympathetic reselection battle and James Lamond
being deselected in favour of a Trotskyist candidate. Renee Short also refused
to face the reselection procedure and stood down prior to the 1987 General
Election.[136] The influence of Militant, within both the CLPs and the NEC,
was expressed when Tony Benn, Eric Heffer, Joan Maynard and Dennis
Skinner organised a walk-out of left-wingers on the NEC in support of
Militant, thus leaving the body impotent without a quorum.[137] Other left-
wingers, described by Butler and Kavanagh as 'the old white left', were to be
deselected in the name of positive discrimination. For example, Norman
Atkinson was forced out of his Tottenham seat to make way for Bernie
Grant. While this provided the Tottenham constituency with a more representative MP, it clearly showed that the extreme views held by the pro-
Soviet strand were losing appeal at every level. The Militant-inspired manual
on selection encouraged CLPs to produce a spreadsheet recording how
their MPs had voted in parliament.[138] While this did benefit all left-wing MPs
it became clear that the pro-Soviet members were at a disadvantage. As an
ideological battle raged within the party it became clear that all factions were
opposed to their ideas.

The pro-Soviet sympathisers became increasingly isolated even within
a left dominated party. The Bennite left saw them as mavericks and opposed
their attachment of socialism to Soviet communism. The centre-left and
right wing argued that they, together with Militant, were damaging to the
party's electoral credibility. Thus Kinnock's attacks on the radical sections were
welcomed by a majority of the parliamentary and extra-parliamentary
membership. The isolation of the pro-Soviet MPs, and their maverick status,
can be recognised by the lack of cohesion over the party's direction. Allaun,
Atkinson, Lamond, Mikardo, Richardson and Thorne backed Benn in his
challenge for the deputy leadership, but Brown, Ross, Short and Wilson
wavered in their support of Benn but could put forward no suitable alternative
candidate.[139] This lack of cohesion impaired their opportunity to gain influence,
however, the broad left-wing consensus, while it lasted, did make the party
leadership a hostage to left-wing activism. Tudor Jones indicated that

Kinnock, during his first years as leader, saw himself as restricted in reforming the party. His mission was to break the left's cohesion and undermine its position at all levels of the party. It was only following the enforced deselection of pro-Soviet and Militant candidates that Kinnock, and later Smith and Blair, enjoyed a "time of tranquillity when party members were finally prepared to let [the leader] get on with his job."[140]

The consistent attack on left-wing strongholds, the creation of a centrally approved candidate list and a complete policy review, a procedure which was to see the party accept what some left-wing critics argue to be a new right agenda,[141] also saw the ideas of pro-Sovietism removed from the party. Ernie Ross was to be the only MP referred to in this study that survived into the Blair parliament. Some of their less radical allies, however, were to maintain the stance developed by Victory for Socialism. These individuals, numbering no more than twenty, were to be a faint voice opposing the support for the American bombing campaign against Iraq.[142] Unilateralism was abandoned under Kinnock and nuclear weapons were once again accepted as a necessary part of Britain's defence capabilities by a Labour government.[143] With the collapse of Soviet communism came the abandonment of many of the socialist tenets that drew those with pro-Soviet sympathies to the Labour Party. It is unlikely that such ideas will resurface in the foreseeable future given the current trajectory of the party.

7

THE PERSPECTIVES OF PRO-SOVIETISM

The case studies of pro-Soviet MPs show that there were nuances between their individual activities and motivations. This indicates that the Soviet Union played a different role within the political thought of each individual. Some individuals were convinced that the Soviet model of socialism represented their practical ideal and, on the strength of this conviction, sought to protect the regime. In contrast others employed the Soviet Union purely to express opposition to the Cold War rationale. They rejected the rationale that the Soviet Union posed a military threat, arguing that the United States had created a myth surrounding Soviet foreign policy aims. This chapter suggests a framework for understanding these differing perspectives and seeks to explain why individuals who held contrasting perspectives pursued differing types of pro-Soviet activity. Understanding the nuances between the individuals helps to explain why there was a lack of cohesion between these politicians. While they shared a common focus for their critique of the Cold War, they did not share a framework of reference, because of their differing perspectives of the Soviet Union, and therefore they lacked unifying objectives.

Having assessed their arguments it appears that some British Labour Party MPs supported the Soviet Union because they believed that the Soviet Communist system represented a positive alternative to the politics and policies that were native to their own party. The strengths of belief differ and can often be contextualised within the periods in which they were developed. This is the primary reason for this study being carried out chronologically. However the nuances between individual's beliefs, and their activities, cannot always be confined within one definite historical period. Some beliefs emerged out of a specific period, and were reactive to events in the international order or the Labour Party. However, other pro-Soviet perspectives developed into traditions that would shape the beliefs of the pro-Soviet strand in later periods, thus becoming an aspect of Labourist thinking. While the study has focused on individuals as case studies, determining the specifics

of their beliefs and influences, this penultimate chapter will focus on the
ideological strands within the pro-Soviet movement.

Many socialists and liberals, who espoused pacifism and social equality, saw the Russian Revolution as a great emancipatory event. This spirit
underlined the agenda for the 1917 Peace Convention. In contrast, the
Bolshevik coup received a more reserved reception. The Soviet political
system, which emerged following the Civil War, became a curiosity, an image Stalin exploited to the full. However, it would be inaccurate to assume
that Soviet marketing techniques provided the sole impetus for pro-
Sovietism. Developments in relations between the Soviet Union and the
West, and failures within the Western social democratic model, chiefly dictated how the Soviet Union was perceived. In those sparse periods of domestic stability and international harmony the Soviet Union received little
attention, however this was limited to a brief period during the 1920s.

Events overtook the Soviet propaganda campaign; making the Soviet model the focus of a movement over which the ideological leaders of
international communism had little control. For example in the 1930s a
movement formed calling for a popular front to emerge within the European socialist movement. The CPGB were drawn into this movement but
did not stand as the ideological leader. The lack of Communist control
over the pro-Soviet coterie was also weak during the Cold War. The peace
movements, which revolved within a pseudo-pro-Soviet orbit, opposed
Communists control,[1] but did not specifically oppose the Soviet Union.
This meant that the Communist Party succeeded by following entryist tactics, gaining influence within movements, but failed to attain ideological
control over policy.

Labour Party left-wingers chaired many of the organisations that fell
within the pro-Soviet orbit. This appears as something of an anomaly con-
sidering the policy of the party that they represented. Studying the individuals themselves however, in isolation, it appears an obvious path for them to
select. They stood as individual thinkers, motivated by ideals that surpassed
the traditional party political dichotomy. Equally they seldom sought real
power, only the power to influence. They attempted to be agents of influence for their cause and took on the role of change agent. Due to the un-
popularity of the focus of their arguments they became almost self-defeat-
ing, despite the fact that their objective was to legitimise their cause. They
were an embarrassment to both the Militant left and the centre-right of the
Labour Party and were considered by the leadership, alongside Militant, as a
serious threat to party cohesion. Kinnock, and arguably many of his predecessors, saw the removal of those who promoted the left-wing agenda as a
necessity. Kinnock attacked the ideologues stating that:

> Implausible promises don't win victories [but] start with far-fetched
> resolutions… [which] are then pickled into rigid dogma, a code, and
> you go through years sticking to that, outdated, misplaced, irrelevant
> to the real needs.[2]

This statement encapsulates the ideological mindset of the pro-Soviet strand, but the expression of this opinion did not convince the pro-Soviet left that they should alter their course. To the pro-Soviet MPs these 'far-fetched' resolutions were deep-seated ideals.

Any attempt to group these individuals into neat compartments can obscure the nuances in their thinking. However, categorising the perspectives they held of the Soviet Union allows us to discuss the subjacent denominators within pro-Soviet thinking. A discussion of the commonalties that are evident in their arguments provides an indication of how the Soviet Union figured in each individual's thinking and how this perspective acted as a prism through which the beholder viewed the world.

After cursorily examining these figures it can be argued that the Soviet Union played a different role to each sympathetic observer. However we can group the differing perspectives under one single assumption, that the Soviet Union represented a positive alternative to capitalism and so stood as an example to socialists the world over. Not all within the pro-Soviet strand argued that the Soviet model should be adopted *in extenso*. Therefore we can separate the beliefs into subdivisions. These subdivisions will be contextualised with regard to the individuals to whom they are relevant and, where possible, the historical period in which they were developed.

THE SOVIET UNION AS THE SOCIALIST EXAMPLE

The Soviet Union's claim to be the first socialist state certainly provided the stimulus for left-wing interest. Some awarded the Soviet Union the unique status of representing the core of the socialist world and, though the Soviet model was copied, it remained the model and, during the Cold War, was able to establish itself as the protector of the international socialist movement. China, Cuba or any other independent or semi-independent Communist state managed to achieve similar prominence or status among British MPs. Despite the fact that the majority of influential Western socialists rejected the Soviet model, others were unable to separate the Soviet Union from the ideals of the global socialist movement. Thus, while Trade Unionists and intellectuals denounced the socialist, and indeed Marxist, aspects of the Soviet Union, others argued that the Soviet Union was socialist in various respects, a description they did not award to Britain under Labour.

The Wall Street Crash, and the economic repercussions, led to one of the high watermarks of this ideal. Capitalism, the system founded upon never-ending accumulation, neared apparent collapse. Socialists, like G D H Cole, Jennie Lee and John Strachey, with previously diverse beliefs, agreed that the world was destined to progress towards socialism. This appeared to be proven by the fact that the Soviet Union was thriving, a factor that led many theorists to develop a theory for the establishment of socialism based upon the Soviet model. There were differing strengths of belief in the Soviet Union as a model. While some confined themselves to arguing that a Soviet-style centrally planned economy was the key to establishing a socialist society, others confidently argued that all aspects of Soviet society were socialist and that the Soviet model should become the blueprint for all socialist movements. Planners, such as John Maynard Keynes and GDH Cole, lent reserved support to the Soviet model in a revised form. Within the zero-sum context of the Cold War, MPs Frank Allaun and Stan Newens argued that there was an interdependent relationship between the Soviet model and international socialism, and hinted that the success of socialism relied upon the success of the Soviet model. While these figures exhibited a restrained support for aspects of the Soviet model, there were those who expressed an almost devout belief. Ron Brown, Alex Kitson, Renee Short, the Webbs and William Wilson all placed the Soviet Union on a pedestal as an example to the British Labour movement.

Those figures that did express a belief in the Soviet Union as a model for socialism utilised this belief as a mirror to reflect the inequalities and inconsistencies within western democracy and Labour Party policies. Issues such as unemployment, education and free access to welfare were highlighted. The purpose for their comparativist analysis was to hypothesise that if the Soviet Union could achieve clear advances, despite unfavourable circumstances, why were the British Labour Party's achievements so limited. This analysis was activated particularly in response to claims that the western system was superior. This was the case after the 1931 debacle, but was also expressed following the unravelling of key aspects of the 1945-50 welfare reform programme. MPs like Allaun and Short used the Soviet Union as a stick with which to beat those socialists who suggested further cuts to benefits awarded the British proletariat, particularly when the cuts were made to finance 'unnecessary' defence spending. The Soviet Union, they argued, had achieved quantitative results in a very short period, while Britain was constrained by a cross-bench consensus despite having had an established socialist government. This reflected the necessity for change. Those who espoused change did not wish to disband democracy, but wanted the Labour Party to harness the reins of government and break the economic power of the capitalist class. This would allow for swift reforms that would establish Britain as a socialist state.

This was socialism in the most idealistic and dogmatic form. Arguably, had a British Labour government been guided firmly by its founding principles then these individuals would have been satisfied. However this was not, and could not be, the case. Forces beyond governmental control ensured that a pro-capitalist consensus was maintained. This led to mounting dissatisfaction among the left-wing of the party. It was within this dissatisfied left, many of whom felt estranged from the party and parliament, that notions of pro-Sovietism emerged. Those who developed the pro-Soviet critique of the party highlighted the achievements of the Soviet Union and exhibited the belief that if the Soviet experiment failed then socialism across Europe would be perceived as an obsolete ideology. Therefore they protected the model. This notion was an aspect of the mindsets of many of those who actively opposed the Cold War, particularly Allaun, Hutchinson, Kitson, Platts-Mills, Short, Swingler and Wilson. Therefore their arguments developed a dual motivation; they spearheaded a campaign for co-existence that also aimed to protect the system in which they vested their hopes.

This motivation was shared by others who were even more proactive in their pro-Soviet activity. Melita Norwood, the employee of the British Non-Ferrous Metals Association who willing passed secrets to the KGB regarding the British nuclear weapons development programme, explained:

> I thought they should somehow be adequately defended because everyone was against them, against this experiment... it was unfair to them that they shouldn't be able to develop their weaponry.[3]

This attitude was not particular to Norwood, or to others proven to be agents of the KGB. Konni Zilliacus also characterised the Soviet Union as a beleaguered nation forced into acting defensively by a hostile world and Allaun argued that the Soviet experiment should be allowed to evolve unhindered. Thus by attaching 'Socialist' to the national title, the Soviet Union was able to become an embodiment of the illusory Marxist-Socialist state.

THE SOVIET UNION AS A POSITIVE ALTERNATIVE

Russia was epitomised as the model for alternative action after the revolution of February 1917. Later this trend was exemplified by the Popular Front Movement. The world was perceived as divided between opposing political ideologies of right and left, defined in their most extreme forms as fascism and communism. This dichotomy led some left-wing ideologues to be drawn to embrace the ideas of the Soviet Union as the only alternative to fascism and imperialism. The argument was put forward that if there was a choice between fascism and communism, communism must be the victor. This was particularly espoused by G D H Cole, but featured in the arguments of Aneurin Bevan, Stafford Cripps and S O Davies. Bevan and Davies had received financial aid from the Soviet Union in their roles as strike leaders in the South Wales coal mines.[4] Therefore it stood, albeit for a short time in Bevan's case, as their natural ally as the embodiment of proletarian power. This led to the perception of the Soviet Union as the enemy of governments that supported capitalism, but the ally of the working class of every nation. This notion was transposed into the political ideas of many of those who went into politics through the Trade Unions.

    This analysis was extended during the Cold War era. The Soviet Union was seen as the positive alternative to the United States. The left-wing would not accept the subjugation of British foreign and defence policy to the White House and opposed any attempt to allow the United States hegemony over Europe. The Soviet Union's history was analysed sympathetically within a subjectivist framework. This reflected the ideals of the analyst and the conclusion was determined by the perception that the Soviet model was fundamentally correct. If the Soviet government had deformed the Marxist-Leninist model, Zilliacus in particular argued, then this was due to the anti-Communist campaign pursued by the capitalist world. If attempts to develop an understanding of the character and implicit aims of the Soviet system were made then the Soviet model would evolve along socialist rather than totalitarian lines. All un-socialist activity within the Communist bloc was excused by activating this analysis. Zilliacus, in *I Choose Peace*, was a major exponent of this view however G D H Cole, who put forward a similar argument during the 1930s, laid much of the groundwork for this analysis. This alternative analysis allowed socialists to view the Soviet Union as a socialist nation that had become disfigured by the international order in which it functioned. Later sympathisers such as Wilson adopted a similar view in retrospect, therefore this was one of the traditions that developed within pro-Sovietism.

    As outlined above there were those who argued that the Soviet Union was socialist. This argument was activated at times when a Labour government was forced to adopt a conservative agenda. The condemnation of the Callaghan budget of 1974, by Atkinson, Newens and Short, was peppered with comparisons to Soviet economic policy. Those individuals who held the view that the Soviet Union was socialist developed a comparative analysis of British Labourism. Their conclusion was that the British model was deficient. Thus the idealised image of the Soviet Union became a fixture within the mindset of the pro-Soviet MPs. They vested their hope in the Soviet Union as the driving force behind world socialism and were unable to recognise the failings of the Soviet regime because, to them, it embodied their hopes for the future.

These radical figures desired a society without poverty, unemployment or inequality and believed that that society had been created in the Soviet Union. This tradition can be traced back to the Webbs but was also promulgated by Kitson, Short and Wilson. The popularisation of this notion created a certain degree of support for the Soviet Union, this was not vested in the Soviet leadership but in Soviet socialism as an ideology with a practical dimension. It is important to note that none of these individuals ever extolled the virtues of Stalin or Brezhnev and that those who initially supported Khrushchev were part of a short-lived minority. It was a belief in the socialist societal basis that was the impetus for support and this, in turn, led them to support the governmental policies in an attempt to protect the regime.

These individuals supported the idea of socialism with religious fervour. They believed that they alone recognised the true potential of socialism as a governmental model. All they had to do was convince others of that potential. They thus employed the Soviet Union to show what could be achieved by maintaining a commitment to socialism, while highlighting the fact that these were attained under an atmosphere of hostility. They failed to realise that much Soviet propaganda was false because they wanted to believe with an almost religious fervency. Therefore they allowed themselves to be convinced. Thus their beliefs and perceptions acted as a prism through which they viewed the world.

THE SOVIET UNION AS A GOVERNMENTAL ALTERNATIVE

As cursorily explored in earlier chapters there was a strand of thought within pro-Sovietism that supported the notion of authoritarian socialism. This remains largely unstated in any of the cases under examination apart from Ron Brown and Lester Hutchinson. Oleg Gordievsky, however, linked the whole body of pro-Soviet thought with a support for totalitarianism. In an article for *The Spectator* he asked:

Why were totalitarian inclinations so very characteristic of the Old Left, and why did so many of its members participate so enthusiastically in the operations of the Soviet propaganda machine?[5]

This question can be answered, to an extent, by reviewing the arguments many of the pro-Soviet figures put forward in support of the Soviet political model.

From the now infamous 'betrayal' of socialist principles by Ramsay MacDonald in 1931 onwards, there was a recognition that certain aspects of British democracy enforced the subjugation of socialism to capitalism. Those who opposed the Bernsteinian model, which argued that socialists could only create a reformed version of capitalism until history ran its full course,[6] proposed that their leaders should act with greater resolve and that the principles of socialism should not merely guide, but dominate, policy formulation. Cole, in 1941, hypothesised about the redundancy of social democracy and used the achievements of Soviet society to illustrate his argument. Others developed a similar analysis. Therefore some pro-Soviet MPs were explicit in their support for committed, decisive and de-termined leadership in implementing socialism and eradicating capitalism.

The Labour Party has only twice had a sufficiently significant majority to dominate parliament. The first ran from 1945-50, the second began in 1997. In the former period opposition from the left was based upon the notion that the time had arrived to implement a socialist policy and make such a policy irreversible. While Attlee's domestic reforms were indeed so-cialist, they were also consensual. The left wanted far more than what was on offer, particularly in the field of foreign policy. The fact that this too was based on a consensus between left and right caused the dissent described in this study and led to a continued and deepening polarisation within the party. Some critics of the government, particularly G D H Cole, Lester Hutchinson and Stephen Swingler also became, at key junctures, critics of the democratic system. They argued that it precluded radical reform and was opposed to any pro-socialist advancement.

This allows speculation as to what type of political system did they argue would allow the creation of a socialist society? The examples they offered to us, both prior to and after the Second World War, indicate that it was only when the leadership had absolute power that society could be totally reformed. A determined socialist leader had to be able to suppress the reactionary elements, particularly when they hold economic, if not governmental, power. The strict economic centralisation enacted by Stalin could not have been accomplished under a liberal democratic parliamentary system. Equally the programme that the left prescribed for 'cradle to grave' welfare and full employment could not be achieved when capitalists retained economic power. The pro-Soviet strand did not enquire whether the British public would want such reforms. Their understanding was that a socialist society was mankind's ultimate desire. The evidence they presented argued that those living under Communism had a better standard of living than their British counterparts. Kitson, Short and Wilson all promoted this argument in the press; therefore we can enquire whether these figures also believed that Labour should become authoritarian when in government.

Though it is tenuous to propose that any section of the Labour Party had an inclination to recreate Stalinist politics in Britain, there are indications that a desire existed among the left for greater dedication from their leadership. Many of the precedents they discussed were set by the Soviet Union and these were utilised to explain how the world could be changed for the better and indicate an inclination towards the authoritarian socialist model. The fact that their chosen vehicle for change, the British Labour Party, was trapped within a consensual parliamentary democracy appears to have given them a feeling of deep frustration. This was felt particularly when, despite holding positions within the party hierarchy, they still lacked any real influence over, or access to, the policy formulation process.

This led to a situation whereby authoritarian socialism could not be denounced because, by linking socialism to the Soviet Union, it could not be separated from the notion of implementing 'true socialism'. The Soviet leadership, it was argued, had displayed true resolve, the quality which domestic Labour leaders lacked. This led some British socialists to lavish praise on the achievements of the Soviet Union, using Soviet achievements as a mirror to reflect the inadequacies of British socialism and the political system. The majority hoped implicitly that democracy would evolve within the Soviet Union, but excused this failing upon the aggressive stance of the international order. There is, however, recognition, exhibited in the work of the Webbs and Zilliacus, that the authoritarian nature of the regime was initially necessary, and even desirable, for the installation of socialism.

There are other factors that led to unswaying support, particularly the desire to protect the Soviet socialist model, and this can explain why the authoritative nature of the regime did not deter democratic socialists. In their analysis the regime was authoritative for a reason, to install socialism. But the withering away of the bureaucracy had been hindered by the continual external threat. Therefore, the nature of Soviet Communism could only progress to a more democratic stage once the world had accepted the regime as an ally rather than an enemy. Since many believed that the threat was ideological, not military, they argued that the United States was prolonging the war to defeat communism; not the Soviet expansionist policy as Western propaganda argued.

Returning to the premise of this argument, we can understand the dual notions of accepting and even supporting authoritarianism, providing the dictator was a socialist. This refutes, to an extent, the premise of Gordievsky's enquiry but explains why this perception can be adopted. It is difficult to find any elected individual who argued that the Labour Party should, once in government, establish a dictatorship and install socialism regardless of the short term hardship. However, we do see individuals calling for greater resolve and opposing their leaders when they were seen to dissemble under capitalist pressure, an accusation that could never be levelled against the Soviet leadership. Thus those who were committed to the installation of a 'true' socialist political system, and were predisposed to believing that the Soviet model represented the ideal of socialism, were able to excuse the authoritarian nature of the Soviet political system. This led them, at key junctures, to highlight the virtues of the Soviet leadership's commitment to socialist aims. The analysis of their support for authoritarian socialism indicates the deep complexity of the movement and the contradictions that existed in these figures' thinking. Equally, it shows why it was simple to view pro-Soviet activists as apologists for Stalinism. Their beliefs are shrouded within traditions of British socialism that have remained largely unexplored. Without a deeper understanding of the roots of these arguments it is easier to view it, on face value, as an aberration rather than a continuity.

THE SOVIET UNION AS THE PROPONENT OF PEACE

It would be a simple process to categorise the peace movement as pro-Soviet because the arguments of the movement, and of Soviet propaganda, were often identical during the Cold War period. To make this judgement, however, would be largely erroneous. The peace movements attempted a policy of non-alignment and were largely successful in maintaining this position. Soviet sponsored groups such as the World Peace Council undermined the non-aligned position arguing that non-alignment meant ineffectuality and intransigence.[7] WPC publications enquired, when the world is torn between 'good and evil' and 'right and wrong', is it possible to be neutral? Neither camp believed this was possible and therefore attempts were made to force individuals to decide which side they would support. Soviet propaganda led some pro-peace activists to believe that the Soviet Union, the nation that produced volumes of material supporting disarmament and rapprochement, was indeed opposed to the nuclear stand-off. This was arguably an accurate perception. Volkogonov testified that the Soviet Union could not compete on equal terms in the arms race, and Gordievsky recalled that paranoia was prevalent among the Politburo during the early 1980s. The Soviet propaganda campaign, however, was not a mechanism that affected everyone in a positive way. Diana Collins remained profoundly anti-Soviet and found that the cynical methods of Agitprop reinforced her perceptions.

The majority of left-wingers who engaged in studies of the foreign policy objectives of the Communist bloc did so because they were already sympathetic to the ideas of pro-Sovietism. Therefore they were predisposed to conclude that the Warsaw Pact was a defensive mechanism. This trend began in the popular front era, however the *magnum locus* came following the ideological demarcation of the world. Zilliacus was the first, and arguably most prominent, exponent of the idea that the Soviet leadership desired an end to hostilities. His influence was passed down to Allaun and Newens, representatives of a younger generation of anti-war left-wingers. The arguments of these figures were not confined within the pro-Soviet analysis of events, but did largely agree with the central tenets of the Soviet line. Others like Lamond, Short and Wilson also made the transition to pro-Sovietism, produced adulatory articles and voluntarily joined the pro-Soviet peace movement. Those already within the pro-Soviet orbit reinforced these beliefs, as did front organisations such as the WPC. Thus the pro-Soviet left and the Soviet Union spoke with essentially one voice. Both called for an end to the arms race, the decommissioning of nuclear weapons and rapprochement with the Communist bloc. Within the pro-Soviet milieu the notion that the Soviet Union favoured peace, while the United States opposed any move to end the Cold War, was popularised.

Soviet foreign policy was also argued to be the positive alternative to the Atlanticist model adopted in Britain during the Cold War. In the 1930s the Soviet Union was characterised as the bastion of anti-fascism, during the Cold War it provided the impetus for détente and rapprochement and stood as the anti-imperialist force in the world. Despite United States President Roosevelt promoting the notion of self-determination at the Bretton Woods Conference, and its codification in UN resolution 637 as "a prerequisite to the full enjoyment of all fundamental human rights",[8] left-wingers argued that United States foreign policy undermined the concept completely. The Soviet support for progressive movements, such as the Greek Democrats, enhanced Soviet anti-imperialist credentials and led figures like Leslie Solley to fall within the pro-Soviet orbit. The progressive nature of Soviet foreign policy was reinforced by Soviet support for the anti-Apartheid cause and the protection of Castro's Cuba. This perception led figures like Ron Brown to promote the Soviet analysis of Afghanistan and join pro-Soviet organisations like the World Peace Council. Therefore the Soviet Union was able to establish itself, among a minority of left-wingers, as the positive alternative to the capitalist, imperialist and, importantly, anti-socialist United States of America.

THE SOVIET UNION IN HUMANIST PERSPECTIVE

There was equally a trend which focussed upon the people, rather than the government or ideology, of the Soviet Union. John Platts-Mills retained great faith in the Russian and East European public, a belief that he gained when producing propaganda during the Second World War. Similar ideas emerged as a tradition within pro-Soviet thinking. These were a particular feature of arguments put forward by Lamond and Short. These figures appear to have been unable to separate the Russian general will from Soviet governmental policy. They believed that the Soviet model of decision-making operated as an upward stream of directives that were translated into policy by the Politburo. This belief led them to argue that the lack of public enmity to the West, exhibited by the Eastern European Communists they met, would be expressed as foreign policy if co-existence was pursued by NATO. This led them to support friendship and cultural exchange societies and to produce propaganda aimed at countering the anti-Soviet rationale.

This was particularly important for those, like Ian Mikardo and Julius Silverman, who were of Russian extraction. They had a link to Soviet Jewry and to the revolutionary traditions of Russian society. Ian Mikardo's family fled the Tsarist pogroms of pre-Revolutionary Russia, therefore he possessed a sympathetic view of the regime that overthrew Tsarism. More importantly, he could not accept the dehumanisation of the people of Eastern Europe because of his hereditary ties to the region and its peoples.

It was a humanist outlook that led others to oppose anti-Russian propaganda. Had there been a change in the Western governmental perception of the Soviet people, it is doubtful whether some of these individuals would have shown any support for the regime. Mikardo, for example, did express opposition to the regime, but was able to explain why it had evolved into a totalitarian state. Therefore he encouraged the regime to be accepted, in order to allow the regime to become more democratic, while countering the official anti-Soviet propaganda. This led him to attempt to establish an economic bridge between Britain and the Soviet Union and actively support Gorbachev as a reformist Communist leader. Many others within the pro-Soviet milieu also attempted to change public opinion. Through the development of economic and cultural links between Britain and the Communist bloc, they attempted to alter the 'sterile' anti-Communist propaganda perspective of the Eastern European peoples and encourage an atmosphere for rapprochement between East and West.

CONCLUSION: THE SOVIET UNION AS A FOCUS FOR ALTERNATIVE ACTIVISM

The British parliament is arguably a forum where competing political ideas can be debated and a reasoned conclusion reached that has the support of a majority of members. However, to those within the pro-Soviet left, it was a forum in which they had little influence. They were continually defeated by the consensus between the major parties on issues very dear to them and thus felt compelled to pursue extra-parliamentary activities. These figures argued for an alternative to the Cold War and attempted to achieve this through establishing themselves as conduits for understanding between the opposing ideologies. Arguably it was during détente and the Second Cold War that this methodology was taken to the extreme. Brown, Lamond, Mikardo, Short and Wilson all acted with a view to 'lighting a candle in a dark corner of the world'. This led them to join friendship societies, reach out to diplomats of the Soviet Embassy and generally evoke the image of co-operation and co-existence. In an ideologically divided world, they attempted to maintain a middle ground and attached themselves to groups of like-minded individuals, be they liberals, humanists or communists.

Within these forums of discussion, existing in opposition to the governmental structures, strategies for change were developed. These forums, usually extra-parliamentary societies, included a variety of individuals; from Pritt and Platts-Mills to Ilya Ehrenberg or Dmitri Shostakovich. Whatever their composition, they expressed 'progressive' ideals. The individuals who participated in these forged links beneath governmental level in the name of those higher ideals to which their lives appear to have been dedicated. The results of their extra-parliamentary contacts were brought back to parliament where, despite eloquent arguments, they found a wall of hostility to their alternative stratagem. In the course of their activities it appears that some could have been used as pawns by operatives of the Soviet Union. However, it appears doubtful that any of those studied ever acted against their personal principles. Therefore, it can be argued that, though they were of use to KGB officials this was to a minor degree and on their own terms. They enjoyed forging links with members of Soviet society, reconstructing the person behind the one-dimensional propaganda image, and finding that they shared an outlook on the world. KGB agents often used these friendly overtures, if only to gain approval from the centre. Furthermore these contacts allowed the possibility of gaining an insight into British politics and the inner machinations of the Labour Party. However, the principles on which these relationships were founded were far removed from the image that is created by the unsympathetic Cold War perspective of these activities.

The political activities of these individuals were geared towards changing the ruling rationale that encapsulated anti-Communism, the Cold War and the nuclear stand-off. Therefore the Soviet Union became a focus, or a lever, that could be used to bring pressure to bear upon the government. However, the result of this activity was only a devaluation of their arguments. The failure to remain non-aligned meant that they could be, and were, written off as agents, fellow travellers and crypto-Communists, their words being lost in a plethora of slurs. Though in many cases they became blinkered to reality by their adherence to an ideal of 'true' socialism, they campaigned continually with their sights set on a higher goal, a peaceful, prosperous and socialist world. This vision is one that became a powerful motivational force, but remained a dream that could not be made reality despite the constant campaigning and activism engaged in by these internationalist, socialist politicians.

CONCLUSION

This study has developed an analysis that allows historians and political scientists to understand how pro-Sovietism developed as a tradition within British Labour Party politics. Through a study of the individuals who were sympathetic with the Soviet socialist experiment, we are able to understand how their perspective of the Soviet Union acted as a guide over their political activities and drew them into adopting an oppositional stance against the Labour Party leadership and successive British governments. This conclusion will respond to some of the questions that are raised by the study, but which could not be addressed within any single chapter or through any one case study.

Four questions can be identified. Firstly, why did these figures invoke the Soviet Union as the model for a socialist world order. Secondly, why did they use the Labour Party as a vehicle through which to change the perception of the Soviet Union and establish a 'socialist peace'. Thirdly, what were these individual's long term objectives and finally, what effect did they have on the Labour Party, the socialist movement in general and on the Cold War, all of which they attempted to change in line with their objectives. The last section will reintroduce the roles ascribed to them in the introduction, the change agent and conduit of understanding, and assess how these definitions capture the individual's essence as politically motivated individuals.

WHY THE SOVIET MODEL?

Any history of socialist thought is a history of the interaction between many complex, varied and competing notions of the socialist state, many of which were represented within the ethos of British Labour Party members. The complexities within socialist theory were often reflected in the contradictions within an individual's own socialist convictions. For example, G D H Cole criticised socialists who harboured non-libertarian tendencies, yet he perceived the socialist movement as a single body of ideals and rejected any analysis that dwelt upon "narrow and sectarian manifestations."[1] This perception, which was expressed by many within the British socialist movement, enforced the view that the Soviet model was one competing theory of socialism and, more importantly, that it was the only theory with a practical dimension. In the most basic terms it was the first socialist state and claimed to be successful in implementing a socialist economic system. Only the Bolsheviks could lay claim to this achievement.

The fact that any attempt to establish socialism had limited success outside of the Soviet sphere of influence meant that the Soviet Union became of significant symbolic value to one strand of the socialist movement. If Lenin and Stalin were able to create socialism, within a proto-industrial, peasant society, what had hindered MacDonald, Attlee, and the other leaders of British socialism, from doing likewise? Thus the Soviet Union became a model for socialists who wished to make significant socialist achievements, they rejected the Bernsteinian theory of historical inevitability, arguing that by adhering to this philosophy a socialist future may remain beyond mankind's grasp forever. They argued it was achievable and should be established, not in a piecemeal form, but in totality and now! The use of a model of socialism was not particular to the pro-Soviet strand. Perry Anderson, and some also argue Antony Crosland, looked to Swedish social democracy as a model for British socialists.[2] However the Soviet model held a special significance to some individual thinkers. It was the first and, though beset by problems, represented a fledgling making its first tentative steps. It was also constantly under threat from a world order hostile to its ideology, therefore, continuing the fledging metaphor, the Soviet model needed protection if it was to evolve properly. Most importantly, however, the Soviet leaders expressed a devout commitment to the socialist ideology, they did not debase their ideas to gain support and had no inclination to allow either endogenous or exogenous anti-socialist forces to damage the integrity of the socialist regime. Therefore, within the work of a minority of socialists the Soviet Union became of an iconic significance.

The Soviet Union laid claim to socialism as a political, economic and social form of government, this led some to perceive a link between their personal political objectives and those of the Communist bloc. Why this link was established is complicated and reliant upon individual experiences. For example; the Soviet Union was perceived as the victor against fascism, the protector of Spanish republicanism, the opponent of American hegemony, the nation opposed to war and the nuclear arms race and a nation excluded and demonised due to its adherence to socialism. All these factors are represented in the mindsets of those individuals studied, the perceptions were awarded differing prioritisation but became normative beliefs within the culture of pro-Sovietism. This appears to have deep cultural significance within the British socialist movement. On consecutive programmes for BBC Television's *Campaign Confessions* Labour candidates made a link between their ideals and the idea of the Soviet Union. Bob Marshall-Andrews, when waving a hammer at the camera he was about to use to knock in posts, jokingly commented: "I'm just missing the sickle"[3]; John O'Farrell, when distributing campaign leaflets outside Maidenhead railway station, told one supporter: "You're wearing a Russian hat, I knew you were one of ours."[4] While both candidates possess 'old lefts' credentials, and are unsympathetic to the Blairite reforms of the party, neither have ever expressed support for the Soviet Union. Therefore this link can be argued to be an aspect of the culture of the left. The idea of the Soviet Union as one arm of the socialist movement, that shared the same ideals of public ownership, social equality and worker's control, became a powerful motivator.

This mindset meant that many were unable to condemn the Soviet Union, that would mean falling into the trap laid by the exponents of anti-Communism. This minority attempted to change the anti-Soviet rationale and establish an atmosphere in which the Soviet Union could be discussed without pejorative connotations being automatically conjured. The Soviet Union, using the phraseology developed by Goldstein and Keohane, became a potent sign on these individuals route through politics, determining their behaviour as political actors. The theory that ideas act as road maps, though intended to predict the actions of leaders,[5] is useful in explaining the adherence to the pro-Soviet line. This hypothesis argues that there are, concerning each political choice, a series of alternatives. Ideology earmarks those which can be adopted and those which cannot. Ideas, it is argued, "can stipulate what is right and wrong" moreover "principled ideas enable people to behave decisively... [and] can shift the focus of attention to moral issues and away from purely instrumental ones focused on material interests and power."[6] The latter has, historically, formed the basis of foreign policy formulation. Those studied herein abandoned material interests and power, their ideas focussed on moral issues and; "determined the tracks along which [their] action [was] pushed by [their] dynamic of interest."[7] This ideological stance placed moral, socialist and humanist principles above those of national security, national interest or power politics. While they can be accused of being erroneous over their choice of focus, their political stance can be explained in this way.

The socialist politician, when constrained by ideological strictures, is limited in the political choices available. This became a particularly potent factor in an ideologically divided world. Those who believed that the Soviet Union was socialist appear to have been drawn to choosing the Communist side and the political activities associated with pro-Sovietism. This was clearly one of the chief motivational forces that led those with a dogmatic adherence to the socialist ideology and a desire to establish 'true' socialism in Britain, to forge an ideological alliance with Soviet Communism.

WHY LABOUR?

The idealised view of the Soviet Union was one aspect of a mindset that focussed upon objectives that were untenable, particularly within the hostile atmosphere of the Cold War. The anomaly is that these individuals chose the Labour Party as the vehicle through which to change the world order. The party was historically anti-Communist, proscribed any organisation that held pro-Soviet links and had been instrumental in the establishment of the framework for the containment of Communism. Equally Labour was reformist and subscribed to gradualism, rejecting revolutionary socialism as a doctrine that inevitably lead to totalitarianism. Yet, within the writings of many of these figures, we find a belief that the Labour Party would change British policy towards the Communist bloc and that Britain could stand as an example to the world, both by standing as an non-nuclear power and by providing the impetus for co-existence.

Had the Labour Party been the only socialist party in Britain during the Twentieth Century, or the Cold War period, it would not be surprising for it to be a broad church that contained a complex array of competing ideas. However a viable alternative existed that was sympathetic to the Soviet Union and espoused similar objectives to these individuals. Curiously, however, they saw the Communist Party as anathemic to their ideals and objectives. All those figures interviewed denounced the CPGB as unsocialist, controlled by Moscow and anti-democratic. =This appears as a contradiction within their thinking, however there is, perhaps, logic to this position. None of these figures were slavish to the Soviet line and liked to perceive themselves as independent regardless of how closely their arguments matched those of Cominform or the CPGB. Equally they did not propose that the Soviet Union should rule Europe or Britain, they espoused an independent and democratic route towards socialism. Furthermore they did not view the world in the same way as the Communists, the pro-Soviet Labour MPs spoke of co-existence, not alliance, with the Soviet Union. They also argued that the world order should consist of independent and equal socialist states, there should not be one superpower or a single ideological guide. Their support for the Soviet model became contextualised within the Cold War rationale, but it was not a support based upon a strong ideological attachment. Their attachment was weak and flexible, it was their opposition to the Cold War anti-Soviet rationale, and the role of the United States as a hegemon over the non-Communist world, that caused their support for the Soviet Union to become accentuated.

There was also a highly idealistic view held of the Labour Party that figured as a symbolic constraint upon their thinking. The left believed that the party could be 'steered' to becoming a vehicle for the worker's, a notion enforced by the Trade Union link. This led the left to amalgamate around organisations which sought to influence the constituency and Conference level of the party organisation. This was largely successful as once Conference became left-wing oriented, a greater number of left-wingers were elected to the NEC. The campaign to steer the party into a leftward trajectory had been begun by the Bevanites using *Tribune* as a platform. Activity was increased by Victory for Socialism, the Campaign for Labour Party Democracy and the Labour Co-ordinating Committee, all of which attempted to heighten support for the left-wing agenda. These left wingers, who included the pro-Soviet MPs and Trade Union leaders, sought to establish the party as a radical, socialist party. This was an unrealistic campaign, the central tenets they promoted had been only been expressed during the formative years of the party's history. However these notions held enormous symbolic significance to these individuals.

The Labour Representation Committee, in the manifesto written for the 1900 General Election, declared its objectives were:

> the Socialisation of the Means of Production, Distribution and Exchange, to be controlled by a Democratic State in the interests if the entire Community, and the Complete Emancipation of Labour from the Domination of Capitalism and Landlordism with the Establishment of Social and Economic Equality between the Sexes.[8]

The 1929 manifesto, in less precise terms, committed the party to: "making Britain a happier and more contented land, and establishing peace in the world."[9] It was these ideals that underpinned Labour's ethos and governed the activism of many left-wing figures. The party constitution, and particularly Clause IV, held greatest significance. Tony Benn described it as "the clearest and best possible statement of the democratic, socialist faith", one that "must... remain at the core of our work."[10]

The socialist project in Britain was often referred to in terms of a faith, particularly among left-wingers who maintained a perpetual myth of betrayal by the party leadership. They also linked the success of the socialist project in Britain, which was often referred to in personal terms reminiscent of the language of a religious crusader, with the establishment of socialism across the globe. This was often expressed in idealistic terms and expressed the belief that socialism would solve all mankind's ills and that it was the ultimate desire of all people, whether they knew it or not:

> the ugliness and squalor which now meets you at every turn in some of the most beautiful valleys in the world would disappear, the rivers

would run pure and clear as they did of yore… and in the winter the log would glow on the fire… the youths and maidens made glad the heart with mirth and song, and there would be beauty and joy everywhere.[11]

The creation of this society was the ultimate objective of all party members and, as one former General Secretary declared:

No socialist worthy of the traditions of the Labour movement should refuse, on occasions, to go against a strong current of public opinion if in doing so he believes that such a course is necessary for the purpose of social progress.[12]

The pro-Soviet MPs believed it also necessary to oppose party policy and national legislation, but equally saw that this was in keeping with the traditions of the party and its ethos, arguing that it was the leadership's stance that was antithetical and anti-socialist.

THE FUTURE IDEAL: A MOVEMENT'S OBJECTIVES

Summun bonum, or the highest good, appears as a prescient term to use to describe the all-embracing goal to which the pro-Soviet strand aimed towards in their activity. Arguably they worked neither for party or nation, but for *res publica*, the common wealth. They expressed the notion that there was a greater good that a government should attain for her subjects. These internationally minded politicians extended this ideal to encapsulate the common wealth of the world's people. The future they campaigned for was socialist, as expressed by the Labour Party constitution and successive manifestos, and peaceful, which necessitated co-existence between all states rather than competition and containment. As the Cold War rationale opposed both these ideals these individuals worked to undermine anti-Sovietism, either by parliamentary or extra-parliamentary means. The individuals provided a good account of their personal objectives, either through their writings or in hindsight during interviews. The evidence indicates that these individuals shared a significant number of ideals and motivations and all focussed upon an abstract goal in the name of humanity. This was rationalised as a positive alternative to Cold War, and the arguably inevitable nuclear war, and unconstrained capitalism. To these individuals it was only the Soviet Union that represented these ideals.

FOOTPRINTS IN THE SNOW

A more complex question asks what effects these figures had. In terms of altering the course of the Cold War the answer appears to be that they had no effect at all. Communism, and Marxist socialism, was defeated;

as was the ideology as a blueprint for society. However during the Cold War supporters of the Soviet model existed as a group that could not be ignored by the Party leadership. Therefore, as one strand within the left-wing of the party, they established themselves as an anchor, maintaining a link between the pragmatic approach to government adopted by the PLP and the party's traditional left-wing ethos. Therefore, while the party subscribed to the Cold War rationale, it could not have become as deeply Atlanticist as Conservative governments. Apart from the 1945-50 period parliamentary majorities were too weak to allow backbench rebellions to take place. The very fact that a force existed who opposed the activities of the western secret services meant care had to be taken.= In practice this usually meant greater secrecy,[13] but policies were also enacted as a result of pressure from the left. For example, the caution with which Harold Wilson handled the issue of Vietnam was the result of having to balance the demands made by the United States and those of the party's left-wing.

Left-wing pressure was constantly brought to bear against the Party leadership. *Hansard* is peppered with demands that a peaceful settlement be negotiated between Britain and the Warsaw Pact. This escalated during the diplomatic process that culminated in the Helsinki Conference of 1972. This was a joint venture between the member nations of the European Economic Community and of the Warsaw Pact, a venture the left saw as being a positive step toward rapprochement. It seems unsurprising, given the groundswell of support for rapprochement on the back benches, that it was a Labour government which entered into this venture, rather than continuing British reliance on the United States to ensure European security.

Equally as the power of the left grew, during the late 1970s and early 1980s, manifestos were increasingly dominated by key tenets of the left-wing agenda. This is particularly the case with defence policy. Unilateral disarmament, an argument with roots in both the Bevanite and Zilliacus traditions, dominated the agenda. Ironically though, this was the beginning of the end for left-wing influence. Gerald Kaufman described the 1983 General Election manifesto as the "longest suicide note in history". It was rejected in totality by the electorate and contributed to Labour's consignment to fourteen years in the political wilderness.[14] To become electable again meant a long process of policy reform and modernisation. Therefore, we can say that the pro-Soviet strand, as activists within the left-wing, did have an impact upon the party, but it is difficult to describe this effect as positive.

In general the pro-Soviet strand made little impression on governmental policy or the course of world history. Their radicalism was as unpopular with the public as it was in parliament. Few could see a link between socialism and Soviet communism and even less could accept that adopting any Soviet-style mechanisms would benefit them. This was the framework in which the party had to operate. These individuals were unable to work within these strictures, and thus their marginalisation was inevitable if the party was to maintain itself as an electoral force.

While their domestic influence was marginal, it can be asked whether they had any effect upon the Soviet regime they sought to protect. In the long term the answer is again no, however, in the short term it is possible that they contributed to the longevity of the regime. In acting as a counter to the anti-Soviet rationale they were able to alter the perceptions of some toward the Soviet Union. For example without their alternative political strategy British businesses would not have been encouraged to aid the Soviet economy, valuable information may not have aided the Soviet arms race and there would have been no direct line of communication between the Politburo and the British Parliament. While these may appear trivial in the light of the events of 1989, they amount to quantitatively more than was hoped when Munzenberg established the mechanisms to create a fifth column. British politicians were actively supporting the Soviet Union, albeit with a focus on a higher goal, and attempting to protect the integrity of the regime. This point is reinforced by the definition of pro-Soviet activity provided by Northedge and Wells. They described the multi-faceted activity of the pro-Soviet strand as having "at times... the effect of weakening the vigilance of [Britain] against Soviet pressures within the international system". They do not over exaggerate this effect, however, stating; "this can never have been more than minimal."[15]

Furthermore, building upon the Northedge and Wells argument, the support for the Soviet Union did reinforce and enhance the perception of the Soviet Union, though to differing degrees, held by the Western public, members of governments and the international community. While few believed Soviet leaders when they declared that Soviet policies were purely protectionist and that the nation sought peaceful co-existence, a British politician, when reiterating these declarations, could convince a broader audience. This is highly debatable. Through studying the individuals it would seem that, despite the eloquence of their argument, they did not add any weight, nor give credence, to the Soviet arguments. It would be more accurate to state that in reiterating Soviet arguments to emphasise the necessity to change policy they devalued their own position. Thus pro-Sovietism became one characteristic exploited by the anti-Labour tabloids when coining the phrase 'loony left'. It seems clear, therefore, that they had as little tangible effect on international relations as they did on the domestic policies of the western nations. Equally they drew little support from public opinion, the dominant anti-Soviet rationale held sway across the western alliance. It can be extrapolated from interviews and scant writings on their careers the majority recognised that they failed but exhibited a degree of pride in the fact that they alone tried. In their opinions, through the maintenance of their ideals, they remained true to the ideals of peace and a secure future for mankind the world over. When placing yourself on this lofty pedestal it appears that failure is immaterial, what matters is that the fight was just.[16]

CHANGE AGENTS AND CONDUITS OF UNDERSTANDING

In pursuing their objectives it is clear that these figures sought to alter Labour's domestic and foreign policies and the governmental perception of the Soviet Union. While they were not alone in the former activity, they spearheaded the latter campaign. They personally attempted to position themselves as the agency through which a co-existent future was attained between the two ideological blocs. In pursuit of this goal they helped establish links between Britain and the Soviet Union that would facilitate mutual understanding of the political systems. They also promoted Soviet foreign policy objectives in an attempt to gain support for the alternative, sympathetic, perspective of Soviet aims. Therefore they stood as repositories for this perspective, and attempted to ensure that it was received by the widest possible audience. Furthermore, in establishing Anglo-Soviet links, they also attempted to encourage Communists to understand British politics. The main aim of this activity was to prevent war through nurturing an atmosphere based on mutual understanding.

The alternative analysis of these figures, as supported by Chapman Pincher, Brian Crozier, Blake Baker, Oleg Gordievsky and, most recently, Vasili Mitrokhin, argues that pro-Soviet left wing MPs amounted to little more than "Soviet spies and saboteurs".[17] However, using the cases of Kitson, Lamond, Short and Wilson as examples, their ideological motivations and philosophies do not earmark them as traitorous. In fact, their ideals appear as patriotic as those who argued the case for strong defence. To them it was an issue of national survival and prosperity, standing in opposition to a foreign power, the United States, which opposed their ideology, taking control. They believed that United States ideological hegemony over Britain would mean the abandonment of socialism and the subordination of British Labourism to American capitalism, therefore to these figures the choice was clear, better Communist than capitalist. In the case of the pacifist pro-Soviet strand, and to turn a well-used aphorism on its head, 'better red than dead'.

Due to the openly sympathetic support displayed by some of these individuals it is certain that the Soviet Union believed they had agents in Parliament. This perception was exacerbated by the clear willingness of some left wingers to encourage relationships with representatives of the Soviet government. Once again this is a question of perceptions. Konni Zilliacus, who talked to Khrushchev and published a favourable account, would have been perceived as a propagandist. However, from his perspective, he was presenting a researched argument as to why the West should improve relations with the post-Stalinist Soviet Union. This is equally the case with Frank Allaun, Ian Mikardo and Stan Newens who consulted Soviet diplomats and Eastern bloc leaders, thus building a more two dimensional picture of world affairs. As Norman Atkinson argued, it was perceived acceptable for a right wing MP to consult an Eastern European Embassy, but not for a left winger; particularly one who was sympathetic to the Communist model of socialism.

Equally the cases of Renee Short and Alex Kitson, who visited the Soviet Union and extolled the virtues of Communist society, indicate that they were fighting for a higher cause, the creation of a socialist society. However by using the Soviet Union as a benchmark for socialist achievement they provided the right wing with the ammunition to denounce their politics. It is clear that they acted as change agents and conduits of understanding as they actively campaigned to alter the ruling rationale and public perception of the Soviet Union. This led some to be viewed, in some cases correctly, as confidential contacts and to become associated with the pejorative connotations attached to that definition. They openly supported many causes which furthered Soviet foreign policy objectives, not simply because it would benefit the Soviet Union but, because there were, in their analysis, clear benefits for the future of humanity resultant from the pursuit of these objectives. They were drawn to front organisations because, as Sapper indicated, to support the progressive side meant you had to join the pro-Soviet orbit. The pro-Soviet strand became the living embodiment of their own meta-narrative; they viewed themselves as the frontline in the campaign to provide humanity with a better future.[18]

. This political strand were largely impotent, both in changing British governmental policy and in protecting the Soviet Union from either military or economic attack. Therefore, it can be asked what is the importance of these individuals. They were individuals who were prepared to stand for an unpopular cause and opposed the politics of the party for which they were elected in the name of future generations. They rejected the party line, negated their own chances of career prospects and, it would seem, ignored common sense in pursuit of a goal that remained permanently beyond their reach. In different circumstances they may have been extremely influential, but not in a world divided by a zero-sum ideological perspective. Equally, outside the Cold War ideological dichotomy, the context within which they operated, they would not have been as highly motivated. Therefore they stand as a distinct group of principled individuals who refused to be cowed by the opposition they faced. It is doubtful that such politicians will emerge again. They remain one aspect of the history of the Cold War, and therefore cannot be separated from the context of the events of the period. However, if a similar conflict developed, one which separated mankind because of ideas many felt were an aspect of their personal ideology, that encouraged irrational hate and fear to govern the minds of the people, and threatened the security of the future generations of the peoples of the world, then similar arguments may well be raised again in parliaments across the democratic world.

APPENDIX
BIOGRAPHICAL DETAIL

Below represents a brief biography of the key individuals discussed within this book.

FRANK ALLAUN (1913-2002)
Labour MP: East Salford 1955-83. PPS to Secretary of State for the colonies Oct 1964-March 1965 (resigned). NEC Member 1967-83, Deputy Chairman of the Party 1977-8, Chairman 1978-9. Editor Northern Voice 1951-67. Previously correspondent with Manchester Guardian, Manchester Evening News and Daily Herald. Founder of Labour Action for Peace, Founder member of Victory for Socialism, member of the Tribune Group and CND. Organised the first Aldermaston March. Lifelong campaigner for peace and opponent of nuclear weapons.

NORMAN ATKINSON (1923-)
Labour MP: Tottenham 1964-87. Labour Party Treasurer 1976-81. Left-wing MP once tipped to be the successor to Aneurin Bevan.

ARTHUR BAX (DIED 1961)
Head of the Labour Party Press Department 1945-61. Committed suicide after confessing to passing information on internal party affairs to the StB.

GEOFFREY BING (1909-77)
Labour MP: Hornchurch 1945-55. Assistant Government Whip 1945-6. Later Constitutional Advisor to the Prime Minister of Ghana 1956-7; Attorney General of Ghana 1957-61; Advisor to President Nkrumah 1961-66. Self-confessed fellow traveller of Zilliacus and left wing socialist. Lawyer.

A FENNER BROCKWAY (1888-1988)
ILP MP: East Leyton 1929-31; Labour MP: Eton and Slough 1950-64. Chairman: Labour and Socialist International 1926-31, British Centre for

Colonial Freedom 1942-7, British, Asian and Overseas Socialist Fellowship 1959-66, British Council for Peace in Vietnam 1965-9, Congress of Peoples against Imperialism 1948-88, CND 1964-95. Executive member Anti-Apartheid Movement 1964-92. Lifelong anti-war demonstrator, conscientious objector and campaigner for peace and an end to the arms race. Created Baron Brockway of Eton and Slough 1964.

RON BROWN (1940-)

Labour MP: Leith 1979-92. Formerly Chairman Pilton Branch AUEW. One time confidential contact of KGB resident Oleg Gordievsky, after losing his seat he found a job exporting Coca-Cola to North Korea. He has since returned to politics and has fought elections to the Scottish Parliament as a member of the Scottish Socialist Party.

G D H COLE (1889-1959)

Chairman of the Fabian Society 1939-46; 1948-50. President, Fabian Society 1952-9. Member, Fabian Society 1912-59; ILP 1912-45; Labour Party 1913-59. Socialist, influential political theorist and Lecturer. Supported the Soviet Union 1930-45 on the basis of socialism and anti-fascism.

TOM DRIBERG (1905-1976)

Labour MP: Maldon 1942-55; Barking 1959-74. NEC member 1949-72, Party Chairman 1957-8. Journalist to the Daily Express, 1928-43, BBC 1943-5, later Editor Reynolds News, New Statesman and Tribune. Notorious homosexual and alleged double agent for MI6 and the KGB. Created Baron Bradwell 1975.

RAY FLETCHER (1921-90)

Labour MP: Ilkeston 1964-83. Leader UK Delegation to Council of Europe 1974-6, Executive member, UK group Western European Union 1974-6. Times Columnist. Alleged to have been a KGB agent by the Mitrokhin papers.

KEN GILL (1927-)

General Secretary TASS, AUEW. Member of the General Council of the TUC 1974-92. Member of the Committee for Racial Equality. Member, British-Soviet Friendship Society, World Peace Council, British Peace Assembly.

HUGH LESTER HUTCHINSON (1904-?)

Labour MP: Manchester Rusholme 1945-9, Labour Independent Group 1949-50. Participant in the Communist-led Meerut conspiracy 1929. Expelled from the Labour Party July 1949. Became a teacher in Lichfield and dropped out of political life.

HUGH JENKINS (1908-)
Labour MP: Putney 1964-79. Minister for the Arts 1974-9. Member of the Public Accounts Committee, Executive Member of the Arts Council, Chairman of the Theatres Advisory Board 1964-74, Vice-President 1976-86, President 1986-95. Chairman of Society for Cultural Relations with the USSR 1985-91. Chairman of Victory for Socialism 1956-60. Vice-President of CND 1981-, Aldermaston Marcher. Peace and anti-Nuclear campaigner. Created Baron Jenkins of Putney 1981.

ALEX KITSON (1922-97)
NEC member 1978-83. Party Chairman 1980-1. Deputy General Secretary Transport and General Workers Union 1980-5, Acting General Secretary 1980-1. Executive member World Peace Council, Chairman British Peace Assembly, member CND, Labour Action for Peace, Committee for Peace and Security in Europe. Frequent visitor to the USSR and supporter of a united industrial front with the CPGB.

JAMES LAMOND (1928-)
Labour MP: Oldham East 1970-83, Oldham Central and Royton 1983-92. Chairman No. 1 Divisional Council of DATA 1965-70, Executive member TASS/MSF 1944-. Vice-President World Peace Council 1974-96. Lord Provost of Aberdeen 1970-1, Lord Lieutenant 1970-1. Justice of the Peace.

JOAN LESTOR (1931-1998)
Labour MP: Eton and Slough 1966-83; Eccles 1987-97. Parliamentary under-secretary: Department of Education and Science Oct 1969-June 1970 (resigned), under-secretary to FCO 1974-5 to DES 1975-6. NEC Member 1967-82, Party Chairman 1977-8 and 1987-97. CND National Council member 1983-98. Previously a nursery school teacher. Left wing parliamentarian once accused by Brian Crozier of acting as a confidential contact of the KGB; the resultant libel action led to Crozier withdrawing 'Free Agent' from the shelves. Created Baroness Lestor of Eccles 1987.

ALF LOMAS (1935-)
Labour MEP: London NE 1979-99. Political Secretary London Co-operative Society 1965-79. Chairman Committee for Peace and Security in Europe. Member British Soviet Friendship Society, British Peace Assembly.

JOAN MAYNARD (1921-98)
Labour MP: Sheffield Brightside 1974-87. NEC member 1972-87. Vice-President National Union of Agricultural and Allied Workers 1966-72. Chairman British Peace Assembly, Troops Out Movement. President Labour Committee on Ireland. Vice Chairman Northern Ireland Group of MPs. Chairman, Campaign Group. Left wing activist her main causes were the end to imperialism in Ireland and for enhanced rights to the farming community.

IAN MIKARDO (1908-1993)
Labour MP: Reading 1945-59; 1964-87.NEC member 1945-59; 1964-87. Party Chairman 1970-1. Chairman; Tribune Group; Campaign Group. Member Poale Zion, Society for Cultural Relations with the Soviet Union. Pioneer of East-West trade. Entrepreneur; traded as Ian Mikardo Ltd.

STAN NEWENS (1930-)
Labour MP: Epping 1964-70; Harlow 1974-83; MEP London Central 1988-99. Foreign Affairs Group 1992-3. Chairman of Tribune Group 1982-3. Vice-Chairman Labour Action for Peace. Director London Co-operative Society 1971-7. Anti-NATO and anti-American propagandist, supported the foreign policy of Nicolae Ceausescu.

WILL OWEN (1901-81)
Labour MP: Morpeth 1954-70. Secretary East-West Trade Committee. Chairman, Anglo-GDR Parliamentary Group. Tried and acquitted on charges of espionage 1970. Later Lecturer and Chairman of Sutton and Carshalton CLP 1974-81.

JOHN PLATTS-MILLS (1917-2002)
Labour MP: Finsbury 1945-48. Labour Independent Group 1948-50. Founder Labour Independent Group 1948. Expelled from the Labour Party 1948. President of Society for Cultural Relations with the USSR 1990-. Chairman, League for Democracy in Greece 1972-7, Haldane Society of Progressive Lawyers 1972-, International Association of Democratic Lawyers 1969-84. Made Queen's Counsellor 1964, Bencher of the Inner Temple 1970. Lawyer.

DENIS NOWELL [D N] PRITT (1887-1972)
Labour MP: Hammersmith North 1935-40, Independent 1940-9, Labour Independent Group 1949-50. Expelled from the Labour Party March 1940. Chairman of Labour Independent Group 1949-50, League for Democracy in Greece 1949-72, Society for Cultural Relations with the USSR 1927-72,

Haldane Society of Progressive Lawyers 1949-72. Executive member of International Association of Democratic Lawyers. Lawyer. Winner of the Stalin Peace Prize 1954.

JO RICHARDSON (1923-94)
Labour MP: Barking 1974-94. Member NEC 1979-91. Served on Select Committees dealing with Home Affairs; Nationalised Industries, Expenditure and Procedure. Member, Keep Left, Tribune Group, Victory for Socialism, CND, Campaign Group. Ian Mikardo's Private Secretary 1951-65. Secretary, Victory for Socialism. Partner in Ian Mikardo Ltd. Campaigner for women's and lesbian rights.

ERNIE ROSS (1942-)
Labour MP: Dundee West 1979-. Chair of Foreign Affairs Committee 1997-. Member of TASS/MSF. Member British Peace Assembly. Left wing anti-NATO and anti-nuclear campaigner during the 1970s and 80s.

ALAN SAPPER (1931-)
General Secretary Association of Cinematograph, Television and Allied Technicians 1969-91. Member General Council of the TUC 1970-64, British Copyright Council 1964-74. Governor British Film Industry 1974-94. Chairman League for Democracy in Greece 1970-. Influential pro-Soviet Unionist and Labour activist.

JULIUS SILVERMAN (1905-96)
Labour MP: Birmingham Erdington 1945-55; Birmingham Aston 1955-83. Chairman, Anglo-Russian Parliamentary Group; Parliamentary Chess Club. Executive Member, Society for Cultural Relations with the Soviet Union. Member, Tribune; Victory for Socialism. Frequent visitor to the Soviet Union. Lawyer.

SYDNEY SILVERMAN (1895-1968)
Labour MP: Nelson & Colne 1935-68. Member NEC 1956-68. Member, Society for Cultural Relations with the Soviet Union. Left-winger, opponent of capital punishment, supporter of Cuba. Lawyer.

RENEE SHORT (1919-2003)
Labour MP: Wolverhampton NE 1964-87. NEC member 1970-81, 1983-8. Vice-Chairman Parliamentary East-West Trade Group 1968-87. Chairman, British-GDR Parliamentary Group 1972-87, British-Soviet Parliamentary Group 1984-7. Secretary, British-Soviet Parliamentary Group 1972-84. President, British-Romanian Friendship Association, Nursery Schools

Association 1970-80, Campaign for Nursery Education 1970-83. Numerous other affiliations concerning women's health, prisoner's welfare and East-West relations. Executive member Victory for Socialism. Member British-Soviet Friendship Society.

LESLEY J SOLLEY (1905-1968)
Labour MP: Thurrock 1945-9, Labour Independent Group 1949-50. Expelled from the Labour Party May 1949. Treasurer of the League for Democracy in Greece 1945-55. Vice-President of the Songwriters Guild of Great Britain 1952-68. Formerly Research Physicist and Lawyer.

JOHN STONEHOUSE (1925-88)
Labour MP: Walsall North 1957-76. PPS Ministry of Aviation 1964-6. Parliamentary under-secretary of state for the colonies 1966-7, Minister of Aviation 1967, Minister for Technology 1967-8, Postmaster General 1968-9, Minister for Post and Telecommunications 1969-70. Imprisoned for fraud and theft 1976-9. Later charity worker and writer. Named by Josef Frolik as an agent of the Czech StB.

BARNET STROSS (1899-1967)
Labour MP: Hanley 1945-50; Stoke-on-Trent 1950-66. PPS to Minister for Health 1964-5. Formerly medical practitioner. Honarary citizen of Lidice, Czechoslovakia 1957. Commander Order of the White Lion of Czechoslovakia 1957. Named by Josef Frolik as an agent of the Czech StB.

STEPHEN SWINGLER (1915-1969)
Labour MP: Stafford 1945-50; Newcastle-under-Lyme 1951-69. PPS to Ministry of Transport 1964-7, Minister for Transport 1967-1968, Minister for Health and Social Security 1968-9. Founder of Victory for Socialism, Chairman 1960-8. Previously Lecturer in Adult Education. Marxist, CPGB member during 1930s

STAN THORNE (1918-)
Labour MP: Preston South 1974-83; Preston 1983-7. Member British-Soviet Friendship Society, Troops Out Movement. Left-wing activist and Trotskyist MP.

WILLIAM WARBEY (1903-1980)
Labour MP: Luton 1945-50; Broxtowe 1953-5; Ashfield 1955-66. Executive Director of the Organisation for World Political and Social Studies 1965-80. Secretary World Studies Trust 1966-80. Executive member Victory for

Socialism. Member British Council for Peace in Vietnam. Anti-Vietnam and anti-NATO campaigner.

BEATRICE WEBB (1858-1943)
Husband of Sydney Webb (see below) Co-founder of the LSE 1895, member of the Royal Commission on the Poor Law 1906-9. Co-published works on Soviet society but held private doubts regarding the regime.

SYDNEY WEBB (1859-1947)
Labour MP: Seaham 1922-29. Secretary of State for Dominion Affairs 1929-30, for the Colonies 1929-31. Founder of the Fabian Society, the LSE, the new Statesman. Wrote the 1921 Labour Party constitution. Pro-Soviet propagandist in his latter days. Created Baron Passfield 1929.

WILLIAM WILSON (1913-)
Labour MP: Coventry South 1964-74; Coventry SE 1974-83. Member Commons Select Committee on Race Relations and Immigration 1970-9. Chairman, British-Soviet Friendship Society 1977-83. Deputy Lieutenant of the County of Warwick 1967. Lawyer. Self-confessed confidential contact of the KGB.

KONNI ZILLIACUS (1894-1967)
Labour MP: Gateshead 1945-49; Independent 1949-50; Labour MP: Manchester Gorton 1955-67. Expelled from the party 1949, readmitted 1952. Formerly, Royal Flying Corps 1914-18, Information Officer, Secretariat of the League of Nations 1922-39, Ministry of Information 1939-45. Pro-Soviet foreign affairs expert, peace and anti-nuclear campaigner.

NOTES

Introduction

1 T Wright, , London & New York, Routledge, 1996, pp 125-6.
2 A Thorpe, , London, Macmillan, 1997, p 4.
3 E Shaw, , Manchester, Manchester University Press, 1988, p 1.
4 For an account of labourism and its critics see P Allender, London, Merlin, 2001.
5 P Hennessy, , London, Victor Gollancz, 1996, pp 171-81.
6 In particular see P Seyd, , 1987, pp 172-86.
7 M Jenkins, , Nottingham, Spokesman, 1979.
8 John Callaghan, , Oxford, Basil Blackwell, 1984, pp 3-6 and pp 68-9.
9 D Keohane, , Leicester, Leicester University Press, 1993, p 4.
10 M Jenkins, , 1979, p 12
11 G Foote, , Third Edition, London, Macmillan, p 5.
12 K O Morgan, , Oxford, OUP, 1984, p 58.
13 K O Morgan, , 1984, p 60.
14 K O Morgan, , Oxford, OUP, 1987, p 156.
15 K O Morgan, , 1987, p 153.
16 R Hattersley, Fifty Years On: A prejudiced history of Britain since the war, London, Little, Brown & Co, 1997, p 294.
17 R Hattersley, Fifty Years On: A prejudiced history of Britain since the war, 1997, p 295.
18 See O Gordievsky, , London, Macmillan 1995; C Pincher, , London, Sidgwick & Jackson, 1981; C Pincher, , London, Sidgwick & Jackson, 1985.
19 Pen-name for one time Conservative MP Rupert Allason
20 C Pincher, , 1985, p 263. Pincher's comments could also be a veiled accusation against Michael Foot, party leader 1980-3 given that a large section of the book refers to the 1983 Labour Manifesto as being 'tailor-made for Moscow'. C Pincher, pp 15-33.
21 Head of the KGB's information gathering and agent control within a foreign country.
22 Interview with Gordievsky 15/11/98.
23 A Weinstein & A Vassiliev, , New York, Random House, 1999, p 145.

24 See J Frolik, , London, Corgi, 1975.

25 C Pincher, , 1985, p 170.

26 Interview with Gordievsky, 15/11/98.

27 O Gordievsky, , 1995, p 243.

28 J Frolik, , 1975, p 123.

29 J Frolik, , 1975, p 124-5.

30 C Andrew & V Mitrokhin, , Middlesex, Penguin., 1999, pp 528-9.

31 The Telegraph, 14/9/99, p 23.

32 See O Gordievsky, , 1995, pp 216-7.

33 Interview with Gordievsky, 15/11/98.

34 Interview with Gordievsky, 15/11/98.

35 J Frolik, , 1975, p 124.

36 C Pincher, 1981, pp 226-7.

37 C Andrew & V Mitrokhin, , 1999, p 125.

38 C Pincher, 1981, p 244.

39 Quoted in C Andrew & V Mitrokhin, , 1999, p 126.

40 O Gordievsky, , 1995; Interviewed with Oleg Gordievsky, 15/11/98.

41 Interview with Oleg Gordievsky, 15/11/98.

42 Shaposhnikov was a local CPSU apparatchik in the Ukraine Soviet. He had extensive contact with Labour MPs, particularly during the twinning of his home town Gorlovka, with Barnsley.

43 O Gordievsky, , 1995, p 292.

44 Interview with Norman Atkinson, 1/12/98.

45 Stan Newens recalled debates between himself and officials from various Soviet bloc nations on matters of policy, Interview with Stan Newens, 10 December 1998. There is also evidence that Alex Kitson argued with his contacts over, for example, the treatment of Jews in the Soviet Union., Kitson's debates are detailed in, 6 January 1981. Shaposhnikov recalled that this type of contact was very common with left-wing British MPs and officials and was always chronicled to ensure that the Soviet official appeared to have attempted to influence his contact and that they were justified in continuing their relationship, this enabled increases in expense budgets and, if the official was working in Britain, meant they were able to remain 'at station' rather than being recalled to the Soviet Union. Interview with Vladimir Shaposhnikov, 19 November 1998.

46 Interview with Norman Atkinson, 1/12/98. Interview with Anne Swingler 14/11/98. Interview with Jan Zilliacus, 8/7/98.

47 O Gordievsky, , 1995, p 287.

48 B Crozier, , London, Harper Collins, 1993, p 115.

49 Interview with Oleg Gordievsky, 15/11/98.

50 Interview with John Platts-Mills, 4 July 1998. Platts-Mills referred specifically to the Rambo-style movies that devalued the life of the Communist, he argued that this made war seem justified as long as we were "killing Commies. [...] that is how Hitler got away with killing Jews" he claimed.

51 It was often intellectuals and writers which were seen as the most influential. Gordievsky argued that those who produced key pro-Soviet texts were responsible for creating a number of sympathisers within the Universities. This was also stressed in S Koch, , London, Harper Collins, 1995.

52 Vic Allen, former lecturer at the University of Leeds, and writer of pro-Soviet analyses of international affairs, is widely seen as fulfilling such a role.

53 Speech delivered at the First Soviet Writers' Congress, quoted in D Caute, , 1973, p 10.

54 For a full explanation of the phrase and its' roots see D Caute, , 1973, pp 1-2.

Chapter One: Building a Pro-Soviet Fifth Column

1 K Marx & F Engels, The Communist Manifesto, London, Phoenix, p 55.

2 The title of the book by Vic Allen; V Allen, The Russians are Coming, Shipley, The Moor Press, 1987 which refuted anti-Communism as based upon prejudice and assumption.

3 A very unsympathetic appraisal is provided in D N Pritt, The Labour Government 1945-51, London, Lawrence & Wishart, 1963, pp 390-402; for a more academic but equally critical appraisal of the investigations into the affiliations and activities of the Labour left see S Dorril & R Ramsay, Smear: Wilson and the Secret State, London, Harper Collins, 1991, pp 36-43.

4 V I Lenin & G Zinoviev, Against the Stream, Moscow, Progress, 1925, p 156.

5 D Shub, Lenin, Harmondsworth, Penguin, 1948, pp 444-5.

6 Lenin's speech to the Supreme Soviet, September 1920, reproduced in V I Lenin, Collected Works, Vol. XXIII, Moscow, Novosti, 1946, p 292.

7 V I Lenin, Collected Works, Vol. XVII, Moscow, Novosti, 1946, pp 386-7.

8 V I Lenin, Collected Works, Vol. XVII, Moscow, Novosti, 1946, p 142.

9 I Phelps-Fetherston, Soviet International Front Organisations: A Concise Handbook, London, Frederick A Praeger 1965, p 1.

10 Karl Radek quoted in The Report of the Fourth Congress of the Communist International, p 53, Communist Party Archive.

11 See S Dorril, MI6: Fifty Years of Special Operation, London, Fourth Estate, 2000; S Dorril & R Ramsay, Smear: Wilson and the Secret State, 1991; P Lashmar & J Oliver, Britain's Secret Propaganda War: 1948-1977, Stroud, Sutton, 1998.

12 V Segodnya, 'Russia's image in the West - two views', Daily Review, 23 January 2001.

13 Quoted in C Rose, The Soviet Propaganda Network: A Directory of Organisations serving Soviet Foreign Policy, London, Pinter, 1988, p 9. Andropov was not the first to make such a statement, however this is indicative of Soviet policy towards the democratic West at an important juncture in East-West relations.

14 This international organisation, controlled by Comintern [the Communist International] and after 1948 Cominform, did carry out this task as far as possible. The CPGB was hindered by its slavishness to Stalin which caused divisions, particularly following the Nazi-Soviet Pact 1939.

15 T H Qualter, Propaganda and Psychological Warfare, 1962, p 27.

16 See, for example R P Dutt, World Politics 1918-36, London, Gollancz, 1937, contrasted with H Pollitt, How to Win the Peace, London, The Communist Party, 1945.

17 For a recent discussion of the British equivalent, the Information Research Department, is P Lashmar & J Oliver, Britain's Secret Propaganda War: 1948-1977, 1998.

18 B A Hazan, Soviet Propaganda: a case study of the Middle East Conflict, New Brunswick, Transaction Books, undated, p 49.

19 Zhurnalist, No. 1, 1972, p 5.

20 The majority of front organisation officials represented Warsaw Pact nations, though Britain, France and Germany also had seats on various councils. Aside from these, other Communist nations were represented: particularly Cuba, North Korea and North Vietnam, and countries undergoing struggles of independence in which Moscow had an interest: South Africa, India and Palestine. The Palestine Liberation Organisation had a seat on the Presidential Committee of the World Peace Council since 1954, though this was not always filled.

21 Interview with Jane Rosen, 8 July 1998.

22 P Johnston, Daily Telegraph, 25/9/99, electronic version.

23 J Stalin, Economic Problems of Socialism in the USSR, Simon & Shuster, New York, 1952, p 30.

24 See S Webb & B Webb, Soviet Communism: A New Civilisation?, special limited edition printed by the authors for the subscribing members of the Transport and General Workers Union, 1935.

25 Pilgrimage was Beatrice Webb's terminology, see M Cole, Beatrice Webb's Diaries 1924-32, London, Longmans, Green & Co, 1956, p 305. David Caute used the phrase 'Socialist Mecca' when discussing the desire among intellectuals to visit the Soviet Union; D Caute, The Fellow Travellers, London, Quartet, 1973, p 117.

26 For a review of the motivations of intellectuals who visited the Soviet Union, and the arguments they produced on their return, see D Caute, The Fellow Travellers, pp 60-131; B Dent, 'Moscow Travellers', New Statesman, 6 July 1984, pp 10-11; P Hollander, Political Pilgrims: Travel of the Western Intellectuals to the Soviet Union, China and Cuba, 1928-1978, New York, Harper & Row, 1981.

27 For details of Shaw's visit, and an analysis, see M Holroyd, Bernard Shaw: Volume 3: 1918-1950: The Lure of Fantasy, Middlesex, Penguin.1991, pp 233-248.

28 The Guardian, 10/10/72.

29 J F F Platts-Mills, 'Law in the Soviet Union', Anglo Soviet Journal, Vol. XXIV, No. 2, Summer
1963, pp. 8-11.

30 Interview with Philip Crees, formerly Chairman of Birmingham Branch of BSFS, 12 May 1999,

31 Interviews with former employees of Webster's Tools, Wakefield. See D G Lilleker, Against the Cold War. PhD Thesis, University of Sheffield, 2001, pp 52-3.

32 Reproduced in A Koestler et al, The God That Failed, London, Andre Deutsch, 1960, and more recently in MacArthur, Brian, (Editor), The Penguin book of Twentieth Century Protest, Middlesex, Penguin, pp 123-5.

33 Interview with Alan Sapper, 25 July 2000.

34 Interview with John Platts-Mills, 4 July 1998.

35 It is documented that Pritt was seen as a GRU asset. See N West, The Illegals: the Double Lives of the Cold War's Most Secret Agents, London, Hodder & Stoughton, 1993, p 35; p 109.

36 Pritt was expelled from the party in 1939 for his support of the Nazi-Soviet Pact and subsequent Soviet invasion of Finland.

37 Letter from William Wilson, 19 May 1999.

38 The name has gone through many variations i.e. World Peace Congress, World Peace Council and World Council for Peace. This is due in some part to translation, but mainly to the banning of the World Peace Congress in 1953 following which the name and headquarters in an attempt to disguise the fact that it was the same organisation.

39 Cominform directive of 29/11/49, quoted in I Phelps-Fetherston, Soviet International Front Organisations: A Concise Handbook, 1965, pp 17-18.

40 R H Shultz and R Godson, Dezinformatsia: Active Measures in Soviet Strategy, Washington, Pergamon Brassey's, 1984, p 112.

41 Articles in Tribune denounce both United States and Soviet actions, Reynolds News, in contrast, developed a pro-Soviet perspective and was able to explain Soviet actions while condemning the United States.

42 This particularly argued by Russian historian Volkogonov. See D Volkgonov, The Rise and Fall of the Soviet Empire: Political Leaders from Lenin to Gorbachev, London, HarperCollins, 1998, p 217; pp 276-7.

43 E R Goodman, 'The Soviet Union and World Government', The Journal of Politics, Vol. 15, No. 2, May 1953, pp 231-253, p 250.

44 Advertisement, World Government News, May 1951, p 9.

45 World Peace Council, What it is and what it does, 1978, p 6.

46 R Chandra, 'The Soviet Union and the arms race', World Marxist Review, January 1981, p 35.

47 Hansard, Vol. 978, Written Answers, Col. 219.

48 Interview with James Lamond, 17/2/99.

49 Interview with John Platts-Mills, 4 July 1998.

50 P Mercer, Directory of British Political Organisations: 1994, Essex, Longman, 1994.

51 See M Ormerod, What About the USSR: Labour and East-West Détente, London, LAP, 1987,

52 See Morgan Phillips papers, National Museum of Labour History for examples.

53 Unpublished History written by Diana Pym for King's College London Archive.

54 Letter J Fraser MP to Diana Pym, 30th November 1967.

55 See King's College Archive, League for Democracy in Greece, Letters, MPs, files A-L and M-Z.

56 There are numerous letters to the MPs who either joined or agreed to name the situation in Greece as an area of special interest in the King's College Archive, League for Democracy in Greece, letters, MPs, files A-L and M-Z.

57 C Rose, The Soviet Propaganda Network: A Directory of Organisations serving Soviet Foreign Policy, 1988, pp 255-276.

58 Sapper was at the time President of the Confederation of Entertainment Unions, Secretary of the Federation of Film Unions, Treasurer of the Federation of Broadcasting Unions and a member of the British Copyright Council.

59 Interview with Alan Sapper, 25 July 2000.
60 Letter S Chakraborty to Diana Pym, 3rd November 1967.

Chapter Two: From Emancipatory Revolution to Grand Alliance

1 See W P Coates & Z K Coates, A History of Anglo-Soviet Relations, London, Lawrence & Wishart, 1945; S R Graubard, British Labour and the Russian Revolution 1919-1924, Cambridge, Harvard University Press, 1956; B Jones, The Russia Complex: The British Labour Party and the Soviet Union, Manchester, Manchester University Press, 1977; A Thorpe, A History of the British Labour Party, London, Macmillan,1998; A J Williams, 'The Labour Party's Attitude to the Soviet Union 1927-35: An Overview with Specific Reference to Unemployment Policies and Peace', in The Journal of Contemporary History, Volume 22, 1987, No 1, pp 71-90, 1987 and A J Williams, Labour and Russia: the attitude of the Labour Party to the USSR 1924-1934, Manchester, Manchester University Press, 1989.
2 See G Cohen, 'Sentimental Socialism versus Revolutionary Marxism? A biographical analysis of Communism and the Independent Labour party', paper presented to the 'People of a Special Mould Conference on the biography and prosopography of the Communist party', University of Manchester, 6-8 April 2001. For an account of the split in British Socialism and consequent emergence of the CPGB see R Challinor, The Origins of British Bolshevism, London, Croom Helm Ltd, 1977.
3 W P Coates & Z K Coates, A History of Anglo-Soviet Relations, 1945, pp 744-50.
4 K Laybourn & D Murphy, Under the Red Flag: A History of Communism in Britain, Stroud, Sutton, 1999, p xvi.
5 For particular examples see D Healey, The Time of my Life, Middlesex, Penguin, 1989, pp 36-38; E Heffer, Never a Yes Man: The Life and Politics of an Adopted Liverpuddlian, London, Verso.1991, pp 16-19.
6 J T Murphy, 'How a Mass Communist Party Will Come in Britain', Communist International, No. 9, 1924, pp 13-14.
7 J T Murphy, 'How a Mass Communist Party Will Come in Britain', 1924, p 14.
8 W Gillies, The Soviet Solar System, London, Labour Party, 1925.
9 E Dell, A Strange Eventful History: Democratic Socialism in Britain, London, Harper Collins.2000, p 52.
10 J Lawrence, 'Labour - the myths it has lived by', Thane, Tanner and Tiratsoo, Labour's First Century, Cambridge, CUP, 2000, pp 341-366, p 352.
11 The Council of Workers and Soldiers' Delegates, What happened at Leeds, London, CWSD, 1917, p 5.
12 See speeches by Snowdon and Sylvia Pankhurst, The Council of Workers and Soldiers' Delegates, What happened at Leeds, London, CWSD, 1917, p 7.
13 The Council of Workers and Soldier's delegates, What happened at Leeds, London, 1917, 11.
14 The Council of Workers and Soldier's delegates, What happened at Leeds, London, 1917, 3.

15 The Council of Workers and Soldier's delegates, What happened at Leeds, London, 1917, 13.

16 See W Gallacher, Revolt on the Clyde, London, Lawrence & Wishart, 1936, p 137.

17 See particularly K Zilliacus, I Choose Peace, Harmondsworth, Penguin, 1949, p 41.

18 A Bullock, The Life and Times of Ernest Bevin: Vol. 1 Trade Union Leader 1881-1940, London, Heinemann, 1967, pp 74-5.

19 R Miliband, Parliamentary Socialism, London, George Allen & Unwin, 1961, pp 56-7.

20 W P Coates & Z K Coates, A History of Anglo-Soviet Relations, 1945, pp 1-25.

21 Labour Party, Report on the Annual Conference of the Labour Party held in the Albert Hall, Nottingham, on Wednesday, Jan 23rd 1918, and two following days, and the Adjourned Conference held in the Central Hall, Westminster, London, on Tuesday, Feb 26th 1918, The Labour Party, London, 1918, pp 60-1.

22 See W P Coates & Z K Coates, A History of Anglo-Soviet Relations, 1945, pp 149-152; F Williams, Magnificent Journey: The Rise of the Trade Unions, London, Odhams, 1954, pp 331-3.

23 F Williams, Magnificent Journey: The Rise of the Trade Unions, 1954, p 331.

24 Labour Party, Report of the British Labour Delegation to Russia, The Labour Party, London, 1920, p 6.

25 ILP, Resistance Shall Grow: The story of the 'Spies for Peace' and why they are important, London, Independent Labour Party, 1922, p 57.

26 Hansard, 29/7/19, Cols. 1979-1980.

27 W P Coates & Z K Coates, A History of Anglo-Soviet Relations, 1945, p 152 footnotes. This also includes a full list of the members of the committee.

28 See C Andrew, Secret Service: The Making of the British Intelligence Community, London, Heinemann, 1985, pp 301-16; G Bennett, A most extraordinary and mysterious business: the Zinoviev letter of 1924, London, Library and Records Department, Foreign & Commonwealth Office, 1999. For the debate on its effect on the party see A Thorpe, A History of the British Labour Party, 1997, p 60. The effect on Anglo-Soviet relations is discussed in W P Coates & Z K Coates, A History of Anglo-Soviet Relations, 1945, pp 197-206.

29 The role of the bankers over Macdonald's policy is reviewed in P Williamson, 'A "Bankers' Ramp"? Financiers and the British Financial Crisis of August 1931', English Historical Review, No. 99, 1984, pp 770-806. For detail on the crisis, MacDonald's response and the subsequent split in the Labour Party see A Thorpe, A History of the British Labour Party, 1997, pp 73-8. The left-wing perspective of MacDonald is provided in W Thompson, The Good Old Cause: British Communism 1920-1991, London, Pluto, 1992, pp 49-50.

30 See D Caute, The Fellow Travellers, London, Weidenfeld and Nicolson, 1973; P Hollander, Political Pilgrims: Travel of the Western Intellectuals to the Soviet Union, China and Cuba, 1928-1978, New York, Harper & Row, 1981.

31 J Lee, This Great Journey: A Volume of Autobiography 1904-45, London, MacGibbon & Lee, 1963, p 156.

32 J Strachey, 'Editorial', Left Review, Dec 1934, p 68.

33 A Gromyko, Memories, London, Hutchinson, 1989, p 160.

34 E Heffer, Never a Yes Man: The Life and Politics of an Adopted Liverpuddlian, 1991, p 17.

35 R P Dutt, Labour Monthly, Jan 1936, p 14.

36 N Mackenzie, [Editor], The letters of Sidney and Beatrice Webb; Book III: The Pilgrimage 1912-1947, London, Cambridge University Press, 1978, p 207.

37 M Cole, [Editor], Beatrice Webb's Diaries 1924-1932, London, Longmans Green & Co, 1956, p 265.

38 N Mackenzie & J Mackenzie, [Editors], The Diary of Beatrice Webb; Volume Four 1924-1943: The Wheel of Life, London, Virago in association with the London School of Economics, 1985, p 249.

39 The 1935 edition was released with a question mark, on later editions the question mark was tellingly omitted.

40 S Webb & B Webb, Soviet Communism: A New Civilisation?, special limited edition printed by the authors for the subscribing members of the Transport and General Workers Union, 1935, p 7.

41 A L Strong, Dictatorship and Democracy in the Soviet Union, New York, 1934, p 17.

42 S Webb & B Webb, Soviet Communism: A New Civilisation?, 1935, p 449

43 This is admitted in a report produced for BBC Radio, see The Listener, Vol. III, No 194, 28 September, 1932, p 429.

44 See L Radice, Beatrice and Sidney Webb: Fabian Socialists, London, Macmillan, 1984, p 295 for a synthesis of this point. The argument also appears in letter and diary entries for the period prior to visiting the Soviet Union, see M Cole, [Editor], Beatrice Webb's Diaries 1924-1932, 1956; N Mackenzie, [Editor], The letters of Sidney and Beatrice Webb; Book III: The Pilgrimage 1912-1947, 1978 or papers in the Passfield Collection, BLPES Archive.

45 N Mackenzie & J Mackenzie, [Editors], The Diary of Beatrice Webb; Volume Four 1924-1943: The Wheel of Life, 1985, p 318.

46 A J Kidd, 'The State and Moral Progress: The Webb's case for social reform c1905-1940', Twentieth Century British History, Vol. 7, No. 2, 1996, pp 189-205, p 203.

47 C Seymour-Jones, 'Webbs of intrigue', New Statesman & Society, 17-31 December 1993, pp 50-51, p 51.

48 Letter from Maisky to Webb, 21 April 1933, Passfield Papers.

49 A J Kidd, 'The State and Moral Progress: The Webb's case for social reform c1905-1940', 1996, pp 204-5.

50 Keynes was arguably influenced by the Soviet economic model, however he was not pro-Soviet or a Communist. He did however support the state-controlled model and linked this to strong centralised leadership, this has led some to criticise his work as being close to an adoption of the pro-Soviet position.

51 S Koch, Double Lives: Stalin, Willi Munzenberg and the Seduction of the Intellectuals, London, Harper Collins, 1995, p 181.

52 A Thorpe, A History of the British Labour Party, 1997, p 79.

53 H Harmer, The Longman Companion to the Labour Party 1900-1998, London, Longman, 1999.

54 R Taylor, The TUC: From the General Strike to New Unionism, London, Palgrave, 2000, pp 50-2; D Hyde, I Believed, London, The Reprint Society, 1952, pp 41-5; N Branson, History of the British Communist Party of Great Britian 1927-1941, London, Lawrence & Wishart, 1985, pp 74-82.

55 J M Roberts, A History of Europe, London, Helicon, 1996, pp 486-492.

56 M Almond, Revolution: 500 years of struggle for change, London, De Agostini, 1996, pp 138.

57 J Callaghan, Rajani Palme Dutt: A Study in British Stalinism, London, Lawrence & Wishart, 1993, p 149.

58 It should be noted that only the Popular Front was seen as a Communist front organisation, the People's Front was based upon similar ideas but was not of similar significance due to the lack of international support. The Popular Front was associated with supporting the international socialist movement in the anti-fascist fight. This identified with Comintern and governmental coalitions in France and Republican Spain.

59 R P Dutt, Labour Monthly, August 1932, p 17.

60 E Estorick, Stafford Cripps; A Biography, London, Heinemann, 1949, pp 140-141.

61 For full text of Cripp's speech see Labour Party, Report of Annual Conference, Brighton 1935, extracts can be found in E Estorick, Stafford Cripps; A Biography, 1949, p 143.

62 G D H Cole, The People's Front, London, Victor Gollancz, 1937, p 17.

63 D N Pritt, The Autobiography of D N Pritt; Part One; From Right to Left, London, Lawrence & Wishart, 1965, p 114.

64 E Shinwell, Conflict without Malice, London, Odhams Press, 1955, p 143.

65 E Estorick, Stafford Cripps; A Biography, 1949, p 282.

66 J Platts-Mills, Muck, Silk & Socialism, London, Paper Press, 2002, pp 146-9.

67 D Lilleker, 'Collective Action: When Government's shape Populist Support' in Fifth International Conference on Alternative Futures and Popular Protest: Conference Papers Vol. II, 1999, pp 91-102.

68 Hansard, 23 October 1941, Col 271.

69 J Callaghan, Rajani Palme Dutt: A Study in British Stalinism, 1993, pp 194-5.

70 R Thurlow, 'The Evolution of the Mythical British Fifth Column, 1939-46', 20th Century British History, Vol 10, No 4, Pp 477-98, 1999, p 495.

71 The People's Convention, We Must Act Now, London, 1941, p 5. See also D Lilleker, 'Collective Action: When Government's shape Populist Support' in Fifth International Conference on Alternative Futures and Popular Protest: Conference Papers Vol. II, 1999.

72 The final accounts for these funds are documented in the General Council's Report drafted for the Annual Trade Union Congress, 1946, p 224. Details of the fundraising activities can also be found in the SCR Archive and in the archived papers of local organisations, see D Lilleker, 'Collective Action: When Government's shape Populist Support' in Fifth International Conference on Alternative Futures and Popular Protest: Conference Papers Vol. II, 1999.

73 G Gallup, The Gallup International Public Opinion Polls: Great Britain 1937-1975, Volume One 1937-1964, Random House, 1976, p 89.

74 J Callaghan, Rajani Palme Dutt: A Study in British Stalinism, 1993, pp 207-9.

75 Letter, Pollitt to Mr J S Middleton, 18/12/42, CP Archive, Pollitt papers.

76 On this point see F Beckett, The Enemy Within: the Rise and Fall of the British Communist Party, London, John Murray, 1995; A Thorpe, 'The Communist International and the British Communist Party', Rees & Thorpe [Editors], International Communism and the Communist International 1919-43, Manchester, MUP, 1998. K Laybourn & D Murphy, Under the Red Flag: A History of Communism in Britain, 1998, pp 187-8.

77 R Thurlow, 'The Evolution of the Mythical British Fifth Column, 1939-46', 20th Century British History, Vol 10, No 4, 1999, pp 494-8.

78 Anglo-Soviet Journal, Vol. II, No. 4, p 294.

79 G D H Cole, Great Britain in the Post-War World, London, Victor Gollancz, 1942, p 422.

80 See particularly G D H Cole, 'A Disturbing Book', in Aryan Path, September 1938. However his critiques are also to be found in a myriad letters and articles to journals and newspapers and in the relevant chapters in G D H Cole, A History of Socialist Thought Volume IV: Communism and Social Democracy 1914-1931, London, Macmillan, 1958 and G D H Cole , A History of Socialist Thought Volume V: Socialism and Fascism, 1931-1939, London, Macmillan, 1960.

81 G D H Cole, Great Britain in the Post-War World, London, Victor Gollancz, 1942, p 37.

82 G D H Cole, Europe, Russia, and the future, London, Victor Gollancz, 1941, p 16.

83 G D H Cole, Europe, Russia, and the future, 1941, p 182.

84 G D H Cole, 'Europe, Russia, and the future: A Reply', Left News, March 1942.

85 For an account of this argument see E F M Durbin, The Politics of Democratic Socialism: An Essay on Social Policy, London, Routledge & Kegan Paul, 1940, p 271.

86 G D H Cole, Great Britain in the Post-War World, 1942, p 164.

87 G D H Cole, Great Britain in the Post-War World, 1942, p 160.

88 G D H Cole, Great Britain in the Post-War World, 1942, p 164.

89 G D H Cole, Great Britain in the Post-War World, 1942, p 163.

90 G D H Cole, The Meaning of Marxism, Michigan, University of Michigan Press, 1948, p 103.

91 G D H Cole, The Meaning of Marxism, 1948, p 140.

92 G D H Cole, The Meaning of Marxism, 1948, p 209.

93 G D H Cole, The Meaning of Marxism, 1948, p 285.

94 G D H Cole, The Meaning of Marxism, 1948, p 288.

95 H Pollitt, How to Win the Peace, London, The Communist Party, 1944, see Chapter V, pp 14-18 particularly.

96 C Churchill, My Visit to Russia, London, Hutchinson & Co, 1945, p 58.

97 M Mazowar, Dark Continent: Europe's Twentieth Century, London, Penguin, 1997, p xi.

Chapter Three: Konni Zilliacus and Labour's Adversarial Voices from the Left

1 The notable exception is J Schneer, Labour's Conscience: The Labour Left 1945-51, London, Unwin Hyman, 1988.

2 T A Koelble, 'Recasting social democracy in Europe: a nested games explanation of strategic adjustment in political parties', Politics and Society, Vol 20, 1, 1982, p 52.

3 A Thorpe, A History of the British Labour Party, London, Macmillan, 1997, p 107.

4 K O Morgan, Labour in Power, 1945-51, Oxford, OUP, 1984, pp 94-5.

5 Labour Party, Let Us Face the Future: A Declaration of Labour Policy for the Consideration of the Nation, Labour Party, London, 1945, p 7.

6 P Piratin, Our Flag Stays Red, London, Lawrence & Wishart, 1978, pp vii-viii; see also D Childs, Britain since 1945, 3rd Edition, London, Routledge,1992, p 18; Lord Morrison, Herbert Morrison: an Autobiography, London, Heinemann, 1960, pp 250-1.

7 Quoted in A Sked, and C Cook, Post-War Britain', New Edition 1945-92, Middlesex, Penguin, 1993, pp 20-21.

8 D Childs, Britain since 1945, 3rd Edition, 1992, pp 2-3; A Sked and C Cook, Post-War Britain', New Edition 1945-92, 1993, pp 21-22.

9 A Thorpe, A History of the British Labour Party, 1997, pp 112-3.

10 The Guardian, 3 March 1984; see also K O Morgan, Labour in Power, 1945-51, Oxford, OUP, 1984, p 8.

11 For example see I Mikardo, The Second Five Years: A Labour Programme for 1950, London, Fabian Society, 1948; I Mikardo, The Labour Case, London, Allan Wingate, 1950. On the consensus, see E Shaw, The Labour Party since 1945, Oxford, Blackwell, 1996, pp 46-8; P Kerr, 'The Postwar Consensus: the woozle that wasn't?' in D Marsh et al, Postwar British Politics in perspective, Cambridge, Polity, 1999, pp 66-86.

12 A Sked and C Cook, Post-War Britain', New Edition 1945-92, 1993, p 95.

13 See C Moorehead, Troublesome People: Enemies of War 1916-1986, London, Hamish Hamilton, 1987; particularly Ch 8, pp 203-231 and Ch 12, pp 308-326.

14 K Zilliacus, The Mirror of the Past; Lest it Reflect the Future, London, Gollancz, 1944, p 15.

15 See H J Morgenthau, 1952, 'Another 'Great Debate': The National Interest of the US' in The American Political ScienceReview, Vol. XLVI, No. 4, pp 971-8.

16 Interview with Mrs Jan Zilliacus, widow of Konni Zilliacus, 10th March 1998.

17 K Zilliacus, I Choose Peace, Harmondsworth, Penguin, 1949, p 15.

18 P M Williams, Editor, The Diary of Hugh Gaitskell 1945-1956, London, Jonathan Cape.1983, p 455.

19 R H B Lockhart, Memoirs of a British Agent, London, Putnam, 1934.

20 On Trade Union opposition to interventionism see F Williams, Magnificent Journey: The Rise of the Trade Unions, London, Odhams, 1954, p 331. For the brief Commons debate on intervention, including Labour members supporting he Bolshevik position, see Hansard, 29/7/19, Cols. 1979-1980.

21 K Zilliacus, I Choose Peace, 1949, p 41.

22 W S Churchill, speaking in Rome 20 January 1927 on the occasion of formal recognition of the Mussolini government, quoted in K Zilliacus, I Choose Peace, 1949, p 47.

23 K Zilliacus, I Choose Peace, 1949, p 68.

24 G D H Cole, The People's Front, London, Victor Gollancz, 1937.

25 See particularly G D H Cole, Europe, Russia, and the future, London, Victor Gollancz, 1941.

26 K Zilliacus, I Choose Peace, 1949, pp 313-320.

27 K Zilliacus, I Choose Peace, 1949, pp 211-273.

28 K Zilliacus, I Choose Peace, 1949, p 400.

29 K Zilliacus, Blue Print for a World Peace Union, unpublished Fabian Society report, Fabian Society Archive, BLPES, 1939, p 13.

30 K Zilliacus, I Choose Peace, 1949, p 429.

31 K Zilliacus, I Choose Peace, 1949, p 445.

32 See R W G Mackay, Peace Aims and the New Order, London, Michael Joseph, 1941, pp 115-6; pp 140-1.

33 R W G Mackay, Peace Aims and the New Order, 1941, p 140.

34 J Schneer, Labour's Conscience: The Labour Left 1945-51, London, 1988, pp 52-78.

35 K Zilliacus, Britain, USSR and World Peace, London, British-Soviet Society.1946, p 3.

36 K Zilliacus, I Choose Peace, 1949, pp 466-470.

37 Labour Party, Let Us Face the Future, Labour Party, 1945, p 7.

38 K Zilliacus, I Choose Peace, 1949, p 509.

39 K Zilliacus, I Choose Peace, 1949, p 315.

40 K Zilliacus, A New Birth of Freedom: World Communism after Stalin, London, Secker & Warburg, 1957, pp 7-12.

41 K Zilliacus, A New Birth of Freedom: World Communism after Stalin, 1957, p 8.

42 Konni is referred to by many contemporaries as either Zilly or Zill, the moniker used often indicates their fondness towards him.

43 B Pimlott, [Editor], The Political Diary of Hugh Dalton 1918-40,1945-60, London, Jonathan Cape in association with the LSE & PS, 1986, p 166.

44 B Pimlott, [Editor], The Political Diary of Hugh Dalton 1918-40,1945-60, 1986, p 199.

45 S Koch, Double Lives: Stalin, Willi Munzenberg and the Seduction of the Intellectuals, London, Harper Collins, 1996, p 171.

46 For details on Kravchenko, and his career in the Soviet Union prior to his defection, see V Kravchenko, I Chose Freedom, London, Robert Hale, 1946.

47 N Tolstoy, Stalin's Secret War, London, Jonathan Cape, 1981, pp 165-6.

48 Interview with Jan Zilliacus, 8/7/98.

49 Interview with Gordievsky, 15/11/98.

50 C Pincher, Their Trade is Treachery, London, Sidgwick & Jackson, 1981, p 252.

51 C Pincher, Their Trade is Treachery, 1981, p 253.

52 H Pelling, The British Communist Party: a historical profile, London, Adam & Charles Black, 1958, p 132.

53 H Pelling, The British Communist Party: a historical profile, 1958, p 163.

54 D Hyde, I Believed, London, Heinemann, 1952, p 201.

55 D Hyde, I Believed, 1952, p 201. The only definite Communist Party member was Percy Bairstow who stood as Labour MP for Pontefract 1945-51. Bairstow left the Labour Party in 1952 and declared himself a Communist in the local press.

56 D Hyde, I Believed, 1952, p 202.

57 D Caute, The Fellow Travellers, London, Quartet, pp 103-4.

58 Quoted in J Schneer, Labour's Conscience: The Labour Left 1945-51, 1988, p 121.

59 Interview with Jan Zilliacus 8/7/98.

60 Letter Laski to Woolf, 11/11/43, Leonard Woolf papers.

61 Interview with Jan Zilliacus, 8/7/98.

62 Interview with Jan Zilliacus, 8/7/98.

63 For evidence of Zilliacus's opinion of Stalinism and the 'Personality Cult' see Konni Zilliacus, A New Birth of Freedom: World Communism after Stalin, 1957, pp 20-65 passim.

64 Interview with Jan Zilliacus, 8/7/98.

65 Letter Zilliacus to Frank Cousins, 29/6/59; Frank Cousins papers.

66 See S Dorrill, and R Ramsay, Smear: Wilson and the Secret State, London, Harper Collins, 1991, pp 24-29 passim.
p 95.

67 K Zilliacus, A New Birth of Freedom: World Communicsm after Stalin, 1957, p 95.

68 Hansard, Vol. 451, Col. 454.

69 Labour Party Annual Report Conference, 1949, p 121.

70 New Statesman and Nation, 30th October 1948, p 372.

71 See Lost Sheep file, General Secretary's Papers.

72 Letter Dalton to Phillips, 1/11/48, General Secretary's papers.

73 Letter Phillips to Maurice Evans, 30/6/49, General Secretary's papers.

74 The other possible expellees were, in the order provided in the Phillips file: J Mack, S Silverman, B Stross, W Warbey, G Bing, S Swingler, G Wigg, H Austin, G Cooper, H Davies, I Mikardo, J Silverman, C G P Smith, W Vernon, R Chamberlain.

75 Interviewed by Daniel Weinbren in 1983, scripts at the National Sound Archive, ref. C609. See D Weinbren, Generating Socialism: Recollections of Life in the Labour Party, Stroud, Sutton, 1997, p 149; p 198.

76 Hansard, Vol. 413, Col. 80.

77 Hansard, Vol. 448, Col. 1245.

78 Hansard, Vol. 419, Col. 1322

79 J Schneer, Labour's Conscience: The Labour Left 1945-51, 1988, Appendices, pp 227-235.

80 For the debate on the Nenni Telegram, and the extent to which it was engineered by Platts-Mills, see J Schneer, Labour's Conscience: The Labour Left 1945-51, 1988, pp 113-117.

81 Anonymous memo attached to the 'Lost Sheep' file, possibly written by General Secretary Morgan Phillips, General Secretary's papers, National Museum of Labour History.

82 Interview with Jan Zilliacus, 8/7/98.

83 Hansard, Vol. 413. Col. 1116.

84 Hansard, Vol. 427, Col. 1543

85 Hansard, Vol. 459, Col. 765.

86 Hansard, Vol. 450, Col. 2463.

87 John Platts-Mills, unpublished autobiography, p 8.

88 John Platts-Mills, unpublished autobiography, pp 6-7.

89 Interview with John Platts-Mills, 4/7/98.

90 D Weinbren, Generating Socialism: Recollections of Life in the Labour Party, 1997, p 105.

91 D Weinbren, Generating Socialism: Recollections of Life in the Labour Party, 1997, p 115.

92 Interview with John Platts-Mills, 4/7/98.

93 Interview with John Platts-Mills, 4/7/98.

94 Interview with John Platts-Mills, 4/7/98.

95 Letter Lord Callaghan of Cardiff to D G Lilleker, 25/8/98.

96 For a full description of the IADL see I Phelps-Fetherston, Soviet International Front Organisations: A Concise Handbook, London, Frederick A Praeger 1965, pp 126-136.

97 S Koch, Double Lives: Stalin, Willi Munzenberg and the Seduction of the Intellectuals, 1996, p 38; pp 154-5.

98 D Healey, The Time of my Life, Middlesex, Penguin, 1989, pp 34-7.

99 Interview with John Platts-Mills, 4/7/98.

100 Though John Platts-Mills recalled the fight, and that it was started by the Conservative MP for Brighton calling Piratin a bastard, he could not recall the name of the MP. The MP for Brighton was Luke William B Teeling (1903-1975) a staunch anti-Communist who had led delegations in 1947 to Finland and Japan lecturing on the dangers of spreading Communism. It is likely that this was the individual Platts-Mills recalled, however, there is only his vague recollections as proof.

101 Interview with John Platts-Mills, 4/7/98.

102 Letter John Platts-Mills to Ivor Montague 10/8/59.

103 J Platts-Mills, 'Labour Incentives in the Soviet Union', in Anglo Soviet Journal, Vol. III, No. 2, Summer 1946, pp 7-10, p 7.

104 D N Pritt, 'In Memoriam', in Anglo-Soviet Journal, Vol. XIV, No. 1, Spring 1953, p 3.

105 Interview with John Platts-Mills, 4/7/98.

106 W Gallacher, Rise like Lions, London, Lawrence & Wishart, 1951, p 72.

107 Interview with John Platts-Mills, 4/7/98.

108 E A Roberts, The Anglo-Marxists: a study of Ideology and Culture, Oxford, Rowman & Littlefield, 1997, p 66. See also H Pelling, The British Communist Party, London, Macmillan, 1958, p 92; N Wood, Communism and the British Intellectuals, New York, Columbia University Press, 1959, pp 1-83; E A Roberts, The Anglo-Marxists: a study of Ideology and Culture, 1997, pp 55-102.

109 E A Roberts, The Anglo-Marxists: a study of Ideology and Culture, 1997, pp 68-74.

110 M Cole, Editor, Beatrice Webb's Diaries 1924-1932, London, Longmans Green & Co, 1956, p 14.

111 Interview with John Platts-Mills, 4/7/98.

112 Platts-Mills indicated that much of his campaigning was, after 1987, personally funded, previously he had been "given grants from international bodies who fought for justice". Interview with John Platts-Mills, 4/7/98. See also J Platts-Mills, Muck, Silk & Socialism, London, Paper Press.

113 For his account see H Lester Hutchinson, Meerut 1929-1932, Manchester, 1932. A further useful source on Hutchinson's role, and the involvement of the CPGB in supporting the Indian Communist Party, is N Branson, History of the Communist Party 1927-41, London, Lawrence & Wishart, 1985, pp 59-60.

114 J Callaghan, Rajani Palme Dutt: A Study in British Stalinism, London,Lawrence & Wishart, 1993, pp 46-7; pp 102-4.

115 N Branson, History of the Communist Party 1927-41, 1985, pp 59-60.

116 See Labour Party, Meerut: Release the Prisoners, London, Labour Party, 1933.

117 H Pelling, The British Communist Party: a historical profile, 1958, pp 106-7.

118 Letter Norman L Stevens to Phillips, 2/3/49.

119 H L Hutchinson, MP, 'Marxism and the Post-War World', in Left, No. 114, April 1946, pp 89-92, p 91.

120 H L Hutchinson, MP, 'Marxism and the Post-War World', 1949, p 92.

121 H L Hutchinson, MP, 'Marxism and the Post-War World', 1949, p 92.

122 Soviet Monitor, 1949, No. 10, p 3.

123 Letter Norman L Stevens to Phillips, 2/3/49.

124 Labour MP for Dartford, 1945-50.

125 Letter Solley to Phillips, 5/5/48.

126 K O Morgan, Labour in Power, 1945-51, 1984, p 61.

127 Gateshead Post, 5/3/50, p 4.

128 D Healey, The Time of my Life, 1989, p 101.

129 K Zilliacus, Why I was Expelled: Bevinism v Election Pledges, Socialism and Peace, London, Narod Press, 1949, pp 62-3.

130 John Platts-Mills, unpublished autobiography, p 9.

131 This is evident from arguments presented in K Zilliacus, Why I was Expelled: Bevinism v Election Pledges, Socialism and Peace, 1949.

132 K Zilliacus, Tito v Stalin: Yugoslavia and the Cold War, London, Perspective, undated pamphlet.

133 K Zilliacus, Tito v Stalin: Yugoslavia and the Cold War, undated pamphlet, p 33.

134 See particularly K Zilliacus, Tito of Yugoslavia, London, Michael Joseph, 1952; K Zilliacus, A New Birth of Freedom: World Communism after Stalin, London, Secker & Warburg, 1957.

135 S Ferguson, Labour Party Politics 1935-45: A Case Study of Konni Zilliacus and the Gateshead Labour Party and Trades Council, M.Sc. Dissertation, The University of Cambridge, 1986, p 39.

136 The Daily Worker, 21/11/52, p 1.

137 W Gallacher, Rise like Lions, 1951, p 159.

138 K Zilliacus, A New Birth of Freedom: World Communism after Stalin, 1957, p 10.

139 K Zilliacus, A New Birth of Freedom: World Communism after Stalin, 1957, p 281.

140 K Zilliacus, A New Birth of Freedom: World Communism after Stalin, 1957, pp 283-4.

141 K Zilliacus, Arms & Labour, London, Labour Campaign for Nuclear Disarmament, 1965, p 20.

142 K Zilliacus, Arms & Labour, 1965, pp 11-13.

143 K Zilliacus, Arms & Labour, 1965, p 17.

144 K Zilliacus, Labour's Crisis, Its Nature, Causes and Cure, London, Tribune Group, 1966.

145 This is highlighted particularly in M Jenkins, Bevanism: Labour's High Tide, Nottingham, Spokesman, 1979, pp 285-306.

146 See S Berger and D Lilleker, 'Blutrünstige Diktatur, das bessere Deutschland, oder Stolperstein auf dem Weg zu einer friedlichen Koexistenz? Die DDR im Blick der britischen Labour Party, 1949-1973', in A Bauerkamper, Britain and the GDR: Relations and Perceptions in a Divided World, Potsdam, Zentrum fur Zeithistorische Forshung, 2001, pp 235-66.

147 K Zilliacus, Labour's Crisis, Its Nature, Causes and Cure, 1966, pp 10-13.

148 D Watson, 'From 'Fellow Traveller' to 'Fascist Spy': Konni Zilliacus MP and the Cold War', in W Thompson, (Editor), Socialist History No 11: The Cold War, London, Pluto Press, pp 59-87, p 83.

149 For a debatoe on Wilson's foreign policy see, P Jones, America and the British Labour Party: the special relationship at work, London, Tauris, 1997, p 139; C Ponting, Breach of Promise: Labour in Power 1964-70, Middlesex, Penguin, pp 218-226; C Wrigley, 'Now you see it, now you don't: Harold Wilson and Labour's Foreign Policy 1964-70' in Coopey, Fielding and Tiratsoo, The Wilson Governments 1964-1970, London, Pinter, 1993, pp 123-135. As yet there has been no thorough review of Wilson's attempts to hasten the process of détente.

150 W Warbey and K Zilliacus, Flashpoint: Vietnam-Indo China and Britain and Vietnam, London, New Gladiator, 1962, p 3.

151 D Volkogonov, The Rise and Fall of the Soviet Empire: Political Leaders from Lenin to Gorbachev, London, HarperCollins, 1998.

152 K Zilliacus, Labour's Crisis, Its Nature, Causes and Cure, 1966, pp 15-16.

153 Particularly see K Zilliacus, A New Birth of Freedom: World Communism after Stalin, 1957, pp 83-95.

154 E J Meehan, The British Left Wing and Foreign Policy: A Study of the Influence of Ideology, New Jersey, Rutgers University Press, 1950, p 31.

155 See Gateshead Post, 22/11/46, p 6; 10/1/47, p 10, Zilliacus Archive, Gateshead Central Library for examples.

156 For an example of this see M Foot, Dr Strangelove, I Presume. London, Gollancz, 1999.

157 K Zilliacus, Dragon's Teeth: The background, contents and consequences of the North Atlantic Pact, London, Narod Press, 1949, p 24.

158 D Watson, 'From 'Fellow Traveller' to 'Fascist Spy': Konni Zilliacus MP and the Cold War', pp 81-3.

159 This had been argued by Trotsky in his critique of Stalinism, see L Trotsky, The Revolution Betrayed, London, Verso, 1956.

160 E Mandel, From Stalinism to Eurocommunism: The Bitter Fruits of 'Socialism in One Country', Paris, Francois Maspero, 1978, p 188.

161 C Boggs, 'The Democratic Road: New Departures and Old Problems', C Boggs and D Plotke, The Politics of Eurocommunism: socialism in transition, London, Macmillan, 1980, pp 431-471.

162 For a review of the emergence of Eurocommunism, and its national variants, see G Schwab [Editor], Eurocommunism: The Ideological and Political Foundations, London, Aldwych Press, 1981. On Italian Eurocommunism see C Boggs, 'The Democratic Road: New Departures and Old Problems', 1980, pp 433-440. The Spanish variant is outlined in S Carrillo, Eurocommunism and the State, London, Lawrence & Wishart, 1977.

163 Quoted in E Mandel, From Stalinism to Eurocommunism: The Bitter Fruits of 'Socialism in One Country', 1978, p 220.

164 S Carrillo, Eurocommunism and the State, 1977, p 172.

165 K Zilliacus, A New Birth of Freedom: World Communism after Stalin, 1957, p 92.

166 S Carrillo, Eurocommunism and the State, 1977, p 174.

167 C Boggs, 'The Democratic Road: New Departures and Old Problems', 1980, p 432.

168 C Boggs, 'The Democratic Road: New Departures and Old Problems', 1980, p 439.

169 C Boggs, 'The Democratic Road: New Departures and Old Problems', 1980, p 439; E Mandel, From Stalinism to Eurocommunism: The Bitter Fruits of 'Socialism in One Country', 1978, p 188.

170 M Jones, 'Konni Zilliacus', obituary printed in New Statesman, 14/7/67, pp 43-4.

171 W Gallacher, Rise like Lions, 1951, p 161.

172 See S Carrillo, Eurocommunism and the State, 1977, p 141; G Schwab, 'Introduction', G Schwab, Eurocommunism: The Ideological and Political Foundations, 1981, pp xxi-xxvi.

173 See E A Roberts, The Anglo-Marxists: a study of Ideology and Culture, 1997.

174 K Zilliacus, A New Birth of Freedom: World Communism after Stalin, 1957, p 9.

175 W Churchill, quoted from a radio broadcast 1/10/39.

176 K Zilliacus, letter to Tribune, published 17/1/47.

177 Interview with Jan Zilliacus, 8/7/98.

178 K Zilliacus, quoted in the Gateshead Post, 1/11/46, p 6.

Chapter Four: Victory for Socialism

1 K O Morgan, Labour in Power, 1945-51, Oxford, OUP, 1984, p 503.

2 E Shaw, The Labour Party since 1945, Oxford, Blackwell, 1996, p 46.

3 A Thorpe, A History of the British Labour Party, London, Macmillan, 1997, p 135.

4 A Thorpe, A History of the British Labour Party, 1997, p 135.

5 See T Bale, Sacred Cows and Common Sense, Aldershot, Ashgate, 1999, passim particularly 232-5.

6 A Thorpe, A History of the British Labour Party, 1997, p 154.

7 On the internal conflict in the party see R Desai, Intellectuals and Socialism: 'Social Democrats' and the Labour Party, London, Lawrence & Wishart, 1994, pp 99-126.

8 R Winstone, [Editor], The Benn Diaries, (new single volume edition), London, Arrow, 1995, pp 78-80.

9 See sections on the Gaitskell leadership in D Coates, The Labour Party and the Struggle for Socialism, London, C U P, 1975; P Jones, America and the British Labour Party: the special relationship at work, London, Tauris, 1996.

10 S Dorril & R Ramsay, Smear: Wilson and the Secret State, London, Harper Collins, 1992, p 27.

11 A Sked & C Cook, Post-War Britain, (New Edition 1945-92), Middlesex, Penguin, 1993, pp 183-4.

12 S Dorril & R Ramsay, Smear: Wilson and the Secret State, 1992, pp 12-35.

13 D Keohane, Labour Party Defence Policy since 1945, Leicester, Leicester University Press, 1993, p 3.

14 M Foot, Aneurin Bevan; Volume 2, 1945-1960, London, Paladin, 1973, pp 579-81; R Taylor, Against the Bomb: the British Peace Movement 1958-1965, Oxford, Clarendon Press, 1988, pp 279-282; A Thorpe, A History of the British Labour Party, 1997, p 143.

15 R Desai, Intellectuals and Socialism: 'Social Democrats' and the Labour Party, pp 100-2.

16 See P Duff, Left Left Left, London, Allison & Busby, 1971.

17 P Duff, Left Left Left, 1971, p 47.

18 E Shaw, Discipline and Discord in the Labour Party, Manchester, M.U.P, 1988, p 97; see also NEC Election Sub-Committee minutes 18 July 1961, Labour Party Archive, National Museum of Labour History.

19 E Shaw, Discipline and Discord in the Labour Party, 1988, p 93; see also NEC Election Sub-Committee minutes 3 May 1955, Labour Party Archive, National Museum of Labour History.

20 Interview with Anne Swingler, 14/11/98.

21 L Scott, 'International History 1945-90', Baylis & Smith (Editors), The Globalization of World Politics, Oxford, OUP, pp 71-87, 1997, p 76.

22 S E Ambrose, Rise to Globalism: American Foreign Policy since 1938, Middlesex, Penguin, 1993, pp 128-9.

23 D Volkogonov, The Rise and Fall of the Soviet Empire: Political Leaders from Lenin to Gorbachev, London, HarperCollins, 1998, p 236.

24 D Volkogonov, The Rise and Fall of the Soviet Empire: Political Leaders from Lenin to Gorbachev, 1998, pp 235-247.

25 M Kenny, The First New Left: British Intellectuals after Stalin, London, Lawrence & Wishart, 1995, pp 172-9.

26 See particularly M Hatfield, The House the Left Built: Inside Labour Policy-Making 1970-75, London, Gollancz, 1978.

27 Victory for Socialism, Executive Council Meeting minutes, undated. Jo Richardson papers; National Museum of Labour History.

28 The Foreign and Commonwealth Committee 1958-1966 was chaired by Zilliacus and included Ian Mikardo, Frank Allaun, Harold Davies and Robert Woof. There are no recorded changes to this Committee during this period.

29 Interview with Jan Zilliacus, 8 July 1998.

30 Tribune, 21/2/58, p 4.

31 Labour Party Annual Conference Report, 1949, p 120.

32 Interview with Stan Newens, 10/12/98.

33 Letter to The Times, 9 March 1981, William Wilson papers; The Times, 14/3/81, p 15.

34 Hansard, 19 February 1958, Col. 1241.

35 See Kaldor, Smith & Vines, Democratic Socialism and the Cost of Defence, London, Croon Helm, 1979; D Keohane, Security in British Politics 1945-99, London, Macmillan Press, 2000, pp 136-154.

36 P Hennessy, Muddling Through: Power, Politics and the Quality of Government in Postwar Britain, London, Victor Gollancz, 1996, p 99.

37 D Keohane, Labour Party Defence Policy since 1945, 1993, p 28.

38 Quoted in K Zilliacus, (undated pamphlet), Home on the Bomb and Labour's Alternative to Genocide, London, New Gladiator Press, p 8.

39 Morning Star, 5/10/71.

40 K Zilliacus, Home on the Bomb and Labour's Alternative to Genocide, p 11, (undated pamphlet).

41 H Davies, Bull's Eye Island, London, Union of Democratic Control, p 9, (undated pamphlet).

42 See K Laybourn & D Murphy, Under the Red Flag: A History of Communism in Britain, Stroud, Sutton, 1999, p 158-162; W Thompson, The Good Old Cause: British Communism 1920-1991, London, Pluto, 1992, pp 134-160.

43 M Foot, 'Bevan and the H-bomb', Tribune, 11/10/57.

44 M Foot, Aneurin Bevan; Volume 2, 1945-1960, 1973, pp 579-583.

45 New Statesman, Editorial, 12/10/57, p 4.

46 D Coates, The Labour Party and the Struggle for Socialism, 1975, p 193.

47 Labour Party Annual Conference Report, 1960, p 68.

48 See S Dorril & R Ramsay, Smear: Wilson and the Secret State, 1991, pp 26-7.

49 Hugh Gaitskell, Labour Party Annual Conference Report, 1960, p 74.

50 Alleged by Chapman Pincher, see C Pincher, The Secret Offensive: Active Measures; A Saga of Deception, Disinformation, Subversion, Terrorism and Assassination, London, Sidgwick & Jackson.1985, pp 15-33.

51 R Taylor, Against the Bomb: the British Peace Movement 1958-1965, 1988, p 314.

52 S Swingler, An outline of Political Thought since the French Revolution, London, Victor Gollancz, 1939, p 86.

53 S Swingler, An outline of Political Thought since the French Revolution, 1939, p 86 and footnotes.

54 S Swingler, An outline of Political Thought since the French Revolution, 1939, p 86, footnotes.
55 A Croft, 'The Young Men are Moving Together: the Case of Randall Swingler', paper presented to the 'People of a Special Mould? International Conference on comparative communist biography and prosopography', University of Manchester, 7 April 2001.
56 Interview with Anne Swingler, 14/11/98.
57 Interview with Anne Swingler, 14/11/98.
58 Interview with Bill Alexander 2/2/99.
59 Interview with Anne Swingler, 14/11/98..
60 Interview with Vladimir Shaposhnikov, 19/11/98.
61 Interview with Stan Newens, 10/12/98.
62 Letter from Anne Swingler, 11/10/98.
63 Many Communist experienced similar crises of faith in 1956, see F Becket, Enemy Within: The Rise and Fall of the British Communist Party, 1995, pp 124-140.
64 See N H Twitchell, The Tribune Group: Factional Conflict in the Labour Party 1964-70, London, Rabbit, 1998.
65 Labour Party, The New Hope For Britain, London, Labour Party, 1983, p 36.
66 S E Ambrose, , Rise to Globalism: American Foreign Policy since 1938, 1993, p 150.
67 Letter from Frank Allaun, 28/10/98.
68 F Allaun, The Struggle for Peace: A personal account of 60 years campaigning inside and outside Parliament, Manchester, Labour Action for Peace.1992, p 18.
69 Letter from Frank Allaun, 15/2/99.
70 The Sun, undated cutting from 1981, Frank Allaun papers.
71 Letter from Frank Allaun, 15/2/99.
72 Morning Star, 5/12/97.
73 F Allaun, The Struggle for Peace: A personal account of 60 years campaigning inside and outside Parliament, 1992, p 19.
74 Brezhnev particularly published many pamphlets, many of which were amalgamated into Our Course: Peace and Socialism, Moscow, Novosti Press Agency, 1977. These were aimed directly at influencing the peace movements of Europe and were recommended reading for members of front organisations.
75 Letter from Frank Allaun 15/2/99.
76 See M Gorbachev, Memoirs, London, Doubleday, 1995, pp 359-367, on 28th Congress of CPSU, Allaun's criticism is found in Morning Star, 5/12/97.
77 Letter from Frank Allaun, 15/2/99.
78 Letter from Frank Allaun, 15/2/99.
79 Letter from Frank Allaun, 15/2/99.
80 F Allaun, The Struggle for Peace: A personal account of 60 years campaigning inside and outside Parliament, 1992, p 8.
81 Labour Weekly, 12/5/72, Frank Allaun papers.
82 F Allaun, The Struggle for Peace: A personal account of 60 years campaigning inside and outside Parliament, 1992, p 16.

83 Letter Allaun to Harry Pollitt, 7/11/39, Pollitt papers, Communist Party Archive, National Museum of Labour History.
84 F Allaun, The Struggle for Peace: A personal account of 60 years campaigning inside and outside Parliament, 1992, p 3.
85 Allaun Interviewed by Richard Taylor, Jan 1978. Quoted in R Taylor, Against the Bomb: the British Peace Movement 1958-1965, 1988, p 311, footnotes.
86 R Taylor, Against the Bomb: the British Peace Movement 1958-1965, 1988, p 275, also discussed by founder of CND in Canon L J Collins, Faith under Fire, London, Merlin, 1966, pp 324-6.
87 J Hinton, Protests & Visions: Peace Politics in 20th Century Britain, London, Hutchinson Radius, 1989, pp 44-49.
88 Victory for Socialism leaflet, 1958, Jo Richardson papers, National Museum of Labour History.
89 Salford Reporter, 31/10/58, Frank Allaun papers.
90 Huddersfield Daily Examiner, 13/9/58, press-cuttings, Allaun archive, National Museum of Labour History.
91 Lancaster Guardian, 23/9/60, press-cuttings, Allaun archive, National Museum of Labour History.
92 Also recognised by Diana Collins, wife of CND Chair Canon John Collins. Letter to Peace News, Vol. 1, No 3.
93 K Zilliacus, in Tribune, 24/1/59, p 12.
94 Letter to the Daily Telegraph, 7/10/67, Frank Allaun papers.
95 See E Shaw, Discipline and Discord in the Labour Party, 1988, pp 89-100 on the endorsement and deselection of MPs and parliamentary candidates.
96 Financial Times, 3/9/66, Frank Allaun papers.
97 Labour Party, Time for Decision, London, Labour Party, pp 25-6.
98 Letter to The Guardian, 17/10/63, Frank Allaun papers.
99 Morning Star, 9/12/72, p 6.
100 There was a large amount of literature aimed to exacerbate fears of Soviet invasion, for example see W S Churchill, Defending the West, London, Temple-Smith, 1981.
101 Morning Star, 8/11/78, p 5.
102 Morning Star, 5/10/77, p 7.
103 Lancashire Evening Telegraph, 16/12/67, Frank Allaun papers.
104 Labour Party Annual Conference Report, 1959, p 131.
105 P Seyd, The Rise and Fall of the Labour Left, Basingstoke, Macmillan, 1987, pp 14-15; pp 24-33.
106 See P Jones, America and the British Labour Party: the special relationship at work, 1996; E Shaw, The Labour Party since 1945, 1996, p 46, 1994.

Chapter Five: Beneath Détente

1 J Coles, Making Foreign Policy, London, John Murray, 2000, pp 70-5.
2 S E Ambrose, Rise to Globalism: American Foreign Policy since 1938, Middlesex, enguin.1993, pp 224-253.
3 C Ponting, Breach of Promise, Middlesex, Penguin, 1989, pp 99-106.

4 C Ponting, Breach of Promise,, 1989, p 221.

5 P Jones, America and the British Labour Party: the special relationship at work, London, Tauris, 1997, p 156; J Dumbrell, A Special Relationship: Anglo-American Relations in the Cold War and after, Basingstoke, Macmillan, 2001, pp 62-73.

6 See HMSO, Command paper 6932, pp 59-60.

7 G P Tank, The CFSP and the Nation State' in K A Eliassen, (Editor), Foreign and Security policy in the European Union, London, Sage, 1998, p 15.

8 HMSO, Command paper 6932, p 105.

9 For a full transcription see HMSO, Command paper 6932, pp 107-112.

10 See J C Q Roberts, Speak Clearly into the Chandelier: Cultural Politics between Britain and Russia 1973-2000, Richmond, Curzon, 2000, pp 7-18.

11 D Volkogonov, The Rise and Fall of the Soviet Empire: Political Leaders from Lenin to Gorbachev, London, Harper Collins, 1988, p 292.

12 See G D H Cole, Europe, Russia, and the future, London, Victor Gollancz, 1941; G D H Cole, Great Britain in the Post-War World, London, Victor Gollancz, 1942.

13 Interview with Stan Newens, 10/12/98.

14 Interview with Stan Newens, 10/12/98.

15 M Crick, Militant, London, Faber and Faber, 1984, pp 22-23, p 39.

16 See Newens contribution to Jacques & Mulhern, The Forward March of Labour Halted? London, Verso, 1981, pp 59-63.

17 Jacques & Mulhern, The Forward March of Labour Halted? 1981, p 63.

18 Interview with Stan Newens, 10/12/98.

19 Interview with Stan Newens, 10/12/98.

20 Interview with Stan Newens, 10/12/98.

21 Interview with Stan Newens, 10/12/98

22 S Newens, Nicolae Ceausescu: The Man, his Ideas and his Socialist Achievements, Nottingham, Russell Press, 1972, pp 18-19.

23 S Newens, Nicolae Ceausescu: The Man, his Ideas and his Socialist Achievements, 1972, p 27.

24 S Newens, Nicolae Ceausescu: a selection from his speeches and writings, Nottingham, Spokesman, 1973, p 8.

25 Many speeches expressing similar arguments were published by Novosti, see particularly L Brezhnev, Our Course: Peace and Socialism, Novosti, Moscow, 1977, pp 44-8. Commentary can be found in many studies of Twentieth Century Russian History, for the most recent and possibly most informed example see D Volkogonov, The Rise and Fall of the Soviet Empire, Harper Collins, 1998, pp. 262-328

26 Quoted in P Martin, 'Sham of Romania's Brave New World', in Readers Digest, January 1986, pp. 60-64, p 63.

27 S Newens, Nicolae Ceausescu: a selection from his speeches and writings, 1973, p 5.

28 S Newens, Nicolae Ceausescu: a selection from his speeches and writings, 1973, p 5.

29 S Newens, Nicolae Ceausescu: a selection from his speeches and writings, 1973, p 5.

30 S Newens, Nicolae Ceausescu: a selection from his speeches and writings, 1973, p 6.

31 S Newens, Nicolae Ceausescu: The Man, his Ideas and his Socialist Achievements, 1972, p 28.

32 For commentaries on these works see M Kenny, The First New Left: British Intellectuals after Stalin, London, Lawrence & Wishart.1995, p 172 and bibliography.

33 Labour Weekly, 5/1/73, p 11.

34 Interview with Anne Swingler, 14/11/98.

35 Letter from Frank Allaun, 15/2/99.

36 Interview with Stan Newens, 10/12/98.

37 Interview with Stan Newens, 10/12/98.

38 Interview with Stan Newens, 10/12/98.

39 Interview with Stan Newens, 10/12/98.

40 S Newens, The Case Against NATO: The Danger of the Nuclear Alliances, 1972, p 11.

41 S Newens, The Case Against NATO: The Danger of the Nuclear Alliances, 1972, p 13.

42 S Newens, The Case Against NATO: The Danger of the Nuclear Alliances, 1972, pp 14-15.

43 Interview with Stan Newens, 10/12/98.

44 Interview with Stan Newens, 10/12/98.

45 Interview with Stan Newens, 10/12/98.

46 Interview with Stan Newens, 10/12/98.

47 Socialist Group of the European Parliament, The Socialist Campaign for Human Rights, Disarmament and Development Co-operation: Principles and Activities, Brussels, SGEP. (undated pamphlet), p 15.

48 Interview with Stan Newens, 10/12/98.

49 R Radosh, Commies: A Journey Through the Old Left, the New Left and the Leftover Left, San Francisco, Encounter Books, 2001, p 203.

50 S Dorril & R Ramsay, Smear: Wilson and the Secret State, London, Harper Collins, 1991, p 20.

51 R Deacon, The British Connection, London, Hamish Hamilton, 1979, p 234.

52 S Dorril & R Ramsay, Smear: Wilson and the Secret State, 1991, pp 18-21.

53 Plummer, in his role as Vice Chairman of the East-West Trade Parliamentary Group, wrote several articles for the Daily Worker and the Morning Star arguing for increasing East-West trade. See for example L Plummer, 'A Peace Treaty: Socialist countries mean business', Daily Worker, 9 August 1961, p 2.

54 J Haines, Maxwell, London, Futura, 1988, p 220.

55 J Dumbrell, A Special Relationship: Anglo-American Relations in the Cold War and after, 2001, p 59.

56 United States Government Publishing Office, Foreign Relations of the United States 1961-63, Vol. 9, Washington DC, USGPO, p 649.

57 A P Dobson, 'The Kennedy Administration and Economic Warfare against Communism', International Affairs, 64, pp 599-618, p 608.

58 I Waller, 'Pressure Politics', Encounter, August 1962, p 12.

59 Information gained from scant details of Ian Mikardo Ltd in Jo Richardson papers; interviews with Margaret Webster and former employees of Websters Tools, Wakefield, 25/6/1998

60 Birmingham BSFS papers; interview with Philip Crees, 12 May 1999.

61 Interview with Philip Crees, 12 May 1999; Interview with Vladimir Shaposhnikov, 19 Nov. 1998.

62 Interview with Margaret Webster 25 June 1998.

63 See J C Q Roberts, Speak Clearly into the Chandelier: Cultural Politics between Britain and Russia 1973-2000, 2000, pp 19-36.

64 I Mikardo, Back-Bencher, London, Weidenfeld & Nicolson, 1988, p 25.

65 Interview with Anne Swingler, 14/11/98.

66 I Mikardo, Back-Bencher, 1988, p 88.

67 I Mikardo, Back-Bencher, 1988, p 97.

68 I Mikardo, Back-Bencher, 1988, p 91.

69 I Mikardo, Back-Bencher, 1988, p 97.

70 I Mikardo, Back-Bencher, 1988, p 95.

71 I Mikardo, Back-Bencher, 1988, p 102.

72 I Mikardo, Back-Bencher, 1988, p 121.

73 Labour Party, Sense About Defence, London, Labour Party, 1977.

74 E Shaw, Discipline and Discord in the Labour Party, Manchester, M U P, 1988, pp 185-200.

75 See I Mikardo, The Second Five Years: A Labour Programme for 1950, London, Fabian Society, 1948; I Mikardo, The Labour Case, London, Allan Wingate, 1950.

76 I Mikardo, The Second Five Years: A Labour Programme for 1950, 1948, p 2.

77 Letter Mikardo to Morgan Phillips, 21/9/50, General Secretary's Papers.

78 Details and reports on CESC events can be found within the Jack Jones papers, MSS 126/JJ, Modern Records Centre. A statement of objectives was produced by the organisation, see F Brockway, Peace Within Reach, London, CESC, 1973.

79 I Mikardo, Back-Bencher, 1988, p 143.

80 E Shaw, Discipline and Discord in the Labour Party, 1988, pp 92-3.

81 I Mikardo, Back-Bencher, 1988, p 131.

82 See Labour Party: Party or Puppet, London, Tribune Group, 1972.

83 E Shaw, Discipline and Discord in the Labour Party, 1988, pp 181-2, and Chapter Five, pp 89-114 passim.)

84 Interview with Jan Zilliacus, 8/7/98

85 Interview with Anne Swingler, 14/11/98.

86 I Mikardo, Back-Bencher, 1988, pp 91-2.

87 Interview with Oleg Gordievsky, 15/11/98

88 I Mikardo, Back-Bencher, 1988, p 95.

89 I Mikardo, Back-Bencher, 1988, p 141.

90 I Mikardo, Back-Bencher, 1988, pp 115-6.

91 I Mikardo, Back-Bencher, 1988, p 116

92 I Mikardo, Back-Bencher, 1988, 116.

93 I Mikardo, Back-Bencher, 1988, p 117.

94 I Mikardo, Back-Bencher, 1988, p 137.

95 See I Mikardo, Back-Bencher, 1988, pp 138-9.

96 R English, Russia and the Idea of the West: Gorbachev, Intellectuals and the End of the Cold War, New York, Columbia University Press, 2000, pp 99-100.

97 I Mikardo, Back-Bencher, 1988, p 149.

98 I Mikardo, Back-Bencher, 1988, p 149.

99 See C Pincher, The Secret Offensive: Active Measures; A Saga of Deception, Disinformation, Subversion, Terrorism and Assassination, London, Sidgwick & Jackson, 1985, p 152.

100 Interview with Philip Crees, 12/5/99.

101 Interview with James Lamond 17th February 1999.

102 Interview with Nigel Spearing, 16 September 1999.

103 Interview with Philip Crees, 12/5/99.

104 Interview with Audrey Wise, 20/4/00

105 Interview for Sunday Times Magazine, 'Short Stories', The Times, 23/9/90, p 16.

106 R Short, The care of long-term prisoner, London, Macmillan, 1979.

107 R Short, The care of long-term prisoner, 1979, p 53.

108 Hansard, Vol, 722, Col. 27.

109 Labour Minister of State for the Foreign Office, October 1964-January 1967.

110 Hansard, Vol. 722, Written Answers, Col. 185.

111 Hansard, Vol. 753, Col. 412.

112 Hansard, Vol. 750, Col. 2116.

113 Hansard, Vol. 654, Col. 258.

114 Hansard, Vol. 738, Col. 994.

115 Hansard, Vol. 738, Col. 994.

116 Hansard, Vol. 720, Col. 1333.

117 Quoted in B Dent, 'Moscow Travellers', New Statesman, 6/7/84, p 11.

118 Hansard, Vol. 786, Col. 1567.

119 R Radosh, 'The Cuban Revolution and Western Intellectuals', in R Radosh, The New Cuba: Paradoxes and Potentials, New York, University of America Press, 1976, pp 41-2.

120 NEC Minutes, RD.225, Jan 1972.

121 See Letter to the Times, 4/10/86, p 4; 9/11/90, p 15

122 See Shaw, Discipline and Discord in the Labour Party, 1988, p 172, and P Williams, 'The Labour Party: The Rise of the Left', in West European Politics, Vol. 6, 1983, p 33. Minutes of meetings are held in the NEC Archive, National Museum of Labour History, Manchester.

123 Labour Monthly, Feb 1975, p 76.

124 Hansard, Vol. 114, Col. 226.

125 Guardian, 10/10/72.

126 Guardian, 10/10/72.

127 Letter to the Times, The Times, 4/9/89, p 13.

128 Hansard, Vol. 114, Col. 227.

129 Hansard, Vol. 114, Col. 228.

130 Quoted in P Hollander, Political pilgrims: Western Intellectuals in Search of the Good Society, 4th Edition, 1998, p 8.

Chapter Six: Raising the Stakes

1 United States Secretary of State James Baker quoted in M Cox, *Beyond the Cold War*, New York, University Press of America, 1990, p 156

2 M Cox, *Beyond the Cold War*, 1990, pp 160-1

3 J Isaacs & T Downing, *Cold War*, London, Bantam, 1998, pp 271-331; D Volkogonov, *The Rise and Fall of the Soviet Empire: Political Leaders from Lenin to Gorbachev*, London, Harper Collins, pp 293-300.

4 D Keohane, *Labour Party Defence Policy since 1945*, Leicester, Leicester University Press, 1993, p 30.

5 J Dumbrell, *A Special Relationship: Anglo-American Relations in the Cold War and after*, London, Macmillan, 2001, pp 89-95; P Riddell, *The Thatcher Government*, Oxford, Martin Robertson, 1983, p 227.

6 S E Ambrose, *Rise to Globalism: American Foreign Policy since 1938*, Middlesex, Penguin, 1993, pp 127-30

7 P Bolsover, *Civil Defence: The Cruellest Confidence Trick*, London, CND, undated 1980s; L James, 'Defence and British Politics in the 1980s: The Greenham Alternative', *Contemporary Political Studies*, 1995, Vol. II, pp 830-7; E P Thompson & D Smith, *Protest and Survive*, Middlesex, Penguin, 1979. Recent studies on popular culture reinforce the idea that there was a growing fear of nuclear war within the public psyche. Accounts of children experiencing nightmares following information broadcasts based upon the *Protect and Survive* campaign were shown on BBC TV, *I Love 1980*, 2000; Channel 4, *Top Ten of the 1980s*, 2001.

8 For example see F Allaun, *Questions and Answers about Nuclear Weapons*, Nottingham, Russell Press, 1981; P Bolsover, *Civil Defence: The Cruellest Confidence Trick*, London, CND, undated 1980s.

9 E Shaw, *The Labour Party Since 1979: Crisis and Transformation*, London, Routledge, 1994, pp 17-19

10 E Shaw, *The Labour Party Since 1979: Crisis and Transformation*, 1994, pp 15-17.

11 A Thorpe, *A History of the British Labour Party*, London, Macmillan, 1997, p 204.

12 Interview with Alan Sapper, 25 July 2000.

13 A distinction first made by Jonathan Schneer when documenting the left-wing of the party in the late 1940s, see J Schneer, *Labour's Conscience: The Labour Left 1945-51*, London, Unwin Hyman, 1988.

14 K O Morgan, *Labour People: Hardie to Kinnock*, Oxford, OUP, 1987, p 286; E Shaw, *The Labour Party Since 1979: Crisis and Transformation*, 1994, pp 36-41; pp 160-4.

15 P Seyd, *The Rise and Fall of the Labour Left*, Basingstoke, Macmillan, 1987, p 15.

16 J Silkin, *Changing Battlefields: The Challenge to the Labour Party*, London, Hamish Hamilton, 1987, pp 55-6.

17 For a historical overview of the latter see John Callaghan, 'Rise and Fall of the Alternative Economic strategy: From Internationalisation of Capital to Globalisation', *Contemporary British History* Vol. 14, No. 3, 2000, pp 105-130.

18 *The British Road to Socialism: Programme of the Communist Party*, 1978 is very similar in places to the programme put forward by the Labour Co-ordinating

Committee and affirmed in the 1983 General Election Manifesto *New Hope for Britain*.

19 *The Independent*, 18 April 1991.

20 T Benn, *Arguments for Socialism*, Middlesex, Penguin, 1979, p164.

21 K Livingstone, 'Uncle Sam's Patsy', *New Statesman and Society*, 12 June 1998.

22 E Shaw, *The Labour Party Since 1979: Crisis and Transformation*, 1994, pp 14-15.

23 E Shaw, *Discipline and Discord in the Labour Party*, Manchester, M U P, 1988, pp 218-53.

24 Interview with Alan Sapper, 25 July 2000. On the LCDTU see J McIlroy & A Campbell, 'Organising the Militants: the Liaison Committee for the Defence of Trade Unions, 1966-1979', in *The British Journal of Industrial Relations*, Vol. 37, No 1, 1999, pp 1-31.

25 K Harris, *Attlee*, London, Weidenfeld and Nicolson, 1982, p 294.

26 D Volkogonov, *The Rise and Fall of the Soviet Empire: Political Leaders from Lenin to Gorbachev*, London, HarperCollins, 1998, pp 280-1.

27 I Mikardo, *Back-Bencher*, London, Weidenfeld & Nicolson, 1988, p 149.

28 Interviews with James Lamond, John Platts-Mills, Alan Sapper and William Wilson.

29 *The Scotsman*, 25/5/19, Press cuttings, Ron Brown file, National Museum of Labour History.

30 D Volkogonov, *The Rise and Fall of the Soviet Empire: Political Leaders from Lenin to Gorbachev*, 1998, pp 389-91.

31 RYAN stood for *Raketno Yadernoye Napadenie*, Nuclear Missile attack. See D Volkogonov, *The Rise and Fall of the Soviet Empire: Political Leaders from Lenin to Gorbachev*, 1998, pp 358-369 for background on the Operation. The policy is fully explored in O Gordievsky, *Next Stop Execution*, London, Macmillan, 1995, pp 244-5, pp 261-2, pp 271-4 and importantly p 377.

32 *The Sun*, 2 February 1981.

33 *Hansard*, House of Lords, Vol. 462, Col 1005.

34 *Hansard*, House of Lords, Vol. 462, Col 1017.

35 *The Times*, 24/4/85, p 1.

36 *The Times*, 24/4/85, p 1.

37 H Porter, *Lord of the Reds*, The Sunday Times, 28/4/85, p 2.

38 Baker named Trade Unionists, Arthur Scargill, Jack Jones, Alan Sapper, Jim Slater, Doug Grieve, Noel Harris and Brian Price, and Labour MPs James Lamond, Ernie Ross sitting MP for Dundee West 1979 to present, Norman Atkinson, Ron Brown, Renee Short, Allan Roberts, and Stan Thorne. Also named was Alf Lomas MEP. See Blake Baker 'When the Red Bear Smiles', Part I, *Daily Telegraph*, 22/4/85, p 22; Part II, *Daily Telegraph*, 23/4/85, p 25.

39 Quoted in D Caute, *The Fellow Travellers*, London, Weidenfeld and Nicolson, 1973, p 5.

40 J McIlroy & A Campbell, 'Organising the Militants: the Liaison Committee for the Defence of Trade Unions, 1966-1979', 1999, pp 23-26.

41 R Taylor, *The TUC: From the General Strike to New Unionism*, Basingstoke, Palgrave, 2000, p 231.

42 See D Childs, *Britain since 1945*, 3rd Edition, London, Routledge, 1992, pp 179-185; A Sked & C Cook, *Post-War Britain*, New Edition 1945-92, Middlesex, Penguin, 1993, pp 220-8. On the Communist role in the strike see S Dorril & R Ramsay, *Smear: Wilson and the Secret State*, London, Harper Collins, 1991, pp 128-132.

43 For examples see M Paton, 'Trade Union education in the Soviet Union' in *The Draughtsman*, Vol. XL111, No. 1, Jan 1960, pp 16-18; T Elliott, 'The President's Address: A message to the membership', in *The Draughtsman*, Vol. XLIII, No. 5, May 1960,pp 8-9; Editorial, *The Draughtsman*, Vol. XLIV, No. 10, Oct 1961, p 23.

44 *Data News*, 1 February 1963, p 5.

45 For example see *Data News*, 12 Febuary 1965, p 4.

46 *TASS Journal*, June 1976, p 6.

47 *TASS Journal*, November 1974, p 8.

48 *TASS News & Journal*, January 1979, p 1.

49 TASS News & Journal, January 1979, p 5.

50 *TASS News & Journal*, August 1979, p 5.

51 E Ross, 'Say No to NATO Cruise Missiles', in *TASS News & Journal*, September 1980, p 9.

52 *Report of RC Annual Conference of DATA*, 28/4-2/5 1969, p 143.

53 *TASS RC Conference proceedings*, 1972, p 94.

54 *TASS RC Conference proceedings*, 1973, pp 162-3.

55 *TASS RC Conference proceedings*, 1973, p 164.

56 Letter, Forsyth to Ayrshire Branch Secretary, undated but believed to be from 1963. MSS 411 box 75, Modern Records Office.

57 Letter, Lamond to Forsyth, November 1968. MSS 411 box 75, Modern Records Office.

58 Interview with James Lamond, 17/2/99.

59 *TASS News & Journal*, June 1980, p 8.

60 Letter, Jones to Gordon Schaffer, 5 November 1974.

61 Interview with Alan Sapper, 25 July 2000.

62 Interview with Alan Sapper, 25 July 2000.

63 *Daily Telegraph*, 9/8/97, online version.

64 *Morning Star*, 7/11/77, Press cuttings, Kitson file, National Museum of Labour History.

65 Quoted in *Sunday Express*, 7/10/79, Press cuttings, Kitson file, National Museum of Labour History.

66 *The Scotsman*, 6/1/81, Press cuttings, Kitson file, National Museum of Labour History.

67 *Glasgow Herald*, 30/1/80, Press cuttings, Kitson file, National Museum of Labour History.

68 *The Scotsman*, 6/1/81, Press cuttings, Kitson file, National Museum of Labour History.

69 *The Scotsman*, 6/1/81, Press cuttings, Kitson file, National Museum of Labour History.

70 *The Scotsman*, 6/1/81, Press cuttings, Kitson file, National Museum of Labour History.

71 *Hansard*, Vol.114, Cols. 219-220.

72 Interview with James Lamond, 17/2/99.

73 *Hansard*, Vol. 114, Col. 222.

74 Interview with James Lamond, 17/2/99.

75 *Hansard*, Vol. 77, Col. 1054.

76 *Hansard*, Vol. 77, Col. 1054.

77 Interview with James Lamond, 17/2/99.

78 Interview with James Lamond, 17/2/99.

79 *Hansard*, Vol. 77, Col. 1035.

80 *Hansard*, Vol. 56, Col. 1228.

81 J Lamond, 'Prospects for Peace', *Labour Monthly*, March 1979, pp 111-2.

82 J Lamond, World Peace Council Delegation to Vietnam and Kampuchea, *Labour Monthly*, January 1980, pp 5-9.

83 Interview with James Lamond, 17/2/99.

84 *Coventry Evening Telegraph*, 5/9/74, Press cuttings, W Wilson file, National Museum of Labour History.

85 *Morning Star*, 9/9/74, Press cuttings, Kitson file, National Museum of Labour History.

86 Interview with Philip Crees, 12 May 1999.

87 Interview with Philip Crees, 12 May 1999.

88 *Morning Star*, 19/3/67, Press cuttings, W Wilson file, National Museum of Labour History.

89 *Morning Star*, 3/7/71, Press cuttings, W Wilson file, National Museum of Labour History.

90 *Morning Star*, 19/3/67, Press cuttings, W Wilson file, National Museum of Labour History.

91 *Morning Star*, 19/3/67, Press cuttings, W Wilson file, National Museum of Labour History.

92 *Morning Star*, 11/9/71, Press cuttings, W Wilson file, National Museum of Labour History.

93 *Morning Star*, 30/7/75, Press cuttings, W Wilson file, National Museum of Labour History.

94 *Morning Star*, 2/10/75, Press cuttings, W Wilson file, National Museum of Labour History.

95 Interview with William Wilson, 24/5/99.

96 Letter from William Wilson, 19/5/99.

97 Interview with William Wilson, 24/5/99.

98 Letter from William Wilson, 19/5/99.

99 Interview with William Wilson, 24/5/99.

100 Interview with William Wilson, 24/5/99.

101 Interview with William Wilson, 24/5/99.

102 Interview with William Wilson, 24/5/99.

103 Interview with Oleg Gordievsky, 4/6/99.

104 Labour MEP for London North East 1979-1999.

105 Interview with Oleg Gordievsky, 4 June 1999.

106 Interview with William Wilson, 24/5/99.

107 Interview with William Wilson, 24/5/99.

108 Letter from William Wilson, 19/5/99.

109 Letter from William Wilson, 19/5/99.

110 MP for Doncaster 1979-87.

111 See S Milne, *The Enemy within: MI5, Maxwell and the Scargill Affair*, London, Verso, 1994, p 118. Platts-Mills involvement is detailed on p 37, 118 and p 230.

112 O Gordievsky, *Next Step Execution*, 1995, p 284.

113 N Jones, *Soundbites and Spin Doctors: How Politicians Manipulate the Media - and Vice Versa*, London, Indigo, 1996, pp 63-4.

114 *Hansard*, 1981-2, Vol. 23, Col. 140.

115 R Brown, 'Afghanistan: Eyewitness Report', *Labour Monthly*, March 1981, pp 127-133.

116 R Brown, 'Afghanistan: Eyewitness Report', 1981, p 129.

117 R Brown, 'Afghanistan: Eyewitness Report', 1981, p 131.

118 R Brown, 'Afghanistan: Eyewitness Report', 1981, p 132.

119 R Brown, 'Afghanistan: Eyewitness Report', 1981, p 132.

120 O Gordievsky, *Next Step Execution*, 1995, pp 283-4.

121 *The Times*, 15/12/96, p 8.

122 *The Scotsman*, 23/10/79, Press cuttings, Ron Brown file, National Museum of Labour History.

123 *The Scotsman*, 25/5/79, Press cuttings, Ron Brown file, National Museum of Labour History.

124 *The Scotsman*, 17/5/79, Press cuttings, Ron Brown file, National Museum of Labour History.

125 *The Scotsman*, 20/8/79, Press cuttings, Ron Brown file, National Museum of Labour History.

126 *The Times*, 26/2/95, letters, p 35.

127 *The Times*, 26/12/94, p 3.

128 *The Times*, 26/12/94, p 3.

129 *The Times*, 26/12/94, p 3.

130 *Tribune*, 15/1/37, p 7.

131 Quoted in E Shaw, *The Labour Party Since 1979: Crisis and Transformation*, 1994, p 111.

132 R Hattersley, Fifty Years On: A prejudiced history of Britain since the war, London, Little, Brown & Co, 1997, pp 294-5.

133 R Harris, *The Making of Neil Kinnock*, London, Faber & Faber, 1984, pp 167-181.

134 G Bish, 'Future Policy Development', RD 2806, July 1983.

135 For a full description of the organisational reform procedure see E Shaw, *The Labour Party Since 1979: Crisis and Transformation*, 1994, pp 108-123.

136 D Butler & D Kavanagh, *The British General Election of 1987*, London, MacMillan, 1988, p 57.

137 D Butler & D Kavanagh, *The British General Election of 1987*, 1987, p 53.

138 C Mullin & D Atkins, *How to Select and Reselect your MP*, London, Labour Party, 1982: for a narrative see D Butler & D Kavanagh, *The British General Election of 1983*, 1984, pp 220-1.

139 J Silkin, *Changing Battlefields: The Challenge to the Labour Party*, London, Hamish Hamilton, 1987, pp 55-6.

140 T Jones, *Remaking the Labour Party: From Gaitskell to Blair*, London, Routledge, 1996, p 130.

141 See for example M Barratt-Brown and K Coates, *The Blair Revelation: Deliverance for Whom?* Nottingham, Spokesman, 1996.

142 This was the number of supporters claimed by George Galloway MP when arguing that participation in Operation Desert Fox should be put to a vote. *Hansard*, 17/12/98, Col. 1160.

143 D Lilleker, 'Labour's defence policy: from unilateralism to strategic review', R Little & M Wickham-Jones, [Editors], *New Labour's foreign policy: A new moral crusade?*, Manchester, MUP, 2000, pp 218-233.

Chapter Seven: The perspectives of pro-Sovietism

1 This was clearly stated by Marjorie Thompson, CND Chairman 1990-3, see P Johnston, *Daily Telegraph*, 25/9/99, p 25

2 N Kinnock, Speech at the Labour Party Conference 1985, *Labour Party Annual Conference Report*, London, Labour Party, 1985; P Gould, *The Unfinished Revolution*, London, Little, Brown & Co, 1998, p 4.

3 D Rose, interview with Melita Norwood, *Sunday Telegraph*, 12/9/99, p 5.

4 See R Griffiths, *S O Davies: A Socialist Faith*, Dyfed, Gomer Press, 1983, p 78; J Campbell, *Nye Bevan*, London, Richard Cohen, 1997, p 59.

5 *Spectator*, 22/5/99, p 35.

6 E Bernstein, (1899) *Evolutionary Socialism*, New York, Schocken, 1961; T Wright, *Socialisms: old and new*, London & New York, Routledge, 1996, p 10; pp 45-46.

7 Diana Collins, (wife of Canon Collins, leader of CND) in a letter to the Editor of *Peace News* 18/3/63. See also G Wernicke, 'The Communist-Led World Council for Peace and Western Peace Movements: The Fetters of Bipolarity and Some Attempts to Break Them in the Fifties and Early Sixties', *Peace and Change*, Vol. 23, No. 3, July 1998, p 290.

8 R H Jackson, 'The Weight of Ideas in Decolonization: Normative Change in International Relations', J Goldstein & R O Keohane, *Ideas and Foreign Policy: Beliefs, Institutions and Political Change*, Ithaca, Cornell, 1993, pp 111-139, p 124.

Conclusion

1 S Mukherjee & S Ramaswamy, *A History of Socialist Thought: From the Precursors to the Present*, New Delhi, Sage, 2000, p 225.

2 P Anderson, 'Mr Crosland's Dreamland: part one', *New Left Review*, No. 7, 1961, pp 4-12; P Anderson, 'Mr Crosland's Dreamland: part two', *New Left Review*, No. 9, 1961, pp 34-45.

3 BBC 2, *Campaign Confessions: Fighting the Marginals*, BBC TV, 10 July 2001.

4 BBC 2, *Campaign Confessions: Losing my Maidenhead*, BBC TV, 11 July 2001.

5 J Goldstein & R O Keohane. 'Ideas and Foreign Policy'. in J Goldstein & R O Keohane, [Editors] *Ideas and Foreign Policy: Beliefs, Institutions and Political Change*, Ithaca, Cornell University Press, pp 3-30.1993, pp 13-17.

6 J Goldstein & R O Keohane. 'Ideas and Foreign Policy', 1993, pp 16-17.

7 Weber quoted in J Goldstein & R O Keohane. 'Ideas and Foreign Policy', 1993, p 12.

8 F W S Craig, (ed) *British General Election Manifestos, 1900-1974*, London, Macmillan, 1975, p 4.

9 Quoted in P Allender, *What's wrong with Labour?*, London, Merlin, 2001, p 154.

10 T Benn, *Arguments for Socialism*, Middlesex, Penguin, 1980, pp-39-44.

11 Keir Hardie's definition of the state under socialism, quoted in D Coates, *The Labour Party and the Struggle for Socialism*, London, CUP, 1975, p 98.

12 Jim Mortimer quoted in J Lees-Marshment, *Political marketing and British political parties: the party's just begun*, Manchester, MUP, 2001, p 131.

13 For example in the creation of the Information Research Department by Bevin, see P Lashmar & J Oliver, *Britain's Secret Propaganda War: 1948-1977*, Stroud, Sutton, 1998, pp 24-9.

14 See D Lilleker, 'Labour's defence policy: from unilateralism to strategic review', in R Little & M Wickham-Jones [Editors] 'New Labour's foreign policy: A new moral crusade?', Manchester, Manchester University Press, 2000, pp 218-233.

15 F S Northedge & A Wells, *Britain and Soviet Communism: The Impact of a Revolution*, London, Macmillan., 1982, p 193.

16 Anne Swingler commented that on seeing the lone student standing in front of the tank in Tianamen Square she thought that is how socialists everywhere feel; indicatively this was after she had lost all faith in Communist variants. Interview with Anne Swingler 14/11/98.

17 C Pincher, *Their Trade is Treachery*, London, Sidgwick & Jackson, 1981, p ix.

18 For a further discussion on the choices involved in putting political beliefs into political action see P Dunleavy, *Democracy, Bureaucracy and Public Choice: Economic Explanations in Political Science*, Hemel Hempstead, Harvester Wheatsheaf, 1991, pp 54-7; R Barker, 'Hooks and Hands, Interests and Enemies: Political Thinking as Political Action'. *Political Studies*, Vol. 48, No. 2, pp 223-238, 2000, p 226.

BIBLIOGRAPHY

ARCHIVAL COLLECTIONS

Anglo-Soviet Journal Archive, Society for Co-operation in Russian & Cultural Studies Archive, 320 Brixton Road, London.

AUEW, Technical and Supervisory Section Archive, MSS 101, Modern Records Centre, University of Warwick.

Birmingham British-Soviet Friendship Society, Birmingham City Archive. MS 1829. Used by permission of Philip Crees.

British Soviet Friendship Society Archive, Stanley Evans papers, NRA 17262, Brynmor Jones Library, University of Hull.

Campaign for Labour Party Democracy (Campaign) papers, Brynmor Jones Library, University of Hull.

Communist Party of Great Britain Archive; NRA/CP

Letters Frank Allaun to Harry Pollitt, CP/IND/POLL/3/9

Letters between John Platts-Mills and Ivor Montague, CP/IND/MONT/7/10, National Museum of Labour History, Manchester.

Frank Cousins papers, MSS 282, Modern Records Centre, University of Warwick.

Coventry Labour Party papers, MSS 11, Modern Records Centre, University of Warwick.

Maurice Edelman papers, MSS 125, Modern Records Centre, University of Warwick.

R A Etheridge papers, MSS 202, Modern Records Centre, University of Warwick.

Fabian Society Archive, London School of Economics Archive.

Future Magazine, National Museum of Labour History, Manchester.

Gateshead Post, Konni Zilliacus collection, Gateshead Central Library.

General Secretary's Papers, The Labour Party Archive, National Museum of Labour History, Manchester.

Jack Jones papers, TGWU Archive, MSS 126/JJ, Modern Records Centre, University of Warwick.

Hugh Jenkins papers, British Library of Political and Economic Science, London School of Economics Archive.

League for Democracy in Greece Archive, Kings College, London.

Ian Mikardo Papers, Annual Return 1993, National Museum of Labour History, Manchester.

MSF Archive, DATA correspondence with James Lamond, MSS 411; Box 75, Modern Records Centre, University of Warwick.

Jo Richardson Papers; including Victory for Socialism Archival Collection, Annual Return 1994, National Museum of Labour History, Manchester.

Passfield Papers, Private papers of Beatrice and Sidney Webb, British Library of Political andEconomic Science, London School of Economics Archive.

D N Pritt papers, British Library of Political and Economic Science, London School of Economics Archive.

Society for Co-operation in Russian & Cultural Studies Archive, 320 Brixton Road, London.

TGWU Archive, MSS 126, Modern Records Centre, University of Warwick.

William Wilson papers, MSS 76, Modern Records Centre, University of Warwick.

Leonard Woolf papers, The University of Sussex.

UNPUBLISHED DOCUMENTS

Collette, C, (1992), *Internationalism and officialdom in the British labour movement: Labours attitude to European socialism 1918 to 1939, with special reference to the role of the International Secretary of the Labour Party*, unpublished M.Litt thesis, University of Oxford.

Ferguson, S, (1986), *Labour Party Politics 1935-45: A Case Study of Konni Zilliacusand the Gateshead Labour Party and Trades Council*, M.Sc. Dissertation, The University of Cambridge.

Letter Platts-Mills to Jonathan Schneer, Sept 1983.

Platts-Mills, J, unpublished autobiography held by family of John Platts-Mills.

Rayner, S F, (1997), *The classification and Dynamics of sectarian forms of Organisation: grid/group perspectives on the far-left in Britain*, PhD thesis, University College London.

Rikihisa, M, (1991), *Labour's Nuclear Defence Policy: The Rise and Fall of Unilateralism 1945-91*, MA dissertation, The University of Sheffield.

Webb, S, (1932), *Russian Trip*, diary of visit to Russia, Passfield Papers.

Webb, Sydney, *Trade Agreements*, pamphlet circulated in House of Lords, with notes, May 1933. Passfield Papers.

Webb, S, (1935), Five volumes of notes on visit to Russia, Passfield Papers.

Zilliacus, K, *Blue Print for a World Peace Union*, abortive Fabian Society project, Fabian Society Archive

Zilliacus, K, *The Tories and Victory for Socialism*, National Museum of Labour History.

Zilliacus, K, *The Challenge to Fear*, unpublished autobiography, in care of widow Jan Zilliacus.

ANONYMOUS PAMPHLETS

British Labour and the Russian Revolution: The Leeds Convention: a report from the Daily Herald *with an introduction by Ken Coates*, Documents on Socialist History No. 1, Spokesman Books.

Dialogue on Security and Disarmament in Europe, International Liaison Forum of Peace Forces, Stockholm, March 11-13, 1984.

'Election Rhymes', in, *Gateshead Local History Society Bulletin*, Vol. 1, No. 9, Jan 1973.

Labour - Party or Puppet?, Tribune Group, London, July 1972.

NATO or Neutralism: which way to peace?, Report of the Labour Peace Fellowship Conference, 1st April 1962.

Resistance Shall Grow: The story of the 'Spies for Peace' and why they are important, London, Independent Labour Party.

The Laski Libel Action: Verbatim Report, London, Daily Express, undated.

The World Peace Council: What It Is and What It Does, Information Centre of the World Peace Council, Helsinki, December 1978.

PUBLISHED TEXTS

Addison, P, (1975), *The Road to 1945*, London, Jonathan Cape.

Allaun, F, (1958), *Stop the H-Bomb Race: Before it's too late let Britain give the lead*, London, UDC.

Allaun, F, (1959), *New Moves in the H-Bomb Struggle*, London, Union of Democratic Control.

Allaun, F, (1981), *Questions and Answers about Nuclear Weapons*, CND, Nottingham, Russell Press.

Allaun, F, (1992), *The Struggle for Peace: A personal account of 60 years campaigning inside and outside Parliament*, Manchester, Labour Action for Peace.

Allaun, F, (nd) *Disengagement and Peace*, London, UDC.

Almond, M, (1996), *Revolution: 500 years of struggle for change*, London, De Agostini.

Ambrose, S E, (1993), *Rise to Globalism: American Foreign Policy since 1938*, Middlesex, Penguin.

Anderson, P and K Davey, (1995), 'Moscow Gold', *New Statesman & Society*, 7 April 1995, pp 25-38.

Andrew, C and O Gordievsky, (1990), *KGB: the inside story of its Foreign Operations from Lenin to Gorbachev*, New York, Harper Collins.

Andrew, C and O Gordievsky, (1991), *Instructions from the Centre: Top Secret Files on KGB Foreign Operations 1975-1985*, London, Sceptre.

Andrew, C and V Mitrokhin, (1999), *The Mitrokhin Archive: The KGB in Europe and the West*, Middlesex, Penguin.

Bale, T, (1999), *Sacred Cows and Common Sense*, Aldershot, Ashgate.

Barbe, E, (1997), 'European Values and National Interests', in Landau & Whitman (Editors), *Rethinking the European Union: Institutions, Interests and Identities*, London, Macmillan, pp 126-46.

Barker, B, (1972), *Ramsay MacDonald's Political Writings*, London, Penguin.

Barker, R, (2000), 'Hooks and Hands, Interests and Enemies: Political Thinking as Political Action'. *Political Studies*, Vol. 48, No. 2, pp 223-238.

Barratt-Brown, M and K Coates, (1996), *The Blair Revelation: Deliverance for Whom?* Nottingham, Spokesman.

Barron, J, (1974), *KGB: The Secret Work of Soviet Agents*, London, Hodder & Stoughton.

Barron, J, (1983), *KGB Today: The Hidden Hand*, Sevenoaks, Hodder & Stoughton.

Beckett, F, (1995), *Enemy Within: The Rise and Fall of the British Communist Party*, London, John Murray.

Berger, S & D Lilleker, (2001) 'The British Labour Party and the 'socialist' Germany: Perspectives on the German Democratic Republic' in Arnd Bauerkamper, [Editor], *Britain and the GDR*, Potsdam, Zentrum fur Zeithistorische Forshung.

Bittman, L, (1972), *The Deception Game: Czechoslovak Intelligence in Soviet Political Warfare*, Syracuse University Research Corporation.

Bittman, L, (1985), *The KGB and Soviet Disinformation: An Insider's View*, Washington, Pergamon Brassey's

Boggs C, & D Plotke, (1980), *The Politics of Eurocommunism: socialism in transition*, London, Macmillan.

Bornstein, S, & A Richardson, (1986), *Against the Stream: A History of the Trotskyist Movement in Britain 1924-38*, London, Socialist Platform.

Bower, T, (1989), *The Red Web: MI6 and the KGB Master Coup*, London, Arum.

Branson, N, (1985), *History of the Communist Party 1927-1941*, London, Lawrence & Wishart.

Brezhnev, L I, (1977), *Our Course: Peace and Socialism*, Moscow, Novosti Press Agency.

Brockway, F, (1938), *Workers' Front*, London, Secker and Warburg.

Brockway, F, (1942), *Inside the Left: Thirty Years of Platform, Press, Prison and Parliament*, London, George Allen & Unwin Ltd.

Brockway, F, (1946), *Socialism over Sixty Years: The Life of Jowett of Bradford (1864-1944)*, London, George Allen & Unwin.

Brockway, F, (1973), *Peace Within Reach*, London, CESC.

Brockway, F, (1977), *Towards Tomorrow*, London, Harts-Davies, MacGibbon Ltd.

Brockway, F, (1986), *98 Not Out*, London, Quartet.

Brockway, F and F Mullally, (1944), *Death Pays A Dividend*, London, Victor Gollancz.

Brown, G, (1986), *Maxton*, Edinburgh, Mainstream.

Brown, R, (1981), 'Afghanistan: Eyewitness Report', *Labour Monthly*, March 1981.

Burgess, R G, (1984), *In the Field*, London, Allen & Unwin.

Burridge, T D, (1976), *British Labour and Hitler's War*, London, Andre Deutsch.

Butler D, & D Kavanagh, (1984), *The British General Election of 1983*, London, MacMillan.

Butler D, & D Kavanagh, (1988), *The British General Election of 1987*, London, MacMillan.

Callaghan, J, (1987), *Time and Change*, Glasgow, Collins.

Callaghan, John, (1984), *British Trotskyism: Theory and Practice*, Oxford, Basil Blackwell.

Callaghan, John, (1993), *Rajani Palme Dutt: A Study in British Stalinism*, London,Lawrence & Wishart.

Callaghan, John, (2000), 'Rise and Fall of the Alternative Economic strategy: From Internationalisation of Capital to Globalisation', *Contemporary British History* Vol. 14, No. 3, pp 105-130.

Carrillo, S, (1977) *Eurocommunism and the State*, London, Lawrence & Wishart.

Caute, D, (1973), *The Fellow Travellers*, London, Weidenfeld and Nicolson.

Challinor, R, (1977), *The Origins of British Bolshevism*, London, Croom Helm Ltd.

Childs, D, (1992), *Britain since 1945*, 3rd Edition, London, Routledge.

Churchill, W S, (1981), *Defending the West*, London, Temple-Smith.

Clayton, J, (1926), *The Rise and Decline of Socialism in Great Britain 1884-1924*, London, Faber & Gwyer.

Clews, J C, (1964), *Communist Propaganda Techniques*, London, Methuen & Co Ltd.

Cliff , T, and D Gluckstein, (1996), *The Labour Party: A Marxist History*, London, Bookmarks.

Coates, D, (1975), *The Labour Party and the Struggle for Socialism*, London, C U P.

Coates, W P and Z K Coates, (1945), *A History of Anglo-Soviet Relations*, London, Lawrence & Wishart.

Cole, G D H, (1920), 'Lenin on Bolshevism', in *The Guildsman*, March 1920.

Cole, G D H, (1936), 'The Truth and Russia', in *New Statesman*, 18/7/36.

Cole, G D H, (1937), *The People's Front*, London, Victor Gollancz.

Cole, G D H, (1938), 'A Disturbing Book', in *Aryan Path*, September 1938.

Cole, G D H, (1941), *Europe, Russia, and the future*, London, Victor Gollancz.

Cole, G D H, (1941), 'Europe, Russia, and the future: A Reply', in *Left News*, March 1942.

Cole, G D H, (1942), *Great Britain in the Post-War World*, London, Victor Gollancz.

Cole, G D H, (1945), *Welfare & Peace*, London, National Peace Council.

Cole, G D H, (1948), *The Meaning of Marxism*,

Cole, G D H, (1958), *A History of Socialist Thought Volume IV: Communism and Social Democracy 1914-1931*, in two volumes, London, Macmillan.

Cole, G D H, (1960), *A History of Socialist Thought Volume V: Socialism and Fascism, 1931-1939*, London, Macmillan.

Cole, M, Editor, (1952), *Beatrice Webb's Diaries 1912-1924*, London, Longmans Green & Co.

Cole, M, Editor, (1956), *Beatrice Webb's Diaries 1924-1932*, London, Longmans Green & Co.

Cole, M, Editor, (1974), *The Webbs and their Work*, Brighton, Harvester Press.

Coles, J, (2000), *Making Foreign Policy*, London, John Murray.

Cook, R & D Smith, (1978), *What Future in NATO?*, Fabian Research Series 337, London.

Cooke, C, (1957), *The life of Richard Stafford Cripps*, London, Hodder & Stoughton.

Coopey, R, S Fielding & N Tiratsoo, (1993), *The Wilson Governments 1964-1970*, London, Pinter.

Council of Workers and Soldiers' Delegates, The, (1917), *What happened at Leeds*, London, CWSD.

Cox, M, (1990), *Beyond the Cold War*, New York, University Press of America.

Crang, J A, (1996), 'Politics on Parade: Army Education and the 1945 General Election', *History: The Journal of the Historical Association*, Vol 81, No 262, April 1996.

Crankshaw, E, (1959), *Khrushchev's Russia*, Harmondsworth, Penguin

Crick, B, (1987), *Socialism*, Minneapolis, University of Minnesota Press.

Cripps, Sir S, (1936), *The Struggle for Peace*, London, Victor Gollancz.

Crozier, B, [Editor], (1970), *We Will Bury You: Studies in Left Wing Subversion Today*, London, Stacey.

Crozier, B, (1993), *Free Agent: The Unseen War 1941-1991; The Autobiography of an International Activist*, London, Harper Collins.

Curtis, S, [Editor], (1998), *The Journals of Woodrow Wyatt; Volume One*, London, MacMillan.

Dalton, G, (1974), *Economic Systems & Society*, Harmondsworth, Penguin, 1975.

Dalton, H, (1935), *Practical Socialism for Britain*, London, George Routledge & Sons.

Dalton, H, (1953), *Call Back Yesterday: Memoirs 1887-1931*, London, Frederick Muller.

Davies, H, (1957), *Death Stands at Attention: A protest against the H-bomb tests*, London, Housmans.

Davies, H, (1960), *Why NATO?*, London, VfS.

Davies, H, (nd), *Bull's Eye Island*, London, UDC.

Deacon, R, (1979), *The British Connection*, London, Hamish Hamilton.

Deane, H A, (1954), *The Political Ideas of Harold J Laski*, New York, Columbia University Press.

Dell. E, (2000), *A Strange Eventful History*, London, Harper Collins.

Dent, Bob, (1984), 'Moscow Travellers', *New Statesman*, July 6th 1984, pp 10-11.

Desai, R, (1994), *Intellectuals and Socialism: 'Social Democrats' and the Labour Party*, London, Lawrence & Wishart.

Dodds, N, S Tiffany and L Solley, (1946), *Tragedy in Greece*, London, The League for Greek Democracy.

Dodson, C and R Payne, (1984), *The Dictionary of Espionage*, London, Collins.

Donoughue, B, and G W Jones, (1973), *Herbert Morrison: Portrait of a Politician*, London, Weidenfeld & Nicolson.

Dorril, S, (2000), *MI6: Fifty Years of Special Operation*, London, Fourth Estate.

Dorril, S, and R Ramsay, (1991), *Smear: Wilson and the Secret State*, London, Harper Collins.

Driberg, T, (1953), *The Best of Both Worlds: A Personal Diary*, London, Pheonix House.

Driberg, T, (1956), *Guy Burgess: a portrait with background*, London, Weidenfeld and Nicolson.

Driberg, T, (1964), *The Mystery of Moral Re-Armament: A Study of Frank Buchman and His Movement*, London, Secker & Warburg.

Duff, P, (1971), *Left Left Left*, London, Allison & Busby.

Dumbrell, J, (2001), *A Special Relationship: Anglo-American Relations in the Cold War and after*, London, Macmillan.

Duncan, R and A McIvor, (Editors),(1992), *Labour and Class Conflict on the Clyde 1900-1950: Essays in Honour of Harry McShane 1891-1988*, Edinburgh, John Donald.

Dunleavy, P, (1991), *Democracy, Bureaucracy and Public Choice: Economic Explanations in Political Science*, Hemel Hempstead, Harvester Wheatsheaf.

Durbin, E F M, (1940), *The Politics of Democratic Socialism: An Essay on Social Policy*, London, Routledge & Kegan Paul.

Dutt, R P, (1935), *Fascism and Social Revolution*, 2nd Ed, London, Martin Lawrence.

Eastwood, G, (1977), *Harold Laski*, London, Mowbrays.

Edwards, R, (1947), *World Survey and War Warning*, London, Independent Labour Party.

Edwards, R, (nd), *War is not Inevitable*, London, Independent Labour Party.

Edwards, R, & K Dunne, (nd), *A Study of a Master Spy (Allen Dulles)*, London, Housmans.

Estorick, E, (1949), *Stafford Cripps; A Biography*, London, Heinemann.

Fielding, S, (1995), 'The Second World War and Popular Radicalism: The Significance of the Movement away from Party', *History: The Journal of the Historical Association*, 80: 258, February 1995.

Fletcher, R, (1963), *£60 a Second on Defence*, London, MacGibbon & Kee.

Fletcher, R, (nd), *Russia through Socialist Eyes*, London, ILP.

Foot, M, (1962), *Aneurin Bevan; Volume 1, 1897-1945*, London, Paladin.

Foot, M, (1973), *Aneurin Bevan; Volume 2, 1945-1960*, London, Paladin.

Foot, M, (1999), *Dr Strangelove, I Presume*. London, Gollancz.

Freeman, J, (1991), *Security and the CSCE Process: The Stockholm Conference and beyond*, London, Macmillan.

Freeze, G L, (Editor), (1997), *Russia: A History*, Oxford, Oxford University Press.

Frolik, J, (1975), *The Frolik Defection*, London, Corgi.

Gaiduk, I V, (1996), 'Soviet Policy towards US Participation in the Vietnam War', in, *History: The Journal of the Historical Association*, Vol 81, No 261, January 1996.

Gallacher, W, (1936), *Revolt on the Clyde*, London, Lawrence & Wishart.

Gallacher, W, (1951), *Rise like Lions*, London, Lawrence & Wishart.

Garaudy, R, (1969), *The Turning Point of Socialism*, London, Fontana, 1970.

Gillies, W, (1926), *The Soviet Solar System*, London, Labour party.

Glees, A, (1987), *The Secrets of the Service: British Intelligence and Communist Subversion 1939-51*, London, Jonathan Cape.

Goldstein, J, & R O Keohane (1993), 'Ideas and Foreign Policy'. in J Goldstein & R O Keohane, [Editors] *Ideas and Foreign Policy: Beliefs, Institutions and Political Change*, Ithaca, Cornell University Press, Pp 3-30.

Gorbachev, M, (1987), *Perestroika*, London, Collins.

Gorbachev, M, (1995), *Memoirs*, London, Doubleday.

Gordievsky, O, (1995), *Next Stop Execution*, London, Macmillan.

Graubard, S R,(1956), *British Labour and the Russian Revolution 1919-1924*, Cambridge, Harvard University Press.

Griffiths, G, (1993), *Socialism and Superior Brains: The Political Thought of Bernard Shaw*, London, Routledge.

Griffiths, R, (1983), *S O Davies: A Socialist Faith*, Dyfed, Gomer Press.

Gromyko, A, (1989), *Memories*, London, Hutchinson.

Haines, J, (1988), *Maxwell*, London, Futura.

Halliday, F, (1994), *Rethinking International Relations*, London, Macmillan.

Harris, K, (1982), *Attlee*, London, Weidenfeld and Nicolson.

Hatfield, M, (1978), *The House the Left Built: Inside Labour Policy-Making 1970-75*, London, Gollancz.

Hattersley, R, (1997), *Fifty Years On: A prejudiced history of Britain since the war*, London, Little, Brown & Co.

Haynes, J E & H Klehr, (1999), *Venona: Soviet espionage in America in the Stalin era*, New York, Yale.

Haynes, V, & O Semyonova, Editors, (1979), *Workers Against the Gulag*, London, Pluto Press.

Hazan, B A, (nd), *Soviet Propaganda: a case study of the Middle East Conflict*, New Brunswick, Transaction Books.

Healey, D, (1990), *The Time of my Life*, Middlesex, Penguin.

Healey, D, (1991), *When Shrimps Learn to Whistle*, Middlesex, Penguin.

Heffer, E, (1991), *Never a Yes Man: The Life and Politics of an Adopted Liverpuddlian*, London, Verso.

Hennessy, P, (1996), *Muddling Through: Power, Politics and the Quality of Government in Post-war Britain*, London, Victor Gollancz

Hinton, J, (1989), *Protests & Visions: Peace Politics in 20th Century Britain*, London, Hutchinson Radius.

Hirsch, R, (1947), *The Soviet Spies: The Story of Russian Espionage in North America*, London, Nicholas Kaye.

Hobsbawm, E, (1994), *Age of Extremes: The Short Twentieth Century 1914-1991*, London, Michael Joseph.

Hobsbawm, E, (1997), *On History*, London, Weidenfeld & Nicolson.

Hollander, P, (1981), *Political Pilgrims: Travel of the Western Intellectuals to the Soviet Union, China and Cuba, 1928-1978*, New York, Harper & Row.

Holroyd, M, (1991), *Bernard Shaw: Volume 3: 1918-1950: The Lure of Fantasy*, Middlesex, Penguin.

Hughes, E, (1969), *Sydney Silverman: Rebel in Parliament*, London, Charles Skilton Ltd.

Hutchinson, H L, (1946), 'Marxism and the Post-War World', in *Left*, No. 114, April 1946, pp 89-92.

Hyde, D, (1950), *I Believed: The Autobiography of a Former British Communist*, London, The Reprint Society.

Jacques, M, & T Mulhern [Editors], 1981, *The Forward March of Labour Halted?* London, Verso.

Jenkins, C, (1960), *Germany's Balance of Influence: The Changing Situation in NATO*, London, Gladiator.

Jenkins, M, (1979), *Bevanism: Labour's High Tide*, Nottingham, Spokesman.

Jones, B, (1977), *The Russia Complex: The British Labour Party and the Soviet Union*, Manchester, Manchester University Press.

Jones, P, (1997), *America and the British Labour Party: the special relationship at work*, London, Tauris.

Jones, T, (1996), *Remaking the Labour Party: From Gaitskell to Blair*, London, Routledge.

Jupp, J, (1982), *The Radical Left in Britain 1931-1941*, London, Frank Cass.

Kampfner, J, (1998), *Robin Cook*, London, Pheonix.

Kaufman, G, Editor, (1966), The Left, London, Anthony Blond.

Kenny, M, (1995), *The First New Left: British Intellectuals after Stalin*, London, Lawrence & Wishart.

Keohane, D, (1993), *Labour Party Defence Policy since 1945*, Leicester, Leicester University Press.

Keohane, D, (2000) *Security in British Politics 1945-99*, London, Macmillan Press.

Khrushchev, N, (1990), *Khrushchev Remembers: The Glasnost Tapes*, London, Little Brown and Co.

Koch, S, (1995), *Double Lives: Stalin, Willi Munzenberg and the Seduction of the Intellectuals*, London, Harper Collins.

Koelble, T A, (1982) 'Recasting social democracy in Europe: a nested games explanation of strategic adjustment in political parties', *Politics and Society*, Vol 20, 1, 1982.

Kolakowski, L, (1990), *Main Currents of Marxism; Book 3: The Breakdown*, Oxford, Oxford University Press.

Kravchenko, V, (1946), *I Chose Freedom*, London, Robert Hale.

Labour Party, (1918), *Report on the Annual Conference of the Labour Party held in the Albert Hall,Nottingham, on Wednesday, Jan 23rd 1918, and two following days, and the Adjourned Conference held in the Central Hall, Westminster, London, on Tuesday, Feb 26th 1918*, The Labour Party, London.

Labour Party Annual Conference Reports 1918-1989. London, Labour Party.

Labour Party, (1920), *Report of the British Labour Delegation to Russia*, The Labour Party, London.

Labour Party, (1945) *Let Us Face the Future: A Declaration of Labour Policy for the Consideration of the Nation*, Labour Party, London.

Labour Party, (1977), *Sense About Defence*, London, Labour party.

Lamond, J, (1979), 'Prospects for Peace', *Labour Monthly*, March 1979.

Lamond, J, (1980), World Peace Council Delegation to Vietnam and Kampuchea, *Labour Monthly*, January 1980.

Lashmar, P, & J Oliver, (1998), *Britain's Secret Propaganda War: 1948-1977*, Stroud, Sutton.

Laski, H J, (1927), *Communism*, London, Williams & Norgate.

Laski, H J, (1958), *An Introduction to Politics*, London, George Allen & Unwin.

Laybourn, K & D Murphy, (1999), *Under The Red Flag: A History of Communism in Britain*, Stroud, Sutton.

Lee, J, (1941), *Our Ally Russia: The Truth*, London, W H Allen & Co.

Lee, J, (1963), *This Great Journey: A Volume of Autobiography 1904-45*, London, MacGibbon & Lee.

Lenin, V I, (1902), *What is to be done?*, Moscow, Progress Publishers, 1978.

Lenin, V I, (1905), *The Revolution of 1905*, London, Lawrence & Wishart Ltd, 1941.

Lenman, B P, (1992), *The Eclipse of Parliament: Appearance and Reality in British Politics since 1914*, London, Edward Arnold.

Levy, B W, (nd), *Britain and the Bomb: The Fallacy of Nuclear Defence*, London, CND.

Lilleker, D, (1999), 'Collective Action: When Government's shape Populist Support' in *Fifth International Conference on Alternative Futures and Popular Protest: Conference Papers Vol II*, pp 91-102.

Lilleker, D, (2000), 'Labour's defence policy: from unilateralism to strategic review', in R Little &M Wickham-Jones [Editors] 'New Labour's foreign policy: A new moral crusade?', Manchester, Manchester University Press, pp 218-233.

Loch Mowat, C, (1968), *Britain between the Wars: 1918-1940*, Cambridge, Cambridge University Press.

Lockhart, R H B, (1932), *Memoirs of a British Agent*, London, Putnam.

Lyman, R W, (1957), *The First Labour Government: 1924*, New York, Russell & Russell.

Lynch, M, (1991), *Scotland: A New History*, London, Macmillan.

MacDonald, J R, (1911), *The Socialist Movement*, London, Williams and Norgate.

Mackay, R W G, (1941), *Peace Aims and the New Order*, London, Michael Joseph.

Mackenzie, N, Editor, (1978), *The letters of Sidney and Beatrice Webb; Book III: The Pilgrimage 1912-1947*, London, Cambridge University Press.

Mackenzie, N & J Mackenzie, Editors, (1985), *The Diary of Beatrice Webb; Volume Four 1924-1943: The Wheel of Life*, London, Virago in association with the London School of Economics.

Mahon, J, (1976), *Harry Pollitt: a biography*, London, Lawrence & Wishart.

Mandel, E, (1978), *From Stalinism to Eurocommunism: The Bitter Fruits of 'Socialism in One Country*, Paris, Francois Maspero.

Marquand, D, (1977), *Ramsay MacDonald*, London, Jonathan Cape.

Marquand, D, (1999), *The Progressive Dilemma: From Lloyd George to Blair*, London, Pheonix Giant.

Marsh, D et al, (1999) *Postwar British Politics in perspective*, Cambridge, Polity.

Martin, K, (1953), *Harold Laski: A Biographical Memoir*, London, Gollancz.

Martin, P, (1986), 'Sham of Romania's Brave New World', in *Readers Digest*, January 1986, pp. 60-64,

Maxton, J, (1932), *Lenin*, London, Daily Express Publications.

Maxton, J, (1935), *If I were Dictator*, London, Methuen & Co.

Mazowar, M, (1998), *Dark Continent: Europe's Twentieth Century*, London, Penguin.

McAllister, G, (1935), *James Maxton: The Portrait of a Rebel*, London, John Murray.

McIlroy & Campbell, (1999), 'Organising the Militants: the Liaison Committee for the Defence of TradeUnions, 1966-1979', in *The British Journal of Industrial Relations*, Vol. 37, No 1, pp 1-31.

McNair, J, (1955), *James Maxton: The Beloved Rebel*, London, George Allen & Unwin.

Meehan, E J, (1960), *The British Left Wing and Foreign Policy: A Study of the Influence of Ideology*, New Jersey, Rutgers University Press.

Middlemas, R K, (1965), *The Clydesiders: A Left Wing Struggle for Parliamentary Power*, London, Hutchinson.

Mikardo, I, (1948), *The Second Five Years: A Labour Programme for 1950*, London, Fabian Society.

Mikardo, I, (1950), *It's a Mug's Game*, London, Tribune.

Mikardo, I, (1950), *The Labour Case*, London, Allan Wingate.

Mikardo, I, (1988), *Back-Bencher*, London, Weidenfeld & Nicolson.

Miliband, R, (1961) *Parliamentary Socialism*, London, George Allen & Unwin.

Milne, S, (1984), *The Enemy within: MI5, Maxwell and the Scargill Affair*, London, Verso.

Minnion, J, & P Bolsover, (1983), *The CND Story*, London, Allison & Busby.

Moorehead, C, (1987), *Troublesome People: Enemies of War 1916-1986*, London, Hamish Hamilton.

Moran, Lord, (1966), *Winston Churchill: The Struggle for Survival 1940-1965*, London, Constable.

Morgan, K O, (1984), *Labour in Power; 1945-51*, Oxford, OUP.

Morgan, K O, (1987), *Labour People: Hardie to Kinnock*, Oxford, OUP.

Morgan, K, (1993), *Harry Pollitt*, Manchester, MUP.

Morgenthau, H J, (1952), 'Another 'Great Debate': The National Interest of the US' in *The American Political Science Review*, Vol. XLVI, No. 4, pp 971-8.

Morris, A J A, (1972), *Radicalism Against War 1906-1914*, London, Longman.

Moser K & M Kalton, (1971), *Survey Methods in Social Investigation*, London, Heinemann.

Mullin C & D Atkins, (1982), *How to Select and Reselect your MP*, London, Labour Party.

Newens, S, (1972), *The Case Against NATO: The Danger of the Nuclear Alliances*, Nottingham, Russell Press.

Newens, S, (1972), *Nicolae Ceausescu: The Man, his Ideas and his Socialist Achievements*, Nottingham, Russell Press.

Newens, S, (1973), *Talking with Nicolae Ceausescu: An interview with Stan Newens*, London, London Co-operative Political Committee.

Newens, S, (1973), *Nicolae Ceausescu: a selection from his speeches and writings*, Nottingham, Spokesman.

Newman, M, (1993), *Harold Laski: A Political Biography*, Basingstoke, Macmillan.

Northedge, F S & A Wells, (1982), *Britain and Soviet Communism: The Impact of a Revolution*, London, Macmillan.

Orwell, S & I Angus, Editors, (1970), *The Collected Essays, Journalism and letters of George Orwell; Volume 4; In Front of your Nose; 1945-1950*, Harmondsworth, Penguin.

Parkin, B, (nd), *Multilateral Disarmament: What are we doing about it?*, London, UDC.

Parkin, F, (1968), *Middle Class Radicalism: The Social Bases of the British Campaign for Nuclear Disarmament*, Manchester, Manchester University Press.

Parkinson, C N, (1967), *Left Luggage*, London, John Murray.

Philby, K, (1969), *My Silent War*, London, Panther.

Peace Pledge Union, (nd), *Conversation Peace*, London, PPU.

Pelling, H, (1958), *The British Communist Party: a historical profile*, London, Adam & Charles Black.

Phelps-Fetherston, I, (1965), *Soviet International Front Organisations: A Concise Handbook*, London, Frederick A Praeger

Phillips, J, (1999), *Labour and the Cold War: the TGWU and the politics of anti-Communism, 1945-55*, in *Labour History Review*, Vol. 64, No 1, Spring 1999, pp 44-61.

Pimlott, B, [Editor], (1986), *The Political Diary of Hugh Dalton 1918-40*, London, Jonathan Cape in association with the LSE & PS.

Pimlott, B, [Editor], (1986), *The Political Diary of Hugh Dalton 1945-60*, London, Jonathan Cape in association with the LSE & PS.

Pimlott, B, (1992), *Harold Wilson*, London, HarperCollins.

Pincher, C, (1978), *Inside Story; A Documentary on the Pursuit of Power*, London, Sidgwick & Jackson.

Pincher, C, (1981), *Their Trade is Treachery*, London, Sidgwick & Jackson.

Pincher, C, (1984), *Too Secret Too Long; The Great Betrayal of Britain's Crucial Secrets and the Cover-Up*, London, Sidgwick & Jackson.

Pincher, C, (1985), *The Secret Offensive: Active Measures; A Saga of Deception, Disinformation, Subversion, Terrorism and Assassination*, London, Sidgwick & Jackson.

Piratin, P, (1978), *Our Flag Stays Red*, New Edition, London, Lawrence & Wishart.

Platts-Mills, J, (1946), 'Labour Incentives in the Soviet Union', in *Anglo Soviet Journal*, Vol. III, No. 2, Summer 1946, pp 7-10.

Platts-Mills, J, (1963), 'Law in the Soviet Union', in *Anglo Soviet Journal*, Vol. XXIV, No. 2, Summer 1963, pp. 8-11.

Platts-Mills, J, (2001), *Muck, Silk and Socialism*, London, Paper Press.

Pollitt, H, (1944), *How to Win the Peace*, London, The Communist Party.

Pollitt, H, (1945), *The Crimea Conference: Safeguard of the Future*, London, The Communist Party.

Pollitt, H, (1951), *Negotiate Now*, London, The Communist Party.

Ponting, C, (1989), *Breach of Promise*, Middlesex, Penguin

Pritt, D N, (1940), *Light on Moscow: Soviet Policy Analysed; with a New Chapter on Finland*, Harmondsworth, Penguin.

Pritt, D N, (1963), *The Labour Government 1945-51*, London, Lawrence & Wishart.

Pritt, D N, (1965), *The Autobiography of D N Pritt; Part One; From Right to Left*, London, Lawrence & Wishart.

Pritt, D N, (1966), *The Autobiography of D N Pritt; Part Three; The Defence Accuses*, London, Lawrence & Wishart.

Pritt, D N, (1970), *Employers, Workers and Trade Unions*, London, Lawrence & Wishart.

Pritt, D N, & R Freeman, (1958) *The Law versus The Trade Unions*, London, Lawrence & Wishart.

Qualter, T H, (1962), *Propaganda and Psychological Warfare*, New York, Random House.

Radzinsky, E, (1996), *Stalin*, London, Hodder & Stoughton.

Radice, L, (1984), *Beatrice and Sidney Webb: Fabian Socialists*, London, Macmillan.

Rees, T & A Thorpe, Editors (1998), *International Communism and the Communist International 1919-1943*, Manchester, Manchester University Press.

Roberts, E A, (1997) *The Anglo-Marxists: a study of Ideology and Culture*, Oxford, Rowman & Littlefield,

Roberts, J C Q, (2000), *Speak Clearly into the Chandelier: Cultural Politics between Britain and Russia 1973-2000*, Richmond, Curzon.

Rose, C, (1988), *The Soviet Propaganda Network: A Directory of Organisations serving Soviet Foreign Policy*, London, Pinter.

Russell, B, (1961), *Has Man a Future*, London, George Allen & Unwin.

Saunders, F S, (1999), *Who Paid the Piper: The CIA and the cultural Cold War*, London, Granta.

Schneer, J, (1988), *Labour's Conscience: The Labour Left 1945-51*, London, Unwin Hyman.

Schwab, G, Editor, (1981), *Eurocommunism: The Ideological and Political-Theoretical Foundations*, London, Aldwych.

Selznick, P, (1960), *The Organizational Weapon: A Study of Bolshevik Strategy and Tactics*, Illinois, The Free Press of Glencoe.

Setton-Watson, R W, (1938), *Britain and the Dictators: A Survey of Post-War British Policy*, London, Cambridge University Press.

Seyd, P, (1987), *The Rise and Fall of the Labour Left*, London, Macmillan.

Seymour-Jones, C, (1993), 'Webbs of Intrigue', *New Statesman & Society;* 17 December, pp 50-51.

Shaw, E, (1988), *Discipline and Discord in the Labour Party*, Manchester, Manchester University Press.

Shaw, E, (1994), *The Labour Party Since 1979: Crisis and Transformation*, London, Routledge.

Shaw, E, (1996), *The Labour Party since 1945*, Oxford, Blackwell.

Shaw, T, (1998), 'The British Popular Press and the Early Cold War', in, *History: The Journal of the Historical Association,* Vol. 83, No 269, January 1998.

Shinwell, E, (1955), *Conflict without Malice*, London, Odhams Press.

Shipley, P, (1976), *Revolutionaries in Modern Britain*, London, The Bodley Head.

Short, R, (1979), *The care of long-term prisoner*, London, Macmillan.

Shub, D, (1948), *Lenin*, Harmondsworth, Penguin, 1966.

Shultz, R H, & R Godson, (1984), *Dezinformatsia: Active Measures in Soviet Strategy*, Washington, Pergamon Brassey's.

Silkin, J, (1987), *Changing Battlefields: The Challenge to the Labour Party*, London, Hamish Hamilton.

Sked A & C Cook, (1993), *Post-War Britain*, New Edition 1945-92, Middlesex, Penguin.

Socialist Group of the European Parliament, (nd), *The Socialist Campaign for Human Rights, Disarmament and Development Co-operation: Principles and Activities*, Brussels, SGEP.

Solley, L J, (nd), *Greece: The Facts*, London, The League for Democracy in Greece.

Spaulding, W, (1985), 'Communist Fronts in 1984', in *Problems of Communism*, Vol. 34, No. 2, March-April 1985.

Strachey, J, (1938), *What are we to do?*, London, Victor Gollancz Ltd.

Strachey, J, (1960), *The Pursuit of Peace*, Fabian Tract 329, London, Fabian Society.

Swingler, S, (1939), *An outline of Political Thought since the French Revolution*, London, Victor Gollancz.

Sworakowski, W S, (1965), *The Communist International and its Front Organisations: A Research Guide and Checklist of Holdings in American and European Libraries*, Stanford, The Hoover Institution on War, Revolution and Peace.

Taaffe, P, (1995), *The Rise of Militant*, London, Militant Publications.

Tank, G P, (1998), 'The CFSP and the Nation State' in K A Eliassen, (Editor), (1998), *Foreign and Security policy in the European Union*, London, Sage.

Taylor, R, (1988), *Against the Bomb: the British Peace Movement 1958-1965*, Oxford, Clarendon Press.

Taylor, R & N Young, Editors, (1987), *Campaigns for Peace: British peace movements in the twentieth century*, Manchester, Manchester University Press.

Taylor, R, (2000), *The TUC: From the General Strike to New Unionism*, Basingstoke, Palgrave.

Teichmann, J, (1986), *Pacifism and the Just War: A Study in Applied Philosophy*, London, Basil Blackwell.

Thompson, W, (1992), *The Good Old Cause: British Communism 1920-1991*, London, Pluto Press.

Thompson, W, (1997), *The Left in History: Revolution and Reform in Twentieth-Century Politics*, London, Pluto Press.

Thorpe, A, (1997), *A History of the British Labour Party*, London, Macmillan.

Thorpe, A, (1998), 'Stalinism and British Politics', in *History: The Journal of the Historical Association*, Vol. 83, No. 272, Oct 1998, pp 608-627.

Thurlow, R, (1999), 'The Evolution of the Mythical British Fifth Column, 1939-46', in *20th Century British History*, Vol. 10, No 4, pp 477-98.

Tolstoy, N, (1981), *Stalin's Secret War*, London, Jonathan Cape.

Tracey, H, (1948), *The British Labour Party: its history, growth, and leaders*, London, Caxton Publishing.

Trory, E, (1974), *Between the Wars: Recollections of a Communist Organiser*, Brighton, Crabtree Press.

Twitchell, N H, (1998), *The Tribune Group: Factional Conflict in the Labour Party 1964-70*, London, Rabbit.

Ulam, A B, (1966), *Lenin and the Bolsheviks*, London, Secker & Warburg.

Vigilantes, (1935), *Inquest on Peace*, London, Victor Gollancz.

Volkogonov D, (1998), *The Rise and Fall of the Soviet Empire: Political Leaders from Lenin to Gorbachev*, London, HarperCollins.

Waller, I, (1962), 'Pressure Politics', *Encounter*, August 1962, p 12.

Warbey, W, (1946), 'Towards a Socialist Foreign Policy', in, *Left*, No. 118, August 1946, pp 173-5.

Warbey, W, (1960), *This Changing World*, London, VfS

Warbey, W, (1965), *Vietnam: The Truth*, London Merlin Press.

Warbey W & K Zilliacus, (1962), *Flashpoint: Vietnam-Indo China: Britain and Vietnam*, London, New Gladiator.

Watkins, E, (1951), *The Cautious Revolution*, London, Secker and Warburg.

Watson, D, (1997), 'From 'Fellow Traveller' to 'Fascist Spy': Konni Zilliacus MP and the Cold War', in W Thompson, (Editor), *Socialist History No 11: The Cold War*, London, Pluto Press, pp 59-87.

Webb, B, (1926), *My Apprenticeship*, London, Longmans Green & Co.

Webb, B, (1948), *Our Partnership*, London, Longmans Green & Co.

Webb, S & B Webb, (1920), *A Constitution for the Socialist Commonwealth of Great Britain*, London, Longmans Green & Co.

Webb, S & B Webb, (1935), *Soviet Communism: A New Civilisation?*, special limited edition printed by the authors for the subscribing members of the Transport and General Workers Union.

Webb, S & B Webb, (1936), *Soviet Communism: Dictatorship or Democracy?*, London, The Left Review.

Webb, S & B Webb, (1942), *The Truth about Soviet Russia*, London, Longmans,

Weinbren, D, (1997), *Generating Socialism: Recollections of Life in the Labour Party*, Stroud, Sutton.

Weinstein, A & A Vassiliev, (1999), *The Haunted Wood: Soviet espionage in America – The Stalin Era*, New York, Random House.

Wernicke, G, (1998), 'The Communist-Led World Council for Peace and Western Peace Movements: The Fetters of Bipolarity and Some Attempts to Break Them in the Fifties and Early Sixties', in *Peace and Change*, Vol. 23, No. 3, July 1998.

West, N, (1993), *The Illegals: the Double Lives of the Cold War's Most Secret Agents*, London, Hodder & Stoughton.

West, N & O Tsarev, (1998), *The Crown Jewels: The British Secrets at the Heart of the KGB Archives*, London, Harper Collins.

West, N, (1999), *Venona: The Greatest Secret of the Cold War*, London, Harper Collins.

Wetter, G A, (1962), *Soviet Ideology Today*, London, Heinemann.

Wheen, F, (1990), *Tom Driberg: his life and indiscretions*, London, Chatto & Windus.

White, J B, (1948) *The Soviet Spy System*, London, Falcon Press.

Whitehead, A, (1992), 'I was one of the Glory Boys', from *New Statesman & Society*, 6 November 1992, pp 28-29.

Widgery, D, (1976), *The Left in Britain 1956-68*, Middlesex, Penguin.

Williams, A J, (1987), 'The Labour Party's Attitude to the Soviet Union 1927-35: An Overview with Specific Reference to Unemployment Policies and Peace', in *The Journal of Contemporary History*, Vol. 22, 1987, No 1, pp 71-90

Williams, A J, (1989), *Labour and Russia: the attitude of the Labour Party to the USSR 1924-1934*, Manchester, Manchester University Press.

Williams, F, (1954), *Magnificent Journey: The Rise of the Trade Unions*, London, Odhams.

Williams P, (1983), 'The Labour Party: The Rise of the Left', in *West European Politics*, Vol. 6, 1983,

Williams, P M, Editor, (1983), *The Diary of Hugh Gaitskell 1945-1956*, London, Johathan Cape.

Wilson, H, (1971), *The Labour Government 1964-70*, London, Pelican, 1974.

Winstone, R, Editor, (1995), *The Benn Diaries*, new single volume edition, London, Arrow.

Wood, N, (1959), *Communism and the British Intellectuals*, London, Gollancz.

Woolf, L, (1947), *Foreign Policy: The Labour Party's dilemma*, London, Fabian Society.

Wright, A W, (1979), *G D H Cole and Socialist Democracy*, Oxford, Clarendon Press.

Wright, T, (1996), *Socialisms: old and new*, London & New York, Routledge.

Wrigley, C, (1997), *British Trade Unions 1945-1995*, Manchester, Manchester University Press.

Young, J W, (1998), 'The Wilson government and the Davies peace mission to North Vietnam, July 1965',

in *Review of International Studies* Vol. 24, pp. 545-562.

Zilliacus, K, (1944), *The Mirror of the Past; Lest it Reflect the Future*, London, Gollancz.

Zilliacus, K, (1946), *Britain, USSR and World Peace*, London, British-Soviet Society.

Zilliacus, K, (1949), *Dragon's Teeth: The background, contents and consequences of the North Atlantic Pact*, London, Narod Press.

Zilliacus, K, (1949), *I Choose Peace*, Harmondsworth, Penguin.

Zilliacus, K, (1949), *Why I was Expelled: Bevinism v Election Pledges, Socialism and Peace*, London, Narod Press.

Zilliacus, K, (1952), *Tito of Yugoslavia*, London, Michael Joseph.

Zilliacus, K, (1957), *A New Birth of Freedom: World Communism after Stalin*, London, Secker & Warburg.

Zilliacus, K, (1965), *Arms & Labour*, London, Labour Campaign for Nuclear Disarmament.

Zilliacus, K, (1966), *Labour's Crisis, Its Nature, Causes and Cure*, London, Tribune Group.

Zilliacus, K, (nd), *Tito v Stalin: Yugoslavia and the Cold War*, London, Perspective.

Zilliacus, K, (nd), *Labour and the Common Market*, London, New Gladiator Press.

Zilliacus, K, (nd), *Our Lives and Cuba: What Britain must do to survive*, London, New Gladiator Press.

Zilliacus, K, (nd), *Home on the Bomb and Labour's Alternative to Genocide*, London, New Gladiator Press.

Zilliacus, Konrad, (1905), *The Russian Revolutionary Movement*, London, Alston Rivers.

(nd) Denotes pamphlets which do not show a publication date.

Index

A

B

C